You Ain't Heard Nothin' Yet

You Ain't Heard Nothin' Yet

Interviews with Stars from Hollywood's Golden Era

JAMES BAWDEN

AND

RON MILLER

UNIVERSITY PRESS OF KENTUCKY

Copyright © 2017 by The University Press of Kentucky

Scholarly publisher for the Commonwealth,
serving Bellarmine University, Berea College, Centre College of Kentucky,
Eastern Kentucky University, The Filson Historical Society, Georgetown College,
Kentucky Historical Society, Kentucky State University, Morehead State
University, Murray State University, Northern Kentucky University, Transylvania
University, University of Kentucky, University of Louisville, and Western
Kentucky University.
All rights reserved.

Editorial and Sales Offices: The University Press of Kentucky
663 South Limestone Street, Lexington, Kentucky 40508-4008
www.kentuckypress.com

Library of Congress Cataloging-in-Publication Data

Names: Bawden, James interviewer, editor. | Miller, Ron, 1939– interviewer,
    editor.
Title: You ain't heard nothin' yet : interviews with stars from Hollywood's
    golden era / James Bawden and Ron Miller.
Description: Lexington : University Press of Kentucky, 2017. | Series: Screen
    classics | Includes index.
Identifiers: LCCN 2017019637| ISBN 9780813174211 (hardcover : alk. paper) |
    ISBN 9780813174228 (pdf) | ISBN 9780813174235 (epub)
Subjects: LCSH: Motion picture actors and actresses—United
    States—Interviews. | Motion pictures—United States—History—20th
    century.
Classification: LCC PN1998.2 .Y67 2017 | DDC 791.4302/80922—dc23
LC record available at https://lccn.loc.gov/2017019637

This book is printed on acid-free paper meeting
the requirements of the American National Standard
for Permanence in Paper for Printed Library Materials.
∞

Manufactured in the United States of America.

Member of the Association of
American University Presses

The authors dedicate this book to the late Robert "Bob" Foster, who was one of America's first regularly scheduled television reviewers and had been a radio columnist before that for the *San Mateo Times* in the San Francisco Bay Area. Not only did Bob introduce us to each other in the mid-1970s, he was a mentor to both of us as we learned to negotiate the television beat while indulging our passion for talking with movie stars from Hollywood's golden era who were then working mainly in TV.

Contents

Introduction

How to Talk to a Movie Star

Ron Miller

After more than half a century doing interviews with movie stars, James Bawden and I think we've finally worked out a fairly reliable way to do the job.

Now, for most people, the first big problem would be gaining access to the movie star you want to interview. That wasn't always a problem for us because most stars are eager to get good publicity for their latest movie, TV show, or stage appearance. As the TV columnist for Canada's biggest and most widely read newspaper, the *Toronto Star,* Bawden actually was sought out by press agents who wanted him to talk with their stars. And because I was a writer whose columns were syndicated in more than a hundred newspapers in the United States and Canada, I was pretty popular with press agents as well.

Of course, we both learned fairly early that nothing is guaranteed when it comes to dealing with celebrities. Some don't want to talk to you, no matter what their press agent thinks. I spent more than twenty years trying to get an interview with James Arness, who didn't want to do any until he really needed a big audience for what turned out to be his final CBS *Gunsmoke* movie. CBS told him he'd get into a whole lot of papers if he talked to me, so I got his only interview.

Bawden still remembers the time he turned up on the set of the 1974 movie *The Towering Inferno* to talk with Fred Astaire and Oscar-winning actress Jennifer Jones. "The minute she saw me take out my notebook, she screamed and took off running," Bawden recalls. Fortunately, Fred Astaire stayed put and Bawden got something worthwhile out of the effort. But Jones never returned.

For me, a classic "no dice" moment came when I sat down opposite the legendary Sylvia Sidney for an interview while she was doing Shaw's *Candida* at the Comedia Repertory Theater in Palo Alto, California. A few minutes into the interview, I asked her if she'd ever been approached to do one of those grotesque horror movies starring older female stars like Bette Davis and Joan Crawford that were currently popular. Sidney grabbed my notebook out of my hand and said, "I don't like these questions!" Her attitude was considerably more negative from that point on. I had touched on a subject area that ticked her off. I had expected her simply to say she'd never do a film like that, but that's a risk you run with any star interview: you never know when you might accidentally step on one of their personal land mines.

Bawden recalls what Julie Harris told him when he approached her on the set of TV's *Knots Landing*: "I hate star interviews!" Thinking quickly, Bawden told her he'd never really understood Shakespeare until, when he was just seventeen, he saw her play a tremulous yet passionate fourteen-year-old Juliet onstage at Canada's Stratford Festival—"and you were already over thirty!"

"You've convinced me," she said and spent the next hour answering his questions.

Yes, it's true: flattery frequently gets you somewhere after all.

Bawden and I are in full agreement on several points when it comes to talking with stars, regardless of their attitude when the interview starts. First, it's essential to prepare yourself fully by acquiring a solid knowledge of the actor's work before you sit down for a chat. This is a lot easier today than it was in the 1950s when I began my career in journalism and first talked with a star. In those days, there were no cable TV channels featuring old movies, no home video copies of movies, and precious few books available at local libraries on the work of film people. If I wanted to see an old Bette Davis movie, for instance, I'd have to wait for it to show up on one of the late, late shows on a local TV station or con a friend with a car to drive me about a hundred miles from my hometown to Berkeley, California, where Pauline Kael ran a pair of repertory cinemas that showed classic movies regularly.

Today you can find complete casts, credits, and other pertinent information regarding any film on the Internet. You can read full biographies of stars with all their films and TV appearances cited. Most of the great films are available on disc or tape and now you can download or stream-view almost everything.

My interview in this book with the great silent comic Buster Keaton was done while I was in college, before any of the current research resources were available. My knowledge of Keaton when I did the interview was based on what I could read in the few film books then available and on my viewing of clips from his silent films in documentaries about the silent era. My first viewings of *Sherlock, Jr.* (1924), *The General* (1927), *Steamboat Bill, Jr.* (1928), and his other classics came long after I met him.

But today there's no excuse for not being well prepared for an interview when you first meet a famous star.

Bawden and I also agree that you must go into an interview with the notion that you're going to show your respect in order to earn your subject's respect. If you were going into an interview with Rock Hudson, for instance, you wouldn't want to start off by asking him to talk about being gay. Hudson never discussed his sex life publicly and most writers respected his wishes and didn't bring the topic up. Does that mean you're not hard-nosed enough? No. What it means is that you're going to avoid annoying the actor or you'll get nothing worthwhile for your efforts.

What's more, stars often will start confiding in you about a lot of personal topics once you gain their confidence. Generally, though, they're going to wait and see what you write after the interview before making up their mind about you. However, some show business notables—the late Farrah Fawcett was a good example—would demand to see a portfolio of your clippings before agreeing to do an interview.

Bawden has an especially bizarre example. He sat down with the great British actress Dame Anna Neagle in 1981 while she was in Toronto for a production of *My Fair Lady.* For a time, it felt like he was having an audience with Queen Elizabeth herself because they were having high tea in her suite and he wasn't allowed to ask any questions, only make comments. Bawden recalls: "So, I'd say something like: 'You must have been very gratified by your success over *Sixty Glorious Years!*' (a 1938 film in which she played Queen Victoria) and then wait for her to respond. Fortunately, she did enough responding to make up an interview." Bawden now thinks Neagle's queenly attitude probably dated from the fact she'd played Queen Victoria twice on-screen.

Bawden also remembers the time he started to interview Burt Lancaster, who was in Toronto to promote his 1980 film *Atlantic City,* and Lancaster insisted on asking the first question himself: "I know you were interviewing Kirk Douglas the day before. What did he say about me?"

Some stars who were plagued by negative tabloid coverage insisted that you sign a form promising not to sell your interview to a tabloid after it ran in your original newspaper or magazine. Tom Selleck did that upon occasion during the height of his popularity. I was happy to sign such a document the one time he asked me to do so because I had no intention of dealing with a tabloid and I respected his paranoia about the topic. Consequently, Selleck and I always had a very warm and friendly relationship that included many private chats over the years.

Bawden ran into that situation with Sharon Stone while she was making *Casino* (1995). He recalls having to sign some kind of waiver promising not to sell his notes to a tabloid, even though it was a group interview with other stars from the movie. Another time, he was asked by Laraine Day to provide "references." Bawden was lucky because he knew Susan Douglas, formerly from TV's *The Guiding Light*, who was a close friend of Day. She intervened on his behalf and Bawden wound up with a luncheon date with Day that lasted all afternoon.

Perhaps the most unusual example of vetting I ever had to go through to meet a star was the time I went for an interview with actress Theresa Saldana, who had been brutally attacked by a stalker not long after playing opposite Robert De Niro in *Raging Bull* (1980). At the time of the interview, she was playing herself in a TV movie about her ordeal called *Victims for Victims: The Theresa Saldana Story* (1984). Not only did the publicity people vet me fully, they also sent me to someone else's house where Saldana was presently staying anonymously. Her fright was palpable and I completely understood everybody's concern. I might add I was grateful I wasn't strip-searched before turning on my tape recorder.

We've both done interviews under rather strange circumstances. Bawden arranged a luncheon interview with producer Hal Wallis and his wife, actress Martha Hyer, while Bawden was staying at the Century Plaza Hotel in Los Angeles. On the morning of the interview, Bawden received a phone call from Wallis, who said, "The limo will be there in half an hour." Bawden naturally assumed Wallis & Wife were in Los Angeles. They weren't. They were in Rancho Mirage—he was in the limo that day for a total of six hours.

And I was thrilled to get an interview with one of my all-time favorites, Sidney Poitier, while he was doing some location shooting for his 1972 film *Brother John* in the northern California area where I worked as a reporter. I dressed up for the occasion in my best suit and tie and my highly polished leather dress shoes and waited to receive directions to the set. Well, turns out Poitier was filming that day in a rugged outdoor setting in the hills above Silicon Valley. I can still hear the laughter when Poitier and crew saw me staggering up a dusty hill, looking like I'd just come through a sandstorm. Worse yet, the film was a parable about the Second Coming of Christ, but they didn't want moviegoers to know that in advance, so Poitier couldn't really tell me much about the movie. He was very nice, but my interview was a major dud.

Bawden and I have no secret formula for how best to gain a star's confidence, but I think we agree that keeping your questions serious is a good way to start. I make it a rule not to ask stars to talk about their private lives unless we agree in advance to do so. If they want to talk candidly about such things, let them bring the topic up. My chief interest has always been their work, not their private affairs—and that earned me a pretty good reputation among press agents.

However, I'm a believer in the theory that stars soon grow tired of being asked the same things over and over, so I always make a habit of asking some "off the wall" questions once the interview is going along well, just to stimulate the star's desire to stay awake. For example, I had been through enough press conferences with George Burns to know that the old-time vaudevillian had developed some standard answers for questions about what it was like to work without his old partner and wife, Gracie Allen, after her death in 1964. So when I got a chance to talk with him, I stayed away from that topic and went for questions that might provoke his famous wit. Though he was in his late eighties when I met him, I asked him if he'd consider doing a nude scene in his next picture. It was a delight to see the grin spread over his weathered face as out came a whole range of wisecracks about nude scenes and how he'd perform in one. I mean, c'mon: the guy was a witty comic and that silly question gave him a chance to show off his skills.

While talking with Bob Hope in his home in Toluca Lake one day, I was wondering what it might be like to have such a famous comedian for a neighbor, so I asked Hope what kind of a neighbor he was. I don't think he'd ever been asked that before and it led to some hilarious stories about his golf balls going into the nearby yard of Jonathan Winters—who didn't like it—and about one thoughtless late-night call he made with a reporter who wanted to meet another famous neighbor, Dorothy Lamour. When Lamour opened the door with her hair up in curlers, he realized he'd violated the standards of good neighborliness quite a bit.

In my one chance to talk with my all-time favorite actress, Barbara Stanwyck, I was uncertain about the wisdom of asking her about Robert Taylor, her former husband and her costar in *The Night Walker* (1964), the last movie she did for theaters. Lots of people dislike talking about ex-spouses, so I didn't want to risk hitting a trip wire on a potentially explosive topic. Instead, I asked her to discuss her favorite leading men from the past and, to my delight, she said, "Oh, Robert Taylor was my favorite, of course." And off we went.

Bawden and I also think it's important to pay attention to the setting of the interview, especially if it's in the home or office of the star. By carefully looking around the room, you often can find little touches that tell you a lot about the person you're interviewing.

I learned that lesson the hard way. While interviewing actress Jacqueline Bisset at her home in Beverly Hills, I noticed a number of items that suggested she had a special interest in ballet. I also had the uncanny feeling that there was someone else in the house who hadn't come forward to be introduced. Still, I never asked her about ballet or why that seemed to be a passion of hers.

Before I went home that day, I stopped at the supermarket for some items and noticed the latest copy of *People* magazine at the checkout stand. On the cover was a picture of Bisset and the news that she was now romantically involved with a world-famous ballet star. I'd missed a grand opportunity to make our interview even more interesting and timely.

Bawden recalls some amusing "atmospheric" details about some offbeat interview situations. One example: while interviewing Janet Leigh in, of all places, a Toronto cemetery at midnight, he noticed she ducked behind a large tombstone to sneak a quick puff or two on a cigarette. She didn't want anyone to know she smoked and told him she'd probably tell her husband that Bawden was smoking if he smelled smoke on her clothes.

Another time, when Bawden was interviewing Lucille Ball, he was surprised to find she insisted on making grilled cheese sandwiches in her kitchen all during the interview. He deduced that she was nervous and needed to keep her hands busy while she was talking.

I have a more touching memory of my last interview with Lucy in her dressing room while she was making her last comedy series, ABC's *Life with Lucy* (1986). I had read that her mother had always been a member of the audience during her famous *I Love Lucy* days. Her mother had died in

1977, so I asked Lucy if it would seem strange knowing her mom wasn't there this time, watching her work in her new show.

"Oh, but she is there," she told me, her eyes brimming with tears. "I see her there every time."

While I think it's nice to develop a friendly relationship with a star, it's customary for writers who also do film or TV criticism to avoid getting so close that you lose your objectivity. There are a couple of notable exceptions in my career. One example: Johnny Sheffield, whose interview with me is in this volume.

Sheffield played Tarzan's son, Boy, in all those jungle action movies of the late 1930s and early 1940s before going out on his own as the star of the *Bomba* jungle movies. Johnny and I had talked on the phone and become so friendly that he also began to write for the website I ran with some fellow columnists. He and his wife visited my wife and me in Washington State and we did a few public appearances together. I didn't feel guilty about becoming friendly with Sheffield because he was long retired from acting and was just a great guy I'd met through our mutual connections to the movies. When he died in 2010, I genuinely mourned him as I would any dear friend.

Another thing that Bawden and I agree upon is not to bring your own political, religious, or social attitudes with you to an interview. If you believe, as I do, that everyone is entitled to his or her own opinion about such matters, it frees you to find out what you may have in common with the person you otherwise might be wary of in an interview situation.

A good example for me was Charlton Heston, whose attitudes about politics and gun ownership were pretty much the reverse of mine. When I went to his home for an interview in the early 1980s, his guard dogs greeted me at the gate of his estate and I suppose I was waiting to hear the sound of an ammo clip clicking into place in a weapon trained on me. Well, Heston turned out to be a warm and gracious host with a deep understanding of filmmaking and a willingness to talk openly and frankly about his work. Wisely, I think, I never mentioned politics or guns. Consequently, I came away from the interview with a solid appreciation of his intelligence and his keen observations.

Another interviewee who surprised me with his warmth, his affable nature, and his articulate ways was Charles Dutton, an African American character actor who had appeared in a number of major films and starred in his own network comedy series, *Roc* (1991–1994). I suppose I had some reason to feel nervous about meeting him: Dutton had served eight years in prison for killing someone in a street fight during his youth. I expected a hooligan with a Hollywood veneer. Though Dutton was an imposing guy from the mean streets of Baltimore, I found him to be a true gentleman who dodged no questions, even about his criminal past, and seemed eternally grateful that his love of acting had saved him from a life that otherwise seemed headed nowhere good.

For both Bawden and myself, the pleasant memories of our interviews far outweigh the infrequent episodes of tension and ill will. My encounters with famous screen bad guys almost always turned out to be a chance to discover how nice some of the screen's great villains could be in person. Several examples are in this collection: Boris Karloff, Lon Chaney Jr., Lee Marvin, Ernest Borgnine, and Jack Elam were among the most hospitable and decent people I've met in a lifetime covering show business.

Bawden's encounters with some very grand leading ladies of the screen have not only produced great interviews, but also built some lasting relationships that have resulted in phone calls and exchanges of letters for years afterward.

I've also had a few special moments with great screen ladies, though not the kind any tabloid would care to print. However, I still remember the heat of that hug lovely Ann-Margret gave me after talking with me in her home about her 1984 performance as Blanche in ABC's 1984 production of *A Streetcar Named Desire*. Being hugged by Ann-Margret? Hey, people, that's the way all interviews should turn out—at least with the pretty ones. Yes, it's nice work, if you can get it.

The title of this book comes from the first line of dialogue spoken by Al Jolson in *The Jazz Singer*, the first feature film of the "talkie" era, after singing his first song, "Dirty Hands, Dirty Face." He says, "Wait a minute, wait a minute! You ain't heard nothin' yet!" and goes on to sing his second song, "Toot, Toot, Tootsie."

I

A Comedy Giant

Buster Keaton

Interview by Ron Miller

When the greatest creative talents of the silent movie era are discussed, there's little debate about whether Buster Keaton deserves a place in the very top ranks of its stars. Indeed, some even consider Keaton worthy of equal standing with the immortal Charles Chaplin among the greatest of all silent movie comedians.

Brought onto the vaudeville stage by his show business family in infancy, Keaton broke into films in 1917 as a supporting player to his friend Roscoe "Fatty" Arbuckle and journeyed to Hollywood with him, where he was given a chance to work on his own at Paramount Pictures. (When Arbuckle's career as a screen comic was ruined because he was accused of manslaughter in the death of starlet Virginia Rappe, Keaton defended him, claiming Arbuckle was innocent. Arbuckle was never convicted, but he never regained his fame.)

A short, slender, sad-faced man, Keaton plunged into the movie business, learning all he could about how things were done. While the great Charles Chaplin later distinguished himself as the director of feature films, his earlier silents mainly recorded his own brilliant slapstick routines, mastered in the music hall comedy traditions of his native England. In contrast, Keaton became an innovator, using the film medium far more creatively than most of his comic rivals, including Chaplin.

His mastery of inventive sight gags was immediately obvious in his short comedies like *The Boat* (1921) and *Cops* (1922), leading him to making his own feature films, starting with *The Three Ages* (1923). His later features, particularly *Sherlock, Jr.* (1924) and *The General* (1927), lifted him to a level of greatness still appreciated today.

Though Keaton made the transition to talking pictures in the 1930s and retained his star quality for a time, he was never again as popular with audiences as he'd been in the 1920s. He was also plagued with personal

Buster Keaton, circa 1929. James Bawden collection.

problems, including drinking. Though he continued to work in movies and television for the rest of his life, it was mainly as a supporting comic player.

Along the way, Keaton worked as a screenwriter, providing comic material for the MGM films starring comedian Red Skelton, and was used as a comedy consultant at Columbia Pictures in the 1940s, where he helped develop actress Lucille Ball's flair for physical comedy.

Among his most enduring cameo performances in the sound era were his appearance as Lonesome Polecat in the 1940 *Lil Abner* movie, his appearance as one of the silent movie pals of Norma Desmond (Gloria Swanson) in Billy Wilder's *Sunset Blvd* (1950), and his very touching and amusing turn with his old rival Charlie Chaplin in Chaplin's *Limelight* (1952).

Setting the Scene

My interview with Buster Keaton came at a very early time in my career. It was 1960 and I was still a college student, working as the editor of *Lyke,* the campus feature magazine at California's San Jose State College (now University). I met the then sixty-four-year-old actor in his hotel room in San Francisco while he was starring in the road version of the stage show *Once upon a Mattress.*

As I recall, an important baseball game was on at the time of our interview and Keaton was getting phone call updates between innings from his old pal comedian Joe E. Brown. Keaton was quite friendly, but seemed to be a little hard of hearing and needed to think over his answers to my questions for some time, which often meant I had started to ask another before he had answered the last one.

For a man whose entire career was an explosion of laughter, Keaton never smiled once. His screen image of dour expression, the "great stone face," was his real-life image, too.

The Interview

MILLER: How did you develop your distinctive deadpan acting style?

KEATON: Well, I was born with a show and grew up with an audience. Through those years, I learned that if I laughed at what I did, the audience wouldn't. So by the time I was seven or eight years old, I worked with a frozen face. By the time I went into pictures, it was mechanical to me.

MILLER: If you had to pick one element in your pictures that's your secret for making people laugh, what would it be?

KEATON: The main thing that makes an audience laugh is that something happens to me that could have happened to them. But it didn't—and they're glad.

MILLER: I'm sorry to say that I've only been able to find a few of your classic films of the 1920s to look at today—and it often means driving a great distance to a big city where there's a theater that revives old films. Now I hear that you are trying to round up all your old films and reissue them for the modern movie audience. Is that true?

KEATON: Yes. And that's why I think I can now retire.

MILLER: Tell me more about that. I want to see the films, but I worry that too many young people today won't sit through a silent movie. Why do you think the public will want to see them now?

KEATON: Well, here's the encouragement I got: some of these exhibitors—especially in Europe—were playing these films like *When Comedy Was King* [1960, featuring a collection of clips from silent comedies] and people liked them and started asking for more. I just made a flying trip to Europe and found out there's a big market there. They told me I could get something like five thousand theaters to distribute [them]. So I just took my negatives to Munich and let them put full orchestration musical tracks on all these prints.

MILLER: Will you try to update them by adding some speaking dialogue?

KEATON: No. I won't use any voices—no moderator, no nothing. Just music. I'll leave the old subtitles in the picture. As soon as we see how they're doing over there, we'll know better how to handle them here.

MILLER: Why don't they make your kind of comedies anymore?

KEATON: I think modern producers are handicapped. It's just their general way of making motion pictures. The cost of production has gone so high. It's all out of proportion.

MILLER: How do you mean?

KEATON: I'll give you an example. I made a picture once called *The Boat*. One of my biggest gags in it was one of the longest laughs [ever] on the motion picture screen. It was when I launched my family cruiser and it went right to the bottom of the sea. They wanted to use that gag in *The Buster Keaton Story* [1957] and they got it. Now, when we originally shot that scene, it took us three days. It wouldn't work. We just kept getting "bugs" out of it. We found out we had to bore holes in the nose of the ship so no air pocket could get in. The rear end had to be a breakaway and collapse with water pressure, so the boat would scoop [water] going down the slide into the

[sea]. Wherever wood is concerned, there's buoyancy and you can't make it go straight to the bottom. So we even put sixteen hundred pounds of pig iron in it. Now we find she won't slide down the ramp. So we had to drop a big sea anchor and a pulley attached to a tug just outside the picture to pull it into the water. By the time we got all these bugs out, it took three days.

Now, when we come to do it for *The Buster Keaton Story,* I had those bugs out before we started. So they got the scene in one take—in one morning. Now get this: when I did it in 1920, the cost of the picture—including my salary—was $22,000. To do just that one morning's work—not more than a few hundred feet of film—it cost the producers of *The Buster Keaton Story* $600,000!

MILLER: Speaking of that movie, starring Donald O'Connor as you, what did you think of it?

KEATON: I didn't much care for it, but Paramount paid a good price for it.

MILLER: If you think your old films will still work today, does that mean you think comedy hasn't changed?

KEATON: The art of comedy has never changed. As long as I can remember, people laughed sixty years ago at the same things we're laughing at today.

MILLER: In one of your films that I have seen—*Steamboat Bill, Jr.* [1928]—the whole front of a two-story building comes tumbling down while you're standing in front of it, but by luck you happen to be standing right where an open window falls and you're not even scratched. That was not only hilarious, but it looked so dangerous that it stunned me. How the heck did you do that?

KEATON: We just did it. We did it just exactly the way you saw it. The front of that building weighed two tons. What we had to be careful of were those big Liberty motors on wind machines. We had six of them to create the typhoon. We experimented with one—drove a truck through in front of it. The truck couldn't have been more than thirty-five feet from the machine when the wind blew it over. So we had to be awful careful none of the drafts from those machines hit the front of the building. It could have warped it or thrown it in any direction. Actually, when the second-story window came down over my head, the clearance on my shoulders was only about two inches and about three inches over my head.

MILLER: Did your luck ever run out on you when setting up a gag like that?

KEATON: Seldom. When we laid out a stunt like that, we were pretty thorough about it. We didn't guess much.

MILLER: Could you get away with doing a risky stunt like that today?

KEATON: Nowadays if a script calls for a stunt, the principals are not allowed to do them. You have to hire a stuntman.

MILLER: But you did your own stunts, right?

KEATON: Yes. We knew from bitter experience in the old days that stuntmen don't get you laughs. That's why we did most of them ourselves.

MILLER: You kept starring in movies in the talkie era. How do you account for the fact that they weren't as popular as your silents?

KEATON: I had a couple that were. But I was warned before I moved out of my own studio over to Metro-Goldwyn-Mayer. They told me: "Everything will be fine except that you're going to have too many cooks—too much high brass and too many writers." And that's what they did. They gave me every writer on the lot, something like eighty-six of them.

MILLER: How many writers did you use for your silents?

KEATON: We always carried a small staff of gagmen and writers. I worked with them as one of them. We figured out the stories and gags and so forth. Then, on the set, we started to shoot and generally came up with 50 percent of our material. There was another thing: none of the features I made—or Chaplin's or [Harold] Lloyd's—ever had a script. We never put our stories on paper. Well, you tell that to anybody in the picture business today and they'd think you dated back to the Stone Age or something.

MILLER: Over all the years, what has been your most enduring single gag?

KEATON: Probably the opening scene in my largest-grossing picture, *The Navigator* [1924]. I shot it in San Francisco, Nob Hill, two beautiful houses up there. In the scene, I come out of my house and get into my car—a big Pierce-Arrow with a chauffeur and footman. They open the door for me. I sit in the back seat and the footman throws a robe over me. The chauffeur gets in and just turns the car around and drives across the street so I could get out and call on my girl who lives there. It was a big laugh—idle rich, you know? That gag must have been repeated fifty times in the years to follow.

MILLER: How have you managed to keep yourself in the public eye for such a long career?

KEATON: Well, to commence with, some stars like Chaplin and Lloyd are very wealthy men. They don't have to care one way or the other. I've

Buster Keaton in *The Navigator* (1924). James Bawden collection.

run into a lot of pitfalls—some bad investments. I've had to keep working. But I'm thinking of retiring now. Just do some commercials and let my films work for me.

Afterword

The year before our interview, Keaton received an Academy Award in special recognition of his contribution to film history. He continued to work throughout the next decade, mostly in comic supporting roles in films like *It's A Mad, Mad, Mad, Mad World* (1963), *Beach Blanket Bingo* (1965), and *A Funny Thing Happened on the Way to the Forum* (1966). At the time of our interview, he was honorary mayor of Woodland Hills, the San Fernando Valley community where he resided. Keaton died February 1, 1966.

II

The Leading Men

Anthony Dexter

Interview by Ron Miller

It took ten days for the newspapers to catch on to the fact that an elderly retired gentleman named Walter Craig who had died in obscurity in the town of Greeley, Colorado, on March 27, 2001, was actually Anthony Dexter, the movie actor marketed as "the new Valentino" back in 1951.

Dexter had long since given up his Hollywood name. It probably wouldn't have made much difference anyway, at least in terms of headlines, since hardly anyone remembered Anthony Dexter, who faded from the limelight almost as fast as he arrived there in an orgy of national publicity centered on the release of Columbia's *Valentino* (1951), in which he played the title role.

If you live a genuinely obscure life, almost nobody gets anything right about you in your obituary because nobody bothers to check the facts. The *Los Angeles Times* obituary listed Dexter's real name as Walter Craig and his age as eighty-eight, but his real name was Walter Fleischmann and his age was probably eighty-one or eighty-two.

In the early 1950s, the movie studios still had most of their stars under contract and controlled the flow of information about them. They often tended to fabricate much of a new star's background, so it's hard to say what the real facts are about the actor called Anthony Dexter, who was picked from a field of about two hundred candidates for the role of Rudolph Valentino (1895–1926).

Dexter was used to that sort of thing. Since he blossomed virtually overnight as a "star of tomorrow," then quickly faded from view with moviegoers, he had lived his life with constant reminders of his "has-been" status. He knew the reason why: he bore an uncanny resemblance to Rudolph Valentino, a Hollywood immortal, and nobody ever let him forget it. His own identity was permanently submerged in the persona of the famous man he portrayed in that one movie appearance.

Anthony Dexter as Rudolph Valentino in the 1951 biopic *Valentino,* which re-created his gaucho-style sequence from the silent classic *The Four Horsemen of the Apocalypse* (1921). Photo by Cronenweth; courtesy of Columbia Pictures.

Setting the Scene

My connection with Anthony Dexter is very ephemeral. I first saw him in *Valentino* and its follow-up, Columbia's *The Brigand,* a 1952 attempt to put Dexter into a role Valentino might have played if he'd been suddenly born again. I was then a junior high school kid. By the time I got to high school, Dexter was no longer starring in big-budget major studio films, but was instead making Poverty Row quickies like *Captain John Smith and Pocahontas* (1953), *Captain Kidd and the Slave Girl* (1954), *The Black Pirates* (1954), and *Fire Maidens of Outer Space* (1955). He was still being forced to mimic Valentino in tawdry swashbucklers that buckled where they should have swashed. In short, he was pretty much finished as a movie star.

A few years later, when I was working my way through college as a freelance writer and doing part-time work as a reporter for my local newspaper in Santa Cruz, California, Dexter wasn't getting much picture work and was doing summer stock to pay his bills. His stage career brought him to nearby Monterey to play the king opposite Patricia Morison in a summer production of *The King and I*. I asked for an interview and he graciously agreed.

Two things struck me right away when I met Dexter and began talking with him in his hotel room: he really did look amazingly like Rudolph Valentino—and he was an incredibly likeable, disarmingly candid sort of guy. He apparently had accepted the cards fate had dealt him.

The Interview

MILLER: Do you regret the barrage of publicity that tried to sell you to the moviegoing public as the new Valentino?

DEXTER: I've never cared much for publicity. I'd rather just go my own way and do my work with no fanfare. The studio publicity people faked virtually every fact about me when they made up my biography for *Valentino*. For one thing, they claimed I'd been found working on a farm and was cast in the leading role in a major studio movie just because I looked exactly like Valentino.

MILLER: What's the true story?

DEXTER: I had a solid background in acting. I have a master's degree in theater arts and had been a college drama teacher. I had plenty of stage experience and had toured with Katharine Cornell, had been in a command performance at the Royal Theatre in Denmark and was, at the time, working on my doctorate in theater arts. I'd been in many Broadway shows, including *The Barretts of Wimpole Street*.

MILLER: Why wouldn't they want to play up your acting experience?

DEXTER: They were more interested in reincarnating Valentino than developing me as a star with my own personality.

MILLER: How could they exert that much control over your career?

DEXTER: I was under contract to producer Edward Small, who made *Valentino*. He wanted me to keep doing roles a young Valentino might have played. I broke my contract rather than do that.

MILLER: So how did that work out?

DEXTER: I guess that's obvious. All the other producers wanted to cash in on the *Valentino* publicity, so they offered me the same roles, only for less money.

MILLER: So breaking your contract was a mistake?

DEXTER: It was the stupidest thing I ever did in my life, [Small] would have pulled me out of the Valentino mold in time and given me career security, too. But I didn't know many answers then.

MILLER: *Fire Maidens of Outer Space* has been proclaimed by some critics as one of the worst movies ever made. Is that the direction your career is now headed?

DEXTER: I made three pilot films for television. Two of them were swashbucklers. But the networks went for westerns at the last minute.

MILLER: What would you like to play?

DEXTER: I've been wanting to do a good romantic heavy, but I still run into the Valentino image wherever I go.

Afterword

After our interview, Dexter appeared in a couple more awful sci-fi pictures from the Poverty Row scene—*Twelve to the Moon* (1960) and *The Phantom Planet* (1961). By then he was billed as "Tony" Dexter. His last appearance in a feature film was a bit part in the 1967 musical *Thoroughly Modern Millie*.

In his later years, Dexter returned to teaching. He taught speech and drama at a Los Angeles–area high school for most of the 1970s. He was living in retirement in Colorado when he died.

For more than fifty years, I've seen at least once every day the photo I took of Anthony Dexter on the day of our interview. I thought it was a pretty good shot, so I framed it and hung it among a few others on the wall behind my writing desk. It also reminds me that he was a good guy, willing

Anthony Dexter strikes a Valentino-like pose in his hotel room during the interview. Photo by Ron Miller.

to help a young journalist even if it meant doing something he really didn't want to do: talk about the ruins of his movie career.

"I suppose you want me like this," he told me that day, turning his face so his profile was in the morning light coming through the window of his room. "That's my best Valentino side."

Henry Fonda

Interview by James Bawden

By any standards, Henry Fonda was one of the great stars of Hollywood's golden age. Born in Nebraska in 1905, the tall, lanky, good-looking Fonda never lost his air of honesty and integrity, which helped him become the quintessential American leading man of the 1930s, first on Broadway in the play *The Farmer Takes a Wife* and quickly thereafter as the leading man to Oscar-winner Janet Gaynor in the 1935 movie version.

Like his good friend and Broadway colleague James Stewart, Fonda projected simple decency, but always combined with a hardy manliness that led him into hero roles in all kinds of settings, from the American frontier to the contemporary urban scene. Fonda was equally at home in romantic comedies like *The Lady Eve* (1941) and *The Male Animal* (1942), outdoor adventure films like *Drums along the Mohawk* (1939), tense dramas like *You Only Live Once* (1937), and costume pictures like *Jezebel* (1938).

Along the way, Fonda created several iconic characters in unforgettable films, among them his Tom Joad in John Ford's 1940 *The Grapes of Wrath*, Wyatt Earp in Ford's *My Darling Clementine* (1946), the conscience-driven cowboy in William Wellman's *The Ox-Bow Incident* (1943) and, perhaps his greatest single character, the cool-headed, rebellious navy officer in both the stage and screen versions of *Mister Roberts* (1955).

In 1978, the American Film Institute presented Fonda with its lifetime achievement award in a dazzling televised ceremony that included presentations by Lucille Ball, Richard Burton, Bette Davis, Kirk Douglas, Jack Lemmon, Charlton Heston, Lillian Gish, and his actor children Peter and Jane Fonda.

In his final year on the screen, Fonda turned in his great Oscar-winning performance as the ailing elderly husband of Katharine Hepburn in *On Golden Pond* (1981), which allowed him to close his career on its highest-ever note.

Henry Fonda reprised his acclaimed Broadway stage role as the title character in 1955's wartime comedy *Mister Roberts*, one of his most memorable screen performances. Courtesy of Warner Bros.

Fonda was also the founder of a modern acting dynasty with daughter Jane, herself a two-time Oscar winner, and son Peter, whose performance in *Easy Rider* (1969) helped make it one of the great films of its era. Peter's daughter, Bridget, has also had a significant movie career.

Setting the Scene

I first interviewed Henry Fonda in Toronto in 1976 as he got ready to go onstage in his one-man show as famed courtroom attorney Clarence Darrow. There was a later, more leisurely encounter in 1977 in his suite at the Century Plaza Hotel in Los Angeles while he was promoting a PBS special he narrated on Mary Pickford. We met again in his trailer in California's Simi Valley in 1979 as he was shooting scenes for the TV miniseries *Roots: The Next Generations*.

The Interview

BAWDEN: Here we are weeks after your wonderful American Film Institute tribute. Have you recovered yet?

FONDA: Oh, I never will. It's overwhelming. So many friendly faces. I just sat there completely stunned. They're sending over a cassette and I'll watch it all months from now if I've recovered by then.

BAWDEN: I asked Jimmy Stewart this same question: did you ever want to attempt the classic stage roles but were held back by your basic Americanism?

FONDA: A great question. I just never had the guts to try, although a friend said I could do Prospero in *The Tempest* well enough. But my accent wouldn't be right. So why try? I know Laurence Olivier once told me he always wanted to ride the range in a John Wayne western. We all have our unrealized projects. And I did play Pierre in *War and Peace* [1956], although in the book he's a big, stocky guy.

BAWDEN: How did you get into movies?

FONDA: In 1935 I needed a job. Broadway was wilting. Came out on my own to scout the joint. And I signed with producer Walter Wanger, who also had Charles Boyer and Sylvia Sidney on contract and promised to build me up and keep me busy forty weeks of every year.

BAWDEN: Your first movie job was opposite Janet Gaynor in *The Farmer Takes a Wife*.

FONDA: She was a year younger but had been in movies since 1927 and won the first Oscar in 1927–1928. Victor Fleming directed. And after a first day I felt pretty confident until Vic showed me the rushes the next day and used the term "hammy." I recoiled. I was awful, projecting right back to the upper balcony. Vic explained in a movie close-up a raised eyebrow can be noticed. He said to speak as slowly and as deeply as I could and that advice has been helping me get by ever since.

BAWDEN: Another early credit is *Trail of the Lonesome Pine* [1936].

FONDA: Third billed to Sylvia Sidney, who was a big star at the time, and Fred MacMurray. On location at Big Bear Lake. I carved the initials "HF LUVS SS" on a tree and director Henry Hathaway found it when he returned to shoot *Woman Obsessed* in the same spot in 1959. It was Paramount's first outdoors Technicolor epic. In 1941 it was rereleased with Fred getting top billing as Sylvia had [temporarily] left movies. Then in 1955 it was rereleased again and I wired Fred: "At last: top billing" because [my] *Mister Roberts* was then a movie hit.

BAWDEN: You made two films squiring Bette Davis and never worked with her again.

FONDA: *That Certain Woman* [1937] was a glossy soap, but *Jezebel* won Bette a second Oscar and she was magnificent. Willie Wyler would do forty takes and then choose the first one, which made her angry, but I liked the experience of working with a top director.

BAWDEN: Another top director you worked with was Fritz Lang.

FONDA: He yelled, he screamed on *You Only Live Once*. Oh, it was agony, but the movie is just great. I was a nobody. By contrast Sylvia [Sidney] was a big star and he left her alone. By the time we made *The Return of Frank James* [1940], I was at Fox and he was the freelancer. He was still nasty as hell but the screaming had toned down. But that film with its use of color is tops.

BAWDEN: How did you get the lead in *Young Mr. Lincoln?*

FONDA: The screenwriter, Lamar Trotti, had seen me in *The Farmer Takes a Wife* a few years earlier and thought I'd make a good young Lincoln by the slow way I spoke. In late 1938 he phoned me up and asked could he come around that night with producer Kenneth McGowan and they'd read the script to me. I'd just seen Ray Massey on Broadway in *Abe Lincoln in Illinois*. A few days later Fox said they'd pay me to do a simple test. It took an hour to get on the false nose and that false beard. They all wanted me, but I thought my voice all wrong. I'd just severed connections with Walter Wanger and I needed work. And about a month later director John Ford's secretary phoned and invited me over. I did so because I was curious—we'd never met. In his office Ford was chewing on a handkerchief and was dressed like a stumble bum. He'd seen the test and asked why I didn't want to work with him. A few months without work had weakened my resolve. Ford kept saying this was the Lincoln twenty years earlier than the play, when he was a completely different fella. He got me so ornery I said I'd take a try.

BAWDEN: What sort of a director was he?

FONDA: Mean, ornery, stubborn. He rarely moved the camera. His direction would consist of a phrase like, "Go for it!" We got on okay and the film got released before Ray Massey's, which was far more accurate.

BAWDEN: Then you made a second film with Ford in the same year— *Drums along the Mohawk.*

FONDA: It's too pretty. The Technicolor made everything seem like a picture postcard. In addition, there was a real battle with Claudette Colbert, who was a huge star at the time. Fox paid a real packet to get her and she was determined to show Ford she was in charge. She'd argue about every close-up, about lighting, what lens was he going to use. He erupted several times but she just kept pressing him.

BAWDEN: How did you get the plum part of Tom Joad in *The Grapes of Wrath?*

FONDA: By mortgaging my soul. Fox head Darryl Zanuck said he'd give it to me if I signed a standard seven-year deal. He said, "Trust me and we'll make great pictures." Ford shot in a very tight fashion so Zanuck wouldn't have footage to play with and ruin the way Ford wanted a scene to be, I mean the basic rhythm. Much was shot at actual migrant camps around L.A. But that famous last scene? Ford had Jane Darwell and I sit around and stew for hours while tension built up. Then he took his one take and it's the best bit of screen acting I think I ever accomplished, and Jane feels the same way.

BAWDEN: Darwell won her Oscar and Ford won as Best Director, but you only got a nomination, the sole one so far in your career.

FONDA: I was told my pal Jimmy Stewart won [for *The Philadelphia Story*] because members felt he should have won for *Mr. Smith Goes to Washington* the year before. Zanuck refused to promote me for *The Ox-Bow Incident* because it lost money. I never even got a nomination for *Mister Roberts.*

BAWDEN: Zanuck's promise didn't turn out so well. Your Fox films were pretty awful.

FONDA: I had a nothing part in *Lillian Russell* [1940]. My character was made up to be with Alice Faye at the beginning and walk off with her at the end. It was terrible, not much more than a cameo. She had romances with a pack of guys including Don Ameche. I felt humiliated.

Henry Fonda as Tom Joad, heading for California in 1940's *The Grapes of Wrath.*
Courtesy of 20th Century-Fox.

BAWDEN: Then he loaned you out all over the place.

FONDA: *The Lady Eve* is one of my best movies. It was made at Paramount. Preston Sturges shot so quickly we'd break for lunch at 1 p.m. at his restaurant and never return until the next day. It was just the most wonderful, freeing part and Barbara Stanwyck was amazing. She got an Oscar nomination. *The Male Animal,* which I made at Warners, was also a fine thinking man's comedy with me and Livvie de Havilland. She's the only leading lady I've costarred in film, onstage [*A Gift of Time*], and on TV [*Roots: The Next Generations*].

BAWDEN: Tell me about *The Ox-Bow Incident.*

FONDA: Zanuck wasn't happy about doing it. I think he felt it might really flop with the public, which it did. So most was shot on standing sets with painted backdrops. It only runs seventy-five minutes long because Zanuck chopped it back, thinking he could run it as the top of a double bill. It really became a commentary on contemporary American society and it propelled Dana Andrews to stardom.

BAWDEN: We don't mention other stinkers along the way?

FONDA: They include *Chad Hanna* [1940], *Wild Geese Calling* [1941], *You Belong to Me* [1941], *Rings on Her Fingers* [1942], *The Magnificent Dope* [1942]. I enlisted [in the military] partly to get away from this awfulness. I mean, patriotism was the real reason—but so many bad pictures!

BAWDEN: You returned with a great western.

FONDA: *My Darling Clementine* is beautiful to watch. I was the martinet in John Ford's *Fort Apache* [1948]. But I was totally miscast as [a priest in another Ford film], *The Fugitive* [1947] and I knew it. And Zanuck had plopped me into a Joan Crawford soap opera, 1947's *Daisy Kenyon*, and I was third billed after Dana Andrews. And I did as I was told so I could walk out that gate and never return.

BAWDEN: Why go back to Broadway at this point?

FONDA: I got the role of a lifetime, the lead in *Mister Roberts*. We opened in February 1948 and I never wanted to leave it. I'd never gotten standing ovations before. And sometimes this happened at matinees. I never tired of it, did over a thousand performances. The days I had two performances I was in heaven. Thought I'd go back to pictures in 1951 when it closed, but *Point of No Return* came along and we played in that for almost a year, closing in November 1952. And then *The Caine Mutiny Court-Martial* [1954] showed up and it ran just over a year. It resurrected the career of John Hodiak and then he died suddenly of a heart attack. We were all shocked.

BAWDEN: Did you think you'd get the movie version of *Mister Roberts?*

FONDA: No! Jack Warner had this crazy policy of buying a Broadway hit and then completely recasting it, and he publicly said he was after Bud [Marlon] Brando. After all, I'd been out of movies for seven years, so I was no longer box office and I was about to hit fifty and Roberts was supposed to be thirtyish. Only when Jack Ford was hired as director was I chosen. Ford said it had to be me or he'd quit. Filming in San Diego was a nightmare. Ford tried to turn it into just another service comedy and I tried to protect its integrity. One night he'd been drinking and we started quarreling in a corner and blows were exchanged. The next day he left the picture for minor surgery. We never worked together again.

BAWDEN: What happened then?

FONDA: Mervyn LeRoy had just rejoined Warners and he directed about half the picture. He redid some San Diego bits back at the studio and saved the picture. After he left, producer Leland Hayward even did some touch-ups. Bill Powell was so unnerved by the process he never made another movie. But because of the bad publicity, I never even got an Oscar nomination.

BAWDEN: You got passed over for other movie versions of your Broadway hits.

FONDA: I did *Two for the Seesaw* in 1958 opposite a darling new actress, Anne Bancroft. I should say she was new to me. She'd done some terrible B films. We really clicked in it, but Bob Wise picked Bob Mitchum and Shirley MacLaine for the movie, which predictably tanked. I did *Critic's Choice* in 1961, but Bob Hope and Lucille Ball did the movie, and their fan bases didn't come to that sort of thing. On the other hand I got *The Male Animal,* which ran on Broadway with Elliott Nugent. And I saw the road company of *Advise and Consent,* which had Farley Granger and Chester Morris in it.

BAWDEN: You were not a fan of Alfred Hitchcock.

FONDA: We shot much of *The Wrong Man* [1957] in New York City in a bitterly cold winter, In one scene at a house, Hitch sat in his warm car and gave his instructions to the assistant director. Then we moved to the Warners back lot and those scenes seem so very obvious. Had everything been shot on actual locations it might have worked. These days he says my reaction to everything in close-up was the same. But he never gave us any tips—just a brief word where the camera was going to be.

BAWDEN: Then you had three political dramas out there almost at once.

FONDA: *Advise and Consent* [1962] still works because Otto Preminger shot on actual Washington locations, and this was tough because crowds gathered everywhere we shot. Don't know how he got permission to shoot in the actual Senate and all those hallways, on the little train that ran underground between the buildings.

In *The Best Man* [1964] I was the Adlai Stevenson candidate for the presidency. The ending was a big surprise to the audience. I liked that. And Lee Tracy was the Harry S. Truman presidential figure from the past, just as Cliff Robertson was the Richard Nixonian figure.

Then there was *Fail-Safe* in 1964, which is more of its time. People think the nuclear issue is over, but it's present today with more countries than ever having the bomb. I think Walter Matthau is just terrific here. It didn't do the anticipated business because *Dr. Strangelove* beat us to the movie theaters and was a more flamboyant production. Yes, I did go see it to check out the competition.

BAWDEN: Did you always know what constituted a hit?

FONDA: No, I watched the first edit of *Spencer's Mountain* [1963] and thought it namby-pamby. And then it made a lot of dough and spawned a TV series, *The Waltons.*

BAWDEN: But you tried a TV series, *The Smith Family,* in 1971–1972.

FONDA: We had thirty-nine episodes over two years. I still blame Fred MacMurray for this one. He kept telling me how easy series situation comedies were. He worked on *My Three Sons* for twenty-two weeks, did all his scenes out of context, and left for his next Disney movie. So I gave it a try and nobody watched. Ronny Howard was my son. I picked Janet Blair as my wife. Jimmy Stewart similarly failed at a TV sitcom and so did Bing Crosby. Fred made it seem so easy, which just wasn't the case.

BAWDEN: You said in one interview you sometimes chose a project purely for the money.

FONDA: I know you are trying to get me to cite a certain Canadian title! I just won't do it! [He was referring to 1979's *City on Fire.*] I look at the offers and accept the best one. It's either that or stay at home and fume about not working.

BAWDEN: Ever had an itch to direct?

FONDA: I have an itch not to direct. On *Sometimes a Great Notion* [1970] the director left and Paul Newman stepped in and he was wonderful. Then years later Joanne Woodward directed me in an episode of *Family* [in 1979]. I knew her from *A Big Hand for the Little Lady* [1966]. And she knew what she was doing. I have no idea how to motivate another actor. It's beyond my capabilities, so why bother?

BAWDEN: Ever watch your old movies on TV?

FONDA: I turned on the set one night and watched a substantial part of *The Moon's Our Home* [1936] and [I] admit my then wife, Margaret Sullavan, enchanted me all over again. And Barbara Stanwyck told me to catch our first film together, *The Mad Miss Manton* [1938], which I always loathed. I watched a bit and I still hate myself in it. And I'm not too happy seeing myself forty years back and how I've aged.

BAWDEN: Future plans?

FONDA: To work until they give me that damned Oscar. My daughter Jane already has two of them, which is as embarrassing as hell.

Henry Fonda with ex-wife Margaret Sullavan in their only film together, *The Moon's Our Home* (1936). Courtesy of Paramount.

Afterword

In 1981 Fonda was awarded an honorary Oscar for his acting, presented by Robert Redford. And in 1982 he finally won an Oscar in competition for *On Golden Pond*, but was too ill to attend the ceremony. He died of heart failure on August 12, 1982, aged seventy-seven.

Victor Mature

Interview by Ron Miller

Theater-trained Victor Mature, a member of the Pasadena Playhouse repertory company, was signed to a contract by film producer Hal Roach in 1939 and quickly given a leading role opposite veteran star Joan Bennett in the 1939 film *The Housekeeper's Daughter,* a comedic murder mystery that was hardly noticed. Then Roach gave Mature the leading role in a most unusual film, the prehistoric adventure saga *One Million B.C.* (1940). As Tumak, the cave man, Mature romanced beautiful Carole Landis and costarred with Lon Chaney Jr., but none of them spoke any dialogue while battling dinosaurs and running from erupting volcanoes.

A big, muscular guy, Mature never looked like a conventional leading man, but he had a strong screen presence and 20th Century-Fox quickly bought up his contract from Roach and, starting in 1941, began to put him into a variety of roles. In that early period, Mature played opposite some of Hollywood's top female stars, including Betty Grable and Rita Hayworth, who were both romantically linked to him. He was married five times and was still with his fifth wife, Loretta, at the time of his death.

Mature's greatest films include the 1941 thriller *I Wake Up Screaming* (with Betty Grable), the 1942 musical *My Gal Sal* (with Rita Hayworth), the 1942 comedy *Seven Days Leave* (with Lucille Ball), John Ford's classic 1946 western *My Darling Clementine* (as Doc Holliday, with Henry Fonda as Wyatt Earp), and the immortal film noir *Kiss of Death* (1947) with Richard Widmark.

In 1949, Cecil B. DeMille cast Mature in the epic *Samson and Delilah* opposite screen siren Hedy Lamarr and permanently moved Mature into the "beefcake" category of movie action heroes. This led to his vivid role as the slave Demetrius in 1953's *The Robe,* the biblical extravaganza that introduced the new widescreen era at the major studios. It was followed by

36

Victor Mature as the slave Demetrius in *The Robe* (1953). Courtesy of 20th Century-Fox.

a sequel built around him—*Demetrius and the Gladiators* (1954)—and other historical epics like *The Egyptian* (1954) and *Hannibal* (1959).

By 1979, Mature had pretty much retired from acting and settled down in his home at Rancho Santa Fe, a Southern California golf resort. He returned to the screen for a final appearance in the TV remake of *Samson and Delilah* in 1984, playing the role of Samson's father.

Setting the Scene

I grew up on Victor Mature movies and the stories about him in the movie magazines. His *One Million B.C.* was sold to television almost as soon as the medium started up, and I suppose I'd seen him in that at least a dozen times in my youth.

One of my editors at my first newspaper job had served in the US Coast Guard with Victor Mature during World War II and remembered him as a very nice guy who had to put up with lots of questions about his sex life with Betty Grable and Rita Hayworth, the top pinup girls for servicemen in the war years. He told me Mature never told anything about those fabulous beauties, which he thought was a sign of a true gentleman.

Having admired Mature's work for years, I naturally eagerly accepted when the ABC network offered me a chance to interview him over the phone from his Rancho Santa Fe home about his participation in the *Samson and Delilah* remake.

Mature turned out to be a very witty, exceptionally likeable fellow on the phone and he even came prepared with a series of corny jokes that he told me before we began the interview. He said he wanted to put me in a good mood. He didn't need the jokes to do that.

The Interview

MILLER: The conventional wisdom is that playing a caveman in *One Million B.C.* got you off on the wrong foot because it emphasized your muscular physique and only let you grunt instead of speak any lines.

MATURE: That was supposed to set me back a long time because everybody thought I was just a grunt and groaner. I did a few more pictures, then decided I'd better get my ass back to New York and do a play. I figured that would put me back on track.

MILLER: Well, you certainly chose well because you wound up costarring with Gertrude Lawrence in a Broadway smash—Moss Hart's *Lady in the Dark* [1941]. How did that work as an image-changer?

MATURE [*laughing*]: Not so well. There was a single line in the play that fixed me good. A woman looks at me and says, "My God, what a beautiful hunk of man!" So the press picks up on that and from then on I was "the beautiful hunk of man!"

MILLER: What's amazing is that you hadn't really played a so-called beefcake role since *One Million B.C.* But then you did *Samson and Delilah.* What was it like working for the famous C. B. DeMille?

MATURE: I never had any personal clashes with him, but he was cantankerous as hell. He would raise hell with somebody like the wardrobe man for twenty minutes, then end up with a line like: "To think they're chopping up little fishes for bait down in San Pedro and leaving you wardrobe men free!" That's the kind of cat he was.

MILLER: How do you think he'd get along today with all the nudity and sexuality in movies?

MATURE: Hell, in reality, he was a wild mother. He loved those orgies in those old movies of his. Everybody was always doing something lascivious with their hands in those scenes. He was quite a character for that kind of stuff.

MILLER: A guy at ABC told me that the European theatrical version of the new *Samson and Delilah* will show Delilah [Belinda Bauer] topless.

MATURE: Well, that's nothing new. If you look quick, you can see a glimpse of Claudette Colbert's tits in the bathtub scene in DeMille's 1934 *Cleopatra.*

MILLER: I understand producer Frank Levy had quite a bit of trouble shooting the temple destruction scene in the new *Samson and Delilah.*

MATURE: So did DeMille in the original version. It cost him $60,000 every time that huge statue fell the wrong way. It was about forty feet tall. They had to build the whole set over again every time it fell wrong. No matter what trouble he had, Levy is still a miracle man. He filmed the whole remake for about $3 million. To do DeMille's version today would cost about $30 million. Anybody who can save $27 million on a movie is a miracle man.

MILLER: You haven't made a picture since 1979. How did he talk you into playing Samson's father?

MATURE: I told him that if the price was right, I'd play Samson's mother. I didn't read the script or anything. When I got down to Mexico [where the film was made] and read the part, I decided I really should have played the mother. [Maria Schell played the mother.]

MILLER: So you think it was a mistake?

MATURE: I don't want to mislead anybody. The original *Samson and Delilah* was a big, big DeMille picture and I don't want anybody to think I have anything like a comparable role in this. Actually, my part is meaning-

Victor Mature in captivity in *Samson and Delilah* (1949). Courtesy of Paramount.

less and unnecessary. Between you and me, I should have phoned it in. It would have spared the TV audience having to see me running around in a kimono with a towel wrapped around my neck. All I do is warn Samson not to marry that Philistine broad. I felt like a Yiddisher mama.

MILLER: Why did you decide to retire from movies in the first place?

MATURE: I never did say to heck with Hollywood. All my life I had a plan to save a certain amount of money until I was about fifty, then take it easy. That's what I did.

MILLER: So, setting aside this little role in a TV movie, what's life like for you today?

MATURE: I spend most of my time on the golf course. I'm usually up at 5 a.m. and take care of my sideline real estate business by 7 a.m. Right now my wife, Lorey, is recovering from surgery, so I've been playing mother to our nine-year-old daughter, Victoria. She'll be bouncing through here any minute now, ready for me to take her to school. I take her to school, to piano and dance lessons, to the library—and then I go stand in line at the supermarket to buy groceries. Those are the exciting things I've been doing lately.

MILLER: Did you have any career advice for Anthony Hamilton, who plays Samson in the new movie?

MATURE: I told him to save his money and not worry about being typecast as a hunk. I gave him a general idea how important it is to have a starring role like this to show around. It's a hell of a lot better than one of those appearances on *The Love Boat.*

Afterword

It's widely assumed that Mature was doing a parody of himself when he played the egotistical retired movie star in the 1966 film *After the Fox,* written by playwright Neil Simon. It's also assumed George Clooney was doing a parody of Mature with his role as a "beefcake" movie star in the Coen brothers' 2016 film *Hail Caesar!*

Married five times, Mature also was twice engaged to marry famous movie stars—Rita Hayworth and Anne Shirley—but didn't tie those knots. He had only one child—daughter Victoria—by his last wife, Loretta.

Mature died at home from leukemia on August 4, 1999. He was buried in his hometown of Louisville, Kentucky.

Walter Pidgeon

Interview by James Bawden

Solemn and exuding strength of character and resolve, Walter Pidgeon was among the most confident and reassuring of leading men in Hollywood for more than a generation.

Curiously, he began his screen career in silent pictures after a stage background that included performing in musicals. He was possessed of a rich baritone singing voice that was rarely heard in his movie career.

Though he had been in dozens of pictures before signing a contract with MGM in 1937, Pidgeon had not become a real movie star and often suffered from miscasting, even at MGM, where he was starred in a series of "Nick Carter" mysteries that seemed all wrong for him. It wasn't until the 1940s that Pidgeon emerged as a strong screen presence, first on loanout to Fox to play the father in the Oscar-winning film of 1941, *How Green Was My Valley*, then in a series of dramas at MGM with Greer Garson, beginning with *Blossoms in the Dust* (1941) and *Mrs. Miniver* (1942), another Oscar-winning Best Picture.

Still, even when he was a film's leading man, Pidgeon almost always seemed to be in support of some other player, like Garson. He had one of his most enduring roles in 1956 at the very end of his days at MGM when he starred in the science fiction adventure *Forbidden Planet*.

In the 1950s, Pidgeon returned to the stage, only occasionally doing film roles. He earned a Tony Award nomination for his part in *Take Me Along* with Jackie Gleason on Broadway.

Pidgeon was very active in the Screen Actors Guild and served as its president from 1952 to 1957.

After the death of his first wife in childbirth in 1921, Pidgeon began a long relationship with his secretary, Ruth Walker, whom he married in 1931. They remained married until his death in 1984 at age eighty-seven after a series of strokes.

Walter Pidgeon circa 1938. James Bawden collection.

Setting the Scene

It was a warm February day in 1972 and Walter Pidgeon was embarking on the most depressing walk of his life. The seventy-four-year-old actor was back on the MGM lot for the first time in a decade and, after a hearty lunch in the mostly deserted commissary, was told there'd be a two-hour delay before the next scene in *Skyjacked* would be shot. "So I decided to revisit my old haunts," he told me. "I sincerely wish I hadn't. Everywhere I went there was desolation, decay. I walked down Main Street and ghosts of the past kept popping up. Park Avenue was in a terrible state of disrepair. Over on the "European" street, I'd once glimpsed Garbo hurrying to the set of *Ninotchka*. Over there was the street leading to the male star dressing rooms. I couldn't find anything or anybody I recognized. Where was the street where I was run over in *Madame Curie*? A few old relics were still around, PR guys and photographers. It was all so very still. My first day on the lot in 1937 all thirty soundstages were bustling with activity. Now only one film was shooting." So Pidgeon turned on his heels and went back to the motor home that doubled as a dressing room and waited to be called for the next shot.

He told me the anecdote the very next year while making *The Neptune Factor* in Toronto. This interview is drawn from that meeting, several subsequent phone talks, and a lovely tea at his home in Beverly Hills.

The Interview

BAWDEN: Tell me about your childhood and youth in Canada.

PIDGEON: I was born in Saint John, New Brunswick, in 1897. Oh, I'd like to pretend it was 1901, but that would be putting one over on you. We lived in a section called Indian Town, very close to the famous Reversing Falls. My father, Caleb Pidgeon, who had a very successful men's clothing store, died when I was six. I had two brothers and two half-brothers. We were very close. My mother kept going back every year to Saint John until she just physically couldn't take it anymore. Mother left in 1925 to come out to California and look after my tiny daughter—my first wife had died in childbirth. Mother slipped away when she was ninety-four, still dreaming of those days in Saint John.

BAWDEN: You tried to enlist during World War I?

PIDGEON: I ran off to join my brother Don in the Canadian Army when war was declared. But my age was discovered and I was sent home. So I enrolled in the University of New Brunswick for several months. Then I finally got in [the army] but was crushed by two gun carriages at Camp Petawawa and caught pneumonia. By war's end I was still recuperating. I was told to take it easy, and what could be easier than a bank teller in Boston? It was the Shawmut Bank and I doubled as a messenger.

BAWDEN: How did the acting start?

PIDGEON: I had always yearned to act—not sing, mind you! But the story is true that Freddie Astaire heard me singing away at a party and got me an agent. I got into E. E. Clive's repertory company, where I really learned to act.

BAWDEN: But in those days you had a young wife to support, so you worked in the brokerage business. Then you were widowed and left with a baby daughter, Edna. What did you do then?

PIDGEON: I heard that Elsie Janis was looking for a singing partner. I auditioned; she liked my voice and then collapsed in laughter when I told her my name. "It's worth thousands of dollars in publicity," she said. "Never, never change it." And I didn't!

BAWDEN: How long did you stay with Elsie Janis?

PIDGEON: I spent six months as her partner, then appeared in the New York sketch musical *Puzzles of 1925*. After that, I appeared in the London revue *At Home* and was signed by First National to appear in a Constance Talmadge movie. But it never happened. I arrived in late 1925 and nobody wanted me. Spent the first six months just getting used to this wonderful new world.

In 1925, L.A. had no traffic jams, no pollution. You'd smell the orange blossoms everywhere, and one might spin down Sunset Boulevard with only a few other cars on the road. First National had a sprawling compound out in Burbank that was just beautiful. Dick Barthelmess was the biggest star, Colleen Moore another. I don't know the logistics but everybody thought it odd this huge studio got absorbed by scrawny Warner Bros. in 1927. I made four or five movies that year, the same every year after that. But I was an abject failure as a silent actor. I needed my voice to act and what's more I hated all that hammy stuff of gesticulating. I finally returned to the stage, only to be brought back a year later for operettas.

BAWDEN: Then Warners put you under contract?

PIDGEON: Yes, but I was back at the First National lot most days. Nobody remembered I'd just wound up a stint there, I was such a bust. Singing in operettas was a big challenge. The mikes were huge and hidden in pots or flower vases and we couldn't move [while] singing because the sound might be distorted. The full orchestra was off to the right and we'd rehearse and rehearse and then try for a full take with the cameraman sweating in an airless booth and those huge lights when it was Technicolor. It was completely stressful and the singers and the musicians would inevitably start mixing everything up.

The day actually came when I was strolling after dining out near home and the theater marquee I passed read, "Walter Pidgeon sings only one song in this picture!" I just knew I had to get out of musicals for good— and I did. The irony is the last of them, *Viennese Nights* [1931], was pretty decent but nobody went to see it. I also did the fastest remake in history— the 1927 *The Gorilla* and the 1931 version—and I had different parts in both!

BAWDEN: I guess the 1931 *Photoplay* profile titled "He Has the Girls Gasping" described you as the fan magazines saw you at the time. It said: "He is like John Boles, neglected by the silent drama. He has just come into his own along with the microphone. . . . He is tall, remarkably well tailored. . . . And Walter has the finest head of hair of any man on the screen." Still, your movie career seemed stalled.

PIDGEON: I finished my Warner Bros. contract with a mere bit in *The Journal of a Crime* [1934] and then I replaced Melvyn Douglas on Broadway in *No More Ladies*. In early 1935, I was with Tallulah Bankhead in the short-lived play *Something Gay* and then played a gangster in the play *The Night of January 16th*.

BAWDEN: Then the movies noticed you again and you stirred up a lot of publicity by turning down the role of Gaylord in the 1936 movie version of *Show Boat*, which came with a salary of $125,000.

PIDGEON: I had no intention of ever playing Gaylord. But I wanted Hollywood bigwigs to know about it and be impressed.

BAWDEN: So instead, you made a bunch of modest programmers for Paramount—*Fatal Lady* [1936], *Big Brown Eyes* [1936]—and Universal— *Girl Overboard* [1937], *As Good as Married* [1937], *A Girl with Ideas* [1937].

PIDGEON: Finally MGM phoned. I'd first visited Metro in 1931 when I was in operettas and had a chance meeting with studio head Louis B. Mayer. He became enraged when I said I was from Saint John and offered to wrestle me to the ground. [Mayer, who was also from Saint John, assumed Pidgeon was fabricating a Canadian background to ingratiate himself with the boss.] But I showed him some of the newspapers Mother used to bring home for me to read. He said at the time he had nothing for me and we'd meet again. It took him six years to live up to that promise. He bought up my Universal contract [in late 1937] and said he wanted me to be a backup Bill Powell. I'd lose the girl in A features but also get to star in programmers.

BAWDEN: The first was the second male lead in *Saratoga* [1937] with Clark Gable and Jean Harlow?

PIDGEON: It was a humdinger of a way to start at MGM, but I instantly felt there was something wrong with Jean Harlow. She was sweating profusely all day, but she told me it was a bad cold. She'd had them before and all would be well. But she deteriorated on a daily basis. Finally, I had to playfully toss her onto a couch and she just lay there, couldn't get up. She passed days later. It was such a shock and the entire company felt so awful. She was such an exceptional girl. Clark [Gable] was completely devastated.

BAWDEN: How did MGM treat you then?

PIDGEON: I was finally getting star treatment. I just loved doing *My Dear Miss Aldrich* [1937] with Maureen O'Sullivan. It showed I could do comedy. And of course I lost Myrna Loy to Gable in *Too Hot to Handle* [1938]. But *Man-Proof* [1938] with Myrna and Roz Russell was very pleasant. And I also had parts in *The Shopworn Angel* [1938], *The Girl of the Golden West* [1938], and *Listen, Darling* [1938], so L. B. had delivered, and when I asked for meaty action parts, he gave me the Nick Carter series. They were my most popular movies yet, really established me, and I was sad when the series was stopped because L. B. argued I'd become too big a name for programmers.

BAWDEN: You also were sought after by other studios and Universal borrowed you for their Deanna Durbin picture *It's a Date* [1940].

PIDGEON: We're both Canadians and she extolled Winnipeg while I talked up Saint John on the set.

BAWDEN: More important, though, were the films you did on loan-out to 20th Century-Fox.

PIDGEON: I thought *Man Hunt* [1941] one of the most exciting movies I'd ever been in and Fritz Lang really got the character down. Then I was asked to stay around by Willie Wyler, who was beginning pre-production on *How Green Was My Valley*. But he's so meticulous he ran out of time and had to be replaced by Jack Ford.

Ford is the greatest director I ever worked with. He kept stressing my character's sheer simplicity, spoke right up if I ever got a bit fancy. He'd watch rehearsals like a hawk, catch something an actor was doing and work to replace it. He gave direct direction such as I never received. This combination of Willie's technical preparations and Jack's sentimentality turned it into my best-ever picture.

BAWDEN: Back at MGM, they had a new partner for you—Greer Garson.

PIDGEON: The first was *Blossoms in the Dust*. People said we acted as if we already knew each other. We did! I'd met her in 1938 when she first came to Metro and spent months twiddling her thumbs. I was asked to do her screen test as a favor and we just hit it off. She was pleasantly surprised I'd do something like this and we kept in touch.

BAWDEN: You rushed through your comedy with Rosalind Russell, *Design for Scandal* [1941], and were back with Garson in *Mrs. Miniver* for William Wyler.

PIDGEON: Willie Wyler took material that was often rather melodramatic and made audiences believe in this family. English? I was Canadian. Greer was Scots-Irish. Teresa Wright and Richard Ney, American. It was a real stew of types. But it worked. We flowered under the Wyler touch, even though that set, the home, was more Californian than English. But Willie got us to believe in the family and then deliver our characters so naturally.

The memorable scene of all the boats assembling in the Thames came as an afterthought by Mr. Mayer. The picture was locked in, prints were being made, but he insisted on the [added scene], which had to be rushed to meet the premiere deadline. It cost a small fortune, but Mr. Mayer never stinted on the costs. It was the scene people remember—plus Mrs. Miniver arresting the German soldier in her garden. Here was a film that gave people hope. Norma Shearer told me later she turned it down because she'd already done an anti-Nazi film [*Escape*] that didn't do well at the box office. So you see it's all in the timing.

BAWDEN: *Mrs. Miniver* was another Oscar winner and a big commercial success. What did it do for you?

PIDGEON: I got a dressing room in the male stars' building. Oh, it wasn't one room, but had a parlor, bedroom, dining room, closets, shower. On difficult night shoots, I'd stay there right through. At day's end, we'd usually congregate in Clark's dressing room, if he was filming: Bob Taylor, Spence Tracy, Bill Powell, Lionel [Barrymore], Frank Morgan. Gable usually left the set right at 5. He'd just stroll off. He'd serve scotch and water and we'd gossip about what was happening. If somebody's picture had

Walter Pidgeon with Greer Garson in *Mrs. Miniver* (1942), playing English civilians on the World War II home front. Courtesy of MGM.

bombed during a badly received preview then everybody would want to talk about that. But it was never malicious. By the way, Spence was the biggest gossip of all.

BAWDEN: What about *White Cargo* [1942]?

PIDGEON: Magnificently wacky. It was all done to show off Hedy Lamarr, but she said it was too silly. Did you know there was an earlier British version with Maurice Evans? He warned me against doing it. We sweated out those African scenes, shot out at the Tarzan jungle. It was unusually hot and that's real perspiration, not glycerin, you see on our faces. I asked Maureen O'Sullivan how she stood it and she said she wore fewer layers of clothes! I thought Dick Thorpe [the director] should have hammed it up a bit, but he was dead serious. The cast I remember as unusually good: young Dick Carlson, Frank Morgan, Reggie Owen. We all thought it quite dreadful. But it made a lot of money based on the adverts—everybody wanted to see Hedy in next to nothing.

BAWDEN: Then you did *Madame Curie* [1943] with Greer Garson.

PIDGEON: This one was all about Metro telling Greer she had become the new First Lady of the lot. The script had been bought for Garbo from Universal [where Irene Dunne was to do it] but I said right away I didn't want to play Pierre Curie. I couldn't get a handle on that man and complained to [director] Mervyn LeRoy that the guy was all science. And he said, "Walter, you've got it!" Pierre had no interpersonal skills at all. He was gauche with women, but there was something about this young Polish girl that made him want to work with her. When I saw it with a preview, they cheered wildly when the couple peer through the glass door at night and see the radium glow. It was quite an exciting moment!

BAWDEN: When did you realize you were now part of a box office team?

PIDGEON: After *Mrs. Parkington* [1944]. I finally gave in. I was part of a big box office team. We were never equals. The films weren't titled *Mr. Miniver, Monsieur Curie,* and *Mr. Parkington.* I knew that much. But as Major Augustus Parkington, I had a really virile part. Here was a man with a past. We even see his former French mistress [played by Agnes Moorehead]. But he is physically attracted to this bright Irish girl whose mother runs a boardinghouse. To him, she is his little Sparrow, his nickname for her. It was a roustabout kind of role, I felt free from all that drawing room stuff. And it became my favorite Garson-Pidgeon performance.

BAWDEN: How about *Week-end at the Waldorf* [1945], the remake of *Grand Hotel* [1932]?

PIDGEON: Calling it a remake of *Grand Hotel* is really stretching it. Ginger Rogers had the Garbo part, not as an aging ballerina but a with-it movie star. Lana Turner was a secretary like Crawford in the original, but was Van Johnson anything like the Lionel Barrymore part? Both had bad hearts and the resemblance stopped there. I wasn't a jewel thief like John Barrymore but a foreign correspondent. It was a big escapist hit for wartime audiences and played mostly for comedy. I would never turn down a hit like that and with Ginger acquired a new lifetime friend.

BAWDEN: How did it feel when studio boss Louis B. Mayer told you that you'd be playing Jane Powell's dad in *Holiday in Mexico* [1946]?

PIDGEON: I said, "Sure, L. B. Where do we start filming?" He looked stern and said, "Walter! You're supposed to get upset. You'll be playing a father, and Janie Powell is the star." I told him I'd already had a similar role opposite Deanna Durbin and I could survive any number of warbling teenagers. It would introduce me to a younger audience and as long as I didn't have to sing, that would be okay. I realized I had him on the defensive and jokingly added, "But never, never ask me to play opposite Lassie! That's where I draw the line—at animals of any sort." And L. B. kept that promise.

As for the girls, [Judy] Garland had the most talent but was always prone to hysteria. Durbin was the one with the operatic voice and she hated her screen image. Jane Powell was all work and her determination has kept her going the longest of all.

BAWDEN: Your other 1946 film, *The Secret Heart,* was supposed to be a ground-breaking dramatic treatise on psychiatry.

PIDGEON: That's what I was promised. But with [director] Bob Leonard at the controls, all that stuff got watered down. Plus having my dear June Allyson as the girl with the complexes made no sense. She was as sweet as apple pie. Claudette Colbert sensed it was going to be a disaster and kept trying to force the story back to the one we'd agreed on. I was warned I'd have a lot of trouble with Colbert, but there was none of the temperamental stuff. During breaks, she talked lenses with the cinematographer! A great technician, she might have made a fine director.

BAWDEN: How did you get your reputation as Hollywood's best-dressed male star?

PIDGEON: It came about after numerous sartorial failures. I learned not to be overdressed. Had about twenty suits and they were expertly tailored. I hate new shirts. They have to look a bit worn to look their best. Shoes were custom made and I watched my weight and used an exercise rowing machine. Violent exercise I never went for. Long walks were good, although the police in Beverly Hills would sometimes insist on accompanying me. I'd smoke a lot to keep the weight off, I confess it, but actually drink very little.

BAWDEN: In 1947, you got top billing in the remake of the A. S. M. Hutchinson novel *If Winter Comes.*

PIDGEON: It was first done as a 1923 silent and my memory serves to remind me we watched it in an MGM screening room. Percy Marmont had the lead. It dealt quite openly with the issue of adultery, which we could not do because of the Production Code. And there were fears audiences might be upset by the very thought of Mr. Miniver chasing somebody other than his wife. Vic Saville [the director] used every trick in the book to keep people watching. But the story was so watered down it was hard to understand just what was going on. Deborah Kerr was the object of my affections, a lovely girl. I think I was downright bad in it. Angela Lansbury was, however, pretty terrific. Imagine, a twenty-three-year-old girl masquerading as a forty-five-year-old and doing so splendidly. Metro packed the cast with scene-stealers: Binnie Barnes, Reggie Owen, Dame May Whitty. It and I were completely unbelievable.

BAWDEN: A year later, you and Garson were back at it again in *Julia Misbehaves.*

PIDGEON: We had more fun on this picture than on any other. Maybe too much fun? We were so glad to be rid of the tears that we both acted a bit goofy. Greer showed off her legs and stood at the top of a human pyramid. I even did pratfalls. Then we watched a rough cut and it all seemed so boisterous.

It was based on a hit novel [*The Nutmeg Tree* by Margery Sharp], but what emerged wasn't the story I'd read at all. The young lovers were played by Liz Taylor and Peter Lawford. That's when Greer and I realized we were slowing down. I even did sing a bit in that one, as I recall. One day Peter Lawford brought this Texan, oil man Buddy Fogelson, on set and Buddy, who had never seen a Garson picture, said, "Aw, heck, I'll take that little redhead up that ladder." It was Greer and he chose her over Liz Taylor, if you can imagine that! [Garson and Fogelson were later married.]

BAWDEN: How do you rate *Command Decision* [1948]?

PIDGEON: It was my best postwar performance. It was quite a gamble because Metro was nervous on two counts. There were no women and [director] Sam Wood proposed filming it just as the Broadway play—no outside scenes of the actual bombing runs which were endlessly debated inside the military board rooms. I still feel Sam was right, although grosses were not as strong as expected. In a military picture, audiences do not expect numerous interior scenes. My character, Major General Roland Kane, was very ambiguous, all hale and hearty but also very ambitious and deeply political. There was something of the likable rogue in him, but I was part of a remarkable troupe. Sam rehearsed us for days on the sets before starting, which wasn't Metro's style but helped get us up to scratch. Clark Gable was excellent—and he should have been all right. He had lived that kind of tension as a bombardier. Van Johnson and John Hodiak were the younger members, along with older members Edward Arnold and Charlie Bickford.

BAWDEN: After that came *That Forsyte Woman* [1949], based on John Galsworthy's novel *A Man of Property.*

PIDGEON: MGM was in a fighting mood. Television was starting to erode the audience base. People were no longer going out to movies once a week as they'd done during the war. So no expense was spared in costumes, in the Cedric Gibbons's sets, and in the cast. Errol Flynn was imported from Warners. He was a lovely fellow despite his roistering reputation, but he was expected to play young Jolyon Forsyte. But he stood his ground and argued successfully for casting against type and he got it and was cast as domineering Soames Forsyte and I got to play Jolyon. I didn't mind it because it gave me a challenge, too, but I just wasn't right and neither was Errol. Audiences were confused. And then there were the other leads: Bob Young and Janet Leigh, when the parts should have been done by English actors. With none of the five leads English no wonder the film lacked conviction. I thought Compton Bennett's direction too pokey. Mervyn LeRoy would have added so much more.

BAWDEN: Then, finally, there was a sequel to *Mrs. Miniver,* the dreary 1950 *The Miniver Story.*

PIDGEON: I argued against it. I just had this feeling. *Mrs. Miniver* wasn't meant to be realistic. It was of a certain time that had passed. To show the couple who had fought off the Nazis being defeated by her cancer, I just felt this was so unfair. We shot on actual locations and London in 1950 was still the site of bomb craters on every other street. It opens on V-E Day with Kay learning she has cancer and goes down from there. Few of the other cast members were back. Clem Miniver lost all his fighting spirit. No wonder nobody came to see it. I shouldn't say this, but a guy I'd worked with before, [director] Hank Potter, wasn't quite right, not imaginative enough. It should have been a British director since we'd come all this way but for what? But I'm pretty sure even [William] Wyler couldn't have fixed this one.

BAWDEN: Then you stayed on in England to do *Calling Bulldog Drummond* [1950].

PIDGEON: It was going to restart the series but be based in Britain to use up the MGM money the British Labour government insisted be spent at home. I think I was okay as the amateur detective, but Margaret Leighton as my Scotland Yard sidekick? Come on now! I just think MGM was losing it. Greer was busy making the third version of *The Last of Mrs. Cheyney,* which was terrible. All the fight had gone out of the studio.

I blamed some of this on old L. B. and his inattention to detail. He seemed more interested in his racehorses during those years. But there was also the ascent of Dore Schary [who eventually took Mayer's place running MGM] and his love of message pictures. I found myself stuck in programmers. When star contracts were up, the studio let the stars go, including Clark Gable. He got into his convertible, circled past the Thalberg building, and drove off. He only returned once and that was to discuss doing *Home from the Hill* [1960] for Vincente Minnelli, but finally he turned it down. With his departure, the studio was never the same.

BAWDEN: But the studio still relied on Garson and Pidgeon and put you in *Scandal at Scourie* [1953].

PIDGEON: It just dragged. There just wasn't enough story. Greer and I were a Protestant couple adopting a little Roman Catholic girl [Noreen Corcoran] in nineteenth-century Ontario. So where was the drama? The studio was really trying and even imported Jean Negulesco as director. It would have worked as a half-hour TV drama. Greer had already had it. I remember on *The Miniver Story* her beau Buddy Fogelson was watching a scene being filmed on the set and said, "It takes less time to drill an oil well!" and he meant it. Greer knew she would have to make a choice between MGM and Buddy. She could see the studio was winding down, so she wisely chose Buddy. I had some years left on my contract and I sincerely tried to keep busy.

BAWDEN: This was about the time when you were placed more into star character roles rather than leading man roles. How did that go over with you?

PIDGEON: It was the age issue. I tried to make the best of it even if that meant slipping down the cast list. But Bill Powell just would not budge. He'd go to number two spot with Liz Taylor in the lead but no farther down. But I actually liked the character parts, like the studio head, in *The Bad and the Beautiful* [1952]. David Selznick hollered that the Kirk Douglas part had been patterned after him, but I actually adopted a few of his characteristics, that touch of condescension, plus a bit of L. B., done with great appreciation, I might add, and it seemed to work. I just laughed at my name, Harry Pebble, and, yes, I was third billed, but this was a huge success.

BAWDEN: But you were billed fifth in *Executive Suite* [1954].

PIDGEON: Another big commercial hit. This was a real acting feast, everyone in high gears, so I played the perennial second best man, Fred Alderson, as very meek, very quiet, and that drew attention. There was Freddie March, whom I never acted with before or since, and Barbara Stanwyck, who later made a terrible movie with me and Jimmy Cagney.

But for all that fury only Nina Foch got an Oscar nomination as the all-knowing secretary who actually says very little.

BAWDEN: That same year you were with Elizabeth Taylor again, this time in *The Last Time I Saw Paris*.

PIDGEON: At the premiere, I nudged the wife and asked her when was it that I'd turned so old looking. Next to Liz Taylor I looked positively ancient. And she said, "Walter, you've looked like this since *The Miniver Story*." And that cutting remark, even from my better half, kind of got to me. The film was awful—terrible back lot shooting that looked phony in color. It didn't hold up under that big screen.

BAWDEN: Around that time you were elected president of the Screen Actors Guild.

PIDGEON: MGM deliberately lightened my workload so I could concentrate on executive decision making. We won residual payments for TV showings of films and that really helped actors no longer in vogue.

BAWDEN: But you finally were leaving MGM after all those years.

PIDGEON: It was actually a relief to finally go. I'd notched my twenty-one years and got the pension. Very few actors got that, and did you know it was all set up in the 1940s just to aid Lionel Barrymore because it was feared he couldn't go on much longer. He died in harness, as did Lewis Stone, so when I left few actors were left except Bob Taylor, who was around another three years. And wouldn't you know it? I had my biggest postwar hit with *Forbidden Planet* [1956] just as I was leaving.

BAWDEN: Discuss that classic sci-fi film.

PIDGEON: [Producer] George Pal kept whispering, "Remember, Walter, it's Shakespeare!" [The film was a sci-fi version of *The Tempest*.] Sure, sure, but if I'm Prospero, was Robby the Robot Ariel? What I remember is the waiting around for the next trick shot to be planned. There was a lot of waiting and playing checkers on that one.

BAWDEN: After *These Wilder Years* [1956] with James Cagney and Barbara Stanwyck, you did *The Rack* [1957], playing Paul Newman's father.

PIDGEON: I thought MGM was fading fast. Why redo a live TV play [*The Rack*] everyone had already seen for free? It was changed so very little I'm convinced it was only made to save some money on more expensive projects. I had my hardest-ever scene here. I had to kiss Paul Newman. Yes, he was playing my son, but we just didn't do that kind of thing in my family and I was up all night before the filming. Did it in one take and that was that. But I never want to go through that again.

BAWDEN: Finally out of MGM, you went back to Broadway in *The Happiest Millionaire* [1956].

PIDGEON: I was cast as eccentric millionaire Drexel Biddle of Philadelphia. We did it as a comedy and not a musical. Walt Disney came backstage during the Broadway run and I told him, "Walt, you'd better film this one quickly because I'll be too old in a few years." And he giggled and said, "Walter, you're too old for it now." When he finally made it [in 1966], he added songs and used Fred MacMurray, who couldn't sing at all. Greer was in it. Not a hit, but I never could bear to see it. It made me feel bad, but what could I do? Toured with the play and we drew crowds everywhere. I'd stand by the stage door and autograph [for] everyone who came with a program. I always hated disappointing people. But those romantic notions about the theater were just about over. It was sheer drudgery, those eight performances a week.

BAWDEN: In 1959, you did a well-received TV revival of *Meet Me in St. Louis* with Myrna Loy as the wife and Jane Powell in the Judy Garland role.

PIDGEON: It was taped in black and white by MGM right on the same sets as the movie. The idea was to redo all the old hits as TV specials and this one ran as a CBS Sunday night spread. I'd never been able to do TV at Metro except for premieres because L. B. thought it competition. I did step in to replace George Murphy on the series MGM made for ABC called *MGM Parade*.

Anyway, I did get to sing a chorus of *Meet Me in St. Louis* with Myrna and those pipes of mine must have sounded remarkably clear because lyricist Bob Merrill caught it on TV, thought my voice fine, and signed me for the musical version of *Ah, Wilderness!* retitled *Take Me Along*, with Jackie Gleason as costar. We had a wonderful time in rehearsals. The cast included Una Merkel, Bobby Morse, and Eileen Herlie, but Jackie has a very low boredom threshold and started interpolating his routines. Audiences loved that kind of stuff and we could have run forever, but Jackie finally left out of sheer boredom.

BAWDEN: Back on the movie screen, you were first billed over Joan Fontaine in *Voyage to the Bottom of the Sea* [1961].

PIDGEON: Was this *Forbidden Planet* underwater with me as Morbius? I sometimes wondered. Joan kept muttering what a comedown this all was, but I told her we'd get a new audience and there was somebody for every segment: Frankie Avalon, Peter Lorre, Bob Sterling, whom I'd known at Metro, Barbara Eden. It made buckets of money and Peter kept us all in stitches. At one point he complained the pet shark was trying to steal all of his scenes!

BAWDEN: How about the all-star *Advise and Consent* [1962]?

PIDGEON: I was warned about [director] Otto Preminger, told he could scream with the worst of them. And he could, but he chose his subjects for abuse very carefully, never attacking the stars. I found him technically efficient at shooting in all those Washington locations despite the crowds we were drawing everywhere. I'd tease Hank Fonda that in this one I had the romantic scenes with Gene Tierney. She was in a very fragile state and Otto was ever so careful not to disturb her. I'd clutch her for a kissing scene and she was shaking like a leaf. I was the majority leader and had one scene set on the Potomac aboard a cruiser with the president [Franchot Tone] and vice president [Lew Ayres]. And Franchot jokes, "Look, it's the MGM Newcomers of 1938!"

I truly enjoyed some very extended shots with Charles Laughton, an actor's actor. He did them all on the first take and got petulant if Otto wanted to try it again. Charles joked that on most sets he had to have his clothes taken out because he ate so much during periods of stress. This time he was losing weight, the first signs of the cancer that would claim his life within a few years.

BAWDEN: In those later years, you finally began to make movies in your native Canada—*Big Red* [1962] in Quebec, *Harry in His Pocket* [1971] in Vancouver, and *The Neptune Factor* [1973] in Toronto.

PIDGEON: Talked about that once to Ray Massey, who hailed from Toronto, and we both agreed we might have stayed at home if there'd been a native movie industry.

BAWDEN: How do you like the pace of TV movies now that you've made quite a few?

PIDGEON: They're done as fast as those old Metro programmers and I can get in there and do my bits and leave. For example, I made one with Joe Cotten called *The Screaming Woman* [1972] opposite Livvie de Havilland. Our scenes were on different days. We never really met, and we finally did on *The Lindbergh Kidnapping Case* [1976] and got along famously. TV became very important to me. It helped remind people I was still around. But I simply would not try a series, although I was offered more than one.

My old pal Ward Bond was killed by *Wagon Train*. The pace was bru-

Charles Laughton (*left*) confronts Walter Pidgeon in the 1962 political drama *Advise and Consent*. Courtesy of Columbia Pictures.

tal. Bette Davis and I replaced Ray Burr on *Perry Mason* when he had his heart attack and we both agreed it was deadly. I had my courtroom speeches written out on my shirtsleeve cuffs. I loved doing *Cinderella* [1965] because it let me get caught up with Ginger Rogers, whose sense of professionalism has never changed. But a series? Never!

BAWDEN: Looking back at your MGM years and movie stardom, what are your thoughts today?

PIDGEON: Maybe it was better never to become red hot. I'd seen performers like that and they never lasted long. Maybe a long glow is the best way. At Metro I was never considered big enough to squire around Norma Shearer or Joan Crawford or Greta Garbo. Well, I outlasted them all at MGM, didn't I? It takes a lot of work to appear easygoing and I tried to avoid being stuffy.

Afterword

Pidgeon gave his last substantial performance on the short-lived NBC series *Gibbsville* in 1976 opposite newcomer John Savage, whom he praised lavishly on the phone to me. Wonderfully cast as an aging but still important writer, Pidgeon wound up his career still a master of his craft.

Subsequently a string of small strokes destroyed his balance and impaired his speech. He complained he'd topple over in his garden because he felt off balance. He died in a Santa Monica, California, hospital on September 25, 1984. He was eighty-seven.

Robert Preston

Interview by Ron Miller

It's impossible to think about actor Robert Preston without remembering him as Professor Harold Hill, the energetic leading character in the Broadway musical *The Music Man* and the 1962 movie version. It was a show-stopping performance and it created a high that Preston was never able to top.

Born Robert Preston Meservey in Massachusetts in 1918, he dropped his real surname when he first began making movies in 1938. After his family moved to Los Angeles, he became interested in acting and studied at the Pasadena Playhouse, which was constantly scouted by talent executives for the movie studios. The tall, rugged-looking Preston seemed ideal for action roles in movies and was signed by Paramount, where he made his debut as a tough seaman in Robert Florey's 1938 *King of Alcatraz*. During World War II, Preston joined the US Army Air Corps and served as an intelligence officer with the 386th Bomb Group of the US 9th Air Force.

Among his most important films were Cecil B. DeMille's *Union Pacific* (1939), a western with Gary Cooper; *Beau Geste* (1939), the classic desert action film, in which he played Cooper's brother; DeMille's *North West Mounted Police* (1940); *Reap the Wild Wind* (1942), DeMille's nautical saga, where he appeared as John Wayne's rival; *This Gun for Hire* (1942), the classic film noir; *Wake Island* (1942), John Farrow's exciting war film; *The Macomber Affair* (1947), Zoltan Korda's safari adventure film with Gregory Peck; *Blood on the Moon* (1948), Robert Wise's noir western with Preston the villain up against Robert Mitchum; and *The Dark at the Top of the Stairs* (1960), Delbert Mann's film from the William Inge play with Preston as an angst-ridden salesman with a troubled marriage.

From the early 1950s on, Preston went back and forth from Broadway shows to Hollywood films, rapidly building a grand reputation both as a stage performer in musicals (*The Music Man, I Do! I Do!, Mack and Mabel*)

Robert Preston in *Finnegan Begin Again* (1985). Courtesy of Home Box Office.

and as an actor in a variety of films, including *How the West Was Won* (1962), *All the Way Home* (1963), *Mame* (1974), *Victor Victoria* (1982), and *The Last Starfighter* (1984).

Above them all, though, was his triumphant performance in *The Music Man*, perhaps one of the most admired characterizations in musical film history.

Setting the Scene

Robert Preston was notoriously private, known for not revealing much about himself in his infrequent interviews. I met him for lunch at the quiet, luxurious Bel Air Hotel in 1985 while I was living in Los Angeles and covering both movies and television. He was doing the interview to promote his new HBO movie *Finnegan Begin Again* (1985), costarring Mary Tyler Moore.

I found Preston to be as lively and energetic as one would expect him to be after living in the character of Professor Harold Hill so long. He was then sixty-five and a very charming and likeable man.

The Interview

MILLER: You're such a veteran of both stage and screen at this point in your life—do you even remember what it was like starting out in pictures?

PRESTON: I was only nineteen when talent executives from Paramount saw me at the Pasadena Playhouse, but I wasn't exactly a babe in the woods. I've been learning my business since I was a child. I always felt I had the ability to play anything they threw at me. The fact that a lot of things didn't get thrown at me was the fault of the situation I was in back then.

MILLER: Explain that a little.

PRESTON: Well, I was doing musical comedy when they spotted me at Pasadena, but Paramount hardly ever used me in anything like that. Why? I think it was because they had Bing Crosby and Bob Hope doing all those musicals and comedies.

MILLER: What did they think you were good for?

PRESTON: I was either the leading man in the small films that nobody ever saw, the token love interest for sarong lady Dorothy Lamour, or the bad guy in the big films.

MILLER: How did the leading man sweepstakes work at the studio?

PRESTON: I stood at the end of a long line. The script went to Alan Ladd and if he didn't like it, then it went to Fred MacMurray. If Fred didn't like it, it went to Ray Milland, then to Bill Holden. And if he didn't like it, it finally went to me.

MILLER: Well, you seemed to be on the wanted list for Cecil B. De-Mille, who used you in several films.

Shirley Jones marches right along with Robert Preston in his signature role as Professor Harold Hill in *The Music Man* (1962). Courtesy of the Movie Channel and Warner Bros.

PRESTON: For the last ten years of his life, DeMille and I never spoke. We had an absolute schism. I simply had no respect for the man and I let him know it. I didn't want to be in another DeMille picture.

MILLER: Your return to theater seems to indicate you weren't happy with the way the movie career was going.

PRESTON: There was no way in the world that I could stay out here and break out of the category they'd put me in. My first chance to get out was when I was offered the role of Sky Masterson in a limited revival of *Guys and Dolls*. It would be my New York debut as a musical comedy star, but I turned it down because I didn't think I could do justice to the songs. I might have been wrong, but my decision not to do it turned out to be divinely inspired.

MILLER: How do you figure that?

PRESTON: If I had done it, just that two-week appearance in a musical would have taken away all the surprise and wonderment and joy that followed with my burgeoning full blown as Harold Hill the following season.

MILLER: I guess the reaction was that you were the obvious choice to play Harold Hill.

PRESTON: Far from it. That part didn't fit me. Nobody knew who the hell Harold Hill was until I put him on his feet. Even Meredith Willson, who wrote it, had no idea that's the way he was going to move, with all that dazzling footwork.

MILLER: As mind-boggling as it seems today, I've heard that Jack Warner, head of Warner Bros., didn't want you for the lead in the movie version, but preferred Frank Sinatra. Is that true?

PRESTON: Yes. Meredith Willson went to bat for me and said it couldn't be done without me in the role.

MILLER: Your interpretation of the role makes one feel that Harold Hill would never settle down for a quiet life in a retirement home.

PRESTON: He's like the character I play in *Finnegan Begin Again* and like Benjamin Franklin, who I played as an eighty-three-year-old on Broadway in *Benjamin Franklin in Paris*. He'd be the sort of man who'd walk into a drawing room, spot another eighty-three-year-old there and say, "What the hell's that old bastard doing here?"

MILLER: You bring lots of vitality to your roles. What's your secret?

PRESTON: Every day of rehearsal and every day you show up on the set, it's back to school time. The whole thing is a learning process and you never, never say you know it all. That's what keeps this thing fun for me at this age.

Afterword

After our chat, Preston made only one more film, the TV movie *Outrage* (1986). He lived comfortably in Montecito, a wealthy suburb of Santa Barbara, California, with his wife, Catherine, but succumbed to lung cancer in 1987 at the age of sixty-eight.

James Stewart

Interview by James Bawden

When people talk of actors who best represented the typical American persona, surely the name James "Jimmy" Stewart will be at the top of the list. The sincere, earnest fellow with the slightly stammering speech was an authentic hero whether he was starring in a comedy like Frank Capra's *Mr. Smith Goes to Washington* (1939), a dark western like Anthony Mann's *Winchester '73* (1950), or a suspenseful drama like Alfred Hitchcock's *Rear Window* (1954).

Born in 1908 in a small Pennsylvania town where his family operated a hardware store, Stewart was educated at Princeton, then went to Broadway, where he made his name in theater, earning a Hollywood contract in the 1930s. He began at MGM, where he was an Oscar-winning Best Actor by 1940, but his career was interrupted by military service in World War I. He distinguished himself as a bomber pilot, winning both the Air Medal and the Distinguished Flying Cross, ending up as a colonel in the air force. He later reached the rank of brigadier general in the reserves.

Stewart's earlier career seemed to prepare him for a life as a light comic actor—he even sang Cole Porter's tune "Easy to Love" to Eleanor Powell in *Born to Dance* (1936)—and his Oscar was for a comic role in *The Philadelphia Story* (1940). He seemed most to exemplify the loveable characters he played in Frank Capra's comedies. But the postwar Stewart risked his beloved all-American image in serious dramas like Hitchcock's *Rope* (1948) and the grim westerns of Anthony Mann, proving he was capable of provocative acting, even in daring films like Hitchcock's *Vertigo* (1958), in which he played a man haunted by his fears and his desires.

The mature Stewart was a bright and articulate man, for all his stammering, and one of America's most loved screen actors.

James Stewart as a reluctant town tamer in the classic western *Destry Rides Again* (1939). Courtesy of Universal Pictures.

Setting the Scene

I first interviewed Jimmy Stewart in 1971 at the Century Plaza Hotel in Los Angeles as he tub-thumped for his first-ever TV series, the NBC sitcom *The James Stewart Show*, which barely lasted a season due to low ratings.

Then I interviewed him in 1973 when he was on location for his CBS series *Hawkins* at the Harold Lloyd estate in Beverly Hills. Stewart was teary eyed, having just glimpsed a photo of himself at a Lloyd party in 1935; he remarked, "I don't remember being that young."

In 1983 I did a phone interview with him to publicize his HBO movie *Right of Way,* his first role opposite Bette Davis.

I've combined highlights of our conversations for this chapter.

The Interview

BAWDEN: What's the biggest public misconception about Jimmy Stewart?

STEWART: That I'm in any way similar to my big parts. Look, I'd like to be as fine as Jefferson Smith [of *Mr. Smith Goes to Washington*]. It never happened. The public wants to think one is the same as the characters played. But that was the studio system. Myrna Loy was never the Perfect Wife in real life. I met Cary Grant first on the set of *The Philadelphia Story* and a more nervous, fidgety actor I never saw. Spence Tracy played the same basic role so often he started to assume some of the characteristics. We'd all repair to Spence's MGM dressing room after a hard day and he'd regale us with the latest studio gossip. Spence was a real chatterbox. You see, the studio system gave you a personality and if you were smart you could parlay that into a life-long career.

BAWDEN: Ever want to break the mold?

STEWART: All the time. But there was a lot of leeway how far I could go. In *Anatomy of A Murder* [1959], I went pretty far and, boy, did I hear it from my fan base. I never ventured that way again, although now I think I should have. The downside is the public can get mighty bored very quickly. Greg Peck told me his career started to slide after his Oscar and all he was offered were Atticus Finch–like roles. Now, I'm a realist to know I could never play Shakespeare. I mean, I think I could, but the public might howl in laughter. It's always been a delicate balancing act—one for me, like doing a *Call Northside 777* [1948]—then one for the fans, like *Harvey* [1950].

BAWDEN: You know Jack Warner's famous line: Jimmy Stewart for president, Ronald Reagan as best friend? Why not tackle the public arena?

STEWART: Well, Ron had a successful start as governor of California and before that he was president of the Screen Actors Guild. I'm trying to think of an example of a politician who tried acting and lasted. Can't off-hand. Maybe they're all actors? But no, I never wanted to become a politician.

BAWDEN: How did you get to Hollywood?

STEWART: I needed a job. As simple as that. I'd started on Broadway in 1932 but by 1934 few new plays were being produced. So I accepted MGM's offer of a standard seven-year contract and I was on my way.

BAWDEN: Describe your first day in Los Angeles.

STEWART: Magical! No freeways. Electric streetcars went everywhere. You could smell the orange blossoms. No smog because few people could afford cars in those days. But I gradually learned L.A. was heavily segregated. Blacks usually sat at the back of the bus. You'd never see them in the big department stores. At MGM there was a separate entrance and lunchroom for the black laborers and maids. It was the dark side of the American dream.

BAWDEN: What did you do at MGM your first day?

STEWART: I had a long chat with Louis B. Mayer, who said he was going to promote me as the all-American boy. I visibly cringed. He liked that my father ran a hardware store, but when I told him I'd studied architecture at Princeton he said that definitely would not go into my studio biography. Then I was taken on a tour of the huge lot. I met Clark Gable, Myrna Loy (who was my favorite), I went out to inspect the Tarzan jungle. It was all so overwhelming for this kid.

BAWDEN: Your first movie was?

STEWART: A short titled *Art Trouble* [1934]. Starred Shemp Howard. Never saw it. Deliberately. Then I had a very tiny part in *Murder Man* (1935), which also was Spence Tracy's first MGMer. He'd been brought in after many programmers at Fox. I remember my name was Shorty. They just wanted to see what I looked like on film. And then I was rushed into *Rose Marie* [1936] as Jeanette MacDonald's brother. I stayed around that set for weeks absorbing the atmosphere. Then I was loaned out to Universal for my first big featured part—*Next Time We Love* [1936]—opposite Margaret Sullavan, who was a mesmerist in the acting department. She was married first to Hank Fonda, so I knew her well and we just clicked and for a few years became a big team.

BAWDEN: You have a story about *Wife vs. Secretary* [1936]? You come in at the ending as Jean Harlow's boyfriend.

STEWART: Well, we had a smooching scene at the end in my character's car and Jean stuck her tongue right down my throat and she kept it there until Clarence Brown yelled, "Cut!" That had never happened to me before.

Then I was Janet Gaynor's gauche sweetie in *Small Town Girl* [1936]. She deserts me for Bob Taylor. I guess *Speed* [1936] was my first big role. Set in the world of speed cars and I was a racer named Terry Martin. Eddie Marin directed and it took three weeks to film. Then I was in the Joan Crawford opus *The Gorgeous Hussy* (1936) with Bob Taylor and her real husband, Franchot Tone. It was all very silly and unhistorical. I do remember my character's name: Rowdy.

Then came *After the Thin Man* [1936]. It was the second in the detective saga and I loved watching Bill Powell work, easily the best actor on the lot. Everybody says how the director, W. S. Van Dyke, directed everything on one take, but I remember how kind and considerate he was with me. I was shaking like a leaf, but the movie was a huge success and some critics say it is definitely the best of the bunch. I was finally in a movie with my dream girl, Myrna Loy, and this one made over $3 million—a huge hit.

BAWDEN: People think of you and Margaret Sullavan as one of the great teams?

STEWART: MGM decided to turn Maggie and me into their latest team. How MGM loved teams: Powell-Loy, Gable-Harlow. But we had a history. We could play off each other. The weakest was *Shopworn Angel* [1938], which was a remake of a 1930 Nancy Carroll Paramount film. In 1940, we had *The Mortal Storm*, directed brilliantly by Frank Borzage, who told me he wanted to make every movie with Maggie. You'll note the film never uses the word "Jew." People assumed this was Mr. Mayer's decision, but it was demanded by the censors, so "non-Aryan" was used, much to the puzzlement of audiences.

Then we played Hungarians in Ernst Lubitsch's *The Shop around the Corner* (1940) and it all worked because of Ernst's magic. He'd rehearse forever and get us itching to do it and then in one take magic happened. It remains one of my favorite parts. Imagine me—a Hungarian! Maggie was always persnickety. A few more films and she went back to Broadway and only came back once in 1950 for a single movie.

BAWDEN: By this time you made your first two Frank Capra classics.

STEWART: I got the part in *You Can't Take It with You* [1938] because I was available and came cheap. But people think on a Capra picture we'd sit around swapping jokes all day. Frank worked us hard. He was a martinet. He knew exactly what he wanted in a scene and you had to deliver or there'd be multiple takes. Never worked harder in my life. Jean Arthur was difficult to crack. Very introverted. She only came alive during filming. She'd be locked in her dressing room between takes. I had to get her to trust me because she was a true comedic talent. I was surprised it won Oscars because it's basically a photographed play, but the acting is on a high plane. And boy, was it popular.

We did shoot some of *Mr. Smith Goes to Washington* in the capital, but the Senate scenes? A huge set constructed at great cost. Frank rode me like crazy and I'm so grateful. Jean was magnificent, but so are Claude Rains and Edward Arnold. Those scenes when Jefferson seems close to collapse during his filibuster? Really felt close to collapse at times. It just all came together and people still tell me they watch it. And I was told I'd win the Oscar for it, but Robert Donat won for *Goodbye, Mr. Chips.*

BAWDEN: Did you consider *The Philadelphia Story* 1940 Oscar win for best actor a case of compensation?

STEWART: Well, I was third billed. Hepburn and Grant do have bigger roles. But this was such a prestigious production. We seemed to shoot forever. The Lords house was completely constructed on the back lot. It's the only one I made for director George Cukor. But let me tell you, on *my* Oscar ballot I voted for my pal Hank Fonda [who was nominated for *The Grapes of Wrath*].

BAWDEN: After five years away on war work, wasn't it expected you would return to MGM?

STEWART: Mr. Mayer thought so. But my contract had expired in 1942. I felt MGM had done everything it possibly could for me. Most of my big hits were made on loan to other companies. *Vivacious Lady* [1938] was at RKO, *No Time for Comedy* [1940] was for Warners, *Destry Rides Again* [1939] was at Universal, *Made for Each Other* [1939] was for David Selznick, and the Capras were for Columbia. At MGM I'd made such stinkers as *Ice Follies of 1939* [1939], *It's a Wonderful World* [1939], and *Come Live with Me* [1941]. My last was *Ziegfeld Girl* [1941], which definitely was not about me. So I declined to return and tried freelance, and gossip hen Hedda Hopper said she'd make it rough for Mayer in her column if he tried legal action.

BAWDEN: You were away from movies for almost five years. The war made you a different person. So why restart your career with *It's a Wonderful Life*?

James Stewart with Donna Reed in the Frank Capra holiday classic *It's a Wonderful Life* (1946). Courtesy of NBC and Liberty Films.

STEWART: I came home to a different America. Everyone did. I wasn't the first choice for *It's a Wonderful Life*. Frank Capra was coming home, too, and he wanted a deeper, darker film than he'd ever made before. But both Gary Cooper and Jean Arthur turned him down. I grabbed onto it, but it was a tortuous shoot made for Frank's new company, Liberty Pictures. Filming dragged on and on. It became impossible for the picture to recoup its $3 million cost. The American public was not enthusiastic. After Auschwitz, were they supposed to believe in an angel named Clarence? I felt there were many outstanding scenes and Donna Reed was everything Frank could want.

I think it's his last good film. It registered as a financial failure and Frank had to peddle his next movie, *State of the Union*, to MGM. He lost control after that completely and became a staff director at Paramount. The Oscars went to *The Best Years of Our Lives* and then Liberty even let the copyright lapse. I was glad I did it, but it wasn't the way my career could proceed. I needed a harder image.

BAWDEN: Is that why you chose *Call Northside 777*?

James Stewart as a frontier peacemaker in *Broken Arrow* (1950). Courtesy of 20th Century-Fox.

STEWART: Yes! Directed in documentary fashion by Henry Hathaway, who told me he'd holler every time I started sputtering. He wanted me to talk as fast as possible. And it was based on the true case of a Chicago journalist who investigated a murder case eleven years old and passionately reported on a wrong man's conviction. The cast was strong: Lee J. Cobb, Helen Walker as my wife and, in bit parts, E. G. Marshall and Thelma Ritter. A new Jimmy Stewart was being born.

BAWDEN: The old Jimmy still made appearances?

STEWART: Oh, yeah, in *Magic Town* [1947], a Capraesque tale, but Billy Wellman wasn't the right director for it. Certainly *Harvey.* The last time the old Jimmy appeared was in *No Highway in the Sky* [1951]. I'd outgrown the old Jimmy in more ways than one.

BAWDEN: *Winchester '73* was another big change.

STEWART: Before the war, I could only make the comic western *Destry Rides Again.* Director Anthony Mann called *Winchester '73* a sort of film noir western. I watched a bit of it recently on TV and had to guffaw when Rock Hudson appears as an Indian named Young Bull. And the box office was tremendous. I then did *Broken Arrow* [1950] for Delmer Daves and then, for Mann, *Bend of the River* [1952], *The Naked Spur* [1953], *The Far Country* [1954], *The Man from Laramie* [1955]. I could have made only westerns because they were so popular. And it got me out of the house and into the vast countryside and some of these really stand up.

BAWDEN: You worked four times with Hitchcock.

STEWART: A strange, roly-poly man interested only in blondes and murder. I'd done *Rope* with him in 1948 after Cary Grant turned it down. I had to have my hair grayed up and I don't think I got it. The sets were on wheels because Hitch was in this crazy phase of using very long scenes. But he did ask me back for *Rear Window,* one of his masterpieces. And it is a sort of love poem to Grace Kelly. The entire set was built on the back lot, but Hitch later said the story could never be remade for modern audiences because, with air-conditioning invented, all Jimmy Stewart would stare at is a bunch of closed windows with the drapes pulled.

The Man Who Knew Too Much [1956] is his only remake. Doris Day was nervous about the project and kept asking Hitch questions, causing him to famously utter, "Doris, it's only a movieeee." I think *Vertigo* best of the bunch, but I don't think Kim Novak quite up to it. Also our age differences caused unease among moviegoers. Until just before filming it was going to be Vera Miles, who became pregnant and bowed out. Hitch blames me for its low box office to this day and thought I was getting too old for such ventures. I really wanted to do *North by Northwest* [1959], but he chose Cary Grant, who actually is four years older.

BAWDEN: You won an Oscar nomination for *Anatomy of a Murder* [1959], but your core base of fans were really shocked.

STEWART: I got tons of letters begging me not to attempt such dirty material again. I mean, it's a trial in which a woman's panties are discussed at length. I'm glad I did it, but passed on similar adult projects. I was looking forward to working with Lana Turner again eighteen years after we did *Ziegfeld Girl,* but on her first day discussing wardrobe Otto Preminger yelled at her so much she just left. Otto then hired Lee Remick and told his publicity staff to mention Lee was Lana's junior by seventeen years! But I still had a reunion with Eve Arden from the same MGM movie. The acting was very high: Arthur O'Connell, Ben Gazzara, George C. Scott—and Otto never yelled once during my scenes. I warned him: one bellow and I'd walk for good.

BAWDEN: You finally got together with John Ford.

STEWART: First for *Two Rode Together* [1961] and *The Man Who Shot Liberty Valance* [1962]. In *Two Rode Together,* Dick Widmark and I tried to get Jack out of bed one morning and the codger just would not budge, saying it looked like rain. But he was plain tuckered out and we let him sleep until noon and it never did rain. Widmark, you know, brought Fred Zinnemann to Ford's Christmas party that year and the two veterans had never met. And Ford immediately asks, "Why the hell do you move your camera so much in a scene?"

On *Liberty Valance,* Ford viciously rode Duke Wayne. He'd say, "No, Duke, that's not the way to hold a rifle. Let Jimmy show you how. After all, he really was in the war while you were prancing around the soundstages." I asked Duke why he put up with such crap and he said, "Jack made me. Took me from B pictures. But one day I'll just lose it and punch the old goat out." But he never did, of course.

BAWDEN: Finally you succumbed to TV, first with *The Jimmy Stewart Show* [1971–1972] and then *Hawkins* [1973–1974].

STEWART: I'm going to continue until I conquer this new medium. On *Jimmy Stewart,* I came too late to the sitcom cycle. Fred MacMurray and Donna Reed came earlier, and Hank Fonda, Bing Crosby and me, well, we just repeated the standard clichés. In *Hawkins,* I never worked as hard—not even on my early B flicks. We did eight ninety-minute episodes and I loved being directed by Paul Wendkos. Strother Martin I insisted on, and there are some great costars, like Julie Harris and Kurt Kasznar. Whether it lasts or not, I'm glad I did it. I don't want to drift into cameos.

BAWDEN: Describe finally working with Bette Davis.

STEWART: She describes herself as an extinct volcano. But I witnessed a few eruptions. We both agreed we no longer understand the picture business. There are some wonderful young actors I truly respect. But there are no quality producers like [David] Selznick and [Samuel] Gold-wyn. Everything seems to be sequels. I was darned lucky to get the breaks I did and I've lasted quite awhile at it—and so has Bette. You can describe me as a guy who always knew my limitations.

Afterword

Despite a few other memorable TV appearances, including a cameo in the ABC miniseries *North and South, Book Two* (1985), James Stewart never really made a big splash in television. Of course, he didn't need to because he was already a screen icon whose appearances on talk shows, awards shows, and various specials invariably saw him treated like Hollywood royalty.

Though Stewart had some great screen roles in his twilight years—he was the physician who diagnosed John Wayne's terminal cancer in Wayne's final film, *The Shootist* (1976)—his final feature film was as a voice actor in the animated film *An American Tail: Fievel Goes West* (1991). Playing a cartoon version of Wyatt Earp called Wyley Burp, he earned rave reviews.

Stewart's only wife, Gloria, who suffered from cancer, died in his arms in 1994. He suffered a fatal heart attack on July 2, 1997. He was eighty-nine.

Cornel Wilde

Interview by James Bawden

Handsome and athletic Cornel Wilde was one of the most popular leading men of the 1940s and 1950s—a capable actor who could play dramatic roles like the composer Frederic Chopin in 1945's *A Song to Remember* or swashbuckling roles like the son of Robin Hood in 1946's *Bandit of Sherwood Forest* or a combination of both, like his trapeze artist in Cecil B. DeMille's *The Greatest Show on Earth* (1952).

In the 1950s, Wilde began to produce and even direct some of his starring vehicles and today is probably best remembered for his arduous performance as both director and star of the grueling African adventure film *The Naked Prey* (1966).

Setting the Scene

My meeting with Cornel Wilde in 1984 was purely serendipitous. I was attending a television critics' convention that January at the Los Angeles area's Century Plaza Hotel and I had a rare night off. In the hotel lobby I bumped into a veteran 20th Century-Fox publicist who invited me to the wrap party for the ABC TV series *Masquerade,* which had been running for two and a half years.

It was on the Fox lot right behind the hotel, so I ventured over and had long chats with the star, Rod Taylor, as well as with the executive producer, Glenn Larson. The soundstage was filled with familiar names who had been guest stars on various episodes, including Lloyd Bochner, Kirstie Alley, Ernest Borgnine, David Hemmings, and Mary Beth Hughes.

Then I spotted a familiar face in a corner: Cornel Wilde, my favorite movie swashbuckler. I walked over, introduced myself, and we chatted for several hours at his table. Here are the highlights of our chat.

Cornel Wilde in *Beach Red* (1967), which he also directed. Courtesy of MGM television.

The Interview

BAWDEN: There are several versions of where and when you were born.

WILDE (*chuckling*): Well, I was born in Austria-Hungary in 1912 in a tiny village that today is part of Slovakia. It was in Hungary at the time. We were Jews and my father was a cavalry officer on the eastern front during the Great War. In 1920, when the country had broken up, he determined to emigrate with his family to New York City, where I was brought up. I became a typical American kid, except my favorite sport was fencing.

BAWDEN: Your Fox biography, then, was made up?

WILDE: [Studio production chief] Darryl Zanuck said I couldn't admit I was Jewish. And to be born in a country which was then with the Axis powers? No way! So he fabricated a new life line and took three years off my age. Whenever I'd bump into Ty Power on the lot, he'd shout, "Hi, youngster!" Because he knew I was after the same swashbuckling parts he was famous for, but the joke was I was actually one year older—[though] he never knew it!

BAWDEN: You originally wanted to be a doctor?

WILDE: The dream of every Jewish boy. After high school I got into the four-year pre-med course at City College in New York and won a scholarship to the Physicians and Surgeons College at Columbia University.

BAWDEN: Did you ever go there?

WILDE: No! I kept putting it off because I was getting bit roles in Broadway plays. Then in 1940 Larry Olivier hired me as fencing coach for his Broadway production of *Romeo and Juliet*. I remember the crowds at the stage door because Larry O and Viv [Vivien Leigh] were the world's sweethearts at the time. I also had the role of Tybalt. Then the reviews came in and it all crashed. The crowds disappeared and, after thirty-six performances, we closed. Larry and Viv limped back to Hollywood and I went along with a stock contract at Warner Bros.

BAWDEN: Then what happened?

WILDE: I got mostly bits. I had a walk-on in *Lady with Red Hair* [1940] and I remember screaming matches between stars Miriam Hopkins and Claude Rains. Then Fox offered me a better deal and I romanced Ida Lupino in *Life Begins at Eight-Thirty* [1942] and Sonja Henie in *Wintertime* [1943], which consisted of her skating and throwing kisses to me. Nice work if you can do it.

BAWDEN: How did you get your breakout role in *A Song to Remember* as Frederic Chopin?

WILDE: Director Charles Vidor saw me in the gym! And he tested me several times before Harry Cohn [Columbia production chief] said okay, and then Columbia had to lend Alexander Knox to Fox in exchange for my services. Knox told me I got the better deal as his role as [President Woodrow] Wilson riled up Republicans so much they tried to get him black-

From left: Cornel Wilde as Frederic Chopin, Merle Oberon, and Paul Muni in *A Song to Remember* (1945). Courtesy of Columbia Pictures.

listed during those HUAC [House Un-American Activities Committee] hearings!

For weeks I had to practice on a silent piano while the real pianist played nearby. But when I asked [costar] Paul Muni to run lines with this newcomer, he barked his interpretation was down pat! Merle Oberon [leading lady] was equally icy. Before it was released, Cohn told Fox he'd take three more pictures from me only out of sympathy. He thought I needed a lot of experience. Fox bought that line and the studio was furious when *A Song to Remember* became one of the year's biggest hits and Harry had me down for three more vehicles.

You can imagine my surprise when I got an Oscar nomination. I thought I was stiff and being at the Oscars as a nominee was so surreal. A few months earlier I'd been completely obscure. I knew Ray Milland would win that night [for *The Lost Weekend*] and he did. I could not have cared less. But I did not know at the time I'd never again be nominated.

BAWDEN: So you stayed at Columbia for *A Thousand and One Nights* [1945].

WILDE: I sang—as Aladdin yet! It was supposed to be a spoof of those dog-awful Maria Montez flicks. We all had great fun and the public loved it because they needed escapism from the war headlines.

Then I made *Leave Her to Heaven* [1945] at Fox with Gene Tierney. It was a real learning experience for me. It was filmed in lush Technicolor to highlight the awfulness of the heroine. I wondered how director John Stahl would do it because we were skirting the Production Code at several occasions. I mean, her character kills my crippled little brother. Stahl was a meticulous craftsman, the slowest director I ever met. He'd take hours to set up a scene and then do just one or two takes. Gene had to drain all emotion from her face. I thought she was sensational and she got her only Oscar nomination. When I started directing, I used Stahl as one example of how to get everything out of a scene.

BAWDEN: Then what happened?

WILDE: Fox suspended me because I didn't want to take a small role in *Margie* [1946]. I settled for *The Bandit of Sherwood Forest* at Columbia, where I played the son of Robin Hood. Innocuous, sure, but it earned $3 million in rentals its first time out.

BAWDEN: Then you were in *Centennial Summer* [1946]—a musical!

WILDE: Jerome Kern's last completed score. But an imitation of *Meet Me in St. Louis* [1944], no doubt about it. Back with Jeanne Crain. Fox was trying to pair us as a screen couple, but it just never happened.

Forever Amber [1947]? We started with Peggy Cummins in the lead, but she looked far too young—she was only sixteen. Production was halted after $500,000 had already been spent. Zanuck finally had to recast and Peggy was naturally distraught. I know they tried for Lana Turner, but MGM asked too much, so Linda Darnell was trotted in. Otto Preminger replaced Stahl [as director] and damned if the whole mishmash didn't make a ton of profit for Zanuck.

BAWDEN: How many times were you suspended by Fox for refusing film offers?

WILDE: Maybe a dozen. I was definitely suspended for refusing to do *That Lady in Ermine* [1948] with Betty Grable. Not that I didn't love Betty, but a picture that covered up her legs? Forget it!

Finally, because I needed a paycheck, I took *The Walls of Jericho* (1948) and it was just fair despite Stahl's touches. Then I did *Road House* [1948], directed by Jean Negulesco, who had just defected from WB [Warner Bros.] to Fox. He last directed at WB a film Jack Warner had so loathed he shelved it for a year: *Johnny Belinda*. When it was finally released [in 1948], Jane Wyman got an Oscar! In *Road House* Dick Widmark gleefully stole scenes as the psychotic [nightclub owner] and Ida Lupino was great as the washed-out singer. That left me as the dull nice guy, I'm afraid. I left Fox after that one, which was a bad mistake.

A few years later I needed the dough and went back for a bad western, *Two Flags West* [1950]. Three years after *Amber*, Linda Darnell is telling me how bad things have gotten on the lot. I think she got bounced slightly after that. I left Columbia after a B called *Shockproof* [1949], which was a little jewel directed by Douglas Sirk.

BAWDEN: How did you get second billing in *The Greatest Show on Earth* [1952]?

WILDE: I had to prove to C. B. DeMille I could fly through the air. Of course, I practiced a bit in advance. But I did a test which he watched and he offered me $50,000 and I said I needed billing over Chuck Heston and he gave it to me! I trained several more weeks before going to the winter headquarters of Barnum & Bailey in Florida. I loved being up there as C. B. bellowed from below about do this or do that. I'd pretend I couldn't hear him. "Come up!" I once hollered, and that really made him angry.

Betty [Hutton] had trained, too; she was supreme. At the last minute Gloria Grahame replaced Lucy Ball, who'd become pregnant. You know, old C. B. had never even got an Oscar nomination as Best Picture, let alone won one. The Academy sensed he was coming to his glorious end and this time he won. RKO had me in a bad swashbuckler, *At Sword's Point*, they'd filmed two years earlier and then they released it [in 1952] to capitalize on the DeMille sensation.

BAWDEN: Why did you go back to Fox at this stage for *Woman's World* [1954]?

WILDE: Money; it's always about the money. Zanuck really got his pound of flesh. He had me billed after Clifton Webb, June Allyson, Van Heflin, Lauren Bacall, Fred MacMurray, and Arlene Dahl, which put me way, way down the cast list. But it was good being in a big hit, which *Passion* [1954] with Yvonne De Carlo was not. I had to go to Allied Artists to make *The Big Combo* [1955]. Just to save some money, I directed *Storm Fear* [1956] myself. I did okay, made all the newcomer directing mistakes, but I proved I could do it.

BAWDEN: Then you say you made your worst mistake.

WILDE: I got too cocky and I actually turned down a choice role old

Betty Hutton with Cornel Wilde in *The Greatest Show on Earth* (1952). Courtesy of Paramount.

C. B. offered me in *The Ten Commandments* [1956]: Joshua. I said it was too small and the money wasn't enough. C. B. never spoke to me again and even one line in such a blockbuster would have bolstered my career momentum. John Derek replaced me. What stupidity! Dumb, dumb!

BAWDEN: How did you get into directing?

WILDE: I was no longer the number one choice for leads. So I directed *The Devil's Hairpin* [1957] for Paramount, costarred with my wife, Jean Wallace, and we had an acceptable A-B, meaning a picture with a B budget but A pretensions. Paramount let me do another, *Maracaibo* [1958], and that one also was turned in under budget and made some money back.

With *Sword of Lancelot* [1963], I had to plow all my money in to top it up. We filmed in Yugoslavia and at [England's] Pinewood Studios. It wasn't exactly inexpensive, but I had everything pre-planned. Jean was a wonderful Guinevere and Brian Aherne was a worldly Arthur. We kept the action flowing and it was a fair-sized hit. Jack Warner, who had *Camelot* in pre-production, was furious and threatened legal action. But I told him, "Jack, we're not bursting into songs here and you can't really copyright the Round Table, can you?"

BAWDEN: I thought *The Naked Prey* the best of your movies as director.

WILDE: Thank goodness I kept myself in shape. We partly shot in the Transvaal and some crew members have the animal bites to show for that. It was based on the true experiences of an American trapper. Maybe I'll do it again with an American background. [He didn't do it, but it was done in 2015 as *The Revenant.*] I mean we had to get the shots right the first time because the animals were uncooperative as well as the natives. We got Oscar nominations for Best Story and Screenplay. We were showing how the natives were perfectly attuned to their land and we, the intruders, were not. After it was over, I had a major physical collapse. It seemed I was running a marathon every day of shooting.

BAWDEN: *Beach Red* [1967] is also sensational.

WILDE: I think it's the best one I directed. It was shot in the Philippines. Again I must mention the budget was necessarily slim. It looked at the Marine landings on a Japanese island. This time I could only use Jean in a flashback as the wife at home. I wanted realism in the fighting; men were expiring, after all. Yes, it was very gory, but that was the whole point. Those who liked those John Wayne actioners where good guys effortlessly triumph were furious I'd dare show the real thing.

BAWDEN: *No Blade of Grass* [1970] followed.

WILDE: I never really liked sci-fi. But this one was different—no special effects. It looked at a future where pollution was dominant and mankind in peril. All the special interests cried foul and the press tended to ignore it. Not a sexy subject, I'm afraid. Ahead of its time, I was told. After such a tepid reception, I was disgusted by the superficiality of modern journalism.

BAWDEN: What happened to swashbucklers?

WILDE: They forgot how to make them. The kids couldn't have cared less. Ty Power was my favorite, so graceful. At a party in the late forties, I met another favorite, Errol Flynn, so debauched he could barely speak. Offered me some dope to smoke. He looked awful and I felt so sad. Stewart Granger was another great swashbuckler. In *Scaramouche* [1952], he was supreme.

Cornel Wilde in one of his last acting roles, with Angela Lansbury in her CBS TV series *Murder, She Wrote*. Courtesy of CBS.

BAWDEN: Any regrets?

WILDE: I should have done a TV series when it was offered to me. I could have made a lot of dough but I had pretensions about making it big as a movie director. I didn't desert the movies; the movies deserted me.

BAWDEN: Later you did do television. I remember talking to you on the phone about *Gargoyles* [1972] as you moved into TV.

WILDE: Well, I'd already done *I Love Lucy* and *Father Knows Best* in the fifties. But that TV movie was pretty special. So [now] I do [shows like] *Love Boat, Fantasy Island.* [TV producer] Aaron Spelling keeps us oldsters occupied. But the movie business I no longer understand. I guess I'm actually getting nostalgic about the studio system, which at least kept us busy and occasionally a great film would actually get made.

Afterword

Wilde was married twice. His first wife, actress Patricia Knight, was his leading lady in *Shockproof* (1949). They wed in 1937 and divorced in 1951. That same year, he married second wife Jean Wallace, former wife of actor Franchot Tone. They costarred in several films but were divorced in 1981.

Wilde died of leukemia complications on October 16, 1989. He was seventy-seven.

Robert Young

Interview by James Bawden

Robert Young was one of the most enduring of all stars from Hollywood's golden age. With some stage experience, he began in movies in the early 1930s as a young secondary leading man whose specialty seemed to be good-natured, reliable chaps whom everybody liked. He soon matured into more complex parts and by the 1940s had a solid background in a wide variety of leading roles in everything from westerns and serious dramas to romantic comedies and love stories.

As the studio system began to crumble in the early 1950s, Young easily made the transition to television, where he gained his greatest popular appeal as the father in one of TV's most acclaimed family series, *Father Knows Best* (1954–1960), following it up with another hit show, the weekly drama series *Marcus Welby, M.D.* (1969–1976), in which he played a family doctor.

Setting the Scene

I was just plain lucky to meet and interview Robert Young on four separate occasions. The first was in June 1974, when the Television Critics Association was meeting at the Universal Sheraton Hotel in Universal City, California. One night MCA held a lavish party for all its stars then on TV series and I was given twenty minutes with Young. We sat together in the corner of the gigantic soundstage. He seemed completely amazed that I never asked him a single question about his current TV hit, *Marcus Welby, M.D.,* but instead wanted to know about such Young film classics as *Death on the Diamond* (1934), *The Mortal Storm* (1940), and *Crossfire* (1947). When the publicist came over with the next scheduled interviewer, Young tapped me on the shoulder and said, "I have a bunch of downtime on the set tomorrow afternoon, so why not come by and we can chat some more."

Robert Young at age twenty-eight. James Bawden collection.

So at 2 p.m., I strolled from the Sheraton onto the Universal back lot—the security gate had my pass all ready—and found Young in his rooms watching his 1938 hit *Three Comrades*. "I got fourth billing," he joked. "But I had the longest career in movies and TV."

In 1977 I met Young at the Academy of Motion Picture Arts and Science's salute to Joan Crawford. Young was part of a galaxy of former Crawford costars lined up at the door to greet the crowd, including Myrna Loy,

John Wayne, Virginia Grey, Ben Cooper, and Jack Jones. We spent much of the night chatting away in a back room until Young came onstage and dazzled the crowd with his Crawford anecdotes. He even held up the leather script binder Crawford had given to him on the 1933 set of *Today We Live,* saying he still used it.

In 1988 I had my last face-to-face interview with Young in a hotel room in Toronto where he was making one of his last TV movies. He chattered away through a long lunch break in the dining room. The very next year he was back on TV in a headache commercial.

Later, I talked to him briefly on the phone, but he seemed tired and said he couldn't make dinner this time. I've combined the highlights of our conversations for this chapter.

The Interview

BAWDEN: How did you get to MGM in 1931, aged just twenty-four?

YOUNG: I'd studied at the Pasadena Playhouse, but in the Depression stage jobs were scarce. I had a bit in a Charlie Chan film, *The Black Camel* [1931], and an MGM talent scout saw it and told [production chief] Irving Thalberg I'd be perfect as Helen Hayes's son in a movie called *The Sin of Madelon Claudet* [1931], then shooting. The original male ingenue hadn't worked out. I was rushed over, talked to Mr. Thalberg in his vast office, and he hired me. Just like that!

My [role] of Dr. Laurence Claudet was very small. Only a few scenes at the end. So I hung around for weeks, absorbing the atmosphere before I did anything. Then we all boarded the MGM streetcar for the first preview and the preview cards had some of the harshest criticism Thalberg could remember seeing. The picture, which was Miss Hayes's talkie debut, was a big mess.

On the streetcar back to MGM, Thalberg said not to worry. He had Hayes's husband, Charlie MacArthur, writing new scenes the next day and we virtually redid the movie and a few months later we were back on that streetcar. And the cards were kinder, but Thalberg ordered a few more rewrites in key scenes. I remember Lewis Stone telling me, "Whatever they say, it's still *Madame X.*" But the picture was a smash and Helen won the Oscar. And Thalberg then put me under long-term contract and had me as Gordon, the grown son of Norma Shearer and Clark Gable, in his next big picture, *Strange Interlude* [1932].

BAWDEN: It is a very strange picture.

YOUNG: It was very tough to make as the actors had to stand around as huge acetate records were played of their inner thoughts. One day Norma got the giggles during one of those scenes and I looked up and Thalberg was at the side of the set and he was not pleased. And then when my character grows up and I come on, it's fifteen years later and Clark and Norma have aged like fifty years and seem in their eighties. Some of these scenes were cut after a jittery first preview. But audiences flocked to it because of the themes of adultery and madness. I think I got away with it but I don't remember it with pleasure.

BAWDEN: I'd like your thoughts on some of your other early films.

YOUNG: In *The Wet Parade* [1932], MGM thought it had a block-buster and plowed a fortune into the film. Victor Fleming came over from Paramount to direct it. Walter Huston was my father and he was so kind and understanding to this youngster, but I think he really hammed it up. *New Morals for Old* [1932]? I just thought it was so stodgy. Lewis Stone and Laura Hope Crews were the parents, Margaret Perry and I the young-sters experimenting at free love. Our director, Charles Brabin, had been directing since 1912, but he was only in his fifties. Charlie loathed what he called "talkers." He'd shout, "Ladies and gentlemen, resume your positions! Now act, please!" At night he would be picked up in his limousine by his wife—vamp Theda Bara. They were such a devoted couple.

Tugboat Annie [1933] had me as the son of Marie Dressler and Wally Beery. Marie said the thought of her and Wally having such a handsome son was shocking. She was very ill with cancer by then and could only shoot a few scenes every morning and then she'd retire exhausted. She acted in the silent fashion, full steam ahead, and for her it worked. Wally loathed being part of a team with her because she was twenty-five years older than he was.

BAWDEN: Did you first meet Joan Crawford on the set of *Today We Live*?

YOUNG: Oh, no. I'd talked to her at several big MGM events, public-ity things. And she was so big, she had cast approval, so I was glad she chose me as her fiancé, Claude. I remember, before filming started, we were in rehearsal and she turned up in some pretty outlandish dresses by Adrian and everybody gasped. But she had costume approval and that's what she wanted to wear, although they were totally unhistorical. No Eng-lish society girl would have worn them in 1917 with a war going on, but

Joan said it's what her fans would want. I was more concerned with getting a dialogue coach, but director Howard Hawks said not to worry. Bill Faulkner had written everything in a very clipped way. No need for an English accent. What Bill had done was cut out the verbs, so Claude always seems to be saying "Rather" or "Quite." It sounded very silly when I watched the first rushes.

By this time Joan and Franchot Tone had fallen in love. He played her brother, but the smooching they did all over the place was anything but brother-sister. I learned a lot from Gary Cooper, who was on loan-out from Paramount to make this one and a Marion Davies movie [*Operator 13*] because his home studio was near bankruptcy and needed cash quickly. Even then Gary was a minimalist. He did as little as possible during a scene and it showed. He got all the attention. He hated both MGM films so much he said he'd refuse to do any more loan-outs.

The big finish in this one is a spectacular naval battle and Hawks told me he took some unused footage from *Hell's Angels* [1930] and no critic ever noticed. The reviews were very nasty about how un-English the cast was and Joan had her second flop in a row—*Rain* [1932] was the first. Her fan base hated her playing an English society girl and Joan learned her lesson. Her next, *Dancing Lady* [1933] brought back the crowds because she played a chorus girl. She was back to being Joan Crawford.

BAWDEN: By 1934, you were being loaned out as much as you worked at MGM.

YOUNG: I had the standard contract. I worked forty weeks a year with twelve layoff weeks. So MGM made sure I was gainfully employed every one of those forty weeks! The studio found they could charge up to $5,000 a week for my services and I was only getting about $1,000 of that so their profit was huge. It was Janet Gaynor who got Fox to borrow me, plus Lionel Barrymore, for *Carolina* [1934]. Lionel remarked she had more clout than Shearer. After a take, director Henry King would look at her and she'd nod if she liked it. If not, we'd do another take. In effect, she was directing the director. And this was the last big year for Janet. She slipped out of the top ten that year, replaced at Fox by Shirley Temple. When the studio was sold in 1935 and merged with Twentieth Century, [production chief] Darryl Zanuck said she was overpriced, and after *Ladies in Love* [1936], she left. When I next saw her at MGM, making *Small Town Girl* [1936], she had a small dressing room befitting a star in decline. After her smash comeback in *A Star Is Born* [1937], she returned to MGM for *Three*

Loves Has Nancy [1938] and demanded and got one of the biggest dressing rooms of all.

BAWDEN: You also made *House of Rothschild* [1934] for Twentieth Century.

YOUNG: Loretta Young and I were the young romantic leads. When Zanuck left Warners earlier that year he had taken Loretta and George Arliss with him. You know it didn't matter who he was playing, Mr. Arliss always had a subplot about his character helping the young lovers get together. I was so nervous on that one I'd do a scene and then walk back to my dressing room to study my lines. He called me out on this and said, "Bob, you are an introvert. Don't run away. Stay on the set as I do. Make friends with the cameraman, sound, editing, anyone who can explain how films are made. Get to understand every facet of the business. It will make you a better actor." Soundest advice I ever received.

His wife, Florence, was always by his side. He always seemed to be feeding her broth. She was slowly going blind from macular degeneration. He was so kind to her. On a night shot they were huddled under blankets holding hands. He told me he had one more film to make [*Cardinal Richelieu*] and that would be that. They then returned to England because he thought the doctors there were better.

BAWDEN: Also in 1934 you made *Spitfire* [1934] with Katharine Hepburn.

YOUNG: At first I was completely beguiled by her. Then exasperated. Who wasn't? She was so completely unbending. She'd just won the Oscar for *Morning Glory* [1933], but typically had refused to pick it up at the ceremony. So now she believed she knew everything about filmmaking. She was playing a mountain girl with a Bryn Mawr accent and every attempt director John Cromwell made to help her was rebuffed.

On the last night of filming, the final scene was done by midnight and Hepburn loudly said she was off to Broadway to star in *The Lake*. She would receive horrible reviews. Cromwell said, "No, I'm going to retake that last scene. You were very bad in it." There was a standoff and Hepburn was given a check by RKO executives and then redid it. But it didn't matter; the film got horrible reviews. And it was all her fault. If only she had listened and bent a bit, Cromwell could have made her shine.

BAWDEN: What about your relationship with [MGM chief] Louis B. Mayer?

YOUNG: Every year I'd have to go up to his office to see if my contract

Katharine Hepburn played an Ozark tomboy smitten with Robert Young in the 1934 film *Spitfire*. James Bawden collection.

was renewed. I always expected to be shown the door. At first he saw me as a Thalbergite, but I never made any waves. I accepted all assignments and he liked that philosophy. Franchot Tone was always on suspension for refusing scripts.

Mr. Mayer kept telling me I lacked sexual appeal and I'd say, "But I'm married with children!" And he'd laugh. Then I'd tell him stories about my little daughters and there'd be tears in his eyes. He was such a sentimentalist. Then I'd get my contract picked up and with the required pay raise. But the tension was huge; I started taking a drink or two before I went into those meetings.

BAWDEN: I remember you once told me a favorite film is *Death on the Diamond* [1934].

YOUNG: Had a load of fun with that one. It was a baseball mystery about gangsters infiltrating the St. Louis Cardinals. With a little more work it could have been so much better. We made it in about three weeks. I played the star pitcher and I got lessons from a pro. That's really me out on the mound. We shot at Wrigley Field in L.A., but a second unit crew shot at the Cardinals' stadium in St. Louis. Madge Evans was the leading lady. She usually worked with Bob Montgomery. When MGM released it that fall, the Cards were surging to the pennant, which they won. Talk about timely. That one was still playing tops of double bills a year later. And look very closely and you can spot Ward Bond and Walter Brennan in bits.

BAWDEN: In 1935 came two with Barbara Stanwyck: *The Bride Comes Home* and *Red Salute*.

YOUNG: One of my favorite actresses. I remember very little about *Bride*. It was on loan-out to RKO. Barbara had just left Warners and I don't think I ever saw this one. I was working so hard in those days. *Red Salute* was a three-week thing made for producer Eddie Small, who certainly got his money's worth. He kept rereleasing it every few years with a new title. Every time I'd see Barbara at an event, I'd shout, "Just saw *Runaway Heiress*"—or whatever the new title was—and she'd raise her eyebrows. When she decided to jump to TV, she phoned me up for advice, but [with] her first show, that anthology [the 1960–1961 NBC series *The Barbara Stanwyck Show*], she was too late getting it started. That fad was over. But she shone in *The Big Valley*, I must say.

BAWDEN: You made two movies with Shirley Temple, but in different eras.

YOUNG: In 1936 [in *Stowaway*], she was at the height of her popularity. And she knew it. She was eight and could get obstreperous very quickly. It was unnatural for such a tyke to have such power. She never had a childhood. Everything was turned into play for her. She usually was letter perfect the first take. After that, she'd become petulant. I worked with her again in *Adventure in Baltimore*, which was thirteen years later. By this time she loathed acting and hated that her childhood had been snatched from her. She and her husband, John Agar, were in it together and quarreling already. She told me she'd just had it, wanted a normal life, if you can call it that, and after one more film she left the movie business completely.

In the sixties I was having a bit of a nap at home and watching Mike Douglas on TV. He asked her [Shirley Temple] if she kept in touch with any of the grand old character stars she was cast opposite and she quipped, "They're all dead!" I sat right up. And later I asked Alice Faye if she knew I was dead and Alice sent a funny letter to Shirley. Later on Shirley had a grand new career as a US ambassador under Richard Nixon and George

Bush. She sat out the Reagan years, once telling me he was the one former costar she truly loathed.

BAWDEN: You once said you thought your career over when in 1936 MGM loaned you out for two pictures to Gaumont British.

YOUNG: It was the fancy right then to plop some American names into British films. Eddie Robinson, Sylvia Sidney, Fay Wray all did it. I thought this was it for me at MGM until I heard from GB they'd paid big bucks. And both films were very successful in the US market. Plus my wife and I got to have a lovely paid vacation far from Hollywood. I returned hotter than before. *Secret Agent* [1936] was early [Alfred] Hitchcock. He was just coming together. He was nice to me in person, but later on, when we met in L.A., he'd just nod and walk on. Never asked me back and he never asked Sylvia Sidney back either. Madeleine Carroll said when she got to L.A., he was frigid. They'd been chums since *The 39 Steps* [1935]. Peter Lorre stole his scenes, I think, John Gielgud looked very uncomfortable. I was the surprise villain. It got a lot of press in the US, definitely a plus for me.

BAWDEN: Then you costarred with England's top musical star, Jessie Matthews. How did that go?

YOUNG: With Jessie Matthews, I joined the film *It's Love Again* already in progress. Vic Saville was directing. He spent the forties producing lavish films at MGM. A top craftsman. She'd work on her dance numbers for months in advance. She worked so hard she had to forgo an offer to join Fred Astaire in *A Damsel in Distress* [1937]. Jessie was very temperamental to others. Every number had to be just so. Her husband, Sonny Hale, was in it for comedy relief. Am I allowed to say I couldn't really stand that man? I later contrasted the tension on this set with the two musicals where I partnered Ellie Powell, who was so businesslike. My wife kept in touch with her over the decades, and when Jessie came to L.A. to perform live in 1969, we gave her a party. She simply couldn't walk away from that fame, but it never really came back. In this business, knowing when to quit is all important.

BAWDEN: Back at MGM you made another Joan Crawford epic.

YOUNG: And another flop. Joan had just been named box office poison. She really needed a hit. This one [*The Bride Wore Red*] was set up as a vehicle for Luise Rainer, who seemed perfect for it, but not Joan. The Molnar play *The Girl from Trieste* [original source of the story] was formula stuff and Joan was way out of her element. But the huge sets were up and Franchot Tone was hot to play the poor postman she finally falls for. I was the socialite who she thinks she should love. MGM imported Dorothy Arzner to direct and the budget was huge. Arzner and Crawford were all buddy-buddy at first until reports circulated the material wasn't working. Then producer Joe Mankiewicz began appearing on the set all the time. Then Arzner virtually disappeared and her contract at MGM was severed. Oh, it was a real mess and the studio didn't try to fix it as Thalberg would have done. They just released it and it sank like a stone.

BAWDEN: You made two movies with Luise Rainer. Why did she fade so quickly?

YOUNG: Bad pictures. She told me the career killer was winning back-to-back Oscars. People expected a level of excellence and MGM put her into trash. [Rainer won her first of two Oscars for 1936's *The Great Ziegfeld*.] Bill Powell, who was in practically every scene as Ziegfeld, wasn't even nominated. And boy, did Bill tease Luise about that. *The Emperor's Candlesticks* was lavishly produced, but American audiences couldn't care at all. *The Toy Wife* was just a misfire and Luise was miscast as a Southern belle. She left Metro because of bad pictures, but also her marriage to Clifford Odets was falling apart. She simply had to get out.

BAWDEN: You have a thesis why 1937 was MGM's worst-ever year.

YOUNG: Thalberg was gone. He was the quality control gatekeeper. Without him at the helm the studio made *Parnell* with Gable and Loy completely miscast. It made *The Emperor's Candlesticks,* which nobody liked, and with the European market closing [because of World War II], it lost a fortune. Garbo in *Conquest* was a huge bore. It was just flop after flop. [Spencer] Tracy had *Big City* as well as the hit *Captains Courageous.* Bob Taylor had *Personal Property.* Ellie Powell had *Rosalie.* Bob Montgomery had *The Last of Mrs. Cheyney.* See what I mean? These were big flops. So Mayer was forced to rejig the process. He hired Mervyn LeRoy as a producer, turned Sidney Franklin into a producer. Anything but have another Thalberg in control. But of course there'd never be another Thalberg. And many of the films in 1938 were equally misdirected.

BAWDEN: MGM was into teams like Powell and Loy. You made five movies with Florence Rice.

YOUNG: She was a lovely girl, daughter of [sportswriter] Grantland Rice. But Mr. Mayer said she, too, lacked sex appeal. After she had the second lead in *Broadway Melody of 1940,* he just dropped her. She went over to Republic and made a batch of real Bs, which she hated. Then she married and never worked again. She simply didn't want to.

BAWDEN: How did you get to costar in *Three Comrades* [1938]?

YOUNG: Well, it was a rare hit for MGM at the time. Frank Borzage asked me and said I'd be replacing Spence Tracy! Frank said, "You don't know how good an actor you are, Bob." How's that for a recommendation! It was Maggie Sullavan's first MGM picture and she won the New York Film Critics Award for her luminous work. But not an Oscar nomination: Mayer insisted it go that year to Norma Shearer for *Marie Antoinette*. I also remember Borzage had Karl Freund sacked for Joseph Ruttenberg as cinematographer early on.

We all knew this one was special. Frank was the kind of director you wanted to work with and he loved actors. There was a chemistry between Bob Taylor and Maggie that was Frank's making. I had the most tragic role and the fact I could deliver it meant a lot to me.

BAWDEN: People often say you made all your best movies from 1937 to 1947.

YOUNG: I was over thirty by then. Time to grow up.

BAWDEN: You made six movies in 1938. You must have worked every one of those forty weeks.

YOUNG: I even managed a quick visit to Fox for *Josette*. [Darryl] Zanuck was determined to turn little Simone Simon into a French-type Janet Gaynor. Didn't work. Movie audiences determine who'll be a star. And they just didn't take to her at all.

BAWDEN: Then came another Crawford opus, *The Shining Hour* [1938].

YOUNG: Frank Borzage again asked me to do it. The original play starring Ray Massey and Gladys Cooper had been a huge hit in London. But it was about a Yorkshire farm family. They transplanted it to Wisconsin, where we sat around every afternoon taking tea! I was the weak brother married to Margaret Sullavan. Best movie actress I ever came across. She and Borzage had a long working relationship. We had some stunning scenes MGM cut to make it more into a Crawford vehicle. Mel Douglas was my older, gullible brother. A lot of it was shot in front of plates. It looked so phony. Maggie was livid her best stuff wound up on the cutting room floor. But that was MGM. And the film flopped anyhow.

BAWDEN: You've said making *Northwest Passage* [1940] was a real experience.

YOUNG: That was only part 1, as the credits say. Part 2 was cancelled because of the war and never made. Part 1 cost over $2.6 million and still made a profit and there were several rereleases. Loved going on location and parts were filmed at Payette Lake, Idaho, and in the Cascade Mountains in Oregon. Whether those places looked like upstate New York I'm not quite sure. Some of the scenes attempted were dangerous, like the men crossing that raging river. Spence Tracy was livid about the days spent in freezing water. And director King Vidor was exact in his direction. If Spence veered at all, King would order a retake. Things got very bitter and then MGM sent them to Florida for *The Yearling,* which was aborted by bad weather. Then Spence said he'd only do *Tortilla Flat* if King was removed as director, which happened. When King came to start *An American Romance* in 1944, he needed Spence as star and Spence flatly refused, so Brian Donlevy had to be imported and the film flopped.

BAWDEN: There was one more with Borzage.

YOUNG: *The Mortal Storm.* I got the script, couldn't see where I fit in as it was a [Margaret] Sullavan–[James] Stewart picture. Frank said he wanted me to be the Nazi, Fritz Marberg. He presented it as a huge challenge. Young people who've seen it on TV ask me why the family is called "non-Aryan" instead of "Jewish." That was at the insistence of the censors and not MGM. Frank said my part would illustrate the banality of evil. It was sold as a tragic romance and audiences ate it up. I'm not sure how well I did, but I tried and the fan reaction was strong, with many letters asking how could I be so evil. But that was the movie's point: the banality of evil. Today the sets seem so false, but the message rings true. It's still a favorite of the young and impressionable. I still get conflicting letters about it. But I'm glad I accepted the challenge.

BAWDEN: Your strangest credit has to be *Miracles for Sale* [1939].

YOUNG: [Director] Tod Browning's last picture. He'd had it and retired for good. I was the young magician and Tod was bitter about the way the horror film had evolved. He said Lon Chaney would have kept it going on a higher plane. I think this one just got through MGM, as so many of its programmers did, without much producer supervision. Some of the tricks were quite fantastic. It was a lot more than a murder mystery.

BAWDEN: You also made two musicals with Eleanor Powell: *Honolulu* [1939] and *Lady Be Good* [1941].

YOUNG: In the first, I played twins. But you could see the budget was far less than her earlier spectaculars. She still got first billing in *Lady Be Good,* but as filming progressed her part was shortened. She doesn't even dance until about thirty minutes into the film. Ann Sothern and I played bickering song writers and we got all the screen time. Ellie stopped speaking to Ann and this feud lasted for over thirty years. When Ellie was sick with cancer, she wrote Ann and said she had misjudged her and that was that. She ended her MGM years plopped into two Red Skelton comedies and just walked away from the business, very bitter.

BAWDEN: Did you get along with director Fritz Lang on *Western Union* [1941]?

YOUNG: Nobody ever got on with him. It was part of his routine to be forever quarrelling. I stayed out of the way and left that stuff to Randolph Scott, who truly loathed him. But on *Western Union* I had a big chat with Darryl Zanuck. My MGM contract was expiring in another year and he offered me a deal where I'd work for both Fox and RKO. He liked those double deals. Dana Andrews had one with Fox and [Samuel] Goldwyn and Maureen O'Hara had one with Fox and RKO. I talked to Mr. Mayer about my future and he halfheartedly offered me a short deal and I knew what that meant. He figured when Gable and the other big stars came marching home [from World War II], he wouldn't need me anymore. So I worked like crazy in 1942 and then left for Fox. I had a picture owed to MGM and that was *The Canterville Ghost* [1944].

BAWDEN: Ironically, in 1942 you got a citation from the National Board of Review for your three MGM pictures of that year: *H. M. Pulham, Esq.; Joe Smith, American;* and *Journey for Margaret.*

YOUNG: I asked King Vidor why he chose me for the lead in *Pulham* and he joked, "Bob Montgomery is at war!" He told me he had to take Hedy Lamarr and give her first billing or Mayer wouldn't agree to the picture. She'd sit with him and they'd talk characterization and it was always her favorite picture because she really acts in it. The screenplay by King's wife, Elizabeth Hill, closely follows the book for once; MGM had a bad habit of rewriting best sellers. I worked closely on how I looked. I start out as a teenager and morph into middle age. Clothes helped, haircuts helped, but it was also a question of speaking. And King tried to shoot chronologically, too. A very satisfying experience.

With *Joe Smith, American,* we had Dick Thorpe as director and he shot fast and without the usual MGM gloss. Lots of stuff filmed outside the studio walls. Yes, there was melodrama when I'm tortured, but it hit a nerve and became one of MGM's top grossers.

Margaret O'Brien became a huge star in *Journey for Margaret.* She was such a lonely little thing, we invited her to the house to play with our girls

Robert Young (*left*) and Margaret O'Brien meet Charles Laughton in MGM's *The Canterville Ghost* (1944). Courtesy of MGM and TV station KTVU in Oakland, California.

and they adored her. It was [director] Woody Van Dyke's last movie. He was in such pain from the cancer that would soon get him. And it was another big hit for MGM, based on a very small budget. A few years later and I was costarred again with Laraine Day. We had both escaped to RKO! My last at MGM, *The Canterville Ghost,* also starred Margaret O'Brien and Charles Laughton, who lauded her as a "pocket [Eleanora] Duse."

BAWDEN: You were also in one of Jeanette MacDonald's last MGM pictures.

YOUNG: In her case, she asked to go. Mr. Mayer was culling the staff of all Thalbergites. Garbo left in 1941, Shearer in 1942. Without Thalberg as guide, their box office plummeted. Jeanette wanted to try opera, she told me, before it was too late, and *Cairo* [1942] was a spy comedy at a time Americans were reeling from the aftereffects of Pearl Harbor. It laid a big egg.

BAWDEN: Everybody who ever worked with Betty Grable seems to have liked her.

YOUNG: It never hurt to be in a Grable picture. *Sweet Rosie O'Grady* [1943] was such a hit. This is the one that made her number one at the box office. Betty had a hotline in her dressing room that went straight to her bookie. She played the horses all day and would walk into a scene and whisper, "I just lost $250 on Smootha Silk in the eighth" or whatever it was.

BAWDEN: You didn't seem to mind taking second billing to Dorothy McGuire in *Claudia* [1943]?

YOUNG: She'd done it on Broadway and this was mostly a photographed play. Ina Claire was wonderful as her mother. It did sensational business and Fox requested a sequel. Dorothy was aghast and said she'd never do a sequel, but technically, she was under contract to Selznick and he simply put his foot down and *Claudia and David* duly appeared in 1946 and was almost as big a hit.

BAWDEN: You also made *The Enchanted Cottage* together in 1945.

YOUNG: At RKO. The silent version with Dick Barthelmess was still around and it was wonderful. I was the disfigured war veteran, Dorothy the very plain little thing. Only a director as careful as John Cromwell could make it work. There are, of course, no stills of the way we actually looked in the film. Placed in the lobby those pictures would have scared away audiences. Just as important are the key performances of Mildred Natwick and Herbert Marshall. It was a huge hit and I still get letters about it.

BAWDEN: That wasn't the end of *The Enchanted Cottage*, was it?

YOUNG: No. After I started *Welby*, Dorothy phoned me up and suggested we remake *Enchanted Cottage* as a TV movie. ABC was contacted and agreed and we got a print and screened it for network brass. This time I'd have Herbert's part and Dorothy would have Millie Natwick's. Well, it was as good as I'd remembered. But Dorothy and I looked at each other and we both shook our heads. It just wouldn't work in the New World. Our age today is filled with cynicism. Back then the horrors of war gripped the public imagination. Now cynics would start a fund to give these people money for cosmetic surgery. So we just suspended the deal.

BAWDEN: Why was *The Searching Wind* [1946] such a box office disappointment after success on Broadway?

YOUNG: The American public was sick and tired of war stories, particularly ones that showed how wrong our diplomacy was in the thirties. It did well in the big eastern cities and bombed in the heartland. I hated my character, who was a wishy-washy diplomat. Producer Hal Wallis told me he'd snapped up rights in a bidding war and then realized he needed Bette Davis as the smart female correspondent to sell it. Hal had just left Warners in a much-publicized feud and Jack Warner said to forget it. Sylvia Sidney is a fine actress, but she lacked box office clout. Our director, Bill Dieterle, made a most impressive picture visually, but nobody wanted to watch it.

BAWDEN: In 1947, you really switched types with *They Won't Believe Me* and *Crossfire*.

YOUNG: *They Won't Believe Me*: the title is prophetic. Nobody would believe me as that lout. I mean, I really tried. But the public was having none of that. This one was killed by adverse word of mouth. Everywhere I'd go, fans would ask, "How could you?" They wanted me as a nice guy. It's funny but I thought Jane Greer was on the cusp of a big career and I thought Susie Hayward might not go the distance because she was so demanding on set. I was wrong on both counts. One more thing: the trick ending. We thought we were being very smart, but it's rather stupid now that I think of it.

Crossfire? I asked [director] Eddie Dmytryk why he chose me and he said I'd be representing the average movie patron. They'd watch the story unfold through my eyes. The original book was about homophobia—not a subject any movie could tackle at the time because of censorship. So it became a study of anti-Semitism. We were right up against Fox's *Gentleman's Agreement*, only our little movie was taut and dug deeper. I thought *Gentleman's Agreement* was, by contrast, namby-pamby. But Fox had a lot of money to spend on promotion and we had virtually nothing. At Oscar time, we lost and *Gentleman's Agreement* won because their damning indictment wasn't very damning after all. I don't think we dealt with the motivation, but this was strong stuff for 1947. Of course, all the attention went to Bob Ryan, who certainly blasted away. But Bob Mitchum told me his part was nothing and he hated doing it. Gloria Grahame was also tops. I think *Crossfire* was one reason the House Un-American Committee investigated our director, Eddie Dmytryk. He'd asked questions usually ignored in our society.

BAWDEN: Did you know *Sitting Pretty* [1948] would be such a hit?

YOUNG: [Director] Walter Lang told me it was a big gamble. All the parts Clifton Webb had tackled since his debut in *Laura* [1944] had been bitchy. Here, he also had to be funny. And sitting with a preview audience I could feel that reserve until the scene where Clifton turns the bowl of porridge on the baby's head. He did that in exasperation after the tyke ruined several takes. It's not in the script. And instantly the audience roared and clapped. Who hasn't wanted to do that to an obstreperous kid? His mother, Maybelle, was always around and one day she waddles up to me and says, "Keep your hands off my Clifton. He's such a beautiful child." And I said, "He's a fifty-six-year-old sissy and I'm a happily married man with four daughters." And she shrugged and waddled off.

BAWDEN: But that wasn't the last you heard of Lynn Belvedere [Webb's character], was it?

YOUNG: In 1962, Fox phoned me up and said there was going to be one last sequel [to *Sitting Pretty*, titled *Hummingbird Hill*] with Belvedere coming back to our home to finally retire. A meeting was set up and Clifton came and we were shocked. He had stopped dyeing his hair; he was physically a mess. Maybelle had just died and he carried on so. Then his last film, *Satan Never Sleeps*, opened and it was apparent he wasn't physically able to act anymore. We had to close down pre-production because using another Belvedere just wasn't in the cards.

BAWDEN: I've seen you in the newsreel clip at MGM in 1949 for the studio's twenty-fifth anniversary luncheon.

YOUNG: I call it the Last Supper at MGM. I was back on a one-picture deal for *That Forsyte Woman* [1949]. I saw Jeanette MacDonald at that lunch and she was back temporarily, too. She told me, "Now I'm singing to Lassie." [She was then making her final MGM film, a Lassie picture called *The Sun Comes Up*.] All production was suspended for the afternoon. An entire soundstage was set up, but nine-tenths of the stars there wouldn't be around for MGM's thirtieth birthday. I'm in my *Forsyte Woman* costume.

BAWDEN: Tell me about *That Forsyte Woman*.

YOUNG: I thought I was pretty poor in the movie. Again I was told not to bother with an accent. I'll tell you who I got to like. It was Errol Flynn, who was warm and witty, a swell guy to hang out with. But Greer [Garson] got irritated with British director Compton Bennett and asked Mayer to replace him with Mervyn LeRoy, but Merv was busy on a Gable film. Walter Pidgeon told me, "I'm Canadian, Greer's Scots-Irish, Errol is Aussie, you and Janet [Leigh] are Yanks and we're supposed to be making a picture about English manners and morals?" It did okay, but wasn't the blockbuster of Greer's past triumphs.

BAWDEN: Why did you get into TV?

YOUNG: Had to. My picture career was petering out after more than two decades. I'd had a great run, but my type wasn't "in" anymore. And besides, I was over forty and it's a kid's business. Also, the movie business was lurching along. Fewer pictures got made every year. I'll give you an example. On *Bride for Sale* [1949], there I was at forty-two running around like a young guy. Claudette Colbert looked lovely, but she was forty-six and the other suitor was played by George Brent at forty-four. And nobody went to see it. Why would they?

BAWDEN: So how did you feel about switching over to TV?

YOUNG: First *Father Knows Best* was on CBS radio, starting in 1949. I never quite liked it because it had to have laughs. And I wanted a warm relationship show. My partner was Eugene Rodney and when we moved to TV I suggested an entirely new cast and different perspective. We shot at Screen Gems, the TV subsidiary of Columbia. The first pilot had Ellen Drew and she told me she just didn't feel right. [The pilot] ran on *Ford Television Theatre* in 1954. My character's name at the time was Tom Warren.

I'd wanted Jane Wyatt all along. She was then living in New York City with her husband and two boys. She'd fallen in love with live TV and Bob Montgomery used her every chance he had. Then a play she was doing bombed and she was out of work. Her husband saw our script on the desk and read it and urged her to do it. So, she did because there was nothing else available. I wanted and got Elinor Donahue as the oldest daughter. She was a few years older than the character she played, but had great experience. Billy Gray was also a bit older, but small for his age and he had movie credits, too. Lauren Chapin came in on an open casting call and aced the part of Kathy because she was so much like my own daughter Kathy.

BAWDEN: You were not an instant success on TV.

YOUNG: We struggled the whole of our first year and finally our sponsor, Kent cigarettes, pulled the plug after twenty-six weeks. In those days sponsors decided everything. I felt the stories were too sitcomy and CBS gave us a horrid timeslot: Sundays at 10 p.m. Which means the kids we were supposed to appeal to were already in bed. But there was a huge outcry over the cancellation and Home Hardware said it would pick us up and NBC gave us a great timeslot of Wednesdays at 8:30 and we grew over the next three years into a hit. Then, for whatever reason, NBC cancelled us, saying the kids were growing up too fast. CBS then picked us up for two more seasons and by 1960 we were often a top 10 hit.

BAWDEN: Why cancel the show then?

YOUNG: It was my decision. I thought we'd gone through all the family themes and I wanted to go out on a high note. And it's very tiring making thirty-nine shows a year. The kids had to have schoolwork factored into their days. We couldn't shoot any faster than we had been doing. Then CBS chairman Bill Paley phoned me and said he'd double all the salaries for one more year. He suggested the Betty character get married and the young couple could live over the garage and that would keep the fresh stories coming in. I polled the cast and Jane was adamant she wouldn't continue, so we closed down production after 196 episodes. But for the next few years CBS ran reruns any time another show failed and then in 1962–1963 ABC picked up the reruns.

BAWDEN: Do you accept the criticism the show sugarcoated the concept of the American family?

YOUNG: No. It was of its time. When I watch old episodes today, I see a show with only whites, but that was the reality of the American suburbs in the fifties. At that time most women wanted to stay at home and look after their families. There was an episode when Constance Ford plays a cousin of Margaret's who is a famous foreign correspondent and visits and says this is all she's ever wanted. That was the prevalent philosophy. And America was doing much better in the fifties than today. I played an insurance salesman and we lived quite well on a sole salary.

BAWDEN: You've said *Window on Main Street* [1961] was a big mistake. Why?

YOUNG: We rushed into it. Reruns of *Father Knows Best* were still on CBS. I was competing with my old image. I didn't realize it at the time. Eve Arden and Loretta Young made the same mistake. I wasn't Bob Young to viewers. I was Jim Anderson. And I discovered this one night as I ran into a shop for smokes and the lady at the counter said, "How could you desert your wife and lovely children, sir?" I thought our premise solid and production values were high. But I was a bachelor here and I played a sort of William White character commenting on the world. But we never really had a chance and after thirty-two episodes CBS just cancelled us.

BAWDEN: Why return seven years later as *Marcus Welby*?

YOUNG: Boredom. I have no hobbies. I was driving the wife crazy. I was drinking excessively. I kept reading the trades and learned ABC had a pilot titled *Marcus Welby*. It was a show about a family doctor and Ralph Bellamy was attached to it. But there was some hesitation about Ralph because he'd already played a psychiatrist on *The Eleventh Hour* and also he kept raising his price. So I booked a meeting with ABC head of development Grant Tinker. He was astonished I'd come in on my own. I argued what the series should be about and agreed to make a TV movie as a pilot. It got huge numbers and we were picked up for fall.

BAWDEN: You brought up the subject. How long were you an alcoholic?

YOUNG: For years, decades. I always will be. I thought I had it discreetly under control until a crew member on *Father Knows Best* told me that the children could sometimes smell liquor on my breath. I felt mortified. Been battling it ever since. I once said I was an introvert in a business of extroverts. Turns out more actors are introverts than I ever imagined. We've established the Robert Young Center for Community Mental Health in Rock Island, Illinois. People are surprised that with my longevity as an actor I'm still insecure. And I'd learned most actors feel this way, whether or not they'll ever admit it.

BAWDEN: During the seven years' run did you ever try to get old pals cast as guest stars?

YOUNG: Rarely. David Victor created the series. We had wonderful directors like Joe Pevney, Herschel Daugherty, even a very young Steven Spielberg. I was content to be the lead actor. That was enough for me. I rarely interfered. But Marguerite Chapman begged for a part. Alcoholism had ruined her career. We got her a small part, one of the last she ever had [in 1971]. There was a script about a chubby lady fighting the pounds and it was perfect for Margaret O'Brien and we had a grand reunion. With Dottie Lamour and Dolores Del Rio, casting office contacted them and they were great. In one episode in 1974 Marcus gets romantically entangled with a fashion designer and producers contacted Jane Wyatt on their own and it worked wonderfully well.

BAWDEN: You're still at it [in 1988], making TV movies. Why?

Robert Young with veteran star Alexis Smith in the 1988 TV movie *Marcus Welby, M.D.: A Holiday Affair.* Courtesy of NBC.

YOUNG: Something to do. I'll try one a year and the ratings are high. *Welby* has even made a comeback in a few of them. Anything more and I get too tired. Remembering lines is another problem. I think the way older people are treated is terrible. I think I can help reverse that image. I'll go on a bit longer, but physically it's all becoming too much.

Afterword

Young made his last professional appearance in Toronto in 1989 peddling headache pills in a series of TV commercials. He was semiretired and in declining health when he tried to commit suicide in his garage in 1991, but voluntarily entered a rehabilitation center. Losing his wife, Betty, in 1994 after sixty-one years of marriage was a major blow. They had four daughters. He died of respiratory failure at his home in Westlake Village, California, on July 21, 1998. He was ninety-one.

III

The Leading Ladies

Bette Davis

Interview by James Bawden

Who was the greatest female star of Hollywood's golden age? If you said Bette Davis, it would be hard to argue with you. Davis rose through the ranks of early sound-era actors and was a major headliner after five years of compelling movie performances. By the end of the 1930s she was a two-time Best Actress Oscar winner and the top female attraction at a major studio, Warner Bros.

Davis was not only a great actress but a charismatic personality with a trademark style on-screen that would make her perhaps the most imitated actress of her time, especially by female impersonators, who doted on her flashy gestures and blunt manner of speaking.

If she was a towering presence on-screen, she was no less impressive off-screen, frequently battling with her nemesis, Warner Bros. studio chief Jack Warner, for the right to blaze her own path in movies, often over his fierce objections and multiple suspensions for refusing the roles assigned to her. Once the golden age was over and film historians began to appraise it, there seemed little doubt that Bette Davis had advanced the cause of show business women in an industry that hadn't paid much attention to them before.

Though Davis won her Oscars for 1935's *Dangerous* and 1938's *Jezebel,* she lifted many more films into the realm of classic cinema with her mesmerizing displays of acting skill, among them *Of Human Bondage* (1934), *Dark Victory* (1939), *The Letter* (1941), *The Little Foxes* (1941), *Now, Voyager* (1942), and most especially *All about Eve* (1950), which contained probably her best-ever work on-screen.

Born Ruth Elizabeth Davis in 1908 in Lowell, Massachusetts, she had a sometimes chaotic life, filled with unhappiness off-screen. She had four unsuccessful marriages, some severe financial setbacks and, in the twilight

Bette Davis as Margo Channing in 1950's *All about Eve*. Courtesy of 20th Century-Fox.

of her career, battled breast cancer and a series of debilitating strokes that almost shut her career down permanently. Yet Davis managed to rise again on numerous occasions—becoming in later years a sort of priestess of scenery-chewing horror roles in films like the box office bonanza *What Ever Happened to Baby Jane?* (1962) opposite her old rival Joan Crawford.

Though she worked primarily in TV movies apart from some dreadful feature films in the last days of her career, Davis had already become a much-acclaimed Hollywood icon and knew, before she died, that her place in cinema history was intact and deliriously rich in magnificent work.

Setting the Scene

I first interviewed Bette Davis in 1976 in her suite at the Century Plaza Hotel in L.A. as she promoted her TV movie *The Disappearance of Aimee* (1976), in which she played opposite Faye Dunaway. In 1979, I met separately with her and costar Gena Rowlands at New York City's Plaza Hotel as each promoted the 1979 TV movie *Strangers: The Story of a Mother and Daughter.*

In 1982 I spent some time on the set of *Little Gloria: Happy at Last* (1982), which costarred Davis as Alice Vanderbilt. I was the one who showed her a copy of the script where her name is misspelled as "Betty"— she cackled with laughter and then shrugged.

Later, together with my colleague George Tashman, I sat with her at the cocktail reception on the Aaron Spelling lot as she was introduced to TV critics as one of the stars of the new series *Hotel* (1983–1988).

For this interview, I have merged the highlights of our conversations.

The Interview

BAWDEN: Do you remember what you said when the *New York Times* recently asked you to define your job as one of the biggest-ever movie stars?

DAVIS: I said I act and then I give interviews and then I act again.

BAWDEN: Did you ever want to be a director?

DAVIS (*shocked*): Women directors were not permitted when I started out, except for Dorothy Arzner, who dressed like a man. To be a great director like William Wyler, one must be a master psychologist. He could get actors to do things they simply did not want to do. A director must know how to motivate other people and that's a talent I lack. I can exasperate others, but not motivate them.

BAWDEN: What motivates you?

DAVIS: Poverty. I came from poverty and I'm always fearful of returning to that state. I can only give my all to every part. I could never telephone in a performance. I have to feel the character and be completely true to her.

BAWDEN: What is your biggest regret?

DAVIS: That I didn't save more of the money I made. Hell, Bob Hope and Fred MacMurray seem to own half the San Fernando Valley. They bought that land in the Depression for $10 an acre. Now it's all shopping plazas and hotels. I had a mother and sister to support in separate residences and later children and ex-husbands. It got so bad in the fifties I had to do those half-hour TV playlets to keep going. CBS's *Playhouse 90* offered me big bucks to do live TV but it scared me, so I kept turning them down.

BAWDEN: Do you keep up with old friends?

DAVIS: Not as I should. I was touring in 1972 in my one-woman show of clips and questions. We sold out in San Diego and I was back in my dressing room. A strange white-haired man got in and I just looked at him. Then he giggled. I knew that giggle. It was George Brent, my frequent costar. For decades he'd been growing avocados in a farm outside the city. I was sad to see him so aged but glad he landed on his feet after movies gave up on him.

BAWDEN: Any others?

DAVIS: Later, I was touring with the show in Australia and, after the clip from *Dark Victory,* I explained how the talented screenwriter, Casey Robinson, had turned a flop play into my favorite movie by inserting the character of Anne [played by Geraldine Fitzgerald] to voice all the sorrow—leaving my character to proceed without all that pity. And I said I didn't know what had happened to Casey. Suddenly an old man jumps up in the auditorium and shouts, "Bette, it's me!" and he runs up on the stage and we embraced. Casey had left L.A. for a new life down under years before. Well, it was a magical moment.

BAWDEN: When I interviewed [director] Curtis Bernhardt he said how much you and Joan Crawford resembled each other.

DAVIS: I read that quote and was shocked at first. Then I read further and he noted we both came from very poor families. And we hardly knew our fathers. Despite what you may have read, we never feuded on the set of *Baby Jane.* There simply was no time. It was shot in just over three weeks. I give full marks to Joan for loving the art of being a movie star. She never stepped out without looking her best. She worked eighteen hours a day at maintaining that stardom and I think later on when she was ignored a lot she was shocked by Hollywood's shabbiness. I always wanted to be an actress and play each character differently. Joan always wanted to be Joan. So I don't think deep down we resembled each other at all.

BAWDEN: But on Oscar night she exacted revenge of a sort.

DAVIS: Joan collected the IOUs of all the nominated female stars who could not make it that year. I was standing in the wings and Anne Bancroft's name was announced and Joan swept triumphantly past me. For *Hush, Hush, Sweet Charlotte* [1964] I think she was genuinely ill with a virus and had to quit. Why ever would she be scared of li'l ole me?

BAWDEN: Don't you have quite a history with Katharine Hepburn?

DAVIS: I've only met her in passing. You mean I stole her Oscar for *Alice Adams* [1935] when my performance in *Dangerous* got the nod? Well, she did give the better performance. We both were up for Scarlett O'Hara in *Gone with the Wind,* but at different times and I don't think either of us was gorgeous enough. We both dated Howard Hughes. Did you know I was going to star in *The African Queen* opposite John Mills for a British company? Then finances fell through, John Huston bought the property and recast with Hepburn and [Humphrey] Bogart.

BAWDEN: You had huge fights with Jack Warner, but today you seem nostalgic for the passing of the studio system.

DAVIS: The studio system made me. I'd been at Universal and got bad parts and the studio head, Carl Laemmle, said I had the sex appeal of Slim Summerville. He dumped me and I thought that was it and was packing to return to New York City. Then I got a phone call from George Arliss, the great British character star, who was at Warners. He'd won the Oscar for *Disraeli* [1929] and his portraits of great men from Voltaire to Richelieu tickled the cinema-going public. He said he thought I had something and asked me to visit him on the lot and discuss a part in his next movie, *The Man Who Played God* [1932]. To say I was all nerves is an understatement. I went and he was very kind, but I thought he was elderly. His wife, Florence, was there, too. She was going blind from macular degeneration. And I made a test and he insisted Jack Warner sign me for a full year. The movie was a huge success and my little part was noticed. For the first time I was photographed with care and my clothes were made especially for me.

BAWDEN: Were you an instant success?

DAVIS: Hardly. In one of those 1932 movies, *Three on a Match*, the director, Mervyn LeRoy, told the press that Ann Dvorak would be a huge star, Joan Blondell would have a long career in support, but there was no hope for me. I stopped speaking to him. We never worked again. Years later he said he had something for me and I said he should try and find Miss Dvorak and have her play it.

BAWDEN: But Warners kept you working and began building you up into a star.

DAVIS: Yes! I used that year to understand the art of picture making. I made seven more pictures that year at Warners, including *So Big!* [1932], which starred Barbara Stanwyck, who was a year older; *The Dark Horse* [1932], a merry spoof of presidential elections; *The Cabin in the Cotton* [1932], where Richard Barthelmess was the sole star. He'd been big in silents and now wore a girdle and was thirty-nine and played a rural innocent vamped by little ole me. That movie has my favorite line of dialogue: "I'd love to kiss ya, but I just washed my hair." What does washing one's hair have to do with kissing?

Then I made *The Rich Are Always with Us* (1932). I was twenty-four and the big star was a Broadway icon, Ruth Chatterton, aged thirty-nine. I remember the day they rolled in what was called "baseball lighting"—the same lights used in night baseball games and intended to wash out all her wrinkles. I never thought about them again until sixteen years later when I was about to start the comedy *June Bride* [1948] and I was aged forty and they wheeled in those same baseball lights and I, too, got teary.

BAWDEN: So you're saying the studio system nurtured you.

DAVIS: Today the young actresses get none of this. For one thing, so very few movies are made. Most of them get their starts in TV soaps or nighttime series. If they're in a big prime-time hit, they play the same character for years on end. The salaries are huge and there's no incentive to quit early. Then they might get some movie roles based on their TV notoriety, but nobody has taught them how to act. And they fade very quickly. TV networks don't want them back and one of them told me with the decline of TV movies she has nowhere to go except back to afternoon soaps. So yes, I'm very grateful for the studio system for nurturing me.

BAWDEN: But the time came when you left for Britain because you couldn't take it anymore.

DAVIS: That was five years later. I'd progressed up the star ladder. In 1934, I got Jack Warner to loan me to RKO for the great part of Mildred in *Of Human Bondage*. Jack was furious I got such great reviews. He said it had made me uppity and he openly campaigned to keep me off the Oscar ballot for Best Actress. But later on a mole at the Academy told me I almost won with the write-in votes permitted at that time. And I won the next year for *Dangerous*, which was viewed as a consolation award. I certainly believed Katharine Hepburn deserved to win that year for *Alice Adams*.

Bette Davis with Franchot Tone in *Dangerous* (1935), her first Academy Award–winning performance. Courtesy of Warner Bros.

And some of my Warners films had been big hits, like *The Petrified Forest* [1936].

But Jack believed in stardom's seven years rule, meaning a star would invariably be fading in her last years. So he tried packing in as many bad movies as possible and I utterly refused to do one stinker, *Garden of the*

Moon [1937], and left for Britain to make movies. [Margaret Lindsay wound up taking the female lead in that movie.] He sued me and there was a British trial which I lost and I went to see Mr. Arliss, who was back in England, and he said take your medicine and return. And I did so and then came a decade of my best hits and I won a second Oscar for *Jezebel*.

BAWDEN: What about your reputation for being difficult?

DAVIS: I always felt I was hardest on myself. After making *Mr. Skeffington* [1944], Jack Warner gave me my own production unit. Then I asked my *Skeffington* director, Vincent Sherman, to direct my first picture, *A Stolen Life* [1946]. He bluntly refused and said I had been too difficult to work with, too bossy. I said it was my nature to challenge a director because it was my name above the title and if the movie flopped I'd get the blame. But after that I never again wanted to be directed by Vincent Sherman.

BAWDEN: You did feud with Miriam Hopkins.

DAVIS: No. She feuded with me. The first day on the set of *The Old Maid* [1939] she flounced in wearing one of my dresses from *Jezebel*. She appeared in the short-lived play before it became my movie hit. She refused to match shots and when I had a close-up, she'd be in the background rolling her eyes. As our characters aged, hers became younger. Eddie Robinson calls her a pig in his book. And I know Errol Flynn stopped speaking to her on the set of *Virginia City* [1940].

When Jack Warner proposed a rematch in *The Great Lie* [1941], I got him to substitute Mary Astor, who went on to win a supporting Oscar. We'd rewrite the dialogue on set and give [director Edmund] Goulding conniptions!

For *Old Acquaintance* [1943], Goulding faked a heart attack to get out of directing us again. I phoned Norma Shearer and tried to get her out of retirement, but she said she'd never play a bitch. Miriam could and did. And a scene came up where I had to slap her face. *Life* magazine asked if they could cover it as a photo spread, but I said no. I really slugged her and her head bobbled and I felt ever so much better. She sent a note in the next day saying she was feeling battered and bruised and booked off sick. Then I felt ever so badly.

You know, when she died in 1972, I was on the set of a TV thing and just blurted out, "God has been very good to us today, he's taken Miriam Hopkins." But there was no response. None of the young actors on set knew who she was anymore.

BAWDEN: People often said you deliberately chose weak directors.

Paul Henreid and Bette Davis share a romantic moment in *Now, Voyager* (1942). Courtesy of Warner Bros.

DAVIS: Well, you critics have ignored Eddie Goulding, who was supposed to be a weak director. And yet he directed my best movie, *Dark Victory*. And is Irving Rapper a weak director? He directed *Now, Voyager,* my second-best-ever movie.

Now, John Huston is considered one of the greats and after making *The Maltese Falcon* [1941], he directed *In This Our Life* [1942] with me and Livvie de Havilland. And it really bombed. Later, I made *Beyond the Forest* [1949] for King Vidor, surely one of the greats. And it was such a stinker I left Warners after eighteen years. So that criticism makes no sense at all.

BAWDEN: In your 1962 book, *The Lonely Life,* you say one of your costars was so ugly you had to close your eyes in a kissing scene. Was that Edward G. Robinson?

DAVIS (*irritated*): Well, he's passed so I might as well admit it.

BAWDEN: How many times have you played a screen character who closely resembled your real self?

DAVIS: Three times. I virtually played myself as Maggie in *The Great*

Lie [1941], Maggie Cutler in *The Man Who Came to Dinner* [1942], and Kit Marlowe in *Old Acquaintance.*

BAWDEN: But not Fanny Skeffington or Regina Giddens or Margo Channing?

DAVIS: Ha! Especially not Margo. When I booked into this hotel [the Plaza] yesterday, the room clerk was quaking in his boots. He said Joan Crawford had sent a list of twenty-one demands from the type of chilled vodka to the threads in the pillow cases and all had to be obeyed or she'd walk out. And I patted him on the shoulder and said softly, "Well, I'm not Joan Crawford. Thank God!"

BAWDEN: I'm wondering if you always got your way in your Warners heyday on specific roles?

DAVIS: The answer is no. Hal Wallis was in charge of WB production and he bought *Now, Voyager* for Irene Dunne, who was freelance and her salary was $200,000 a picture. Irving Rapper was chosen to direct it and he slipped me a mimeographed script. So I stormed into Jack Warner and convinced him I was cheaper. After all, I was already under contract and making only $3,000 a week. And Jack said sure purely on the economic angle.

Later, when I was off for a year on pregnancy leave—that would be 1947—I slipped into the studio late at night to audition for *Life with Father,* but Mike Curtiz was going to direct it and he said I just wasn't right [for the part]. I'd already refused *Mildred Pierce* [1945] because I didn't really want to work with him again. So losing *Life with Father* was okay.

BAWDEN: What was the biggest film you ever turned down?

DAVIS: *Come Back, Little Sheba* [1952]. Hal Wallis was then at Paramount and bought it for me. I made the mistake of going to a Broadway matinee to see Shirley Booth and her genius spooked me. I turned Hal down flat and he had to hire Shirley, who made her movie debut at fifty-four and won the Oscar. I was going through a terrible time personally and I'd momentarily lost my courage.

BAWDEN: Why were most of your final batch of WB films so miserably bad?

DAVIS: Public tastes changed after the war. Also Warners lost its confidence; all the big studios did. As soon as a star's contract was up, Jack Warner dumped her—or him. In just a few years Ann Sheridan, Ida Lupino, Errol Flynn all left. Fewer and fewer pictures were being made every year. Do I think Jack deliberately sabotaged my career? No. He just didn't care anymore. I hit forty in 1948 and such big stars as [Mary] Pickford and [Norma] Shearer retired around that age. Women over forty were not supposed to be sexy. Look at Mary Astor—in 1941 she scored in *The Maltese Falcon,* but she was thirty-four. Two years later she was at MGM playing moms to the likes of Judy Garland.

BAWDEN: But your pictures were awfully thin.

DAVIS: Agreed. In *A Stolen Life,* I was twins and this was based on an old Elisabeth Bergner movie, but the public wasn't buying it anymore. And with *Deception* [1946], Jack wanted to reunite the *Now, Voyager* threesome of me, Claude Rains, and Paul Henreid. The lush classical music disguised the fact this was just a triangle story. *June Bride* [1948] was okay when Robert Montgomery wasn't mugging. But *Winter Meeting* [1948] sank like a stone. I was a spinster poetess and I fell for a war hero who'd seen such carnage he was thinking of becoming a priest. I begged Jack to get Gary Cooper or John Wayne as the story would only work with a real masculine icon. He chose newcomer Jim Davis—later Pa on *Dallas*—and Jim couldn't handle the dialogue. Then Jack forced me to make *Beyond the Forest* [1949]. I was a backwoods temptress married to a slob of a husband I wanted to kill. Jack said he had to use Joe Cotten because he was owed a picture. I pleaded for Eugene Pallette. Halfway through filming I asked for my release. Perhaps that's what Jack wanted all along: to get at me.

BAWDEN: But then you went to Fox for *All about Eve.*

DAVIS: Oh, no, I made *The Story of a Divorce* for Howard Hughes, but he wisely released it only after *All about Eve* came out. [He changed the title to *Payment on Demand*]. I'd finished the Hughes movie when Darryl Zanuck phoned late at night. He said Claudette Colbert had broken her back on the last day of filming *Three Came Home* [1950]. He needed a new actress to play Margo Channing for director Joe Mankiewicz. I said yes without reading the script. But it was so wonderful we never changed a word. It saved my career but the rest of the fifties was bleak. I thought I'd have hits with *The Virgin Queen* [1955] or *The Catered Affair* [1956], but both lost money.

BAWDEN: But you stormed back on Broadway in *The Night of the Iguana* [1960]?

DAVIS: Every night started with a standing ovation. I finally had to take a bow to quiet the audience, which displeased Margaret Leighton, who had insisted on top billing. One day I had such a miserable cold the

Bette Davis as Apple Annie in Frank Capra's 1961 *Pocketful of Miracles.* Courtesy of UA-TV.

doctor told me to skip the matinee. I told my agent to get down to the box office and report back. He phoned in to say fully half the theatergoers had lined up to get their money back. But I was never even considered for the movie. John Huston chose Ava Gardner.

BAWDEN: Hadn't Huston already offered you a plum movie role which you turned down?

DAVIS: In 1960 he phoned up and said would I consider third billing in a western titled *The Unforgiven* to star Burt Lancaster and Audrey Hepburn. I said billing never bothered me. And I sweetly asked what my part would be. Johnny cleared his throat and said, "Burt Lancaster's mother." And I cackled and laughed until tears came to my eyes. I was a mere five years older than Burt. Thanks, but no thanks! [Lillian Gish wound up in the role.]

BAWDEN: How close were you to playing Martha in *Who's Afraid of Virginia Woolf?*

DAVIS: I was back at Warners in 1964 playing yet another twin in *Dead Ringer*. Jack told me he was angling to buy rights and wanted to use me and Henry Fonda. But *Dead Ringer* wasn't a hit and then he told the press he was thinking of Pat Neal. Then when he brought in Mike Nichols [to direct], it was Liz Taylor and Richard Burton. Liz was passable, but Burton gives one of the greatest movie performances. Then I was being touted in the columns to play the countess in *A Little Night Music* [1978], but I was later told Liz thought I would overpower her—and Hermione Gingold got it. But the movie was dreadful, so who cares?

BAWDEN: For years now you've been surviving on TV movies.

DAVIS: It's where the audience is. A two-hour TV movie has a shooting schedule of nineteen days. Some of these were pretty good, including *Skyward* [1980] and *A Piano for Mrs. Cimino* [1982]. But the one that soared was *Strangers: The Story of a Mother and Daughter* with Gena Rowlands as my daughter. Like me, she's completely unsentimental and we really clashed on the screen, an epic duel of equals.

BAWDEN: Why are you doing a TV series, *Hotel*, at this point in your career?

DAVIS: For the money, of course. And the part is pretty terrific. You know, I've done nine TV pilots and none sold. The TV presidents said I was too big for TV, whatever that means. In the movie I'm replacing Melvyn Douglas, which tickles me. I'll be like Jane Wyman in *Falcon Crest*. I'll be in every episode, but some weeks I'll have a scene or two and then I might be the focus of an entire hour. I can stay at my apartment and not have to traipse off to locations. I can wear expensive clothes—no rags for me. And I think if I make enough and the show goes on long enough, it might be it. I don't want to fade away into cameos as Ethel Barrymore did. I'm a brand. You hire me and you get sixty years of professionalism, a few Oscars, and a link both to the past and the present.

Lillian Gish (*left*) cares for her sister Bette Davis in 1987's *The Whales of August.* Courtesy of Nelson Entertainment and PBS.

Afterword

Three weeks after our last talk, Davis checked into a Boston hospital for a double mastectomy. A stroke that changed her facial features followed. She bravely battled back and did act again. After filming the pilot for *Hotel,* she was replaced by her old *All about Eve* costar, Anne Baxter, for the rest of the series. Her final completed feature film was *The Whales of August*

(1987), which teamed her with other screen legends Lillian Gish, Ann Sothern, and Vincent Price. She earned rave reviews.

Davis had begun another film, *The Wicked Stepmother,* when she succumbed to cancer. She died October 6, 1989, in a hospital at Neuilly-Sur-Seine, France. She was eighty-one.

The unfinished film had only a week's worth of Davis footage, but director Larry Cohen rewrote the screenplay to use it, turning her character into a witch who could transform herself into a younger woman. That allowed Cohen to replace Davis with the much younger Barbara Carrera, who finished the film in her role. The film was not successful.

Yvonne De Carlo

Interview by James Bawden

One of the great screen sirens of the 1940s was Canadian actress Yvonne De Carlo, who became a leading lady in westerns like *Salome, Where She Danced* (1945) and exotic "sex and sand" historical movies like *Song of Scheherazade* (1947). Occasionally she glowed even brighter in much classier pictures like Jules Dassin's grim 1947 prison picture *Brute Force,* Robert Siodmak's stirring 1949 film noir *Criss Cross,* the 1953 Alec Guinness comedy *The Captain's Paradise,* and Cecil B. DeMille's 1956 religious epic *The Ten Commandments.* But another generation will remember her best for her comic lady monster Lily Munster in TV's *The Munsters* (1964–1966) and the 1966 movie version *Munster, Go Home!*

Setting the Scene

In 1975 CBC-TV was running a salute to the great Canadian film stars: Norma Shearer, Walter Pidgeon, Deanna Durbin, et al. But the one who truly intrigued me was Yvonne De Carlo, so I arranged to interview her during my summer visit to Los Angeles in 1975 while previewing the fall TV season. De Carlo told me she'd do the interview only if we met at the Polo Lounge of the Beverly Hills Hotel. When I showed up there, the waiter tried to give De Carlo what she considered an inferior booth, so she let him know, pretty vividly, that wasn't going to happen.

The Interview

BAWDEN: You were born in Vancouver, British Columbia?

DE CARLO: That's correct—in 1922. I was christened Margaret Yvonne Middleton. My parents were not married, which was fudged in early studio press releases. My father actually was Samoan and that explains

Yvonne De Carlo in a typically exotic role in *Song of Scheherazade* (1947). Courtesy of Universal-International.

my eyes, doesn't it? Life as a single mom in the twenties was very rough indeed, so [Mom] invented a father for me who just up and left one day.

My mother was the prime force in shaping my career. She was a waitress, but there always was enough money for my singing and dancing lessons. To her, I was a rough, uncut diamond. I sang in the choir at St. Paul's Church as soon as I could walk. I wrote poetry for the *Vancouver Sun*. By fourteen, I was dancing leads at June Roper's School of Dance. Then I was a featured dancer at the Vancouver Little Theater and at fifteen I was dancing in the line at the Palomar Supper Club.

When I was fifteen, we went to Hollywood and found all doors barred. I returned in 1941, aged nineteen, and started off as an extra. My first movie was *Harvard, Here I Come*. You haven't heard of it? Lucky you! But most of the time I was underemployed. Mom waited tables at the Cafe de Paris at 20th Century-Fox studios for 15¢ an hour. She'd slip the unused sandwiches in her handbag and we'd eat off them. I had to get to Bakersfield for dance gigs which gave me $3 a night but bus fare ate into that. In 1941 I was named Miss Venice Beach. We had to return to Vancouver to get legal visas and promptly returned to Hollywood. Earl Carroll hired me for his show at the Aquarius Theater for $40 a week, which was heaven. Then Paramount signed me to a standard day player's contract.

BAWDEN: So your first studio was Paramount?

DE CARLO: In 1941 Dorothy Lamour had burst forth as a huge star, thanks to the *Road* movies with Bob Hope and Bing Crosby. Paramount was scared she was going to defect when her contract lapsed in 1942–1943. So I was hired as a threat. It was common at every studio. Jimmy Craig was at MGM for years as a look-alike for Clark Gable. See what I mean? So you can spot me in *Road to Morocco* [1942], *For Whom the Bell Tolls* [1943], *Let's Face It* [1943]. Hiccup and you'll miss me.

Dottie knew exactly what was going on. On *Road to Morocco* she saw me in the background and laughed, "I got Hope and Crosby—you got a camel." She'd always pat me on the rump in the studio commissary. But when she signed at Paramount in 1944 for seven more years I was no longer needed—and was discarded.

BAWDEN: What did you do next?

DE CARLO: My agent got me an audition at Universal, smallest of the big studios. To our mutual astonishment, I was hired on the spot. Universal was a failing studio. It existed on horror movies and Abbott and Costello flicks. They were even trying to force Deanna Durbin out. They needed a female lead for an opus already shooting: *Salome, Where She Danced*, which had been written for Maria Montez. But her alcoholism and her girth were both too much, so I was in and the costumes fit—that's all that mattered to our director, Charlie Lamont.

I mean, how many movies have you ever seen set during the Austrian-Prussian War of 1866? Of course it was based on the career and legend of Lola Montez and there really was a town with that name in Arizona where she later escaped to. Laurence Stallings, who wrote *What Price Glory?* [1926] was our writer and we did it all on the back lot, mostly in three weeks although it was in Technicolor. I was later told Merle Oberon had been the second choice but she asked for too much money.

I got to dance a lot and I kept my mouth shut as much as I could. Stephen Sondheim later told me it was a campy classic. We had fun making it: Rod Cameron, David Bruce, who was a scream; Albert Dekker, Walter Slezak. It really was camp before that term existed.

BAWDEN: Then what happened?

DE CARLO: They plopped me into a western [1945's *Frontier Gal*] with Rod Cameron also scheduled for Maria Montez. Again it was shot in Technicolor in about three weeks. On location I shared a dressing room with Andy Devine—other "stars" included Fuzzy Knight and Sheldon Leonard. Charlie Lamont was the studio director who tried to do everything on the first take and he added lots of slapstick. I was the female adornment and the ending had Rod giving me a good spanking and me liking it a little too much. It ran the top of double bills. Rod was a charmingly dull guy—when his wife divorced him later, out of boredom, he ran off with his mother-in-law!

BAWDEN: You were groomed to be a big star.

DE CARLO: Cliff Work, vice president of production, sent me to John Robert Powers School in New York to be fine-tuned. I was shown how to eat with knife and fork as if I'd been using my hands all these years! I was taught to walk with a book on my head. And in studio clothes I went out on studio dates with studio male ingenues I never saw before or since. And these fabricated romances were written up in all the movie magazines.

BAWDEN: But you were idle in 1946?

DE CARLO: The studio was reorganized as Universal-International and Bill Goetz took over as president. He tried to phase out the horror flicks, got rid of Deanna Durbin in 1948, and imported talents such as producer Mark Hellinger as well as Burt Lancaster and Joan Fontaine. He told me I was safe. He needed budding talent and he put me into Hellinger's big-budgeted actioner *Brute Force*. Julie Dassin was the director and Richard Brooks wrote the story. [Burt] Lancaster was in it, along with Hume Cronyn, Charlie Bickford, Annie Blyth, Ella Raines. Quite a cast. I was an

Italian girl and Julie was very patient with me, giving me multiple takes, and also I was beautifully photographed.

BAWDEN: And you had the star part in *Song of Scheherazade.*

DE CARLO: The only movie title nobody could pronounce. Very artistic at times. Jean Pierre Aumont, who later was married to Maria Montez, was Rimsky-Korsakov and the cast also included Brian Donlevy—and Eve Arden as my mother, if you can believe it! I mean it's totally and deliberately silly. Audiences were just confused. I can't say my dancing was much, I just felt silly all the time.

BAWDEN: I think *Criss Cross* is your best movie of that era.

DE CARLO: Mark Hellinger threw me a tremendous challenge. The director was Robert Siodmak, who was very meticulous in his details. He'd sometimes act out a whole scene for me. I was back with Lancaster, who was a very sexual man. I mean he was prettier than I was. And he was a yeller. He'd scream at Robert in great frustration. Burt said he'd never do another crime picture and he was off to swashbuckling. I thought Dan Duryea fantastic, Stephen McNally, too. I watched it recently and I held up my part as the wandering wife very well. I was finally an actress!

BAWDEN: Many of your subsequent UI films were programmers.

DE CARLO: That's putting it nicely. With *Black Bart* [1948] I had Dan Duryea and Jeffrey Lynn as my male costars. Then there was *River Lady* [1948] with both Duryea and Rod Cameron. Then there was *Calamity Jane and Sam Bass* [1949] with Howard Duff and Willard Parker. All in color. All shot on the UI ranch and all directed by George Sherman, who was a tough taskmaster. We worked Saturdays until dawn broke.

Then I did *Buccaneer's Girl* [1950], directed by Freddie De Cordova, who now directs *The Tonight Show.* And he also directed *The Desert Hawk* [1950] and then I did *Tomahawk* [1951] with Van Heflin and Preston Foster, directed by—you guessed it—George Sherman. The plots were very similar with all those westerns and they were cut to around eighty minutes each to fit on double bills.

BAWDEN: Then you did a British film, *Hotel Sahara* [1951] with Peter Ustinov. How did that come about?

DE CARLO: I had nothing to do with it; it was a loan-out. I loved the cast, which included David Tomlinson and Roland Culver. I was told I was the American name that would entice US cinemagoers, but in fact it didn't do much business over here at all. But about a year later I went to Morocco to make *The Captain's Paradise* with Alec Guinness. Celia Johnson and I were his two wives, one in Morocco and one in Spain. It was considered shocking in its day. So I did my first scene and the normally passive Sir Alec picked me right up and shouted, "This one can act!" But not many saw this one either.

BAWDEN: You became expert in breaking in new talent, in a manner of speaking.

DE CARLO: In *Criss Cross,* I needed a sexy dancing partner in an early scene and that was Anthony Curtis, who I don't think had any dialogue at all. Boy, was he jittery! Then in *The Desert Hawk* I had an unknown Rock Hudson, who was very nervous and said, "I'm not sure I can walk and talk at the same time." So I said, "Well, you'd better learn quickly, kid." Richard Greene was the nominal hero but the females in the audience really hooted it up when Rock came on screen.

We then made *Scarlet Angel* in 1952 and [Hudson] was on the cusp of something big. This one was a remake of *The Flame of New Orleans* [1941] with Marlene Dietrich. And the very next year he finally got billing as big as mine in *Sea Devils* over at RKO and we had a class A director in Raoul Walsh. He dressed it all up rather fine, although it really was nothing more than an actioner. It was based on Victor Hugo's *Toilers of the Sea* and did big business.

What had happened was in 1952–53 Universal rearranged my contract. The new Universal wasn't doing any better than the old and had to rely on Ma and Pa Kettle, Francis the Talking Mule, and Abbott and Costello to balance the budget. I usually did one for them a year and then took freelance assignments.

In 1953 I chose *Sombrero* just to see what MGM was like. And I found that studio making programmers like the rest of us. This one was a real stinker featuring Ricardo Montalban, Pier Angeli, Vittorio Gassman, Cyd Charisse. I was the backwoods wife of Vittorio and he was expiring of a tumor. I never actually saw it but it wound up turning around my career.

BAWDEN: Explain, please.

DE CARLO: Well, Cecil B. DeMille requested a print from MGM to check out Nina Foch, who he wanted to use as Moses's mom in *The Ten Commandments.* When I came on, he stood up dramatically and shouted, "That's the face I've been looking for as Moses's wife." So his secretary invited me to the great man's office, where he proceeded to act out all the parts for me. His secretary told me to wear sandals and every time I wiggled my big toe he would smile. He had a foot fetish, it turns out. Then he turned and said, "Now we are to be wed—professionally!" The only condition was I had to wear contact lenses to turn my eyes brown. But I kept pulling them out and he never noticed until the premiere when he stood up and shouted at the screen, "The blue-eyed seductress has deceived me."

On the set he wanted florid acting. He was always shouting at me, "More! More!" Eddie Robinson really went all out and C. B. would even shout at him, "More! More!" All that exertion gave him a heart attack and he never directed another movie. I drove past the Westwood Theater months after the premiere and there still were lineups around the block. It saved Paramount from bankruptcy.

BAWDEN: What effect did this have on your career?

DE CARLO: I was hot again. Warners offered me the lead opposite Clark Gable in *Band of Angels* [1957]. Raoul Walsh insisted on me. And Gable agreed and we got on. He had no pretension about his stature. There was a degree of sadness about him. He was closer to sixty than fifty and his role was a variant on Rhett Butler. He was so conscientious, always on time. At first he struck me as a cold fish. But once I convinced him I was a regular guy he'd even talk bawdy to me. I used to kid him about the crowds of women on location who'd even follow him to the washroom. And he'd roar with laughter.

BAWDEN: You were due to make *The Helen Morgan Story* [1957] but lost out.

DE CARLO: *Band of Angels* did bad business and Jack Warner replaced me with Ann Blyth. And that film really bombed and ended Annie's film career just like that. The only work I could get was *Timbuktu* [1959] opposite an actor I call Victor Immature [Victor Mature]. I went out on a nightclub tour and then my husband [stuntman Robert Drew Morgan] lost his leg doing a stunt on *How the West Was Won* and I had to get movie work. I phoned up Duke Wayne and took the [second female lead in *McLintock!* (1963)]. We had a scene where we wrestled on the stairs and I look up and Maureen O'Hara's fuming. Only Maureen wasn't acting; she felt the Duke was her property! Then Bob Hope used me as his paramour in *A Global Affair* [1964]. And I did three quickie westerns for A. C. Lyles at Paramount, all shot in ten days each.

Later, we shot *The Power* [1968] on the MGM back lot, which was all in ruins. George Hamilton was the last MGM contract player and the studio was astonished it made some money. Then [director] Tay Garnett offered me *The Delta Factor* [1970] with such fading names as Yvette Mi-

Yvonne De Carlo as Lily Munster with Fred Gwynne (*left*) and guest star Richard Deacon in an episode of *The Munsters*. Courtesy of CBS.

mieux and Diane McBain and we made it in two weeks. Russ Meyer [a specialist in erotic films] phoned me up and said, "Yvonne, I have always admired your—face." I thought he was going to say "breasts" and so *The Seven Minutes* [1972] was his attempt to go mainstream. I was a novelist named Constance Cumberland.

BAWDEN: I want to jump back and ask what you thought when *The Munsters* was offered to you.

DE CARLO: I'd wanted a TV series. But this? I wasn't sure. I had a hard time getting into the rhythm of it. Then director Joe Pevney suggested I play Lily as a sort of mixed-up Donna Reed character and not overdo anything. When I saw the first pilot in a screening room I cringed at my makeup. But I never estimated it would become this cult thing. It took two hours of makeup to make me seem like that. It ran for two huge seasons, then CBS quarreled with the creators about reruns and we got cancelled. A movie in color in 1966 [*Munster, Go Home!*] showed off everything in reds and greens on my face. Boy, was I ugly.

BAWDEN: Next came TV movies.

DE CARLO: Not really. I started [doing] TV in 1952. I did all the shows from *Ford Television Theatre* to *Burke's Law* to *The Virginian*. When TV flicks came along, I tried them, too.

In the TV movie *The Girl on the Late Late Show* [1974] I met such contemporaries as Van Johnson and Gloria Grahame and made new friends. We had worked at different studios, never knew other. And I was back with Ricardo Montalban in the TV remake of *The Mark of Zorro* [1974].

BAWDEN: You periodically come back to Canada to work.

DE CARLO: Up there I'm Canadian "content," which they need to count for the tax breaks. I had a hilarious role in *It Seemed Like a Good Idea at the Time* [1974] as Stefanie Powers's gun-toting mom. What fun!

BAWDEN: And I have to ask about your Broadway debut in Stephen Sondheim's *Follies*.

DE CARLO: Stephen asked me to come to New York and audition. I sang and danced a bit and he said I wasn't what he wanted. Back in my hotel room I'm packing and the phone rings and he says, "I just wrote a song just for your character, which I'm in the process of creating." It was "I'm Still Here" and when I sang it every night the audience went wild. And it's become my motto because the system hasn't destroyed me. I refuse to be battered. I refuse to break. And I'm still here.

Afterword

De Carlo married stuntman Robert Drew Morgan in 1955. They had two sons, Bruce and Michael, and were divorced in 1974. In 1997, son Michael died. The coroner's report mentioned concerns about foul play. In 1998, De Carlo suffered a stroke and moved to the Motion Picture Country Home in Woodland Hills, California, where she died from heart failure on January 8, 2007. She was eighty-four.

Janet Leigh

Interview by James Bawden

Though Janet Leigh was the star of dozens of comedies, romances, and even some musicals, she will forever be remembered for her most shocking role—as the beautiful prey of serial killer Norman Bates in Alfred Hitchcock's 1960 masterpiece *Psycho.*

The journey this glamorous leading lady made in films from the 1940s into the 1990s represents a classic story of adaptation of a career to the many tides of show business popularity.

Setting the Scene

When I started going to the neighborhood movie palaces in the east end of Toronto as a child in 1953, Janet Leigh rapidly became one of my faves. As I got older and was permitted to visit the great movie palaces downtown, including the cavernous Loews and its companion Loews Uptown, which almost exclusively showed MGM flicks, Leigh was one star I always looked for. I mean, June Allyson was a little too old for me by then and Debbie Reynolds too young. But Janet Leigh was just right. And in 1960, when I was fourteen, I somehow got into the first day's screening of *Psycho* and was knocked for a loop by Leigh's iconic turn as Marion Crane.

Many years later, I got to know her in person in my capacity as a journalist. That's when I discovered she was not only a movie star but also a kind and warm mother. I remember one time when we were chatting at her Los Angeles home during an afternoon in June 1974, a very young Jamie Lee Curtis suddenly ran through the living room, dressed in a bikini, and dived into the pool. "T-t-t-that's my daughter!" said Leigh, who was temporarily at a loss for words.

In 1989, I spent a day with her on the set of *Twilight Zone,* the Toronto-filmed Canadian remake of the original TV series, and noticed that, at

Glamorous Janet Leigh, circa 1951. James Bawden collection.

sixty-two, she remained drop-dead gorgeous. In 1995, we talked again on the phone for an hour as she began publicity for her book about the making of *Psycho.*

The Interview

BAWDEN: You seem to have had the upbringing typical of a Depression-era American child.

LEIGH: Very much so. I was an only child, born in 1927. My real name is Jeanette Morrison. My parents, Helen and Fred Morrison, were from Danish stock, hard workers all their lives. I was born in Merced, California, and grew up in Stockton. We always lived in rented rooms. They poured all their love into my upbringing and I never realized how poor we were until I had grown up.

I was very good in school, [but] very lonely because both my parents had to work long hours. I was pretty good in music and by the time I was eighteen I was studying music and psychology at the University of Pacific, married to a swell guy, Stanley Reames. I thought I'd have a career in some kind of social work that utilized music as a teaching tool for needy children.

BAWDEN: Is the story of how you were discovered by Norma Shearer true?

LEIGH: Completely. My dad was operating the front desk at the Sugar Bowl ski lodge at Truckee in northern California in the winter of 1945 and Norma and her second husband, Marty Arrouge, were there and Norma saw my photo on my father's desk and asked to see it more closely. Without even asking Dad, she took the photo out of the frame and said, "I'm taking this to MGM because they're saying they need new talent." I was then studying at UCLA and living above a garage with my husband.

But Norma knew how MGM worked. [Her first husband, Irving Thalberg, was once head of production there and she was one of its biggest stars.] She first contacted [agent] Lew Wasserman to represent me. And only then did she go out to MGM, in person yet, and contacted talent head Billy Grady. And I was phoned quite a few months later and found myself at Metro in Grady's office.

Right then MGM was embarked on a gigantic hiring spree. Mr. Mayer [MGM production chief Louis B. Mayer] later told me 1946–47 was the last great year at the studio before television started emptying the movie theaters. Billy sent me to photography for stills and makeup tests, which lasted for weeks, before signing me to the standard starlets' clause at $50 weekly for three months. I then got instruction on makeup, how to wear clothes, even how to use a fork and knife!

Next I was taken to see the Metro drama coach, Lillian Burns Sidney—then married to [film director] George Sidney—and she sniffed, "Oh, another 'girl next door.'" Lillian had been an actress in silent days and she was beloved by the younger set at MGM for her candor. After more tests, she gave me a scene from *Thirty Seconds over Tokyo* [1944], which Phyllis Thaxter had done. It was the young wife lamenting her husband being away. [She] told me to come back in two days and do it for her. It was a monologue and I could relate to it, and when I finished I looked up and there was a faint smile on Miss Lil's face.

She sent me to have it recorded on film and gave me another scene, which I read without any study. Turns out it was a scene from *The Romance of Rosy Ridge* [1947]. Then she phoned producer Irving Cumming and director Roy Rowland and said, "I've got your ingenue for *The Romance of Rosy Ridge*." So I read for them and they decided I'd do this picture on location starting the next Monday. Now that really startled me. I didn't think I was prepared as yet.

I burst into tears because I said I didn't have any money for transportation and Miss Lillian laughed and said, "Child, they'll transport you. Now go home and pack. You do have a suitcase, don't you?" I had no idea that all those weeks I was away the studio had another girl, Beverly Tyler, waiting back on the lot to plop in just in case I failed.

BAWDEN: What were your memories of that shoot?

LEIGH: Van Johnson got me through it. He has always been my trusted friend. Every night he worked with me on next day's scenes. [Director] Roy [Rowland] was a tower of understanding. If I flubbed, I'd start crying, so he'd pretend to cry, too. The crew was so supportive but, as I said, I knew nothing. Early on Van looked in at my cabin one night and I was washing out my dress for the next day. "Oh, dearie, they have women for that," he laughed. "You don't want to deprive anyone of a job, do you?" Then one day he looked in and said, "You're in! Turns out the big boys looked at all the footage and they're going to proceed with you." There was no turning back.

I haven't seen it since the premiere. I'm told no complete print exists, just a cut-down version for double bills, and that makes me mad. That was the first time I'd ever thought there was a chance I might be let go. And when we got back to MGM for the interiors I had a little bit of confidence built up. The film was hardly a smash but MGM started promoting me and Van as a team. Next up they announced *The Stratton Story* [1949] for us and Van started practicing baseball on the back lot diamond. Then we were both replaced as Jimmy Stewart said he wanted to do the part and I was too young to be cast opposite him.

BAWDEN: When did they change your name?

LEIGH: While I was away. The checks started coming for Janet Leigh. I'd already told Miss Lil that I hated Jeanette Morrison and she thought it quaint. Mr. Mayer proposed Janet after Janet Gaynor and Leigh after Vivien Leigh. But I wasn't keen on it. Then they proposed Jeanette Reames and Van said, "Absolutely not!" Finally Mayer overruled us all and said Janet Leigh was a light, bright name, a starlet's name. I thought it commonplace at the time but grew to love it.

BAWDEN: Did you keep in contact with Norma Shearer?

LEIGH: Of course. Once back at the studio I did meet Norma and became her friend. She was "only" forty-three by then but already of another era. We gradually lost contact but once very recently [in 1972] I was driving through Beverly Hills and saw her, aged and stooped, walking with Marty. Two oldsters out on an evening's stroll. I stopped the car and ran into her arms and told her how much she had meant to me. She was gracious, but distant. Did she even remember me? She was having mental problems by then. I left in tears, Marty said it was all right. She was just drifting away from reality.

BAWDEN: In 1948 MGM kept you good and busy.

LEIGH: I wanted them to. I would never have dared turn any part down. I needed the money. Even before *Romance of Rosy Ridge* was released I was on the set of *If Winter Comes* [1947] as the village girl who has an ill-fated romance with Walter Pidgeon. What a cast—Deborah Kerr, Angela Lansbury—and it was such a bad movie and I was bad in it with my British accent. Then I rushed to the set of *Alias a Gentleman* [1947], doing costume fittings and then our star, Wallace Beery, booked off sick, so I was given another movie to do. It was *Hills of Home* [1948] and yes, my costar was Lassie. Am I allowed to state Lassie was a boy? But a kinder costar I never did have. Years later he still remembered me. In *Words and Music* [1948] I was Mrs. Richard Rodgers opposite Tom Drake. Word at MGM was that he was on his way out. I remember one day the Rodgers family were on the set and Mary Rodgers looked me up and down. I was only twenty-one.

BAWDEN: How long did it take for *Little Women* [1949] to be filmed?

LEIGH: Well, months and months. Because this was one of those prestigious MGM quarter-century extravaganzas. We did everything inside on studio sets. The whole house was on one set, Sir C. Aubrey Smith's was on the next. David Selznick owned the rights and was selling off all his properties. Rhonda Fleming told me she was going to play my part—Meg—

before he pulled the plug. [Director] Mervyn LeRoy was a tough taskmaster and with June Allyson, Margaret O'Brien, and Liz Taylor as my sisters, a lot of tomfoolery went on, I can tell you. I got fifth billing before Mary Astor and Rossano Brazzi. It was a huge success at the time because America was feeling sentimental for another time and this was a reminder of how a family could flourish even during the Civil War. One thing that bothered me about the story: Liz is supposed to be younger than Margaret—but not with those curves, I can tell you!

But you are right, filming went on and on. I had the smallest part among the sisters, so I had enough time to go down the street and do my scenes as Van Heflin's wife in *Act of Violence* [1948]—as did Mary Astor. You know the story, don't you?—that one day Mary came back to visit and Mervyn was up a crane and hollered down, "Mary, those clothes! People might think you're a slut!" Well, that's exactly what she was playing in *Act of Violence*—and quite brilliantly, too.

BAWDEN: In 1949 you were in five movies.

LEIGH: Well, *Little Women* finished in late '48. Then I did *The Red Danube* [1949], an all-star Cold War thing. I was a Russian ballerina stranded in Vienna! Look, I studied ballet and the dance scenes look authentic. The phony Russian accent, I'm not so sure. My character was hiding out at Mother Superior Ethel Barrymore's convent. The way she focused those big black eyes on me made me most uncomfortable. Peter Lawford, Angela Lansbury, Walter Pidgeon were all in it. It was old home week and that's the trouble. There was no tension and it was supposed to be a thriller.

In *The Doctor and the Girl* [1949] I, naturally, was the girl. Harry Cohn sold off half of Glenn Ford's contract to MGM. And this was the best they could do for him! I remember Nancy Davis [Reagan] was in it well before she met her Ronnie, and she came from a medical background and told me it was too artificial for words. We shot on location, including Bellevue Hospital. It had a big budget but it played on double bills and quickly disappeared.

Then I was rushed into *That Forsyte Woman* [1949]. Greer Garson, Errol Flynn, Walter Pidgeon, Bob Young, and me right up there as one of the stars. I remember the huge Victorian houses built from scratch for this one movie. My first day on set I got a handwritten note from Greer welcoming me onboard. What a gracious lady! Sparks were expected to fly between her and Flynn, but they remarkably got on. Hard to believe he was only forty because between takes he'd sit in a corner and shake visibly. Had trouble remembering the lines. The subject matter was adultery, which could not be mentioned at the time, so the story gets tricky at times and Compton Bennett wasn't the best director for this kind of thing. Greer openly thought [Director George] Cukor might have improved it. Still, it was a success based on its star power.

BAWDEN: Around this time MGM had that huge party to celebrate twenty-five years—I've seen the newsreels.

LEIGH: And what a party it was! We were dragged from the *Forsyte* set for it. Both Greer and I are in our Victorian costumes. Flynn and Pidgeon are there, but as themselves. We were all seated in the biggest soundstage and introduced: Gable, Tracy, Gardner, Hepburn, Astaire, Sinatra, Lansbury—it goes on and on. I'm wedged between Lansbury and Lanza on one side and Jeanette MacDonald on the other. And five years later for the thirtieth? Only a few of us were left—Mayer, Gable, Garland, Hepburn were all gone. I was winding up and so was Greer. They rolled out a cake, I remember, no more than that. The dream factory was running on low by that time.

BAWDEN: The last reunion was for *That's Entertainment!* [1974], right?

LEIGH: We were air-freighted to Vegas [for *That's Entertainment!*] and there were even a few stars not considered MGMers: Merle Oberon and Gloria Swanson. Ellie Powell wouldn't come for fear of meeting her ex, Glenn Ford. Johnny Weissmuller was there but his Jane, Maureen O'Sullivan, was not. I was told Bill Powell was too infirm to make it. Norma simply would not come. What a ragtag bunch we were. I came for the party, although I did my musical films elsewhere.

BAWDEN: How did you get to RKO?

LEIGH: I was out on a Sunday night, slowly dancing around at a party, and I noticed a very strange man looking at me. No matter what I did, his eyes were on me. I asked his name and one of the girls tittered, "That's Howard Hughes!" Then he left. On Monday afternoon Benny Thau comes on the set of *The Doctor and the Girl* and says I've been loaned to RKO for three pictures over the next few years.

And I did *Holiday Affair* [1949], an attempt to make Bob Mitchum into a Cary Grant type. It did not work! He was a department store clerk and I was a spy for the opposition, and when he helps me he's fired. Bob was very uncomfortable in it. And a darling little boy, Gordon Gebert, was my little son. One day during a scene he started playing away and wasn't supposed to be doing that so I stopped the scene. Bad mistake. Director Don Hartman told me I should incorporate such things into the scene to make it appear more natural. It was a great lesson to learn. And, to answer your inevitable next question, Gordon left show biz shortly after that.

BAWDEN: You have no credits listed for 1950.

LEIGH: Much time was spent at RKO making *Jet Pilot,* but Howard didn't get around to releasing it until 1957! Then at RKO I made *Two Tickets to Broadway* [1951]. Not bad, not good. But at least it was a musical role, which I never got to do at MGM. Tony Martin and Ann Miller and Eddie Bracken were in it, too. When we started, Stan Laurel and Oliver Hardy came to the cast reading. Then Laurel got very sick and those two wonderful guys both dropped out. Did you know that? There was just no budget to play with, but I got to sing on the big screen for the very first time.

BAWDEN: You once said you fit the classic mold of an MGM female star. Explain.

LEIGH: First, I came from a poor background, so I was very beholden to Metro. They loaned me money for a car, for a home for my parents. Thus I had to repay them with weekly deductions, so I couldn't get out of line. I don't remember a single role I turned down. Of course, I had Lew Wasserman, the greatest agent around, and he did prod them on occasion. All us girls—[June] Allyson, [Eleanor] Powell, [Debbie] Reynolds—we all had humble beginnings. Only [Katharine] Hepburn was from a wealthy family. After my divorce [in 1949], the studio controlled my dating. They'd make me up at the studio, put studio clothes on me, and promote phony romances. When I married Tony Curtis in 1951, Mr. Mayer was furious. He was no longer in control, you see. And it did get out I'd been married twice before. Hedda Hopper later called us a conniving pair because we got all that publicity, but as I recall it, she was always phoning up for exclusive stories.

BAWDEN: Talk about your 1951–1952 films.

LEIGH: Well, *Mr. Imperium* [1951] was an Ezio Pinza vehicle. I was just the girl, and he was such a ham and the camera caught all that and we were quite an odd couple. *Angels in the Outfield* [1951] was cute, I guess, and I was a sports reporter, if you can believe that. Nobody ever mentions that one to me. I had one story in *It's a Big Country* [a 1951 anthology film made up of different stories] with Gene Kelly, the only time I worked with him. *Fearless Fagan* [a 1952 comedy about a circus lion] was dog awful, bottom of the barrel. I asked why we were making it and was told they had all this talent hanging around they needed to find work for. I mean, Stanley Donen directed it and it had Carleton Carpenter and we made it in weeks. The lion was a real pussy cat. I'd go over to him and he'd turn on his back and purr to be rubbed on the stomach.

I had the second lead in *Scaramouche* [1952] and, no wonder: Eleanor [Parker, who played the leading female role] was the most beautiful woman I'd ever seen. But it was okay to be in a big hit. And I did *Just This Once* [1952], which was a Peter Lawford vehicle, only he was faltering and I got first billing. But he has become a dear friend ever since.

BAWDEN: One of your breakout films as far as I'm concerned was *The Naked Spur* [1953] with Jimmy Stewart.

LEIGH: He's the kind of actor who makes you seem better when acting with him. And he's a great man in real life. No pretensions. He once told me this is one of his favorite roles. Look at it closely: there was such torment in his eyes. He knows he is leading a man back to a certain death. Taking a man to be killed—isn't that a form of murder? And accepting money for it? We did most of it on location. The director, Anthony Mann, had worked with Jimmy before and he knew just when to prod and poke him and when to back off. I loved my tomboy look, I tried desperately to avoid any suggestion of Hollywood glamour. I had [the] makeup [department] shear off almost all my hair and I'd just rub my fingers through it and no real makeup except some powder to stop any sheen. Lew [Wasserman] said it was an indication what I could do. It was the first time I was truly proud of a performance.

BAWDEN: You also did *Confidentially Connie* [1953] that year?

LEIGH: I knew you'd mention that one! A comedy about the meat shortage. I tried watching it on TV one night and couldn't finish it. But I was back with my Van [Johnson] for the last time at MGM. I was loaned out twice that year—MGM figured they could make a lot of money off my popularity.

I did *Houdini* [1953] at Paramount. MGM nixed my idea to bring him [the film's star, Tony Curtis] over to MGM for a picture with me. Negotiations dragged on for weeks because MGM refused to grant Tony top billing, saying I was the bigger star. But it wasn't even an MGM movie! I just wanted to work with my husband and finally a deal was arranged. I wished the movie had been better produced, Historically, it was inaccurate, but it did make a lot of dough.

Walking My Baby Back Home [1953] I loved because I danced with Donald O'Connor. Some scenes were later used in the *Columbo* episode I did. I just had a ball working with Donald. We became best buds. The budget was very tiny on it. I think it was Donald's last Universal picture, outside of those *Francis* [the talking mule] features.

BAWDEN: You made four movies in 1954.

LEIGH: For *The Black Shield of Falworth*, I was on loan to Universal-International, who turned it into another Janet-Tony thing. Those "costumers" were very popular right then, after the success of *Ivanhoe* [1952]. You know, forever after, when I meet Walter Matthau, he'll snort, "Yonda is de castle of me fodder!" But Tony never said anything like that!

Then I was borrowed for *Living it Up* [1954] with Dean Martin and Jerry Lewis. We were always over at Jerry's, where he made amateur feature movies for the fun of it. One could sense on the set this act was starting to break up. The ad-libs could get very vicious. Dean resented Jerry's ascendancy and Jerry resented Dean's easy charm with the ladies. I wasn't surprised they broke up about two years later.

And then the time came to say good-bye at MGM. I finished *Rogue Cop* [1954], a goodish Bob Taylor vehicle, then walked around the lot saying good-bye to everybody. I met Mr. Thau in his office. We looked at each other and we both cried. A lot. He said there wasn't enough work to keep me here. I knew I had to go out in the brave new world of freelancing. But I was still upset. I packed up my dressing room stuff, put it in the car, and drove off the lot by the side door—I was too upset to leave by the big gates.

BAWDEN: But your movies got better.

LEIGH: Right away! I did *Pete Kelly's Blues* [1955] as my first freelance over at WB and it was a terrific hit. Jack Webb shot a lot of it at Fleming Plantation in Lafitte, Louisiana, because it, after all, was set in 1927 and Kansas City had changed a lot in thirty years. Jack could really play the cornet. He'd been playing since he was a boy. Peggy Lee was terrific, Ella Fitzgerald, too. Jack wasn't a great director, I feel, because he rushed along. He was used to the fast pace of making a TV series. And acting-wise, [costars] Eddie O'Brien and Lee Marvin had it all over him. In our scenes, I found him distracted by his many duties and he didn't really give me much. But a big hit it was.

Then, at Columbia, I did the musical version of *My Sister Eileen* [1955] with Betty Garrett and Jack Lemmon, the only time we worked together. I asked [Columbia studio boss] Harry Cohn why he didn't use the 1953

Janet Leigh with then husband Tony Curtis in *The Perfect Furlough* (1958). Courtesy of Universal-International.

score for Broadway's *Wonderful Town* and he barked they asked for too much money and besides he already owned the rights [to the original story]. So he commissioned a brand-new score from Julie Styne and Leo Robin that wasn't as good, I'm afraid. But we did have Bob Fosse and Tommy Rall as our dancers and when you dance with Fosse, you stay danced! The critics preferred *Wonderful Town,* but how many had actually seen it, I wonder?

BAWDEN: Give me your story about *Safari* [1956].

LEIGH: It was part of a two-picture deal Lew [Wasserman] had engineered with Columbia. Vic Mature was a big white hunter sort. He was going after the Mau Maus and I was his sweetie going out on this safari. Vic said he'd only make it on the back lot, but our director, Terry Young, ordered him to accompany the crew to the dark continent. One scene called for Vic to swim across a crocodile-infested river. An hour before, we all gathered along the bank and Vic said he would not do it. Then a shooter appeared and said he'd shoot directly into the crocodiles and so frighten them they'd scatter. And Vic looks up and says, "What if one of them is deaf?" Well, Young lost his legendary English coldness and started ranting and Vic did the shot "under duress," but we all watched with great apprehension. By the way, all the spectacular scenes from stampeding elephants to the Kikyuy warriors were all shot for us. There was no stock footage. It was a big hit, but has since disappeared. I've never seen it on TV.

BAWDEN: In 1957, *Jet Pilot* finally came out.

LEIGH: It would have made a bundle in 1951–52 when it was made and the Cold War was at its height. But Howard fell in love with the aviation footage and every time the US changed a plane he'd insist on shooting it all again. It cost over $9 million, I was told, and when it finally came out, RKO was no more. Universal-International released it. I was a sexy Russian pilot and if it had been shown in 1951 I'd have become a bigger star. By 1957 I looked completely different—I was mature, a blonde, not this cute, curvaceous brunette.

BAWDEN: In my opinion, your first masterpiece was *Touch of Evil* [1958].

LEIGH: When I met Orson Welles in his UI office, I'd just broken my arm the day before. It was heavily bandaged and I said I guessed I should get a cast on it. Orson was enthusiastic at first and then wavered, feeling that would be too kinky. So I usually have a coat or something over it so it could remain rigid.

Here was the first great director I'd worked with. I was blown away in the screening room when I watched the dazzling opening. We shot mostly at night down in Venice [a suburb of Los Angeles]. The sets are amazing in themselves and then there are all those Welles cronies who pop in and out. Marlene Dietrich was down for about four nights and she's marvelous. When she tells him his time is up, I jumped in the screening theater! I didn't understand a lot of it when we were making it. And I still don't. I think my motel scenes with Dennis Weaver came out marvelously. I don't think Chuck Heston ever again was half as good. You know Orson thought of it as the ultimate B movie, which it is, in a way. Nothing quite makes sense or was supposed to. And predictably the studio hated it and refilmed bits and Orson wrote this magnificent fifty-eight-page memo, which I feel could be made into a movie itself.

BAWDEN: And I feel the second masterpiece was Alfred Hitchcock's *Psycho*.

LEIGH: I read the script and saw that I died about a third of the way through. When I met with Hitch, he agreed that I died forty-five minutes

Janet Leigh does a little screaming while undressing for that famous shower sequence in Alfred Hitchcock's *Psycho* (1960). Courtesy of MCA-TV.

into the movie. That was very important because audiences could not quite believe one of the stars of the film would be murdered so quickly. He used his TV camera crew, so the shoot was rapid paced. He didn't expect it to be such a hit. Instead, he inadvertently started the slasher craze, which deeply disturbed him.

Vera Miles was in it because she owed him a picture. When I wrote my book [about making the film], I sent her a letter asking if I could interview her and got no reply. John Gavin told me the movie's success never affected him. And Tony [Perkins] and I at first thought it was just another credit. But I'm now totally identified as Marion Crane. I booked into the Toronto hotel this week and the reservations clerk said, "I assume you won't be wanting a shower?" Well, buster, your assumption is correct. I never take a shower! Never!

The shower scene was pure cinema. Shot for seven days. Every shot was storyboarded. When [art director] Saul Bass says he shot it, boy, is he wrong! And yes, I did have a double while the day's work was being rehearsed. But that body is mine, all mine, once shooting began. At one point, the water was so warm it washed off the pasties and I figured, "What the hell! Let's keep going!" The grips looking on from the overhanging balcony got a great view. Finally, it was all assembled for me to look at—seventy shots—complete with music and the sound of Hitch slicing and dicing a cantaloupe. And that's when it got to me and I had nightmares. By the way, "Mother" wasn't Tony Perkins. He'd left to do a Broadway musical, so it was a stunt double. I've been told it's one of the most famous scenes in movie history.

At the obligatory final cast party, Hitch comes up and embraces me with tears. Says I'm his only leading lady he had killed off. Says we can never work again because people will always remember how he had killed me. And he walked out and it was true. He would never hire me for anything. Not even his TV series.

Oscar night at the Pantages Theater, I was a basket case. [Leigh was nominated for Best Supporting Actress]. I really wanted it. And the way the Academy ignored Psycho! Many voters told me they simply disapproved of the whole thing. There was no Best Picture nomination. And Psycho changed the way we see movies, I mean the way we look at a film. The Apartment [1960] won and it's nearly as great, I guess. Hitch did get a Best Director [nomination], but predictably, Billy Wilder won [for The Apartment.] Tony Perkins was the best actor, as far as I'm concerned, but he was ignored. I lost to Shirley Jones, who was wonderful in *Elmer Gantry*. I wanted to win and I didn't. And I never was nominated again.

BAWDEN: I think your third masterpiece was *The Manchurian Candidate* [1962].

LEIGH: Boy, did I need that one. Hadn't worked in awhile. Going through a tough divorce from Tony Curtis, you know. Then Frank Sinatra [the film's star] took pity on me and told [director] John Frankenheimer to hire me as Rosie. I read the relatively short part and I had a dozen questions. Like, where does she come from? And who is she working for? Some people who saw it thought she was CIA, others a Russian spy. Others said she was just a pickup. That's how John wanted it. I just appear on the train. I talk in highly coded language. What gives?

One of my first days on set I walk in and they're going to do the train scene. John said simply, "Let's do it." No time for diddling around. I had a perfect first take and we did a few more for good measure. Frank aced it as always, great on the first [take], which we ultimately needed. When I saw it all put together, I didn't know what to expect.

Angela Lansbury as the mother was magnificent. She was only three years older than Laurence Harvey [who played her son]. [He] really was as unlikable off camera as he is on. John said James Gregory's character was patterned after Richard Nixon. If you study James you can see that. President Kennedy loved it. Then he was assassinated and the film was shelved on Frank's orders for over twenty-five years. [The film is about an attempted presidential assassination.]

BAWDEN: Is it true you were "in" with both Presidents Kennedy and Johnson?

LEIGH: Jack Kennedy said I should be a congresswoman. But I'd already been married three times. Lyndon Johnson asked me to become ambassador to Finland, but that would mean moving with little children. I did a tour of Latin American countries to promote the Peace Corps. I wish I'd been able to do more.

BAWDEN: You seemed less busy in the sixties.

LEIGH: I remarried [to stockbroker Bob Brandt]. And I decided to avoid long locations because of the kids. One day when we came home from filming *Kid Rodelo* [1966] in Spain, [my daughter] Kelly said, "Mommy, my best friend isn't my best friend anymore." So I stopped that. I had high hopes for *Bye Bye Birdie* [1963] with Dick Van Dyke, but Columbia recut the movie to highlight Ann-Margret and it didn't work. [Director] George Sidney got smitten with her. I think Ann was embarrassed by this. I had a reunion of sorts with Van [Johnson] in *Wives and Lovers* [1963], which was a mere sixteen years after we were in *Romance of Rosy Ridge*. Shirley MacLaine had walked [off the picture] and [producer] Hal Wallis invited me on board on one day's notice. It was a funny movie, but as Van said, our fans were now living in the suburbs, putting their kids through college.

Then, out of the blue, I got offered [the role of] Paul Newman's ex-wife in *Harper* [1966]. It had a great cast: Betty [Lauren] Bacall, Julie Harris, Bob Wagner, Shelley Winters. Not a big part as Susan Harper, but juicy— and who could resist a sort of love scene with Mr. Paul?

BAWDEN: You became a queen of the TV movies.

LEIGH: Because they were shot in L.A. So I did *The Monk* [1969], *Honeymoon with a Stranger* [1969], *The House on Greenapple Road* [1970], *My Wives Jane* [1971], *Deadly Dream* [1971], *Murdoch's Gang* [1971]. I'm sure I left some out. I was on *Bracken's World, Bob Hope's Chrysler Theater,* but my fave is the *Columbo* I did in 1975 where I play a faded star who may be a killer. John Payne was the costar and we had Maurice Evans, Sam Jaffe, quite a gathering. I loved doing Dean Martin's variety shows. He's such a well-rehearsed pro and far from being soused. His drink of preference was always apple juice.

BAWDEN: And now here we are in Toronto [in 1989]. It's past midnight and we are cowering behind a gigantic tombstone in St. John's Cemetery to evade your husband, who doesn't like to see you smoke.

LEIGH: The scene is for a *Twilight Zone* episode and it has to be finished tonight. We're going back to L.A. on the first flight home. I never did get that Broadway hit I always wanted. What I got instead was a long and satisfying marriage. Two great kids and their kids. Tons of friends from the past. And when we get back to the hotel tonight, this girl will be taking a nice long hot bath. No showers anywhere, anytime!

Afterword

Janet Leigh wrote an autobiography, *There Really Was a Hollywood* (1984) and, with writer Christopher Nickens, the book *Psycho: Behind the Scenes of the Classic Thriller* (1995). She had two daughters with Tony Curtis— Kelly and Jamie Lee. Kelly had only a brief acting career, but Jamie Lee became a popular TV and movie star. Janet Leigh costarred with Jamie

Lee in two films, *The Fog* (1980) and *Halloween H20: 20 Years Later* (1998). Altogether, Leigh was married four times. Her first marriage (in 1942) to John Carlisle was annulled. She was only fifteen. Her second marriage (to Stanley Reames) and third marriage (to Curtis) both ended in divorce. She was still happily married to her fourth husband (Bob Brandt) when she died at home from a heart attack on October 2, 2004, at age seventy-seven.

Joan Leslie

Interview by James Bawden

To cinemagoers of a certain generation, Joan Leslie's name evokes warm, nostalgic feelings. During World War II she reigned supreme at Warner Bros. as the girl soldiers had to leave behind.

She had talent as well as beauty. Watching her dance with James Cagney in *Yankee Doodle Dandy* (1942) and with Fred Astaire in *The Sky's the Limit* (1943) is my recipe for sheer delight. As a very young star, she made impressions in *High Sierra* (1941) with Humphrey Bogart, in *The Male Animal* (1942) with Henry Fonda and, most of all, as herself in *Hollywood Canteen* (1944).

Later on, she stole *Born to Be Bad* (1950) from Joan Fontaine and *The Revolt of Mamie Stover* (1956) from Jane Russell—not that there was that much to steal.

Setting the Scene

It was on one of the hottest days of July 1994 that I invited Joan Leslie to high tea at the Ritz Carlton Hotel in Pasadena. I was met by a chic and sophisticated matron who stayed cool throughout the long afternoon.

The Interview

BAWDEN: Didn't you come from a show biz family?

LESLIE: No! That's the publicity talking. My dad worked for a bank in Detroit right up to the [1929 stock market] Crash. Up to that time we were solid, secure, and conservative and completely middle class. Our deep religious values held us together.

I was born—now get this—Joan Agnes Theresa Sadie Brodel on January 26, 1925, in Detroit. I'm the youngest of three sisters and we're still very

Joan Leslie poses with a Thanksgiving turkey in her starlet days at Warner Bros. James Bawden collection.

close and loving to each other. I made my debut at age two—singing "You Are My Sunshine," so there must have been a lot of ham in me.

In 1934, because we desperately needed money, we three went on the road as the three Brodel Sisters, a singing vaudeville act. There! You have an ad for us from Toronto's Shea's theater. I remember our stay was so long I went to parochial school there. I did imitations of Greta Garbo and ZaSu

Pitts. What range! Can't imagine where I picked those up. It was a strange, crazy quilt of a childhood but we all made it because we were together.

BAWDEN: Then came movies?

LESLIE: Hold on a minute! At age ten I became a Powers child model. It was $5 an hour. We were still performing and at the Paradise Club on Broadway there was a knock at the door and it was an MGM talent scout. It's strange but up to then we'd never really thought about Hollywood. I was so much in love with the stage. But the offer was too good, so I made a test.

BAWDEN: And?

LESLIE: For the test Mom wrote my script and even had a part for my little dog. MGM liked it, signed me, and weeks later I was on the set of *Camille* [1937] cast as Bob Taylor's younger sister. And yes, I really did go to the little red schoolhouse on the lot and I remember playing with Mickey Rooney, who smoked a lot, and Freddie Bartholomew.

Of course, my part was not large. I have no Garbo stories to tell. Except one. We were playing jacks outside her dressing room and as she swept past me her gown brushed me. She said in that accent of hers: "Pardon!" That's all. Pardon! So I guess you could say I talked to Greta Garbo. I'd often wondered what my career would have been like had I stayed at MGM. But my option wasn't picked up. I was a has-been at eleven.

BAWDEN: You still got jobs.

LESLIE: We had all moved to L.A. and decided to stay. Sister Mary got a short-term deal at Warner Bros. I had day jobs on the *Nancy Drew* films and in *Love Affair* [1939] and *Susan and God* [1940]. Later I'd get to know Joan Crawford. But not here!

BAWDEN: How did you finally get to Warners?

LESLIE: I was needed. They knew my work in bit parts. The director was Raoul Walsh, a man's man. But look at the performances he got out of his women stars! He needed a fifteen-year-old to star opposite Humphrey Bogart in *High Sierra*. I put on my best dress for the test. My father took me over. I wasn't nervous and I rather liked Bogie from the start. He took care to be soft-spoken around me. Roy [his character] is secretly in love with the girl, you see. I was the cripple, Velma, and I read softly and Mr. Walsh loved it. He told Jack Warner to sign me to a seven-year contract and that was that.

I got a new name, too—Joan Leslie. On the set there was tension between Ida Lupino and Bogie, but there was always tension. I could feel a

Henry Hull (*left*) Humphrey Bogart, and Joan Leslie in the 1941 thriller *High Sierra*. Courtesy of Warner Bros.

rivalry. Maybe it worked in their scenes. And I was noticed in the reviews. I was on my way.

BAWDEN: Any final thoughts about Bogie?

LESLIE: Remember, he wasn't Bogie as yet. Look at the credits for *The Maltese Falcon* [1941]. He and Mary Astor had their names under the title. He still lacked star-billing status. I did make a second film with him—*The Wagons Roll at Night* [1940]—and I found him still wonderful to work with, but restless. The film was [a second feature] and he was billed under Sylvia Sidney. There was such a distance in our ages—more than a quarter of a century—that a real friendship wasn't possible. And he was experiencing marriage problems.

BAWDEN: What do you remember about making *Sergeant York* [1941]?

LESLIE: Well, who didn't love Gary Cooper? But he was twenty-five years older and even treated me as a kid. He gave me a doll! I was playing Gracie York, who was married at the age of fifteen. After the picture was completed, I met Gracie, who had come out to Hollywood to inaugurate the new fighting tank called the Sergeant York. It proved to be a huge bomb, but I knew her as an entirely rustic person, so simple and sweet. She said at the movie premiere in New York City that the couple had been installed in a gigantic hotel and both had had trouble figuring out how the indoor plumbing worked.

BAWDEN: Compare Cooper to Randolph Scott, who starred with you in *Man in the Saddle* [1951].

LESLIE: There's no comparison really. Randy excelled at westerns and I fought with Ellen Drew over him on that one. He was gentlemanly and these movies fit him like a glove. With Coop there were other dimensions at work. He was among the biggest-ever stars. Like Cagney. He was unique.

BAWDEN: Then you had star billing in *The Male Animal?*

LESLIE: I was Olivia de Havilland's kid sister, Hank Fonda my brother-in-law. It was a fun picture to make. Based on the James Thurber play, it just worked from day one. The cast was huge: Eugene Pallette, Jack Carson, Hattie McDaniel. My beau was played by a very talented guy, Herbert Anderson, who later starred on TV's *Dennis the Menace* [1959–1963]. Filming went very fast as Hank had a date to get back to Fox. And Elliott Nugent was a talented director of comedy. Why nobody writes about him these days is anybody's guess.

BAWDEN: Everybody has seen *Yankee Doodle Dandy.*

LESLIE: My one great picture. The cast was huge and the movie was officially directed by Michael Curtiz. But Jimmy Cagney had an awful lot to do with the staging of the numbers and his own interpretation of George M. Cohan. Jimmy supplied the high energy and in some scenes he virtually took control with a lot of help from Richard Whorf. Mike didn't know a thing about American history. Mike was free to concentrate on the look of the film, the camera angles, and had virtually nothing to do with the dancing. Sometimes Jimmy was so pooped after a full day of dancing that he'd stay home part of the next day and not appear until noon. And he was always around when his kid sister Jeanne was doing her stuff. He'd praise her to the skies. I was just mighty proud I could keep up with him.

BAWDEN: Describe life as a teen at Warner Bros.

LESLIE: It was a tough school but taught me a lot about professionalism. I would ride my bike around the lot and be considered just a kid. [Director] Edmund Goulding even turned me down for the lead in *The Constant Nymph* [1943] because he said he could only think of me on my

Joan Leslie with Oscar winner James Cagney as George M. Cohan in *Yankee Doodle Dandy* (1942). James Bawden collection.

bike and not as a repressed little British girl. Joan Fontaine was imported to do it. She was eight years older than me!

I used to sneak onto the soundstages and watch the likes of [Bette] Davis and [Barbara] Stanwyck at work. I never really worked with Joan Crawford, but she liked me and asked me to go with her to Adrian's salon in Hollywood on a clothes-buying spree. She was filled with ideas as how to spruce up my image, but it was from the older woman's point of view.

Stanwyck? Shared a makeup artist and hairdresser with her. One day

I'd forgotten something I needed and phoned Dad to bring it in. He drove like crazy, came flying in, and said, "Here I am" to the woman under the gigantic dryer and Barbara poked her head around the dryer and said something comical like "So what?"

BAWDEN: You were the studio's teen queen.

LESLIE: But Jack Warner was very protective to this kid. Every year he would have a birthday party for me and have gifts. And there were the obligatory parties to meet the theater owners and exhibitors and tout the new product. At one of these affairs, Errol Flynn got too close for comfort and alarm bells rang off in people's heads and he was shuffled away. Because I simply was not that kind of girl. I lived simply at home with my parents and sisters and was normal in every way but one. My day job was as a movie star.

BAWDEN: Your meatiest-ever assignment was in 1943's *The Hard Way*.

LESLIE: I'm not so sure I completely understood what was going on there. Director Vincent Sherman told me it was loosely based on the rise of Ginger Rogers. And I was to be Ginger. Did you know she actually turned it down as an impossible plot? I was the younger sister being driven to the top by her forceful older sister, played to the hilt by Ida Lupino. [Bette] Davis had turned the part down as impossible. There were fireworks between Ida and Vincent. It sported a gritty look, which Mr. Warner did not particularly appreciate. But it was a huge hit and Ida won the New York Film Critics Award and she really was tremendous. I don't think I was hard enough in the drama department. After all, I was only eighteen. At the premiere Ginger actually came over and said, "Why, it could have been my life!" But it was!

BAWDEN: Also in 1943 you were loaned out to RKO to dance with Fred Astaire in *The Sky's the Limit?*"

LESLIE: Fred loved to rehearse. I loved to rehearse. We rehearsed day and night! But there was little camaraderie between us because of the age difference. In fact I celebrated my eighteenth birthday on the set and was Fred's youngest-ever leading lady. He was all of forty-four and a bit touchy on that subject. We tried out some numbers the first time we met and then broke for the weekend. Monday morning I had them all down pat. "You have been practicing!" was how he put it, with a smile, as if others he'd danced with hadn't bothered. I can tell you I studied like crazy with choreographer Hermes Pan. He even looked like Fred! I matched Fred step for step and that made him very happy. I think some of our routines are very lovely indeed and I'm proud to be one of his partners. Why the film didn't do better I just don't know. Fred was already darkly hinting at retirement.

BAWDEN: Then you got top billing in *Hollywood Canteen*. How did that happen?

LESLIE: I was receiving bags of mail every day from servicemen overseas. Warners had a ton of secretaries hired just to answer it. I was getting more mail than anybody else at the time! I'd met some of these wonderful boys at the real canteen where I'd help serve. Everybody was there: [Marlene] Dietrich, [Hedy] Lamarr, [Bette] Davis. It wasn't really me. It was my image as the girl you've left behind. So the whole story was structured around me as the typical average gal. My mate on the picture was Robert Hutton, who was very popular himself. But Bob had one drawback. He was simply far too nice. He never challenged his directors. Did everything exactly as he was told. But he never went as far as he should have. But we kept in touch until his death. He was always very dear to me.

BAWDEN: You had high hopes for *Rhapsody in Blue* [1945]?

LESLIE: Well, it was George Gershwin's life story. But Jack Warner was a cheapskate. It was done in black and white. A musical! I played a totally made-up creature and I felt uncomfortable. I was a singing and dancing gal but I could never relate to her. And I certainly had trouble with [director] Irving Rapper, who simply did not like women. I'd rehearse a scene and he'd say, "Well, Joan, if you're going to play it that way, we might as well go home." That hardly instilled confidence. Also, I'm not sure Alan Alda's father, Robert, a good actor, was the right choice [to play Gershwin]. Irving wanted Cary Grant or John Garfield and Jack Warner said no. The film was a hodgepodge as far as I'm concerned.

BAWDEN: Your Warners fare then sank very low.

LESLIE: I wasn't even considered for the bad daughter in *Mildred Pierce* [1945]. Ann Blyth was imported from Universal! I got to do *Too Young to Know* [1945], which was a very bad picture. *Cinderella Jones* [1946] was pretty dire, with Bob Alda. I hated *Janie Gets Married* [1946], which was a terrible sequel. Jack often did this to players he was trying to dump—put them in stinkers. I couldn't understand what the studio was doing to me. My contract was up in 1947 and they were simply running it out. Then I made *Two Guys from Milwaukee* [1946] and I just couldn't take it anymore. I loved both Jack Carson and Dennis Morgan. We had made *The Hard Way* together. But I didn't want to be the third wheel in their antics. My agent convinced me the time had come to leave Warners.

BAWDEN: The papers had a field day with your lawsuit to break your contract.

LESLIE: It became the saga of a spoiled young girl making $2,000 weekly and she wants out. I think I made a mistake. My agent gave me bad advice. He saw all the work out there for a freelance star, but in 1947 the studios actually began contracting. I argued at the trial that I'd signed as a minor, so the contract wasn't valid. Jack had just been through all of this with Olivia de Havilland and he was in a fighting mood. But I was labeled a troublemaker by WB. The other studios wouldn't touch me. I did win the suit but I lost the war. I lost in terms of getting better pictures.

BAWDEN: But you did freelance.

LESLIE: At minor studios. One I did at Eagle-Lion was *Repeat Performance* [1947], about a woman who has murdered her husband and she gets a second chance. Richard Basehart was wonderful in it; so was Louis Hayward. It was an exciting, demanding movie to be in. But it was never sufficiently promoted. I took a small role just for memory's sake in the recent TV movie remake with Connie Sellecca and I enjoyed that. Then I did a poor western for Eagle-Lion called *Northwest Stampede* [1948]. We initially had high hopes for that one, too, but it was in competition from the big studios and didn't get bookings in the top movie palaces.

BAWDEN: By 1950, though, you were back in the big leagues.

LESLIE: MGM phoned out of the blue and asked if I could come to work next month as a quickie substitute for June Allyson in the Robert Walker comedy *The Skipper Surprised His Wife* [1950]. Junie was pregnant and the studio had a start date and nobody on staff to do it. Bob was just out of rehabilitation for his alcoholism. Such a sweet man, very talented. He was trying to put on a happy face but it was evidently a very tough battle. I lost my mother when the picture was being made and Bob came over to me on the set, very distraught, and said, "Oh, Joan, how terrible. Nothing that terrible has happened to me."

Well, it had. He'd lost wife Jennifer Jones [who divorced him] and his darling boys and he didn't see them as much as he wanted. He had battled the devils of hard drinking. He'd been through fire but wouldn't acknowledge this. And then the very next year he was dead.

BAWDEN: Then you did *Born to Be Bad*.

LESLIE: I had a nice part as counterbalance to the star, Joan Fontaine, who was the conniving one. Joan told me she'd wanted to do it in 1946 but the studio cancelled it. Then Barbara Bel Geddes was hired but the new studio owner, Howard Hughes, fired her. We had Nick Ray as our director. You can see his touches throughout, and the fine cast included Robert Ryan and Mel Ferrer. One critic even said the two Joans should have simply exchanged parts. It's among my favorite performances.

BAWDEN: Then you went to Republic.

LESLIE: Had to. That's where the work was. Republic knew how to make westerns. But I actually enjoyed myself there. It was a very tight family and you worked hard. None of those films was particularly bad and some were pretty good. Everybody always is asking about *The Woman They Almost Lynched* [1952], which has become a kind of cult classic. Audrey Totter and I have a great gunfight. But I even enjoyed working with the boss's wife, Vera Ralston, on *Jubilee Trail* [1954]. [Ralston was married to studio chief Herbert Yates.]

BAWDEN: You also did a lot of live TV.

LESLIE: It was back to my stage roots and I loved doing that kind of stuff. Started out on *Summer Theatre* in 1953, but switched to *The Ford Television Theatre*, which I loved. A full week's rehearsal, then live. Then I was on *Chevron Hall of Stars* [1956] and *Studio 57* and *G.E. Theatre* in 1959.

BAWDEN: Your priorities changed.

LESLIE: Boy, did they ever. I married Dr. Bill Caldwell [on St. Patrick's Day, 1950] and that was that. In 1951, we had adorable twin girls, Patrice and Ellen. My last film was *The Revolt of Mamie Stover* [1956] and it was a pretty bad one, although I couldn't help liking Jane Russell, who never took herself seriously. Saying good-bye was easy after that. I was all of thirty-one. I'd done everything backwards. I'd had a great career and then came the family. We stayed in Hawaii after the film, on vacation, and when we returned found our twins were behaving in a very strange way indeed with a most peculiar nanny. I decided I just had to be a full-time mother and I simply stopped accepting offers.

BAWDEN: Did you miss it?

LESLIE: No, because the biz left me. The big studios were melting down. Just for kicks I did a 1965 episode of *Branded*, but that was it. Spent the whole time wondering how my girls were. Both not only went to college, both have their Ph.D.s in English and are university teachers. But when they left I thought just maybe I might be able to get something in and that started with a cameo as Howard Duff's wife on *Police Story* in 1975. Then I did *Charlie's Angels, The Incredible Hulk, Simon and Simon,* and *Murder, She Wrote.* In 1986, Bob Conrad phones me and says he wants me to play his mother in a police thing to be shot in Fort Lauderdale. We did the pilot but NBC backed out of a series commitment. Then I did a couple of TV movies—*Turn Back the Clock* [1989] and *Fire in the Dark* [1991]—and that's it.

More recently I haven't liked the parts offered. Too depressing. I always thought I excelled at light comedy and dancing and today the parts for one my age are very dark and distressing. The way older people are treated is terrible. The other girls in my age range agree with me. I've worked on charity events with Ann Blyth and June Havoc and we'll joke together about what dull copy we make. Ann and I both married doctors. They make understanding spouses. I came from a vaudeville tradition where you just picked yourself up and went on. And do you know what? I can still ride a bicycle and I still eat apples.

Afterword

Joan Leslie's husband died in 2000. She remained firm in her vow not to accept any more heavy parts. She died at age ninety on October 12, 2015.

Patricia Neal

Interview by James Bawden

Patricia Neal was a theater-trained dramatic actress who won a Tony Award on Broadway, then came to Hollywood in the 1940s, where she carved out a respected movie career that included her Best Actress Oscar win in 1963's *Hud*.

No role she ever played, though, could be as dramatic as the life she lived. First, she engaged in a torrid love affair with a married man—two-time Oscar winner Gary Cooper—then suffered a nervous breakdown when the affair ended. Her youngest son was severely injured when hit by a taxicab and her daughter died at age seven from measles. Neal herself suffered a series of debilitating strokes in 1965 and battled through years of rehabilitation before finally resuming her career.

Her life was filmed as a TV movie in 1981. She was portrayed in that film by two-time Oscar winner Glenda Jackson.

Setting the Scene

Even after a series of strokes Patricia Neal remained quite a life force. I clearly remember how she was on that day I talked with her as we sat on a park bench in downtown Toronto in the late summer of 1973. She looked wan and wistful up close, hardly the dazzler of her long-ago days at Warner Bros. or even in her days as the older seductress in *Breakfast at Tiffany's* (1961).

She was in Toronto to promote a little-seen Canadian movie, *Happy Mother's Day, Love, George,* directed by TV actor Darren McGavin, costarring Cloris Leachman, Ronny Howard as her son, and Neal's own daughter, Tess Dahl, in a small part.

"Everyone wants the story," she sighed meaningfully. She meant the story of how she'd survived multiple brain aneurisms in 1965. Her condi-

Patricia Neal in her young leading lady days at Warner Bros., circa 1951. James Bawden collection.

tion was so serious that *Variety* ran her obit by mistake. "But I survived. I'm still here," she told me. "Well, parts of me, that is."

She looked out at the passing traffic and sipped her hot tea. "The thing is, I want to work. Oh, how I'd love to return to Broadway, but I can't be sure that up there on that stage I could remember all the lines."

The Interview

BAWDEN: You were marvelous as Olivia Walton in the TV movie *The Happening* [1971] and that's why so many think that CBS TV movie was such a hit in the ratings. But the rumor is the network cast Michael Learned in the role when they turned it into the weekly series *The Waltons* because they feared you couldn't deliver on a weekly schedule because of your condition.

NEAL: I could have and I would have.

BAWDEN: You made your screen debut in *John Loves Mary* [1949] opposite Ronald Reagan. Your reaction? [Reagan was governor of California at the time of our interview, but hadn't yet been elected US president.]

NEAL: He was not a good actor, but he was charming, so full of himself, sheer delight to know.

BAWDEN: You've said you weren't impressed with your work in that film and in some of your subsequent roles at Warner Bros.

NEAL: I really lost it. That Jack Warner! He blabbed that Eleanor Parker, Ruth Roman, and I were the new WB stars and we were going to make audiences forget Joan Crawford, Bette Davis, and Barbara Stanwyck. It didn't exactly turn out that way.

BAWDEN: But what about your other film of 1949, *The Fountainhead*, based on the famous Ayn Rand novel?

NEAL: What a stinker! Barbara Stanwyck had gotten Jack to buy it for her. Then he publicly gave it to me. The knives were out for me because all the gossip columnists loved Barbara. I was miscast. The film was terrible. I had that sinking feeling at the premiere that I was going to get it. But I also met Gary Cooper on that one.

BAWDEN: How significant was that?

NEAL: He was my everything. [In her autobiography, Neal said she became pregnant and Cooper insisted she undergo an abortion. She did so and was devastated when he went back to his wife, ending their three-year love affair.]

BAWDEN: How about some reactions to your other films of that period? *The Hasty Heart* [1949]?

NEAL: Good, back with Reagan.

BAWDEN: How about your second picture with Cooper, *Bright Leaf* [1950]?

NEAL: Another dud.

Ronald Reagan as a serviceman and Patricia Neal as his nurse in *The Hasty Heart* (1949). Ron Miller collection.

BAWDEN: *The Breaking Point* [1950]?

NEAL: Quite something. Johnny Garfield's last big film.

BAWDEN: You had more box office disappointments and that was that?

NEAL: Jack Warner dropped me just like that. In less than three years I'd gone from being the next Bette Davis to a has-been. But Fox picked me up.

BAWDEN: You made one of your most enduring classics for Fox, Robert Wise's *The Day the Earth Stood Still* [1951].

NEAL: I still get fan letters for that one. It worked because we were so low-budget there were few special effects, so Bob had to concentrate on story points. And Michael [Rennie] made a wonderful visitor from another place.

BAWDEN: Would you indulge me by saying your famous secret words from that movie? The words that made Gort, the giant robot, come under your control?

NEAL: All right: Gort! Klaatu, Barada, Nikto!

BAWDEN: But your other pictures weren't so hot: *Week-end with Father* [1951], *Diplomatic Courier* [1952], *Washington Story* [1952], *Some-*

thing for the Birds [1952]. Then Fox dropped you and you did some live television until you found another great role, back at WB in *A Face in the Crowd* [1957].

NEAL: I got the part because I was cheap and I could play sexy. I saw it recently. It was such a right-on attack on television and American society. No wonder it was so unpopular.

BAWDEN: Despite the good reviews for that role, it wasn't a hit and you didn't make another US film for four years.

NEAL: Then I got *Breakfast at Tiffany's*. Okay, I thought, so it's Audrey Hepburn's picture. Well, I'm going to play Mrs. Failenson twice as sexy as Audrey and we'll just see whose bed George Peppard prefers sleeping in. And it worked. I was on the screen for a few minutes, but people seemed to remember me. I was one year older than Audrey but I was suddenly an older woman type.

BAWDEN: Then came *Hud,* the role of faded housekeeper Alma Brown, and the 1963 Oscar.

NEAL: It was all Paul Newman's movie. He was so generous to the rest of us, but at an early preview he was shocked. Hud was supposed to be this terrible person and the fans came out really admiring him. Mine really was in support, but the way Paul treated those scenes, it made my part seem bigger. I got an Oscar, so did Melvyn Douglas [in support], but Paul lost out. That's typical of Hollywood.

BAWDEN: For the first time, you could pick and choose your roles. What about *Psyche 59* [1964]?

NEAL: Blah!

BAWDEN: And *In Harm's Way* [1965], opposite John Wayne?

NEAL: It's very comfortable in Duke's arms.

BAWDEN: Then, while you were shooting *Seven Women* [1965] for John Ford, you suffered your stroke. How are you now?

NEAL: One eye is shot. Hell, one side of me doesn't work. I can't remember names and this hand twitches sometimes. But the baby I was carrying was fine. And I got a few good roles after that.

Afterword

Those later roles included the mother part in *The Subject Was Roses* (1968), the British film *The Night Digger* (1971), and another treasure, *Baxter!* (1973). Her autobiography, *As I Am,* was published in 1988.

Patricia Neal at the bus stop in her Oscar-winning performance from *Hud* (1963). Courtesy of Paramount.

In the years after 1973, she worked less frequently—*Ghost Story* (1981), guest spots on such TV series as *Highway to Heaven,* and TV movies like *All Quiet on the Western Front* (1979). She was exceptional in 1999's *Cookie's Fortune.*

When Glenda Jackson played her in *The Patricia Neal Story* for TV, Neal joked she was set to star in *The Glenda Jackson Story.*

When Neal and husband Roald Dahl separated in 1983, the person who helped her through was none other than Gary Cooper's widow, "Rocky" Cooper. Rocky made sure Neal went into retreat at Regina Laudis Abbey in England, where emotional stress is treated.

But Neal still wanted to act even into her eighties. She died of lung cancer after a brave fight at age eighty-four. Talking with her that day, there was every indication she realized her life contained elements of Greek tragedy.

Maureen O'Sullivan

Interview by Ron Miller

The striking beauty of this Irish young lady inspired director Frank Borzage when he saw her attending a horse show in Ireland. He brought her to America in 1930 to play leading lady to singer John McCormack in *Song o' My Heart*.

Though the Fox studio didn't see a great future for her after a few more films, MGM did, and she was signed to a contract there. She starred in several major films of the early 1930s, most prominently becoming Johnny Weissmuller's screen mate in the great *Tarzan* movies of the 1930s and early 1940s.

When O'Sullivan realized her role as the ape man's Jane was ruining her career, she left MGM to raise a family with her husband, director John Farrow.

She returned to the screen later, but played a solid role in only one more truly memorable film, Farrow's classic noir *The Big Clock* (1948). In her older years, she made only brief appearances in films like *Peggy Sue Got Married* (1986). In 1963, O'Sullivan briefly served as cohost of *The Today Show* on NBC.

One of her children—actress Mia Farrow—became as famous as her mother and they appeared together occasionally, most memorably in Woody Allen's *Hannah and Her Sisters* (1986).

Setting the Scene

In 1994, to help promote a showing of her three best *Tarzan* films at the Stanford Theater in Palo Alto, California, O'Sullivan agreed to talk with me on the phone from her home in upstate New York. She was then eighty-three, but still quick-minded and in good humor.

Maureen O'Sullivan as Jane, safe in the arms of Tarzan (Johnny Weissmuller). Courtesy of American Movie Classics.

It was not the best time to ask her any questions about her current private life since the interview took place during the acrimonious battle between her daughter, Mia Farrow, and Woody Allen over child custody issues and Allen's romantic affair with Farrow's adopted daughter.

Still, I found O'Sullivan refreshingly candid about all other topics and we had a most interesting chat.

The Interview

MILLER: I'm guessing that there's at least one thing you and Tarzan's Jane had in common: a spirit for adventure.

O'SULLIVAN: I felt Jane was pretty much me. I was pretty adventurous without any particular ambition except for more adventure. I still think it was pretty adventurous to come to Hollywood from Ireland at eighteen.

MILLER: It seems kind of extraordinary that a young girl with no real film acting experience was their [Fox's] first choice to play the leading lady in a film starring one of the world's most popular singers.

O'SULLIVAN: Well, I wasn't their first choice, you see. They wanted Janet Gaynor, but she wasn't available.

MILLER: The general belief is that Fox didn't see your potential and dropped you after a few films, but some of them were pretty important films, especially *A Connecticut Yankee* [1931] with Will Rogers. What did you think of him?

O'SULLIVAN: He didn't particularly like me. I used to wear slacks and he thought that wasn't feminine. He also thought I was "fast." He always said he never met a man he didn't like, but I don't know about women.

MILLER: Once you were out of work in Hollywood, what did you do?

O'SULLIVAN: I tested for the role of Jane in *Tarzan, the Ape Man* [1932]. I don't think I'd have gotten the role without the help of Felix Feist, who directed the screen test. I'd been playing nothing but wispy, forlorn little things, so that's the way I thought I'd play the test. It was all I knew how to do. But Felix Feist told me to drop all that and be more direct, the way I really was. I guess it worked because the movie's director, W. S. "Woody" Van Dyke, wanted someone else until he saw my test.

MILLER: Before we discuss the *Tarzan* films, I wanted to ask you about another film you made in 1932—one of my favorite films of the period, *Payment Deferred*. In that film, you played opposite Charles Laughton, who was then considered one of England's finest actors. Later, you played his daughter in *The Barretts of Wimpole Street* [1934]. Your take on him?

O'SULLIVAN: Charles was a pain in the ass, but we became very, very good friends. He didn't like me at first. We met on *Payment Deferred*, which he had played on the stage opposite his wife [Elsa Lanchester]. He was upset that I got the role instead of Elsa. When we finished the movie, he told me he hated me. I told him he must be very polite because I wasn't aware of it.

MILLER: Well, if sparks didn't crackle between you and either Will Rogers or Charles Laughton, how did you get on with Johnny Weissmuller, an Olympic athlete with no acting experience who was known for his skirt-chasing propensities?

O'SULLIVAN: I think much of the popularity of those films was due to something called chemistry. Johnny and I were good friends off-screen—nothing romantic or anything like that—but on-screen we had this wonderful chemistry. It's a very indefinable thing.

MILLER: If you want to talk chemistry, I was pretty impressed with the scorching content of those daring scenes between you and Johnny that were originally cut from *Tarzan and His Mate* [1934] but later restored for the home video version of the film. I'm thinking of the scene where you jump into the water from a tree while he's holding onto your outfit—and it comes off in his hand. I mean, aren't you both completely naked in the underwater swimming scene that follows?

O'SULLIVAN: All that was doubles. I hate to tell you, but it was. You see, I'm claustrophobic and I couldn't bear to put my face underwater like that, so they had to get somebody else.

MILLER: Well, there's a pretty good close-up when you bob to the surface of the lagoon and it sure looks like you. I could swear we glimpse a bare breast, too.

O'SULLIVAN: Well, that's probably me in the close-ups. I haven't looked at the film since they restored those scenes, but I'm sure it's all right. I was never a prude. When we were doing them, I thought those "sexy" scenes were fun.

MILLER: Have your grandchildren seen that version of the movie?

O'SULLIVAN: I don't know, but I don't think they'd find it offensive. After all, we were in the jungle and clothes were not natural in the jungle.

MILLER: Aside from the effect the type casting eventually had on your career, were you happy being Jane in so many films?

O'SULLIVAN: Frankly, I got kind of bored with it. They took so long in those days to do anything. It was wait, wait, wait for the second unit to finish or for the monkeys to do something. I was always in a *Tarzan* film. The studio wouldn't let me out to do anything else because I might be needed for a retake.

MILLER: How about working with chimps? I don't imagine that was a picnic in the jungle.

O'SULLIVAN: I know you've heard this a thousand million times, but they were all homosexual. They were crazy for Johnny and jealous of me, so they always tried to bite me if I ever went near him.

MILLER: In the years between films, though, MGM did put you into some pretty substantial films, like *Strange Interlude* [1932] with Clark Gable.

O'SULLIVAN: Clark played an old man in his scenes with me. I wasn't familiar with him, coming from Ireland, so I had this picture of him as an older man. He asked me out one Sunday to go horseback riding in Griffith Park, but I turned him down. I didn't want to go out with such an old guy. Then when I saw him without his makeup, I realized I'd made a *big* mistake.

MILLER: In 1935, MGM also cast you as Greta Garbo's sister in *Anna Karenina*. Did you get to know her?

O'SULLIVAN: I thought she was a legend, so I'd better not talk to her unless she spoke first. When I came on the set, she said, "I'm so happy you're going to play Kitty!" She was very nice. We had lunch together and I liked her very much.

MILLER: You also costarred with Norma Shearer, the queen of the lot and wife of production chief Irving Thalberg. She played your mother-in-law in *Strange Interlude*. Your view of Shearer?

O'SULLIVAN: I loved Norma. We were great, great friends. She was in love with life, with people, with men, but she didn't like Gable talking to me on the set and asked the assistant director to make him stop. Gable told me, "I'm going over there and tell her what she can do!" And he did.

MILLER: I'm almost afraid to ask this one: How did you get along with the comic skirt chaser Groucho Marx while making *A Day at the Races* [1937] with the Marx Brothers?

O'SULLIVAN: He'd come every morning to my dressing room and try out his jokes on me at 8 a.m. I was very fond of Groucho and I thought he was sexy. He was very considerate of others, even Margaret Dumont. [He always insulted and tormented Dumont's characters in their films together.] Off-screen, he was very nice to her.

MILLER: That same year, 1937, you started a romance with director John Farrow, whom you'd met at Fox?

O'SULLIVAN: We renewed our acquaintance when he came in to

direct a sequence for *Tarzan Escapes* [1936] that was never used. I started dating him over the studio's objections. They warned me he was a dangerous ladies' man. I guess he was pretty dangerous, all right. We had seven children together.

MILLER: Were there roles you wanted badly, but couldn't get because you were tied to the *Tarzan* series?

O'SULLIVAN: I lost out on the female lead in *Our Town* [at another studio in 1940] and John Ford had a showcase role for me in one of his films, but I couldn't get free to take it.

MILLER: In 1942, after *Tarzan's New York Adventure,* you decided to leave MGM and the series.

O'SULLIVAN: I just lived day to day and movie to movie. What else could I do? I'd been pregnant in my last several films and they had to hide me behind Cheetah or some palm fronds. I wanted to raise my family.

MILLER: Did you ever have any regrets?

O'SULLIVAN: No, although I really missed working with Johnny. He was a big kid, a really sweet guy. He had fun making those films and didn't care if he was a good actor or not. I thought he was extremely good. He was very sincere and you believed whatever he was trying to say. I don't think he ever got bored with it.

MILLER: We're talking because three of your *Tarzan* films are being revived in a movie theater at a time when they're very popular items on home video, too. Did you ever think they'd be this respected more than half a century later?

O'SULLIVAN: We didn't see any future in the films. We certainly didn't think they'd go on like they have—in perpetuity. They're classic, aren't they?

Afterword

O'Sullivan turned to stage work in her later years and scored a big success on Broadway in the play *Never Too Late* in 1962, the same year husband John Farrow died. She also starred in the 1965 film version of the play. In 1983, she married retired building contractor James Cushing. At the time of our interview, she was preparing to star in a regional theater production of *Love Letters*. Her last screen credit was in the 1994 TV movie, *Hart to Hart: Home Is Where the Hart Is.* She died after heart surgery in Scottsdale, Arizona, on June 23, 1998. She was eighty-seven.

Jane Russell

Interview by James Bawden

Jane Russell was arguably the successor to Jean Harlow as the definitive movie sex symbol of Hollywood's golden age, at least until Marilyn Monroe came along to take her place in the 1950s. A tall brunette whose thirty-eight-inch bust seemed to propel her to Amazonian stature among the more subdued figures typical of female stars in the 1940s, Russell burst onto the Hollywood scene in Howard Hughes's controversial western *The Outlaw,* which was considered so "hot" for its time that it languished on the shelf for two years before going into limited release in 1943.

Though Russell had no acting experience and little preparation for stardom, she eventually began to fulfill her star potential, particularly in Bob Hope's riotous hit comedy of 1948, *The Paleface,* and was a major attraction by the time Fox teamed her with rising star Marilyn Monroe in 1953's *Gentlemen Prefer Blondes.*

Far from a sex symbol in real life, Russell was a devoutly religious woman who led a reasonably scandal-free life. Her buxom figure continued to aid her career in her mature years, however, as she became TV's principal spokesperson for the Playtex brassiere company.

Setting the Scene

I first met Jane Russell in 1984 when she was appearing in the NBC television series *The Yellow Rose* as Sam Elliott's mother. We met at the Century Plaza Hotel in Los Angeles. She was warm and friendly, remembering the times she had sung in my hometown of Toronto, including a solo stint at the Royal York Hotel's Imperial Room.

Three years later I sat next to her at the Sheraton Universal Hotel in Universal City at a gala luncheon in celebration of the premiere of the TV special *The RKO Years.* Russell sported closely cropped silver hair and

Jane Russell in her notoriously sexy film debut in Howard Hughes's *The Outlaw* (1943). Courtesy of the Cinemax cable network.

looked far younger than her sixty-five years; her third husband, John Calvin Peoples, was very attentive. Naturally, Jane was front and center during the show's hour about Howard Hughes. At the celebration, she greeted other RKO stars such as Janet Leigh, Joan Fontaine, and Lizabeth Scott as long-lost friends.

The Interview

BAWDEN: Who created the famous Jane Russell screen personality?

RUSSELL: Certainly not me! Just two guys, both named Howard—[director] Howard Hawks and [producer] Howard Hughes. I'm not at all like that. Never was. It was a great personality to hide behind.

BAWDEN: How would you describe her?

RUSSELL: Well, she had to have a great sense of humor, considering all the predicaments she fell into. I think she had fair looks, a pretty good singing voice. She was a man's woman. She'd drink a pint with them. Did she prefer bad boys? Perhaps. She could ride and shoot with the best of them. A great gal to have on your side.

BAWDEN: And your own personality?

RUSSELL: God-fearing. Family-oriented. Never cared for hoopla. A hard worker. Could handle comedy better than drama. Saw through phonies. A great friend to have when in a tight situation.

BAWDEN: How did you get to be a sensational sex symbol?

RUSSELL: I was nineteen and I needed a job. I'd graduated from high school. I thought I'd get some work in print modeling. Never considered acting because, believe it or not, I'm shy.

BAWDEN: So what happened?

RUSSELL: Well, it was 1941 and director Howard Hawks had a Billy the Kid movie project that he said would be headlined by unknowns, partly to save money, I guess. He found the Kid in Jack Buetel, who was twenty-three and an insurance salesman. And he picked me after numerous tests. I'd done a bit of modeling but had never acted. A photographer had taken some snaps—Howard saw them and I was invited in. There were five female and five male finalists and we all did close-ups of the rape scene. I saw the test and I thought I looked hot and so did Howard Hawks. Jack and I left and there was a strange man standing in the hallway. It was my introduction to Howard Hughes. Hawks took us to the Mocambo nightclub, where he introduced us to Gary Cooper, which was such a thrill.

BAWDEN: How many scenes did Hawks direct you in?

RUSSELL: None. He took us to a cowboy outfitters called Nudie's for costume fittings. Then I met his wife, Slim, who took me to her designer for other clothes. A huge tent city was built in Tuba City, Arizona, where I was introduced to costars Walter Huston and Thomas Mitchell. I wasn't in the first scenes and, just as I was about to start, Hawks left after disagreeing with Hughes, who moved everything back to L.A. I was on my own.

BAWDEN: Then what happened?

RUSSELL: Hughes took over. He didn't know what he wanted. We'd shoot the same thing a hundred times. His idea of direction was to say, "Just go for it." And that's what Walter and Tommy did. It wasn't until I saw it all put together that I realized there were as many breast shots as there were shots of my face. I was never so embarrassed. But the stories I ever did nude scenes are completely false.

BAWDEN: Hughes was a renowned ladies man. Did he come on to you?

RUSSELL: Hughes never really made a pass at me. Oh, he thought about it. But I was engaged to Bob Waterfield, my high school boyfriend, who was a L.A. Rams quarterback. Bob told him, "Howard, I can pick you up with one arm and toss you against that brick wall." So he completely backed off.

BAWDEN: When did filming cease?

RUSSELL: Eighteen months later. He kept shooting new scenes, redoing other shots. He never knew what he wanted. Walter and Tommy were being paid by the week and made more money off it than any ten other films of theirs. It really wasn't finished until 1943, at a huge cost.

BAWDEN: Then you became a sensation.

RUSSELL: I got a paycheck every week. I married Bob in 1943. I expected that would be that for my movie career. Finally, it was released in 1946–47 and the censor had conniptions. But people who lined up to see it were disappointed. There's no nudity at all. I thought I looked good. My acting was nonexistent. I thought Jack looked terrific. Howard got all these gobs of publicity, but he told me in 1950 that it had yet to make a profit because it was so costly to make. Of course, the shot people remember has me rolling in the hay. You want my critical opinion? I think it stinks.

BAWDEN: You finally got a second film with *Young Widow* [1946].

RUSSELL: The first time most moviegoers saw me was in this very bad film. I was awful. Louis Hayward was ever so helpful, but I froze during every take. Those pros Connie Gilchrist and Cora Witherspoon were really helpful. Marie Wilson is funny. I just thought I stank. So did reviewers! The director, Edwin L. Marin, was tearing his hair out.

BAWDEN: You say Bob Hope saved your career?

RUSSELL: Bob borrowed me [to costar in *The Paleface*]. Howard demanded $200,000 and got it! I went over to Paramount to see Bob. He told me in a Bob Hope picture the gal is the straight man, meaning she tosses him the line and he comically reacts to this. I was given the Paramount beautician treatment. I never looked as good, felt as good. The photography was glistening. This was the way to make a movie. Bob was a dentist in the Wild West. Had a string of his gag writers on the set to polish every scene. The director, Norman Z. McLeod, gave me a lot of takes so I could settle down—and then I just zinged it. If I flubbed a line, Bob would flub a line. It was a huge hit and there was a sequel in 1952 called *Son of Paleface* that was even more popular. That movie made me. I was no longer a laughingstock. And I've stayed very close to Bob and his great wife, Dolores, and done his TV shows many times.

BAWDEN: Then you didn't film again until 1951?

RUSSELL: Oh, no. I made another western for Howard titled *Montana Belle* [1948]. George Brent costarred. But they kept remaking scenes and didn't release it until 1952, which was very typical of him.

BAWDEN: People think of you and Bob Mitchum as a team.

RUSSELL: We're best buds. When I first met him I said to Bob, "You're the male Jane Russell!" And he exploded with laughter. He got it. He was given a screen persona almost entirely at variance to the real man, who is kind and thoughtful. Again we shot for almost a year [on the film *His Kind of Woman*]. Howard ordered a huge new nightclub be built for one scene. John Farrow directed it and delivered a final print. Howard hated it, so he ordered Richard Fleischer to shoot retakes and finally Fleischer reshot the whole thing, including a new ending written by Howard that I hated. Three different actors played Nicky, who was based on Lucky Luciano: Howard Petrie, Robert Wilke, and then Ray Burr. Howard brought in Vinnie Price for a few scenes in the second version and Vinnie says he stayed for six months. There was a boat-sinking scene Howard ordered reshot with Price in it and the cost was over $200,000 to sink that boat again.

BAWDEN: Then you made *Macao* [1952] with Mitchum.

RUSSELL: Of course, we didn't go there. That was a lot of second-unit footage. Howard decided I needed class, so he hired Jo [Josef] von Sternberg, who had directed all those [Marlene] Dietrich flicks. A mean, nasty little man. Instantly hated Bob. And the crew loathed him back. One day he directed: no more coffee or pop or nibbles on the set. The crew seethed. Next day Bob comes in wearing a trench coat and laid it on the floor and plopped several dozen Cokes [on it]. Next day he comes in with baskets of fruit. Jo went ballistic but he stayed his distance. Bob could have flattened him with one plop. He photographed me with lots of shadows on my face and Hughes started ranting, said I looked like Dietrich. [Director] Nick Ray had to come in and do mop-up. Jo wanted me to sing languidly, but that's not me. I've got spunk and personality. But I watched part of it on TV recently and I never looked better, I must admit.

BAWDEN: Did you like *The Las Vegas Story* [1952]?

RUSSELL: I thought Victor Immature [Mature] very funny. He didn't give a damn. Never bothered to cover his shots, from close-up to long shot. Sleepwalked through it and then ran for lunch when the commissary bell sounded. Hoagy Carmichael had this crazy tune, "The Monkey Song," and the crew kept breaking up, it's so wacky. I loved Vinnie Price. But at the premiere I had a swollen face. Bob [Waterfield] slugged me the night before and I had quite a shiner. In those days gals were supposed to grin and bear it. And the Hughes PR staff said I'd been hit by a car door. But everybody knew the truth.

BAWDEN: Who got you together with Marilyn Monroe for *Gentlemen Prefer Blondes*?

RUSSELL: Well, Howard Hawks had always promised he'd be working with me again. And he had just finished *Monkey Business* [1952] with Cary Grant—and Marilyn in a supporting role. The whole Monroe mania was breaking out, so he suggested to [Fox production chief] Darryl Zanuck that I be borrowed from RKO with Marilyn. *Gentlemen Prefer Blondes* had been revived in 1949 as a Broadway musical set in the twenties. But Howard made it all contemporary and set on a gigantic luxury liner. And there was one refurbished for us on one of the gigantic soundstages. I'm not sure if they had just used it in *Titanic* [1953]. I think it was remodeled.

Well, the first thing you do on a musical is go into the recording studios and prerecord the musical numbers. That's when I got to know Marilyn. First, I was surprised that she spoke naturally and not in that silly baby talk she used in movies. I just adored her from the start: so sweet, silly, and drop-dead gorgeous without any makeup and with her hair uncombed. And she had a good singing voice.

Then we went into the dance hall to rehearse the numbers. Did you know, Fox bought it for Betty Grable, but Zanuck pointedly told her she was too old. Hughes said he'd loan me for $200,000, which was a huge amount. Zanuck gulped but told me he needed me as insurance because Marilyn already had this reputation for being untrustworthy. In my big

Marilyn Monroe (*left*) and Jane Russell strutting their stuff in *Gentlemen Prefer Blondes* (1953). James Bawden collection.

number, I'm tossed all over the place by muscle-bound athletes and I told them to aim carefully. I still think the sight of Marilyn in that pink gown shows her off at her best.

You know, Marilyn gave Hawks fits. At the end of each take she'd look at her Russian coach instead of him. And she'd always ask for retakes. After one minor scene when she kept requesting retakes I whispered to Howard, "Isn't this expensive?" He laughed and whispered back, "No. There's no film in the camera." Turns out he'd been filming the rehearsals and using them most of the time because Marilyn was so much more natural. We became great friends. She had no enemies, except among the harassed directors.

BAWDEN: And both of you were married to athletes.

RUSSELL: Tell me about it. The most egotistical people in the world. And my husband liked her husband [Joe DiMaggio]. When they'd meet, they'd talk stats all night and Marilyn would fall asleep on the couch. You know the story: she comes back from entertaining the troops in Korea and says to Joe, "You can't believe it: fifty thousand cheering fans!" And he says, "Yes, I can, honey. I get that all the time."

BAWDEN: Didn't Marilyn once say you tried to talk to her about God and she tried to talk to you about Freud?

RUSSELL [*laughing*]: Well, she did tote around this book by Freud and pretended to read it. But on the set I noticed she was holding it upside down.

BAWDEN: Did the two of you keep in touch?

RUSSELL: It was easier between husbands. Her third, Arthur Miller, thought all Hollywood was disreputable and he took her east, filled her mind with garbage. He wrote that terrible movie *The Misfits* for her—and that's not Marilyn. It's all crazy babble talk. She had this God-given gift of making people laugh and feel better. Why tamper with that?

BAWDEN: When did you last see Monroe?

RUSSELL: A few weeks before her death. It was not a suicide. She came down to the beach house and spent the afternoon running in the sand with the kids. She said she'd settled the suit with Fox. They had fired her from *Something's Got to Give*. She'd be restarting production in about a month. And she had signed with MGM to remake *Of Human Bondage*, to be directed by Henry Hathaway. She looked wonderful and shyly confided there was a new man in her life and he was very powerful, but first he had to divorce his wife. I now think she must have meant John Kennedy. But that crazy idea of a permanent relationship was so Marilyn.

BAWDEN: So you believe she was killed.

RUSSELL: Disposed of. She was threatening to squeal. Of course, she was taking so many drugs it could have been accidental. But about a month later I was in Washington at an affair for my adoption causes and I can feel somebody staring at me across the crowded room. And it was Bobby Kennedy and I think he knew that I knew. And he looked extremely distraught.

BAWDEN: Did you ever meet any of the other so-called sex symbols?

RUSSELL: Liked them all. I was at a party once at Bob Hope's and spent the evening in the study with Dorothy Lamour as we swapped war stories. She had exactly the same experiences at Paramount, her home studio. I know Ava Gardner was having a long affair with Hughes. Maybe I should have phoned her up and warned her off him. Betty Grable I knew when we both were headlining at Las Vegas and, like me, she's a survivor because she never took any of the fame seriously.

BAWDEN: Why are there no sex symbols today?

RUSSELL: Because they take too much off. You can't look sexy when you're buck naked. It was Louis Mayer at MGM who told all his female stars: "Never show your ass." And that's great advice. Jayne Mansfield showed all, so there was no mystery about her. I never even showed my belly button and neither did Lamour. We knew what we were doing because less is always more. If you want more, then go make stag films.

BAWDEN: What do you remember about *The French Line* [1954], the 3-D movie that was considered so scandalous at the time because of your sexy dance number?

RUSSELL: Howard Hughes wanted to put me in a bikini in that movie, but I refused.

BAWDEN: What about your films after that?

RUSSELL: *Foxfire* [1955] is a good one, with Jeff Chandler, and director Joe Pevney churned it out in a few weeks. This was the very last US movie ever to be made in three-strip Technicolor, which is why I still looked great when I watched it on TV. *Gentlemen Marry Brunettes* [1955] with Jeanne Crain needed Marilyn, no doubt about it. It was advertised as "the Big, Buxom Musical." Which is the first time my breasts got mentioned in a movie ad. I had some dance numbers and the choreographer was—get this—Gwen Verdon.

BAWDEN: You kept going back to Fox?

BAWDEN: Well, I was told Clark Gable wanted me. He had cast approval on *The Tall Men* [1955]. Clark wasn't that tall, neither was Bob Ryan. I think the word "tall" meant important. And Gable had just been through Susan Hayward [his costar in *Soldier of Fortune*] and he craved some peace and quiet. So Zanuck had to pony up another $200,000. Raoul

Walsh was the wonderful director. A great old guy who loved it that I asked for no special favors. It was an outdoor CinemaScope production shot on locations and production took many weeks. I used to tease Gable his hair was the same auburn color as mine, which brought guffaws. He was fifty-four and very aware of the passing of time. Did we have chemistry? I think so—I adored that man, so unpretentious and amiable. I adored him, respected him, and so did the audience. It was his biggest hit in the fifties.

BAWDEN: You were all wet in *Underwater!* [1955].

RUSSELL: Very funny. I also exposed my nipple when Dick Egan reaches underwater to free me. At least it seems to be me. I now think it was my double. I had several actually. By the way, the premiere was underwater, too, and I wondered if any of the portly movie critics who went down would fail to bob back up to the surface. At least my wardrobe was inexpensive—just bathing suits. And forget makeup! It was filmed in 3-D but I only saw it flat. It was fun, but I didn't think Dick Egan a strong enough costar. Gilbert Roland was always tops. He knew how to play for the camera. At the time I never realized that this was it for me and Howard. We'd lasted almost fifteen years. It was a huge hit, but my last for Hughes. He subsequently went out of production and sold off RKO. I remained under personal contract for more than twenty years and occasionally he'd phone with a new movie proposed and then there'd be only silence again.

BAWDEN: You kept working.

RUSSELL: *Hot Blood* [1956] I made at Columbia and I can tell you Howard did not get $200,000 this time, but I liked Cornel Wilde [her costar] as a person. And then I made *The Revolt of Mamie Stover* [1956] for Fox. Zanuck demanded me because [director] Raoul Walsh said I was essential. It takes place in 1941, but Raoul said to use contemporary fashions. In the novel, I'm a near prostitute. But here it was all diluted. But it's one of my best performances with Raoul. Women always shone under his assured direction.

RUSSELL: Then you finished your movie career for some time with *The Fuzzy Pink Nightgown* [1957]. Why? Was it your decision?

RUSSELL: No. The audience. After all, I was thirty-six—too old to be a sex symbol. Also my kids were growing up. And I wanted them to be proud of their mommy. The other kids started teasing them at school. Also movies were mostly made on locations by then and I couldn't take them out of school. So I switched gears.

BAWDEN: You had your own production company with Waterfield?

RUSSELL: Russ-Field Productions. We made *Gentlemen Marry Brunettes, The King and Four Queens* [1956] with Clark Gable, *Run for the Sun* [1956], *The Fuzzy Pink Nightgown*. Some hits there, some flops.

BAWDEN: When did you start your separate singing career?

RUSSELL: I formed a group with Connie Haines, Beryl Davis, and Della Russell, who was not a relative. Della quit early and we three just continued. Toured everywhere. Several times in your Toronto. Mobbed everywhere in Italy. I debuted solo in Vegas in 1957 at the Sands. I was on Bob Hope's and Red Skelton's [TV shows] all the time. I toured in summer stock. In 1971 I made my Broadway debut in *Company,* which was a real thrill. I was Sam Elliott's mom on the TV series *Yellow Rose* [1984]. I was always busy, still am.

BAWDEN: You know what the tabs say.

RUSSELL: That I'm a drunk. Well, I did drink. A lot. Loved it. But now I'm a member of AA. And it's very boring, I can tell you.

BAWDEN: Did it bother you to be associated with Playtex bras?

RUSSELL: When you think about it, this was the perfect product for me to push. All us gals my age need support. I mean, Betty Grable peddled multivitamins, June Allyson pushes Depends. I'm perfectly satisfied with Playtex. If Marilyn were still around, she'd have a line of girdles.

BAWDEN: When did you start your adoption agency?

RUSSELL: It's called World Adoption International Fund. We've connected thousands of kids with new parents. It's my most important life's work. I had an abortion when I was eighteen and it was a botched backstreet affair. I found I could not have children. So I adopted three. They're my life. And their children. I wanted to share that with others. Because to be adopted is the most wonderful thing in the world.

BAWDEN: You said you have another gig ready for next week.

RUSSELL: I'm going to a local VA hospital to talk to the guys, thank them for their sacrifices, sing a bit, if they want it, talk them up as my heroes, just say how much I appreciate their sacrifices.

Afterword

Jane Russell made a few more films in her later years, playing mostly supporting roles. The best remembered is *Born Losers* (1967), which was the first in the Billy Jack series of films. Russell was married three times. She divorced Bob Waterfield in 1968 and married actor Roger Barrett that same year, but he died shortly after their marriage. She married real estate broker John Calvin Peoples in 1974 and he died in 1999. Russell had three children—a daughter and two sons—with Waterfield, all adopted. She died of respiratory failure at her home in Santa Maria, California, on February 28, 2011. She was eighty-nine.

Jean Simmons

Interview by James Bawden

"Jean Simmons: An Unforgettable English Rose" was the headline in the prestigious British newspaper the *Guardian* when the British actress died in 2010 at age eighty. Pushed into the limelight in her teens in the mid-1940s, Simmons had come to America and soared to international stardom within a decade. Elegant and beautiful, she was also a superb actress who seemed at home in any role.

Her death was greeted with a slew of remembrances, which was surprising, considering she had lived her last decade out of public view. Critic David Thomson wrote: "Even in the age of Vivien Leigh and Elizabeth Taylor, she was an authentic beauty and there were always hints the lady might be very sexy."

Setting the Scene

I met Simmons twice. Once was at a lunch on the set of ABC's 1983 miniseries *The Thorn Birds,* where she dutifully answered questions about the project then in production in the Simi Valley near Los Angeles. It was a sweltering day. Simmons had been up since dawn and finished several scenes that morning. She looked radiant, but was temporarily taken aback when Ron Miller, my coauthor on this collection of interviews, sneaked in a question about her role as an Indian girl in the classic 1947 movie *Black Narcissus.* She had come a long way since then.

I had my own interview time with Simmons in the summer of 1988 when she sat down in Toronto on the set of the TV revival of *Alfred Hitchcock Presents* for what turned out to be several hours of reminiscing about a film career that first started in 1944 when she was just fifteen.

Jean Simmons in *Great Expectations* (1946). James Bawden collection.

The Interview

BAWDEN: What do you remember about your breakout movie, David Lean's 1946 *Great Expectations*?

SIMMONS: I was only seventeen and here I was in this magnificently mounted motion picture. The Havisham mansion was a real house, not a studio set, although it was redressed so the great room was filled with spiders' webs that would get in my hair. And there were movie rats every-where! They came scampering when one called them for the food. I was plain terrified of Martita Hunt as Miss Havisham. She truly frightened me. She stayed in character and, to this teenager, looked like a witch. My scenes were with young Pip, played wonderfully by Anthony Wager. He was three years younger than me, so I could truly boss him around, as when Estella [her character] asks him if he would like to kiss her. He also was in the 1989 [TV] version.

BAWDEN: And what did you think when asked to play Miss Hav-isham forty years later?

SIMMONS: Well, of course, I saw the connection right away. There's the scene in the [1946] film where [the grown-up Pip] John Mills comes back to the decrepit great house and finds [the grown-up] Estella [Valerie Hobson] there and alone and she's turning into a crazy lady. So it made sense to me and I thought, why not? This one ran on the Disney Channel. I don't think I was as cruel as Martita Hunt, but maybe I was as loony. And the cast was quite good: John Rhys-Davies as Joe, Anthony Hopkins as Magwitch, Anthony Calf as Pip, Ray McAnally as Jaggers. This one ran over three hours—everything was in it. And the director was Kevin Con-nors. But that doesn't stop me from loving the 1946 version, too.

BAWDEN: You made a number of fine British films in those years. Let me throw titles at you.

SIMMONS: *Hungry Hill* [1947]? It was a Daphne du Maurier story nobody remembers. A Margaret Lockwood movie. She was always very nice to this teenager. I was Dennis Price's younger sister—I was always the younger sister in those days. *Uncle Silas* [1947]? It ran in North American cinemas as *The Inheritance,* a very bad title. They cut it down and it makes no sense when played on American television. I had a big part in it as a very naïve young thing whose old uncle tries to kill her off. An old dark house type of story. I was constantly terrified. Derrick De Marney was the codger, but he was only forty. He used buckets of old-age makeup. They remade it for British television with Peter O'Toole [shown as *The Dark Angel* on PBS's *Mystery!* in 1991 with Beatie Edney in Simmons's earlier role]. But it can't be as scary as our version.

BAWDEN: *Black Narcissus*?

SIMMONS: I went into the studio and got painted brown every day. It itched, whatever they used. And yes, I said studio. Every scene was done inside a studio. It was an experiment by [director Michael] Powell and

Jean Simmons (*left*) plays a naïve native girl in *Black Narcissus* (1947) with Deborah Kerr and David Farrar. James Bawden collection.

[codirector Emeric] Pressburger to prove anything can be replicated in a studio. You had to be in the right mood, but the color was stunning, the overall effect was brilliant. My part as an [East] Indian princess was comparatively small and, as I recall, I never say anything. Am I right? I was opposite Sabu, the most entrancing Indian boy, who had been discovered by Alex Korda and taken to England from India. There was something lost about him—his own culture, was that it? Today [the film] might be dismissed as racism, but at the time it was considered a film of high art. I don't think actors do blackface anymore. It's not considered proper. But it was fun!

BAWDEN: At nineteen you won an Oscar nomination for Laurence Olivier's 1948 *Hamlet*.

SIMMONS: Ophelia is a very difficult part, although not a big one. So I needed a lot of training. I think I got it [the role] for my looks and then they peroxided my features because Larry Olivier had gone blond. In his case, it was to wash the wrinkles away, he said, because he was forty-one.

The critics said, "Bravo" for using black and white after the color of [Olivier's] *Henry V,* but Larry always said he was fighting with Technicolor at the time, so color was out. I stayed away from the rest of the cast. I had to remain immersed in my character and I didn't quite understand her. I ran lines constantly, even with Vivien Leigh, as I remember. She'd wanted to play the part as marquee value, but at thirty-six was considered too old. But I only remember the kindness of these two—at the time they were the world's most glamorous film couple. Larry said I had a huge stage career ahead of me, if only I'd go to Bristol and [do] repertory for a few years. But I much preferred the salary of a film star at that stage.

BAWDEN: Then you were off to Hollywood.

SIMMONS: I first made *The Clouded Yellow* [1950], which I've seen again recently. It's a fine chase movie. And I made *So Long at the Fair* [1950] with Dirk Bogarde, who has remained a lifelong friend. It was a tricky plot about a girl and her brother who travel to the 1889 World Exposition in Paris and he disappears without a trace. If you haven't seen it, I won't give you the trick ending, which was based on fact.

BAWDEN: In America you had quite a brawl with Howard Hughes.

SIMMONS: A madman! He bought up my [J. Arthur] Rank contract for five films and threatened to have me blacklisted unless I made the kind of drivel RKO was putting out. I did one, *Angel Face* [1952], and it was pretty fair. I was a psychopath who sends her father over a cliff, as I recall. But there's no doubt Howard stopped my momentum. Finally, he lent me out to do *The Robe* [1953]. Everybody has seen it. I think it's junk, but why argue with its popularity? It was the first CinemaScope picture and they were experimenting as they went along. Scenes would be shot and when we watched them [they] would look gruesome because the lens distorted everything. The director was Henry Koster and he said he'd have to keep the camera perfectly still and could we just walk into the frame, give our lines, then walk out!

BAWDEN: One of my favorite Jean Simmons movies is *The Actress* [1953].

SIMMONS: It's one of mine, too. Also one of MGM's biggest flops. I went to see it at a Westwood cinema and nobody else was there. MGM didn't quite know how to sell it. It was from a memoir by Ruth Gordon about growing up with her unusual father. Spencer Tracy read it first and that meant MGM wanted to make it. [Director] George Cukor signed on and asked me to try it on, but I never completely eliminated my [British]

Jean Simmons with then husband Stewart Granger in *Young Bess* (1953). James Bawden collection.

accent to his satisfaction. Nothing much happened in it. There were vignettes. Perhaps it was too precious for the average moviegoer. Spencer was lord of MGM in those days. When we went on location, his great trailer came along, as did his retinue of servants. Tony Perkins was my young man and it was his first movie and he was just plain scared of Spencer, who could really bellow when provoked. Teresa Wright, who was eleven years older [than me], played my mom! She did so again in *The Happy Ending* [1969]. I loved it when a reporter asked her years later why she'd stopped making movies and she replied, "I guess Jean Simmons no longer needs a mother."

BAWDEN: Didn't you wish you were at MGM instead of RKO?

SIMMONS: Who wouldn't have wanted to be at MGM? I watched how they were grooming Liz Taylor, but I'm guessing there was only one British leading lady allowed under contract at one time. They did the same job of polishing Grace Kelly. I never got such sustained studio treatment. I guess I resented it. I actually made *Young Bess* [1953] at MGM before *The Actress*. A lot of money went into that one, but it just doesn't look right historically. [Director] George Sidney, who usually did musicals, was very meticulous. My husband Jimmy [her husband then was actor Stewart Granger, whose real name was Jimmy Stewart] was there and so was Deborah Kerr, who was so ticked off she bought up her contract and made *From Here to Eternity* [at Columbia] all in the same year. After two iffy pictures, MGM declined to renew my short-term contract and I freelanced.

BAWDEN: You made two movies around that time with Marlon Brando.

SIMMONS: It was supposed to be three. First up was *The Egyptian* [1954]. Marlon just walked out at the last minute, wouldn't do it. I don't blame him—I should have walked, too. If I ever see a bit of it on television, I start howling with laughter. It was rubbish, but expensive rubbish—cast of thousands, huge sets. Victor Mature was again in it and he just loved showing his [physique] off. Edmund Purdom replaced Marlon and he couldn't bring any conviction to the script. Then when Michael Wilding walked out with that huge headdress, Peter Ustinov said he looked like a gigantic salt shaker and we all dissolved in laughter. But it made a ton of money. Anything biblical was selling, but this was, what, a thousand years earlier [in world history]?

BAWDEN: Then you made *Desiree* [1954] with Brando and Merle Oberon.

SIMMONS: He was Napoleon. He's Method, so it meant strutting around, looking coy, berating everybody behind and in front of the camera. The script wasn't right and we were just uncomfortable. Merle Oberon as the aging Josephine was okay, but I just felt so silly. [Simmons played the title role, a seamstress who was Napoleon's lover.] Director Henry Koster wasn't much help, although he is a lovely man. It was one of Marlon's few flops from that time.

BAWDEN: But you and Marlon were delightful in *Guys and Dolls* [1955].

SIMMONS: The idea of casting a British gal as Sarah Brown—why, it was audacious! [Director] Joe Mankiewicz's doing. Some of the Broadway cast was there, but Joe wanted to use Betty Grable as Miss Adelaide. But she was late for an interview with Sam Goldwyn. She stopped to help an injured dog and Sam blew up and refused to see her. I always thought Frank Sinatra should have been Sky Masterson rather than Marlon, and so did Frank. On this set the two male stars feuded, not the women. Michael Kidd staged all the dances. I somehow got through it. The critics were kind of nice to me. But I was never asked to do another screen musical, although I did *A Little Night Music* on the stage.

BAWDEN: Why do you say *Hilda Crane* [1956] was an important picture in Hollywood's history? Explain, please.

SIMMONS: It was the last picture made at Fox or anywhere else in Hollywood where we worked six days. New union rules came in and that was the end of working Saturdays, which really was until dawn broke on a Sunday morning. Other than that, the picture is awful.

BAWDEN: I think in *Home Before Dark* [1958] you give your best screen performance.

SIMMONS: The way Mervyn LeRoy presented it to me was this was not going to be another *Snake Pit* [1949]. It would be a completely realistic study of what gave this girl a breakdown and how she scaled out of it. Mervyn insisted on black and white and he cast meticulously. I thought Dan O'Herlihy stunning as my college professor husband. I got a Golden Globe nomination; so did Efrem Zimbalist Jr., who was superb. Rhonda Fleming still says it was her best acting job. But [studio boss] Jack Warner hated the material and campaigned against any Oscar nominations, if you can believe it. And it never appears on the late show.

BAWDEN: Then came *The Big Country* [1958], a true all-star western.

SIMMONS: Can't talk about that one. Won't. [Director] Willie Wyler was downright nasty and impossible to work with. He always selects a victim to go after on each picture. This time it was me. Charlie Bickford said, "If the little squirt tries anything more, then I'll squash him like a gnat." But Willie would never have dared go after Greg Peck or Charlton Heston or even Charlie, who was over seventy by then.

BAWDEN: How did you prevent Burt Lancaster from overpowering you in *Elmer Gantry* [1960]?

SIMMONS: He was too busy being Elmer. Burt had spent a lot of years angling for the Oscar. This time he really felt he had it. I met my future husband, [director] Richard Brooks, on that one. He shot very slowly, but with all due speed. He knew what to look for and kind of expected actors to take in his detailed direction. Burt was in his glory and Richard got fine performances out of Arthur Kennedy and particularly Shirley Jones, who got a supporting Oscar. It's very long for a drama, over two hours. And nobody expected it would be such a moneymaker. Richard's home studio, MGM, declined to make it and United Artists stepped in.

BAWDEN: How did *Spartacus* [1960] come about?

SIMMONS: Well, I did have this reputation for spectacles. But seriously, I'd just finished *Elmer Gantry* and the word coming from that set was strong. I knew *Spartacus* was Kirk Douglas's project all the way and, after the first scenes were shot, he fired [director] Anthony Mann and switched to Stanley Kubrick. It was in that period I got cast. The first choice was a continental import who did not make it. I was back with Larry Olivier, with Charles Laughton, with Peter Ustinov. All the interiors were done in L.A. So we all bonded and played games on each other and the months passed rather well. Kirk was the king, so we all obeyed him. I still like to tease him that during the crucifixion scene he'd finally been placed up on the cross after hours of adjustments. Right then the assistant director bawled, "Lunch!" So we all trooped off, leaving Kirk to writhe on the cross. It was a huge hit for me, played reserved seats everywhere.

BAWDEN: But after *The Grass Is Greener* [1961], you were gone from movies for several years?

SIMMONS: My agent said why take fourth billing when you've just finished the biggest movie of the year? I said it was the first real comedy role I'd been offered. Same reason Bob Mitchum took third billing. Perhaps we had too much fun on the set. It never translated into a satisfying comedy, did it? It was about adultery, but that subject couldn't even be discussed back then. Cary Grant was in most of my scenes. He was a fussbudget. Everything must be just so. Then he'd come forth with the most amusing, polished take, so seemingly effortlessly. I needed more comedy chances and I rarely got them. Then I married Richard Brooks, had a baby, and luxuriated in not working for the first time since I was fourteen.

BAWDEN: Producer David Susskind once told me the reason *All the Way Home* [1963] was such a monumental flop.

SIMMONS: It was the Kennedy assassination, right? We opened the weekend after President Kennedy was killed. And nobody had the heart to see James Agee's little story about the death of the father figure. It wouldn't have made much money anyway. Today they'd do it for PBS or something. I always considered it something special.

BAWDEN: Critique your later movies.

SIMMONS: I'd lost all career momentum. I took *Life at the Top* [1965] because it was the only offer. Working with Laurence Harvey was difficult. But he was playing a difficult character. *Mister Buddwing* [1966] with Jimmy Garner wasn't coherent. *Rough Night in Jericho* [1967] was a Dean Martin western. *Divorce American Style* [1967] had me in a comedy and I needed comedy by then.

BAWDEN: You won your second Oscar nomination for *The Happy Ending* [1969].

SIMMONS: Critics assailed it as a women's picture. Well, it was from a woman's perspective—although Richard [her husband, director Richard Brooks] was very masculine, he always had terrific parts for women. The moments in it were unmelodramatic. Bobby Darin was wonderful, John Forsythe, too, Shirley Jones. But TV movies were just coming in and people thought it too small for movie screens.

BAWDEN: I'm a big fan of your British film *Say Hello to Yesterday* [1971].

SIMMONS: So you're the one who saw it. It was [Canadian] director Alvin Rakoff's attempt to comment on *Brief Encounter*. I'm a middle-aged London housewife who has a fling with a young nob played by Leonard Whiting from *Romeo and Juliet*. Only this time, there's no guilt. No recriminations. British critics hated it. How dare we go after a true classic? It was all very slight and needed more work, but I rather liked it. Leonard was disturbed by its failure. In this business, you have to roll with the punches, I told him, but he stopped acting a few years later.

BAWDEN: How did you take to life as a TV actress?

SIMMONS: I'm a realist. After forty, the roles generally stop for women. TV offers a lot more. I did two dramas for Bob Hope's series and liked the experience. Tight schedules do not bother me. I guess I finally became a true convert when *The Dain Curse* [1978] did so well and then I did *Beggarman, Thief* [1979] and I had become a TV name. I did *The Thorn*

Jean Simmons (*left*) with Barbara Stanwyck in ABC's miniseries *The Thorn Birds* (1983). Courtesy of ABC.

Birds to meet Barbara Stanwyck. I saw myself in her. She'd lived to act and was a true professional, although faltering in health. The gas lighting bothered her breathing and she wheezed visibly. The day you TV critics came to Simi Valley, she'd done her one scene of the day and to conserve strength had to go home. I got an Emmy for it and then I did another—*North and South* [1985]—and felt it was the best of my miniseries existence.

BAWDEN: My favorite Jean Simmons TV role was in the British-made *December Flower* [1984].

SIMMONS: I was a woman searching for her roots who comes back to Britain and finds she has an elderly aunt who needs caring for and she moves in. That's all the story there was. [Director] Stephen Frears made it on location in a cramped house—a two up, two down thing—and it just worked so beautifully as a study of elderly abuse. Mona Washbourne was the sweet old soul and Mona was so decrepit Stephen said he wasn't sure if she was going to make it. Make it? She'd been stealing scenes left and right! There was the scene where Mona shows her abusive relatives her Mickey Mouse telephone and it was all I could do not to break up, she was so wonderful. You tell me why this one has never been on video.

BAWDEN: You must see the irony of making an episode of *Alfred Hitchcock Presents*.

SIMMONS: Because he never used me? Yes! I saw him at a party and he said I was brunette and that would never do. But he's one of the directors who got away. I do wonder why David Lean never used me again. Why Powell and Pressburger gave up on me so early. Or if I'd taken Larry O's career advice and gone into theater for good.

Afterword

Jean Simmons died of lung cancer in Santa Monica, California, on January 22, 2010. She was eighty.

Alexis Smith

Interview by James Bawden

Alexis Smith was a beautiful and resourceful dramatic actress whose remarkable career took her to movie stardom and leading lady status in the 1940s, a shocking slide to near obscurity in the 1950s, and a sensational rebirth as a Tony Award–winning Broadway musical star in the 1970s.

The Canadian-born redhead costarred with some of Hollywood's top leading men, including Errol Flynn in *Gentleman Jim* (1942), Fredric March in *The Adventures of Mark Twain* (1944), Humphrey Bogart in *Conflict* (1945), Cary Grant in *Night and Day* (1946), and Bing Crosby in *Here Comes the Groom* (1951).

After her movie career as a Hollywood leading lady faded, she astonished her critics by becoming the toast of Broadway in the musical *Follies* in 1971, then returned to Hollywood for a regular role on TV's *Dallas*, among other projects.

Setting the Scene

Because Smith was Canadian and I was a Canadian entertainment writer, I was even more fascinated by the many twists and turns of her career. I'd first noticed Alexis Smith's incandescent beauty on TV's *Late Show* in several of her big hits of the 1940s. And when she came to Toronto's Royal York Hotel for cabaret in 1973, I was there in the audience.

Imagine my surprise when the very next year I was seated next to Smith at a luncheon in L.A. for a TV movie she'd made for CBS, *The Ambassador* (also starring Eddie Albert).

We met again in the summer of 1981 as she was busy packing to storm the Canadian Stratford Festival in a new production of *The Visit*. I walked up to the gigantic white doors of the home she shared with her longtime

Alexis Smith in her starlet days at Warner Bros., circa 1941. James Bawden collection.

husband, actor Craig Stevens, in West Hollywood, and it all seemed so strangely familiar. Turns out the facade was used every week on *The Loretta Young Show:* lovely Loretta would sashay through the doors and twirl her dress for TV viewers. Smith and Stevens had bought the house a decade later and used it as their L.A. base.

The Interview

BAWDEN: I understand you're very proud of your Canadian roots.

SMITH: Always have been. I was born [in 1921] in Penticton, British Columbia, but we moved to Los Angeles when I was eleven months old because my dad thought the dry, warm climate would help Mum, who was not the strongest. That was in 1922. Dad originally was a traveling salesman, selling soda hardware in B.C. Mum was the cultured type. She got us season tickets to the Hollywood Bowl and we'd go at 11 a.m. to watch the rehearsals and return after 5 p.m. so we could get really good seats. Dancing and singing was a good part of my childhood. By fifteen, I knew I was going to be an actress. I won first prize in a state declamation contest, playing both Elizabeth and Essex in a scene from *Elizabeth the Queen.*

BAWDEN: Your parents were very strict, as you were an only child?

SMITH: Yes, they were strict! God bless them! Then a boyfriend gave me a cigarette case as a Christmas present and boom! There was an unholy ruckus that night. Mum hated smoking because of her health, so I got tears, silence. It was awful.

BAWDEN: How did you get into movies?

SMITH: At eighteen I got into Los Angeles City College to study drama. Loved every moment of that. In those days movie actresses were usually petite, and I was five feet, ten inches. I just thought I'd be doing theater mostly. Or if that failed I could go to university and do English teaching. My big play at City College was *The Night of January 16* and a talent scout saw me and instantly dangled a Warners contract. My parents were not rich. We always needed money. I breezed through a screen test and photographed okay and I signed and lasted at Warners almost a decade. Who would have thought that?

BAWDEN: You wanted to change your name?

SMITH: I never really liked my name when growing up. Alexis is a boy's name but my mother hadn't known that. She had wanted to name me Alexander after Dad, so she thought Alexis most closely resembled it. I begged her later on in school days to change it to Audrey or something. But the WB big boys told me Alexis took the sting off Smith and Smith took the curse off Alexis. And I've grown very fond of it. It is short and distinctive.

BAWDEN: Any reasons you can think of why you became a big star so suddenly?

SMITH: I think I just came along at the right point. Jack Warner came to believe by 1940 that Warners was too much of a man's studio. The only big female star he had was Bette Davis. Kay Francis had just been bumped because of her age. Joan Blondell had departed with husband Dick Powell. Bogie [Humphrey Bogart], [James] Cagney, [Paul] Muni, [Edward G.] Robinson, [George] Raft—that was a whole lot of tough guys. Jack had imported Miriam Hopkins and Merle Oberon on short contracts, but that was expensive. He wanted to make his own stars. So he'd been carefully nurturing Ann Sheridan and she blossomed. Jane Wyman was still doing comedy at the time. Then, after my first picture with Errol Flynn, it was decided that's where I belonged.

BAWDEN: You were interviewed by Charles Higham for his book on Flynn. Your opinion?

SMITH: His take is that Errol was some sort of Nazi sympathizer. I can't take that too seriously. Flynnie desperately wanted to get into the war but couldn't because he had a bad heart and lung scars from TB. Two strikes against him. It hurt him when critics got on his back for making so many war pictures shot on the back lot. He was just adorable to me on *Dive Bomber* [1941]. He tried nurturing my affair with Craig Stevens. On our next, *Gentleman Jim,* he suffered his first heart attack after doing those boxing scenes. It was kept hush-hush by the studio, but he was very sick. He told me he wanted to go all out to challenge life and not spend years as an invalid. And that's exactly what he did.

BAWDEN: What films in your early period do you really like?

SMITH: Oh, *The Constant Nymph* [1943] is my favorite. There was tremendous publicity when Joan Fontaine got the lead. She was twenty-seven playing fourteen. But I think I did as remarkable a change. I was just twenty-two and I was playing a sophisticated doll of thirty-five. I loved doing it and being successful. And then there was *The Adventures of Mark Twain* and Freddy March was in the lead. Irving Rapper was the director and he just egged me on. I wasn't just adornment in these movies. And it felt so great. I was just so proud of my work there.

BAWDEN: You then made two movies with Humphrey Bogart and in both movies he was trying to kill his wives for your love.

SMITH: Hey, don't blame that on me! *Conflict* was just a bad movie. Bogie didn't want to do it and harassed our poor director, Curt Bernhardt, whenever he was given direction. He wanted to kill Rose Hobart and then marry me. I was her sister. Did I get to know him? Not at all. He was then with Lauren Bacall and she kept him on a tight leash. He didn't even talk much between takes. Then we immediately made another, *The Two Mrs. Carrolls* [1947], with Barbara Stanwyck. So bad they let it linger for two years before release. Barbara screamed a lot. I was terrified of her. It was shot entirely indoors. The fishing scenes at the beginning? Shot on a soundstage and the entire house was built on another stage. Then I was assigned to work with Bogie again in *Stallion Road* [1947], but the script was so poor Bogie just went on suspension. It became Ronnie Reagan's first postwar film. And it really tanked. Poor Ronnie!

BAWDEN: I want to ask you about two monster musicals you made.

SMITH: Gulp! On *Rhapsody in Blue* [1946], it was all so terribly stupid. I was a completely made-up character George Gershwin was mooning over. And [director Irving] Rapper was no help on this one. He'd wanted John Garfield and not Robert Alda [to play Gershwin]. And the whole thing was overblown. I'm told Al Jolson took a look, shuddered, and then decided to switch the movie of his biography from Warners to Columbia.

On *Night and Day* I was window dressing. I remember asking Cole Porter on set why he chose Cary Grant to play him. And he laughed and said better Cary than Basil Rathbone. Cary made no attempt to ape Cole's effeminacy and he even kept his English accent. The songs made the movie, but Jack Warner was always a cheapskate and when Ethel Merman demanded $50,000 to sing two of her hits, he chose Ginny Simms. And that's why people don't remember it, even though it made a mint at the time.

I was Mrs. Porter. Her story was so sad. Spent most of her day in an iron lung. Wish I'd gotten to know her. I did study Cary and the way he never gave too much to a scene. He was a minimalist. You see, he was making love to the camera. His costars somehow got in the way but he was only interested in how it all looked up on the screen.

BAWDEN: You once made a good point saying everybody at Warners got typed.

SMITH: Irving Rapper was the women's director after [Edmund] Goulding left for Fox. Annie Sheridan always battled for juicy dramas, but that's not how Jack Warner saw her. Jane Wyman languished in comedy until she made *The Lost Weekend* [1945] at Paramount and even after that Jack still used her as a dumb bunny in *Night and Day.*

In 1944 I made a ripe stinker called *One More Tomorrow.* The billing was Ann Sheridan, Dennis Morgan, me, Jack Carson, and Jane in fifth position. By 1946 she had become a major star with *The Yearling* on loan to MGM. By 1948 she had her Oscar [for *Johnny Belinda*] and two years later when Warners purged me, she was number one at the box office. By the time we made *Here Comes the Groom* she was a huge star, deservedly so, and I was billed below the title.

BAWDEN: You've said your sweet temperament stopped you from becoming one of the greats.

SMITH: I guess I started too young. I needed more training. And there was my upbringing. My dressing room was next to Bette's and the language she exchanged with her mother! Crawford and Stanwyck clawed after parts. I had a home life and an absence of ego. I routinely accepted

Alexis Smith with Clark Gable in *Any Number Can Play* (1949). Courtesy of National Screen Service Corp.

every assignment. Didn't party after hours. Went home. Didn't fit the mold of a truly great star. No multiple marriages for me. Warners had been good to me. Never loaned me out until 1949, which indicated my most favored status was ending.

BAWDEN: Then you got to work with Clark Gable in *Any Number Can Play* [1949].

SMITH: I just fell in love with MGM's glamour factory. All of a sudden

I looked so much better. The way I was photographed, the care they took with my wardrobe—what a shame the picture was so disappointing. It had no vitality. I was twenty-eight at the time, but I had a seventeen-year-old son [Darryl Hickman]. In one scene, Clark talked about taking me to the 1933 World Series where our characters supposedly met. I would have been like twelve. Playing an older woman was always part of my persona, I'm guessing. Audrey Totter, who costarred, told me there was only one star MGM would ever give single billing: it was Wally Beery! Even Gable got a costar up there above the title. Wish I'd known him better. But postwar he was a different guy. After a take, he'd go back to his dressing room and shut the door. There was no chance of small talk with the king.

BAWDEN: So what happened at Warners in 1950?

SMITH: Davis left in 1949, Stanwyck had already departed. Bogie left in 1950. Garfield was gone. Flynn held on but left at the end of 1950. Ellie Parker left in 1950. It was no longer the studio I'd loved going to since 1940. Revenues were dropping like crazy. I was in a ripe stinker called *The Decision of Christopher Blake* [1949] and it lost so much dough I was toast at the studio. To get me to break my contract Jack Warner deliberately put me in a terrible western called *Return of the Frontiersman* [1950]. I first was tested with a young man so scared he stammered. Named Rock Hudson. Then they tested me with the musical star Gordon MacRae, who, let's face it, is a squirt at five [foot] six. I towered over him in our test. I deliberately wore tall boots and he looked up to me in our love scene test. Jack said they'd start shooting anyway. So I did the long walk and wound up at Universal.

BAWDEN: What happened there?

SMITH: I started out in a terrible western, *Wyoming Mail* [1950]. Then I got hooked up with a bright new director, Joe Pevney, and we had a huge hit with *Undercover Girl* [1950]. It was shot entirely on the streets, meaning there were no studio sets. A lot was done in ramshackle houses about to be demolished for freeway expansion. Scott Brady, Dick Egan, Gladys George, Connie Gilchrist—a real great cast. And Joe shot quickly and we finished it in fourteen days and it became Universal's most profitable film of the year because it had been made so inexpensively. It was Royal Dano's first movie and we're shooting away at 2 in the morning and he asks plaintively, "Is it always this tough?" I wasn't a passive character. I was avenging the murder of my father, killed by a drug cartel. I just loved doing that one.

BAWDEN: And then?

SMITH: The next year the best I could get was the second female lead in a Bing Crosby–Jane Wyman starrer, *Here Comes the Groom*. In one scene Janie and I are supposed to go at it at a garden party, so I proposed a real tumble and [director] Frank Capra whispers in my muddy ear at the end of a take: "I love it when bitches fight." Then I was back at Universal for *Cave of Outlaws* [1951], which I'm proud to say I never actually saw. I had to make it; that was bad enough.

BAWDEN: You still worked?

SMITH: At reduced prices in films that were often programmers. Oh, *The Turning Point* [1953] was okay. I had Bill Holden as my partner, Eddie O'Brien, Tom Tully. It was an efficient thriller, directed by old Bill Dieterle. It was about corruption in a small midwestern town. I was "the girl." Routine stuff. At lunch one day old Bill launches into a story about the making of *The Hunchback of Notre Dame*, where he'd discovered Eddie. And O'Brien pipes up, "And now look at the drivel we're being given."

BAWDEN: You were steadily going down the ladder?

SMITH: Things got so bad I booked a British film, one I think is great, *The Sleeping Tiger* [1954]. It starred the new Brit heartthrob, Dirk Bogarde, and we've been best buds ever since. Our director, Joe Losey, was blacklisted in the States. Costar Alexander Knox had been booted from Hollywood for leftist leanings. But Losey built up an amazing film noir tale of an errant wife and he really got a good performance out of me. And then one night we're all celebrating at the Dorchester Hotel dining room and who should come flouncing in but Ginger Rogers and her crazy mama, who was a HUAC witness against the Hollywood Ten. And Joe and I both do a nosedive to hide under the table until the Terrible Two depart from the other side of the room!

BAWDEN: I remember seeing you as a kid in *The Young Philadelphians* [1959].

SMITH: My last picture for fifteen years. [Director] Vince Sherman hired me despite the protests of Jack Warner. It was spooky going back. Most of the people I'd worked with had been laid off. The lot was still busy, making TV westerns. I was a sexy wife with an old coot husband played by that wonderful actor Otto Kruger. In the night I get up and walk down the hall in my very best lingerie and into the bed of Paul Newman, who sleeps without a top on. It was done in one continuous shot and boy, was I feeling sexy that day. Paul takes me in his arms and whispers, "Come to Papa." We started at 7 a.m. and Paul says, "Honey, we're going to make love like you've

Alexis Smith embraces Paul Newman in *The Young Philadelphians* (1959). Courtesy of Warner Bros.

never made love before." Then, later on, he says he's all smooched out and what was he going to say to Joannie [Woodward] if she asks for a smooch?

BAWDEN: Then you were in the entertainment wilderness?

SMITH: Did I feel out of it? Yup! Bitter? Nope! Craig's career really took off with *Peter Gunn* [the TV series] and we subsequently moved to New York. There was a whole new world waiting for me there. I'd do some

TV, but not much: *Michael Shayne, The Defenders*—then five whole years before *The Governor and J.J.* That was my big comeback. Stephen Sondheim saw me in that and asked me to audition—multiple times—for *Follies*. And boy, was that a blast! The cover of *Time!* The critics' darling! It was wonderful. To get a Tony Award—I never ever thought that would happen. And for a musical. Movie offers came in but I wanted to tackle cabaret, which is where I first met you in 1973.

BAWDEN: Then came *Once Is Not Enough* [1975].

SMITH: Kirk Douglas was this rich, rapacious guy and I was his extravagant second wife and a lesbian to boot. Who could quarrel with that? I insisted on a closed set with my lover Melina Mercouri for our kissing bout. She, of course, was actually [supposed to be] Greta Garbo. It was cut from the final print, thank goodness. It embarrassed both of us!

BAWDEN: It's been strange meeting with you again.

SMITH: I'm doing a revival of *The Visit* at your Stratford Festival [1981]. I'm a last-minute replacement for Danielle Darrieux, who eventually decided it was too much for her. I was going into a tour of *Best Little Whorehouse in Texas* and it collapsed in Frisco. The Stratford part is choice, I just love it. Because it's unlike anything I've ever done.

Afterword

After our 1981 meeting, Smith stayed busy. In one phone conversation, she admitted turning down a guest spot on TV's *Hotel* because the plot was a thinly redone version of the Lana Turner scandal, "and I know Lana and would never want to hurt her." She was on *Dallas* for two seasons: 1984 and 1990. On the TV movie *Marcus Welby, M.D.: A Holiday Affair* (1988) she enjoyed a lovely autumnal romance with Robert Young. Also in 1988 she was in the short-lived ABC series *Hothouse* opposite Michael Learned and Louise Latham. And on *Cheers* (1990) she played the mentor of Kirstie Alley.

By 1991 she had stopped returning calls and there were rumors she was seriously ill. In fact, she made a very brief, almost wordless appearance in *The Age of Innocence* (1993). Her death from brain cancer came on June 9, 1993. At her bedside were Stevens, her husband of forty-nine years, and life-long friend actress Frances Rafferty. Stevens never acted again and died on May 10, 2000. The couple left $2 million to philanthropic causes. Neither Smith nor Stevens ever got a star on the Hollywood Walk of Fame.

Elizabeth Taylor

My Seven Minutes Alone with Elizabeth Taylor

Interview by Ron Miller

In the spring of 1985, I was ushered into the private dressing room of Elizabeth Taylor where I was privileged to talk privately with her for a period of seven minutes while she ate lunch. Actually, I'm one of these guys who always pushes the envelope, and I pushed it quite severely that day: I'd been warned I was going to be allowed to stay with the star for only five minutes—boldly, I won a full two minutes more. Though I'm pretty certain Miss Taylor didn't mind losing those two minutes to an arrogant lout like me, I wouldn't be surprised if *TV Guide* or *USA Today* resented being cut back to three minutes on my account. Gee, I hope they forgave me.

It's amazing how much mileage a guy can get out of having spent seven minutes alone with Elizabeth Taylor. I don't think she let that many men spend seven minutes alone with her—unless, of course, she married them first. That's why I feel so very special these days when somebody asks me, "Did you ever interview Elizabeth Taylor?" Usually, I smile kind of wisely and just nod my head yes, waiting for them to ask what she was really like in person. I'm not the least bit backward about answering that question either. After all, I did spend a whole seven minutes getting to know her.

First, I'm happy to report that Elizabeth Taylor, who was in her early fifties at the time, was very attractive. Yes, she was a bit overweight, but she still had lovely features and her famous violet eyes were truly mesmerizing. I mean, those eyes were really magical and she knew how to use them.

I also drew the immediate impression that she was down to earth and likeable. I say that because I began our "interview" by cracking a joke that

Elizabeth Taylor in costume for her cameo role as a brothel madam in the TV miniseries *North and South* (1985). Courtesy of ABC.

made her nearly spit out her food, which I'm sure made her glad I wasn't accompanied by a photographer. At the time, her son by second husband Michael Wilding was playing Jesus Christ in a TV miniseries, so I simply asked her if she ever thought, after a career spent on the cover of tabloids, that she'd be known as the mother of Jesus. That notion obviously struck her as pretty funny. And here's an amazing thing: she laughed really big. At that moment, I knew she was the kind of girl who loved dirty jokes. To my credit, I didn't tell her any, though, just to test my hypothesis.

Our interview took place in Charleston, South Carolina, where she was playing a cameo role as a whorehouse madam in the ABC television miniseries *North and South*. I was tempted to run with that a little by asking her what about her made them think she was right for that role, but I didn't want to push my luck and have her toss her lunch at me.

Getting the interview wasn't easy. In fact, the process of getting it turned out to be much more entertaining than actually doing it. In the first place, I had to be approved in advance by the producer of the miniseries, David Wolper, whose works included *Roots* and *The Thorn Birds*. Fortunately, I knew David and he approved me. However, Miss Taylor had agreed to do a few interviews only at the very last minute, and the only way I could get to Charleston in time for her allotted "availability" was to fly there on the Warner Bros. private jet. Only one "press" seat was left.

At the time, my company, Knight Ridder Publications, had a policy that forbade its reporters or columnists from accepting anything free from news sources. I could go on the trip, the company agreed, but I'd have to pay my own way. Well, the studio didn't have fares for its Lear jet, so I had to quickly find out what it would cost to charter a private jet to Charleston and send a check in that amount to Warner Bros. I did it—and I'm sure there is some Warner publicist somewhere who has that check framed.

There were only two columnists on the flight—myself and Tom Green, then the L.A. bureau chief for *USA Today*. As we boarded, we were informed that our ABC network press contact had lost his seat on the flight. Later, we learned he had been bumped from the flight so Elizabeth Taylor could bring her dog with her.

When the time came for us to leave, nothing happened. Turned out the corporate jet had gone to the wrong airport, so we had to wait an extra hour. That worked out fine because Elizabeth was about that late getting there anyway. She finally arrived in a limo with her dog, her male secretary, and a ton of luggage. In contrast, actress Morgan Fairchild, also in the cast, was driven to the airport by her sister and carried on her own small bag.

We then were informed that Miss Taylor would not talk with us on the flight, even though she was sitting across the aisle from us with David Wolper. We were told that we were free to talk all we wanted with the other two actors on the flight—Morgan Fairchild and Hal Holbrook. That, too, was a break because Holbrook and Fairchild are both wonderful people. And I'll have to admit that sitting knee to knee with Morgan Fairchild for more than an hour was extremely pleasant, given that she's a very nice person and awesomely good-looking.

Altogether, it was quite cozy in the plane, which was more like a stretch limo. There were eight of us on board, not counting the crew. Once we were airborne, a male steward plied us with delicacies never served on commercial flights.

Although Elizabeth wouldn't speak to Tom Green or me during the flight, she was facing me and honored me with several radiant smiles that seemed to ask my forgiveness. It was sort of like looking at a *People* magazine cover miraculously come to life.

When we finally landed in Charleston, there was a huge mob waiting to greet us. Well, I guess they were probably there to greet Elizabeth Taylor. That's when I finally realized how big a star she still was, even though she hadn't done anything really significant on the screen for many years.

In our little interview, I spent most of my seven minutes asking her about her upcoming role in *Malice in Wonderland* (1985), a CBS TV movie about the rivalry of former Hollywood columnists Louella Parsons and Hedda Hopper. Taylor played Parsons and Jane Alexander played Hopper. Taylor told me she really had a lot of fun playing a person whom she actually had met in her youthful Hollywood days.

I was surprised that Elizabeth Taylor had no real venom for the gossip press that had victimized her for years. She even had nice things to say about Louella Parsons. I don't think she was just trying to avoid being nasty. I think her attitude may have been really important for someone who lived so much in the public eye for most of her life. I don't think the incessant media attention ever got to her the way it gets to her modern counterparts in show business.

I've heard many negative things about Elizabeth from friends whose opinions I trust. One fellow, who handled the publicity for her CBS movies, told me she had something in her contracts that required the producers to give her a special gift at the start of each day on the set. She always pretended it was a big surprise, he said.

Equally, I've heard positive things. Another fellow I know comes from Wales, where his family was quite friendly with the family of Richard Burton. He told me that when the Burtons were still married Richard always brought Elizabeth with him whenever he visited the home village and she was simply wonderful to everyone, never playing the star or acting like anybody special.

Personally, I liked her. I felt she was open and friendly to someone she could easily have snubbed. I'm sure she behaved like a diva a good deal of the time. In fact, I know she rubbed David Wolper the wrong way by asking him to fly her to New York for the weekend in the studio jet while she was doing her *North and South* cameo.

I got to watch her film her cameo a few hours after our brief interview. She hit all her marks perfectly, blew no lines, and seemed to be very nice to everybody on the set. I came away with a good feeling about her.

Now I'm often asked my opinion of her as an actress. Truthfully, I don't rank her among the top actors. I thought she was very good when she was young and wasn't trying so hard to be impressive. I loved her in *A Place in the Sun* (1951) and *Cat on a Hot Tin Roof* (1958). Though I don't think she deserved her first Oscar for *Butterfield 8* (1960), I thought she was very, very deserving when she got her second one for *Who's Afraid of Virginia Woolf?* (1966). But I admit I lost interest in her career by the 1970s.

Many writers have praised her efforts on behalf of AIDS issues and related causes in her later years. I'm sure this was a sincere effort on her part. She had many male friends who were gay, starting with Montgomery Clift, and three of the male leads in *Giant* (1956) were gay men—Rock Hudson, James Dean, and Sal Mineo.

It's very likely Elizabeth Taylor was the last of the great Hollywood divas of the 1950s. She died on March 23, 2011, of congestive heart failure. She'll be remembered for lots of things by many of us, including her two Oscars and her eight marriages. But I'll remember her most for those very special seven minutes with her in 1985.

Of course, the flight home on a commercial jet brought me down a good deal from my Elizabeth high. There was a two-hour layover in Atlanta. The ride was bumpy, the food inedible, the atmosphere nowhere near as chummy, the company less exalted. And there were no photographers waiting to greet me. I've been sulking ever since.

Esther Williams

Interview by James Bawden

MGM virtually had to invent a new kind of movie—the aqua-musical—in order to make a star out of Esther Williams, a tall, leggy beauty who simply had to be put on a movie screen somehow.

An expert swimmer who first attracted public attention at the age of fifteen by winning swimming competitions, Esther was also so strikingly beautiful that she became a popular model in the Los Angeles area while still in her teens. After a few showcase appearances in its films, MGM seriously groomed her as a major attraction by putting her into expensive Technicolor films that were basically "aquacades" set to music and loaded with romance and comedy.

Williams quickly became a top box office attraction. Her films gained stature and she became more experienced as an actress. This eventually led to her proving she could carry a dramatic role without spending half a movie in a bathing suit, submerged in the studio's special water tanks.

Setting the Scene

I thought I was going to meet Hollywood's most famous of all swimsuit superstars back in 1974. MGM had invited TV critics, who were already at a convention in L.A., to a special screening of their all-star movie attraction *That's Entertainment!* After the movie, there was a lavish buffet dinner and MGM trotted out a legion of its greatest stars. Gene Kelly and Fred Astaire were there. So were Myrna Loy and Cary Grant. And Ann Sothern, Janet Leigh, Vincente Minnelli, George Sidney, Ann Blyth. And when the lights went down, it was rumored that even the legendary 1930 Best Actress Oscar winner Norma Shearer would be wheeled in—and she was. But to my disappointment, there was no Esther Williams. It turned out she was then embroiled in a fight with the studio, believing she should

Esther Williams with water skis at Cypress Gardens in Florida, circa 1953. James Bawden collection.

be paid extra for the scenes inserted into this bonanza of a documentary movie.

So I never got to meet Esther Williams in person. But she did wind up chatting with me on the telephone for more than an hour one day in 2001.

She was available to talk because she was eager to promote a TV documentary about synchronized swimming she was supporting. I phoned her at her Beverly Hills home.

The Interview

BAWDEN: How did you get into the movies?

WILLIAMS: I blame it all on that awful Adolf Hitler. If he hadn't started the war, I would have gone to the 1940 Olympics. But oh, no, he had to invade France and the Olympics were cancelled in both 1940 and 1944. So I needed a new occupation.

BAWDEN: So what happened next?

WILLIAMS: Well, I was in several water shows, one with Johnny Weissmuller where he kept pinching my bottom six times a day. And then I had to get work as a clerk in a department store in L.A. and an MGM agent took me to meet [studio boss] Louis B. Mayer and that was that.

BAWDEN: You swam in your first movie, *Andy Hardy's Double Life* [1942]?

WILLIAMS: Well, I was picked because I towered over Mickey Rooney. Heck, everybody towered over him. And that series was the first step for Lana Turner, Donna Reed, you name it. If you couldn't get noticed after that, then MGM dropped you.

BAWDEN: Didn't they give you a makeover?

WILLIAMS: I was taught how to walk, talk, wear evening clothes, eat properly. Diction, deportment—it was all supervised by Miss Lillian Sidney. And then I got another "straight" part, a small one, in *A Guy Named Joe* [1943].

BAWDEN: Who decided to jump-start your career in swimming films?

WILLIAMS: Old Louis B. Mayer. He told me, "What Sonia Henie did for ice, you'll do for water." That was okay for me—I needed the job. So [1944's *Bathing Beauty*] was all packaged by director George Sidney, and Red Skelton had first billing. Basil Rathbone was our villain, Xavier Cugat supplied the music. The water ballet at the end was tiny by our later standards but it was a huge hit. The boys at war loved me in a bathing suit. But I had a huge female audience, too, because I was athletic. And Mayer ordered my own swimming pool be dug—it had ways that the fire could envelop the water plus portholes for the cameramen.

BAWDEN: You'd do one of these a year?

WILLIAMS: It took months to get the water routines down. Fred Astaire dropped by one day and watched and walked away, shaking his head. He couldn't believe how complicated it could get. The rest of each movie could be photographed in six weeks but the water events took six months.

BAWDEN: You know what Fanny Brice said about you?

WILLIAMS [*laughing*]: "Wet, she's a star; dry, she ain't." And it was very true indeed. I did several straight dramatic pictures and nobody went to see them. I was with Bill Powell in *The Hoodlum Saint* [1946] and in one scene I had to smack him hard on his face. I really slapped away and tore the little invisible strings hanging up that part of his face like a fish net. [This was a makeup trick sometimes used on older actors.] His face suddenly sagged horribly and he had to stagger off to makeup to get that string readjusted!

BAWDEN: You remember what you said when asked to name your favorite costar?

WILLIAMS: I said, "The water. The water never let me down."

BAWDEN: Didn't you wear a false nose in some underwater scenes?

WILLIAMS: Yes! Especially in those diving numbers when I might get bubbles up my nose and that would ruin a take.

BAWDEN: Injuries?

WILLIAMS: I broke neck vertebrae in one dive and was in a cast for six months. Then when making *Million Dollar Mermaid* [1953] for Mervyn LeRoy, he kept me at the bottom of the pool too long and I experienced the Rapture. That's when you know you are drowning and there's nothing you can do about it. And it's the loveliest feeling in this universe. Thankfully, an assistant spotted I was in trouble and dived in to get me to safety with just a few minutes to spare.

BAWDEN: Who among the actors you worked with was actually a good swimmer?

WILLIAMS: Red Skelton could keep up with me. Van Johnson learned how to swim well. Peter Lawford just dog-paddled around. Howard Keel wasn't bad. Ricardo Montalban could fake it.

BAWDEN: I get the titles [of your movies] mixed up.

WILLIAMS: So do I! Van phoned me recently and said, "Esther, I can't remember the difference between *Easy to Wed* [1946] and *Easy to Love* [1953]." And I said, "No? Who the hell cares!"

BAWDEN: Any favorites?

WILLIAMS: Well, *Neptune's Daughter* [1949] was very good, I thought. We were rehearsing the new song "On a Slow Boat to China" when the MGM censor came into the dubbing studio, enraged, and pulled it because of suggestive lyrics. So [the composer] Frank Loesser substituted *Baby, It's Cold Outside,* which really was suggestive and nobody seemed bothered at all. [That tune also won the Oscar for Best Song.]

BAWDEN: As a little kid I liked *Texas Carnival* [1951].

WILLIAMS: You did? We recorded the song "It's Dynamite" with the Red Norvo Trio and that included the great bassist Charlie Mingus. When time came to film it, Charlie had been replaced by a white guy. I was told by an MGM executive, and I'm completely repeating what he said, "You can't have a n—— and two white guys playing together in a family picture. We'd be blacklisted in the South!" So Charlie was substituted, although that's him you can hear playing. I thought it was sick even then.

BAWDEN: You said you enjoyed making *Million Dollar Mermaid?*

WILLIAMS: Because it was the relatively true story of Annette Keller-man. Fanciful for sure, but I had somebody to work off of. And who couldn't adore Victor Mature? He was such a sissy, wouldn't get in the water until it was warmed up for him!

BAWDEN: What happened to your MGM career in 1955?

WILLIAMS: I got a notice saying I was fired. George Sidney had directed *Bathing Beauty* and he directed my last, *Jupiter's Darling* [1955], but the public had become tired of the formula. We had pink elephants. [They really added pink elephants to crank up the spectacle level!] Noth-ing worked anymore. My pictures had made the studio $80 million in pure profits. But the old man [Mayer] was canned. It had become Metro-Gold-wyn-Schary and he [Dore Schary] hated musicals and he especially hated me. I bumped into Mr. Mayer at the Brown Derby and he asked me to join him in independent production. Said he'd build me a new pool twice as large as the old one. I never heard back from him. He died soon after that from a broken heart.

BAWDEN: You then went to U-I as a dramatic actress.

WILLIAMS: In *The Unguarded Moment* [1956] I was a high school teacher tailed by a stalker I thought was student John Saxon. Instead it was his father, Edward Andrews. Roz Russell wrote it! Then I made *Raw Wind in Eden* [1958], another bust. And that was that. Consecutive flops!

BAWDEN: What did you think of *The Big Show* [1961]?

WILLIAMS: Made in West Germany: Cliff Robertson, Robert Vaughn, Nehemiah Persoff. Not quite top drawer. It was called a remake of *House of Strangers* [1949]. But it flopped and that was that.

BAWDEN: You went into business?

WILLIAMS: I sold Esther Williams pools around the world. Thousands for our Canadian affiliate. They have never cracked to this day. I sold Esther Williams bathing suits. I was incorporated. Then when Fernando Lamas came into my life and we married, he asked that I be his wife first and foremost and I helped him in his directing chores.

BAWDEN: Your life today?

WILLIAMS: I swim every day. Everyone should. Swimmer's bodies are wonderfully muscular but still thin. It's the best exercise for me because I'm over eighty and I can still touch my toes. And I say I'll only go to heaven if there's a great big heated pool already set up for me.

Afterword

Among the movie roles Williams turned down was the part Shelley Winters eventually played in the original 1972 version of *The Poseidon Adventure,* which required both swimming and acting.

Williams had three children with second husband Ben Gage. In her autobiography, *The Million Dollar Mermaid* (1999), written with Digby Diehl, she confessed to love affairs with actors Victor Mature and Jeff Chandler. She died on June 6, 2013, at age ninety-one.

Jane Wyatt

Interview by James Bawden

Many children of the 1950s must have given their mothers lots of anguish because they were not more like Jane Wyatt in TV's *Father Knows Best* (1954–1963). Wyatt's Margaret Anderson is certainly one of TV's all-time most beloved moms, a cut above Barbara Billingsley's June Cleaver (*Leave It to Beaver*), Donna Reed's Donna Stone (*The Donna Reed Show*), and Harriet Hilliard's Harriet Nelson (*The Adventures of Ozzie & Harriet*). Wyatt brought a certain regal bearing and a set of patrician airs to her Margaret Anderson. She attended Barnard College and was a member of the Social Register. Wyatt was a warm and kindly person, attributes that readily translated into a long movie and TV career.

Though best remembered by baby boomers for her TV series role, Wyatt was, like so many other stars of TV's first generation, a movie star of enormous talent long before television twinkled in American homes. Anyone who was already a star in Frank Capra's original *Lost Horizon* (1937), played a significant character role in Elia Kazan's Oscar-winning Best Picture *Gentleman's Agreement* (1947), was the female lead in Fritz Lang's classic film noir *The House by the River* (1950), and was still important enough to play Mr. Spock's mother in *Star Trek IV: The Voyage Home* (1986) certainly could lay claim to the descriptive term "legendary actress," which is what Jane Wyatt surely was.

Setting the Scene

I first interviewed Jane Wyatt in Cornwall, Ontario, in 1972 as she was making a TV movie version of *Tom Sawyer* (1973) opposite Buddy Ebsen and Vic Morrow at Upper Canada Village. She was well cast as Aunt Polly, but after work became "one of the guys," attending hockey games at the local ice rink.

Jane Wyatt in a studio portrait from *The Man Who Cheated Himself* (1950). Courtesy of Jack M. Warner Productions.

Telephone interviews followed, and we reconnected in 1984 when we met for lunch in Los Angeles. Wyatt had left a sick bed to make the appointment: a promise, she said, was a promise.

I've merged the highlights of our conversations into the interview that follows.

The Interview

BAWDEN: How do you feel about your identification as one of TV's perfect mothers?

WYATT: I love that I succeeded at that part. But you understand I was never Margaret Anderson. I didn't stay at home. I was out working most days. It was a part I was playing. I had help to dust and cook, I was too busy. Once when the show was on, I took my own two boys out for a Christmas treat and a lady stopped me and said, "Thank you so much, Mrs. Anderson, for staying at home with your family." She didn't seem to notice I was with different children. I thanked her and went on my way. How could I tell her that I had servants to help me at home and that Margaret was merely a fictional character?

BAWDEN: Did you realize that part would change your career?

WYATT: What career? I had been blacklisted in movies for several years. No, not formally. There just were no offers after I made *My Blue Heaven* [1950] and *Criminal Lawyer* [1951]. That left live TV, which was fighting the blacklist and dear Bob Montgomery hated that, although he was very right wing, you know. And he kept using me on his show, *Robert Montgomery Presents.*

I was in New York doing one of his live broadcasts when Bob Young sent over a script for a new TV series called *Father Knows Best.* He'd been doing it for years on radio, but wanted a better-known actress as his TV costar. [June Whitley played the role on radio.] Montgomery had suggested me, but I didn't want to do a series.

When I came home, my husband said he'd read it and thought it pretty good and told me to do it because my inactivity was driving him crazy. But I chose a Broadway play, *The Autumn Garden,* which was a flop, so when I returned, the script was still there. I took it because there was nothing else.

BAWDEN: It had a shaky start?

WYATT: That's putting it mildly. To save money, CBS insisted they use the old radio scripts, and here Bob Young was something of a ninny and on TV he looked uncomfortable. We had a talk and I told him to go back to his original conception for TV—to make Jim Anderson warm and friendly and not a boob. In today's parlance, it would be dubbed a dramedy. But at the end of the first season our tobacco sponsor P. Lorillard cancelled us and I thought that was it. Then Scott Paper Company took us on and we switched to NBC for three seasons [1955–1958] and that's when we matured into a hit.

Then we returned to CBS for the last two years. Bob decided to kill it when it was at its highest popularity. CBS retorted with a new plot that had Elinor Donahue [who played their oldest daughter] married and living over the garage with her new groom, but Bob said no. Oh, how I was scared we might do a seventh season. By that time I was going crazy. To keep myself sane I read the entire Old Testament during time off on set just to keep in touch with something other than our show.

BAWDEN: Young also owned the show?

WYATT: And reaped huge dividends during all those rerun seasons. CBS kept us going years after we had finished. Then it was syndicated, station to station. I couldn't escape it! We only got paid as actors for the first six reruns. We did it as a one-camera show, one a week—had to because the three children had to have four hours of schooling a day. Bob also produced it with his partner Eugene B. Rodney. You know, Bob is very taciturn and has a great work ethic and this was translated to the kids, who hero-worshipped him.

I got close to Billy Gray because he was the same age as my sons. Elinor Donahue was a bit older and very precocious. Little Lauren Chapin came from a tempestuous background. When she married, I paid for the reception. There was nobody else to do it.

BAWDEN: You hardly were a subservient wife.

WYATT: Right on! I was the one who ran that family, Jim Anderson was always at work. Margaret ran everything. One episode she was mad at the family for the whole time. And by the way, I never did vacuuming with my pearls on. That must have been on *Leave It to Beaver*.

BAWDEN: But you had quite an impact.

WYATT: A man stopped me recently and said he'd been raised in an orphanage and he'd fantasized Margaret Anderson was his mother. Then I went to a Crosby, Stills, Nash, and Young concert. Stephen Stills is a second cousin—and the whole audience got up, shouting, "Margaret! Margaret!" Now that was quite an experience!

BAWDEN: When did you know the series had been on too long?

WYATT: At a CBS affiliates meeting. I waltzed over to Bob Young and fixed his tie. His real-life wife, Betty, looked daggers at me. I got the picture. I had become Margaret Anderson! Enough!

BAWDEN: Let's go back to your beginnings. You have an ancestor who signed the Declaration of Independence?

WYATT: Oh, yes! Philip Livingston, on my father's side. On my mother's side there was Rufus Sewell, founder of Columbia University and ambassador to England. I guess we were posh. I was the second of four children [born on August 12, 1910] and I attended Chapin School in New York City. Then I went to Barnard College for two terms. Yes, it's also true [that] when I went into acting I got banned from the Social Register. Then when I married husband Edgar I got restored!

I made my Broadway debut in A. A. Milne's play *Give Me Yesterday* in 1931—the height of the Depression, remember. I had brief runs in several plays, including *The Joyous Season* [1934] and *The Bishop Misbehaves* [1935].

BAWDEN: You were stage crazy?

WYATT: Still am. But the talkies decimated Broadway and then the Depression finished the job. I accepted a short-term deal from Universal and was cast in Jimmy Whale's movie *One More River* [1934] opposite Colin Clive and Mrs. Patrick Campbell. He said I sounded very posh and it got grand reviews, but nobody in America came to see it. People simply had no money. Then I was cast as Estella in *Great Expectations* [1934], but it was very humdrum. The director, Stuart Walker, didn't understand it. Our Pip was Philips Holmes and he was very nervous. We reused streets from *Frankenstein*. But there were two actors in it—Francis L. Sullivan and Valerie Hobson—who also were in the marvelous 1946 version. Valerie was Becky here, Estella in '46, and Francis was the lawyer Jaggers both times.

BAWDEN: Can you tell me what you remember about these films on the list of your movies?

WYATT: *We're Only Human* [1935]? Absolutely no recollection, although I know it's on my résumé.

Lost Horizon? I had flopped in movies, was trying out for another Broadway play, when [director] Frank Capra phoned me up and asked me to visit him at Columbia. He said he needed an unknown, somebody cheap, but a girl with acting experience. He wanted as Sondra a girl who looked like she'd always lived in Shangri-La. I made a test with Ronnie Colman, who was so sweet and helpful, and I got it.

BAWDEN: I read it wasn't such a hit at the time of its original release in 1937.

WYATT: Harry Cohn, head of Columbia, told me the cost was just over $2 million, roughly half Columbia's production budget for the entire year. The first preview there was nervous laughing and Frank was con-

Jane Wyatt with Ronald Colman in *Lost Horizon* (1937). Courtesy of Columbia Pictures.

vinced it was a bust. He cut out the first two reels of the Chinese riots. We ran it again and the audience cheered. Ronnie made it work. You saw everything through his eyes. I was never a fan of those huge Shangri-La sets, but the movie worked as long as Ronnie was front and center.

BAWDEN: Today it's a classic.

WYATT: I have my ideas about that. It came and went uneventfully at the time. Ronnie never even got an Oscar nomination. But today we can see it as one of the greatest productions from Hollywood's heroic age. It's because all those great character stars—Edward Everett Horton, Tommy Mitchell, H. B. Warner—are no longer around. In 1937, they were seen in picture after picture. Now we sit back and appreciate them because that kind of acting will never be seen again.

BAWDEN: But you did not become a big star from it. Why?

WYATT: Oh, I blew it. I did myself in as far as screen stardom was concerned. I haughtily refused a Columbia contract and I went back east and the play flopped. When I did come back, all I got were Bs. My momentum was destroyed. I did that all by myself. My dreams of becoming a big Broadway star never did come true.

BAWDEN: In 1941 you hit Warners with a comedy, *Weekend for Three*. I'm wondering if you bumped into Jane Wyman. Do you ever get confused with her because of the similarity of your names?

WYATT: I don't remember meeting her at that time. But I got many production memos intended for her. I adore her as an actress, but at that time she was also doing B features. I would have loved to have done *Johnny Belinda!* [Wyman's 1948 Oscar-winning role].

BAWDEN: In 1943 you made two pictures at the same time?

WYATT: Yes, two programmers for producer Poppy Sherman. He loved to squeeze every last cent out of his productions. Made mostly westerns, you know. So there I was doing *Buckskin Frontier* and *The Kansan*, both with Richard Dix, a dear, sweet man, but rather overaged to still be a star. We'd shoot all the scenes for both pictures at one location and then go on to the next. I wore the same clothes, hair style, etc. in both. So did Dick. He was so professional about it. I've always considered *The Kansan* the more important of the two. Did they ever appear together on a double bill, I'm wondering? Albert Dekker and Vic Jory were in both, cast in virtually the same parts. To my surprise, western fans write to me all the time about them. It was grand fun!

BAWDEN: Then came an A picture, *None but the Lonely Heart* [1944], opposite Cary Grant.

WYATT: One of my favorites. The nominal leading lady was a very gorgeous British girl, June Duprez. First day of shooting, Cary strolls up to me and says this is the first time on-screen he's ever played himself. Cary truly burrowed inside Ernie Mott. He should have gotten the Oscar. But his film fans hated him as less than glamorous and he never tried that again. It was set in the Depression and now Americans were worried about the war.

Do you know who was nervous? Ethel Barrymore as the mother. Hadn't acted in movies in twelve years. Was over the top until Cary worked with her and got her to be minimalist. She got the supporting Oscar because of his generosity in showcasing her. But I didn't like [playwright] Clifford Odets's direction. It needed the sure touch of a Jack Ford. Clifford wrote it, but he was trying too hard to direct. The camera kept moving all over the place. It was a box office failure, but after all, Cary already had two big hits in *Arsenic and Old Lace* and *Destination Tokyo.*

BAWDEN: You were then in another big one, *Gentleman's Agreement,* but in a cameo.

WYATT: I'll tell you how that happened. I'd lost my momentum again after *Lonely Heart.* I had a baby, Chris, then I did yet another play that flopped. Then the only movie I could get was a B—*Strange Conquest.* I was at a party chattering up a storm with Dorothy McGuire and [director] Elia Kazan saw me. He was then casting *Gentleman's Agreement* and needed somebody to play Dorothy's sister. He was very small and very intense and he came over and offered the part to me, promising that in his next picture, *Boomerang* [1947], I'd have a big juicy co-lead. I played sort of an anti-Semite, which I liked doing, and that got me into trouble eventually.

Then Gadge [Kazan's nickname] came forth with *Boomerang,* which was shot almost entirely in Connecticut. It was based on a *Reader's Digest* article by Richard Murphy. Dana Andrews, who was huge at the time, was a crusading district attorney investigating the trial of a priest. It was hard being on location in those days because the equipment was hardly portable. But there were fine actors in it—Sam Levene, Lee J. Cobb, Karl Malden, Ed Begley.

BAWDEN: And you got into trouble because of it?

WYATT: That's putting it mildly. I was warned I might have to appear before the House Un-American Activities Committee. I know they were investigating me. I asked Harry Cohn about it and he said he'd received a letter from them charging I'd done plays by Voltaire and Chekhov! Harry said both sounded faintly Marxist to him! I said let 'em try to bring me down! After all, my ancestors included a signer of the Declaration of Independence. I never had any political inclinations except those that involved my beloved Catholic Church. Yes, I had gone to Washington in 1947 with a planeload of celebrities protesting HUAC—but Humphrey Bogart, June Havoc, Danny Kaye were also on board. And HUAC seemed to back off. But later I learned I was gray-listed. I was guilty by reason of association.

BAWDEN: Meanwhile, you made a dandy film noir, *Pitfall* [1948] at RKO.

WYATT: I'm still asked about that one. Because it did not have a tacked-on happy ending. Dick Powell was terrific as an insurance investigator and Liz Scott was a parolee being preyed on by Raymond Burr. We shot a lot of it out in the valley and in some scenes you'll see the new housing tracts. I even did a scene in the May Company store on Wilshire Boulevard where Liz was supposed to work. I did see it recently and thought it was so white—no ethnics at all—which was L.A. in those days. It's an artifact of the forties.

BAWDEN: Then it was back to Warners.

WYATT: For *Task Force* [1949]. Gary Cooper had casting approval and he teased me he'd actually asked for Jane Wyman. [Writer-director] Delmer Daves wrote it as an attempt to show where the [aircraft] carriers had come from. Coop's character had been advocating them since the thirties. My character was married to his best buddy, who died in one experiment, and now she's afraid she'll lose Coop, too. After my first take with the big lug, I told Del, "Guess we'll have to do that one again. He was asleep on the job." Del laughed and told me to sit in when the takes were unspooled the next day. So Coop had underacted me and stolen the scene effortlessly. There was just a flicker of his eyebrow, He kept saying on set, "Too much!" I call him a minimalist, the best I've ever worked with. His philosophy was to get the audience to work along with you. Best acting advice I've ever heard.

BAWDEN: During the *Father Knows Best* years you only had a chance to make one movie.

WYATT: In 1957 I flew with son Michael to Salzburg where Douglas Sirk was filming *Interlude* [1957] with June Allyson and Rossano Brazzi. It was a remake of an Irene Dunne starrer, *When Tomorrow Comes.* Universal said all my scenes could be shot within three weeks, so I'd get home for the next season of *Father Knows Best.* And it was wonderful visiting all those historic sites. The movie was just plain awful. Nobody remembers it.

BAWDEN: After *Father Knows Best,* what happened?

WYATT: I was typed as a TV star. I did one movie, a little thing with Eddie Albert [1961's *Two Little Bears*]. But then TV movies came along and I got one of the first ones, 1964's *See How They Run.* Did a lot of those—and guest spots. The movie business had changed too much for me to be a part of it. I was Amanda, Mr. Spock's mom, on *Star Trek*—I still get

Jane Wyatt with Robert Young as the Andersons in TV's *Father Knows Best* (1954–1963). James Bawden collection.

letters about that. And I got to do the 1986 movie *Star Trek IV: The Voyage Home*. My first day and a young man comes up and says, "Miss Wyatt, I think you knew my grandfather. I'm Frank Capra III!"

There were two unfortunate TV movie reunions of the *Father Knows Best* cast, but we had changed, so it was rather sad. I told Bob to stop revis-

Jane Wyatt as the human mother of Mr. Spock (Leonard Nimoy, *right*), and wife of his Vulcan father (Mark Lenard) in *Star Trek IV: The Voyage Home* (1986). Courtesy of CTV Television.

iting the past and he agreed. Then Bob got another series, *Marcus Welby, M.D.* [1969–1976] and I figured, well, that's one show I'll never be asked on. But they wrote a pretty good part for me as an upscale designer. That was in 1974 and Bob's professionalism was still there.

I've been Norman Lloyd's wife on *St. Elsewhere*. But my favorite TV part was on *Hollywood Television Theatre* [in a 1971 episode] called *Neighbors*. Andrew Duggan and I were white old racists contemplating selling their home to a black couple. Cicely Tyson played the black wife. It was my chance to kick the establishment just one more time. I'm so out of it that when they offered me [the TV movie] *Amityville: The Evil Escapes* [1989] opposite Patty Duke, I thought it was a Civil War story.

And then I did *Driving Miss Daisy* on the West Coast stage opposite Ted Lange from *The Love Boat.* I'm still around and still kicking.

Afterword

In Wyatt's last telephone call to me, in 2000, she related the sad news that her husband Edgar had died a day before their sixty-fifth wedding anniversary. Asked to define the secret of her success, she'd once told me, "Being a good wife and mother and a strong Catholic are the big things. The icing on the cake was the career." Jane Wyatt died of heart trouble on October 20, 2006, at her Bel Air estate, aged ninety-six. The year before, she had sent an autographed picture of herself, uncharacteristically decked out in 1942 finery, with the comment, "I wish I looked like this today!"

IV

Child Stars and
How They Grew

Bonita Granville

Interview by James Bawden

Bonita Granville was a marvelous child actress who grew up to find a happy ending for her career outside the acting game.

Film purists will best remember her for her performance as the nasty little troublemaker who spreads rumors about teachers Miriam Hopkins and Merle Oberon in William Wyler's *These Three* (1936), the film version of Lillian Hellman's stage play *The Children's Hour*. That earned her an Oscar nomination in the Supporting Actress category, putting her up against adult performers, then quite unusual for a child actor.

But teen girls who grew up in the late 1930s will always remember Bonita Granville best for her four films, made from 1938 to 1939, in which she played teen sleuth Nancy Drew.

Granville later had a so-so career as an adult performer, but she really prospered after her marriage to producer Jack Wrather, which led to her becoming the producer of TV's long-running *Lassie* series. As a business executive, she eventually became the operator of the *Queen Mary* ocean liner attraction in Long Beach, California.

Setting the Scene

I'd wanted to interview Bonita Granville since catching her malevolent childhood performance in *These Three*. We finally met on a sweltering June afternoon in 1986 at the headquarters of the Wrather Corporation in downtown Beverly Hills. (She was chairman of the board.) A robbery in the jewelry boutique across the street had stopped traffic and I had to sprint the last few blocks to be on time.

Bonita Granville with canine friend on the Warner Bros. lot, circa 1938, during the filming of her *Nancy Drew* films. James Bawden collection.

The Interview

BAWDEN: It seems inevitable, given your background, that you'd become an actress.

GRANVILLE: Well, yes, we were a theatrical family and I acted in stock as a toddler. Children make the best actors, you know. For me it was all pretend. And then when the Depression hit and talkers came in we migrated to Los Angeles for film work. Dad [Bunny Granville] started way back in minstrel shows at the turn of the century. One of his early vaudeville partners was Will Rogers. And he joined the Ziegfeld Follies in 1912 and then served as an aviator with the Second Field Army in combat in northern France. And when he died unexpectedly in 1936, aged fifty, in L.A., it was imperative that I keep acting to support the family. And luckily, Dad did live to see me get my first big part in *These Three*. He died the year after Will Rogers went down in that plane crash in Alaska. That was more than a coincidence, I feel. They had been super close.

BAWDEN: First you did small roles that were almost like work as an extra.

GRANVILLE: I was the little daughter of Ann Harding and Larry Olivier in *Westward Passage* [1933]. I'd fall asleep in Larry's arms after lunch and decades later I came up to him at a Hollywood affair and said, "Mr. Olivier, I slept with you and I loved it." It didn't come out the way I wanted and he blushed mightily but he soon remembered me as his daughter and we had a hug.

I played "Young Fanny" in *Cavalcade* [1933], aged nine, and I remember dancing on a gigantic boulevard in one scene. The sets were grand to this little girl, the huge crowds milling about rather overwhelming. Ursula Jeans played the character grown up. I've never seen it as a grown-up. [It was the Oscar-winning Best Picture that year.]

And I was a classmate of Amy [Joan Bennett] in *Little Women* [1933]. It was a shock to learn dear sweet Amy was really Joan Bennett, who was twenty-three and had already been married several times. And I played in *Anne of Green Gables* [1934] opposite Anne Shirley, who'd been doing little parts like me, but billed as Dawn O'Day until this, her big break. I was in another Ann Harding opus, *The Life of Vergie Winters* [1934], a real sob story. I continued doing these little things and got paid for a few weeks' work on most of them. I'm briefly glimpsed in *The Garden of Allah* [1936] in the girls' school. I didn't know quite what to make of Marlene Dietrich and her painted face.

BAWDEN: Then came *These Three*.

GRANVILLE: There was a big audition. Every girl around came out. They kept narrowing the field and I got it. I came from a very nice family, so I had no idea what being that naughty meant. Sometimes the director,

From left: Alma Kruger, Bonita Granville, and Margaret Hamilton in *These Three* (1936). Granville earned a Supporting Actress Oscar nomination as the spiteful child who upsets a private girls' school with her lies. Ron Miller collection.

Willie Wyler, had to prod me. The wonderful old actress Alma Kruger coached me how to be naughty. She was a real vet. I don't think Mother knew it had been a play about lesbianism on Broadway—or maybe she did.

Listen very closely and in one scene Margaret Hamilton says, "Bonita, come here" instead of my stage name of Mary. Nobody noticed it and I didn't either until it played on TV! I get slapped in the face. Mr. Wyler wanted a retake but my mother forbade it. Marcia Mae Jones was the goody one, but I think Mary was more like average children. Most kids have mean streaks.

About the leads: Merle Oberon, Joel McCrea are average, but Miriam Hopkins does sneak in some of the lesbian undertones. I got an Oscar nomination at thirteen, but I lost to Gale Sondergaard, my only time at bat. [That was the first year of the "Supporting Actress" category.]

BAWDEN: You cornered the market in bad-girl roles.

GRANVILLE: Tell me about that! In *Maid of Salem* [1937] I was a real

Teenage Bonita Granville with Jackie Cooper in *White Banners* (1938). Courtesy of Warner Bros.

bitch! Frank Lloyd, our director, was revered at the time for historical melodramas but didn't even remember me from *Cavalcade*. And remember this was fifteen years before Arthur Miller's play *The Crucible*. Critics said Claudette [Colbert] was the first Puritan miss to sport plucked eyebrows and mascara, but she really tried hard. I was the vindictive teen who accuses her of witchcraft and I had one gloriously hysterical scene. But this was not a Colbert comedy and the audiences did not come.

Then I was Livvie de Havilland's bratty kid sister in *It's Love I'm After* [1937], only Livvie on the set was totally infatuated with Leslie Howard. Two years later they were lovers in *Gone with the Wind* [1939]. I was Billie Burke's spoiled daughter in *Merrily We Live* [1938], but being Connie Bennett's sister was a stretch. I was fifteen and she was thirty-five. I just remember all the fun we had on the set with Patsy Kelly and Alan Mowbray entertaining us with ditties.

BAWDEN: What do you remember about *White Banners* [1938]?

GRANVILLE: Only that it was a medium-budgeted picture, but our wonderful director, Edmund Goulding, gave it such stature. He worked with the cast and especially with Jackie Cooper and me on every little nuance. Often he'd act out all the parts in a scene. Then he'd shoot very quickly, one or two takes, or three at the most. One morning a spy on set told Hal Wallis that Eddie hadn't shot a scene and it was past 11 a.m. so Mr. Wallis appeared and watched the intricate setup that Eddie had ordered. They shot it twice—one for insurance—and Eddie then barked, "Lunch!" What could Wallis do? This was perfection!

I absolutely adored Claude Rains, movies' finest-ever actor, and his teaming with Fay Bainter was memorial, they so respected each other. Fay was nominated twice for the Oscar: for this as Best Actress and for *Jezebel* as Best Supporting Actress, for which she won.

Warners tried to promote a puppy love thing between me and Jackie Cooper. I went on my first date with him to a local malt shop, accompanied by Warners publicists and cameramen. I was horrified Jackie had to plant a moist pucker on my cheek, but that was part of the assignment. Jackie's face was beet red from embarrassment. We became very close, best pals. I was one of the few who knew what he had been through and later, when both of us were at MGM, we hung out together at Mr. Mayer's pool on Sunday afternoon—highly chaperoned, I must add. Judy Garland was there puffing on illegal cigarettes! Oh, all the MGM kids were invited and attendance was mandatory, if one wanted to keep working on the lot. Later on, Jackie got bitter about the way he'd been treated as a kid and we lost touch after I got married. But I still adore him, I really do.

BAWDEN: Did you start the *Nancy Drew* movies after *White Banners*?

GRANVILLE: Yes, I think so. I'd been a fan of the books, so I was absolutely floored at getting the coveted part. They tested every teen gal in L.A. but I had already worked at WB so I had the credentials. The first was *Nancy Drew, Detective* [1938], based on the 1933 book *The Password to Larkspur Lane.* I remember Jimmy Stephenson played the head gangster, which was hardly feasible. He was the most charming British actor, who died a few years later from smoking. John Litel was my dad, a deeply Catholic man who always blessed us each morning. You can see him in dozens of Warners films of the period. Frankie Thomas was my boyfriend, Ted Nickerson.

It was a hit at Saturday matinees and we did three more in 1939. *Nancy Drew, Reporter* was next. I'm trying to remember something about it. I remember Dickie Jones was in it. I think we'd make them in less than three weeks on standing sets and everything was supposed to be around sixty-five minutes because we were at the bottom of double bills.

In *Nancy Drew, Trouble Shooter* [1939], I clear my uncle of murder charges. I think this one was the best. William Clemens directed all of them. They played for the next decade on children's matinees but we only made one more. It was *Nancy Drew and the Hidden Staircase* [1939] and that was it. I wasn't available as I had signed a short-term MGM contract, but WB never offered me any more *Nancy Drews* anyway.

BAWDEN: Didn't you have your own mystery novels collection?

GRANVILLE: Oh, yes! In 1942 Kathryn Heisenfelt wrote *Bonita Granville and the Mystery of Star Island,* published by Whitman Books. It sold like gangbusters because those *Nancy Drew* movies were still out there at Saturday matinees. There were sixteen of these books featuring various movie actresses and mine has me acting about in a decidedly Nancy Drew fashion! I remember getting paid a lump sum but not residuals. I used to have a copy of it somewhere.

BAWDEN: You did six features your first year at Metro?

GRANVILLE: They worked me harder than WB. But most of these were big, prestigious pictures and I only had supporting parts. In *Escape* [1940], I sat around for weeks. I again was malicious, one of Norma Shearer's pupils in her girls' school. Bob Taylor was ever so nice as the male lead, although he was a decade younger than Norma and looked it. And there was Conrad Veidt as Norma's Nazi protector. We shot and shot on this one. Over several months. There were some wonderful actors in it: Blanche Yurka, Philip Dorn, Albert Bassermann, who talked so slow you could eat a sandwich between words. It was a big bomb because people did not want to be reminded that war with Germany was coming.

And a similar movie, *The Mortal Storm,* starred Maggie Sullavan and Jimmy Stewart, about the plight of the Jews in Bavaria. Hitler saw it and expelled all MGM personnel from Germany. That was the impact at the time. But the family is never called Jewish in the movie, only "non-Aryan," so there's some confusion there. When Frank Morgan is imprisoned, there's a "J" on his prison uniform, so there. It was packaged as a romance and was popular because Jimmy and Maggie were a team by then.

BAWDEN: Then you joined another series in *The People vs. Dr. Kildare* [1941].

GRANVILLE: Those movies don't stand the test of time because there have been so many imitations since then. I was a famous ice-skater—think Sonja Henie—and I was injured and everything seems okay, but I can't walk, let alone skate. Dr. Kildare does the operation right on the spot, so I sue him for malpractice. I played a rather nasty character, but at least I had a lead in an MGM hit for once. In fact it was more a courtroom drama than anything else. MGM had a standing courtroom set. I do remember they kept beefing up Red Skelton's part, much to the disgust of Lionel Barrymore. Today malpractice suits are so commonplace. Not then! I loved making it, getting that MGM glamour treatment.

BAWDEN: But you left at the end of 1941.

GRANVILLE: There were so many girls, MGM was filled with ingenues. My last at Metro was *H. M. Pulham Esq.* [1941]. I was the daughter of Bob Young and Ruth Hussey. It was just about Bob's last before he left MGM after ten years there. During the war, there was a rush to get leading men as many of the biggies had gone off to war. But my contract wasn't renewed. It made me more popular with the other studios, if anything.

BAWDEN: Then you were in several huge pictures, but in small roles.

GRANVILLE: *Now, Voyager* [1942] found me back at Warners at the command of producer Hal Wallis. I was the very nasty cousin of Bette Davis in early scenes when she's truly ugly and I'm taunting her, along with Ilka Chase. I remember shooting and shooting but at some point Wallis came on the set and said in effect, "Enough already!" and the scenes with Bette so drab were sliced down. It became a sort of Cinderella story.

Then in *The Glass Key* [1942], Brian Donlevy had top billing, but it turned Alan Ladd into a superstar. Both Alan and Veronica Lake were among the tiniest of stars. Rooms in an Alan Ladd picture were built three-quarter-[sized] so they'd look bigger. I remember my character's name, Opal, and the violence that seemed to be in every scene. It was a real smash.

BAWDEN: I really liked *Syncopation* [1942].

GRANVILLE: It was the history of American music—jazz, blues, beginning before Prohibition. Bill Dieterle directed, so it was a big production. It was Jackie Cooper's first as a fully grown lead and then he went into the service and got forgotten for awhile. I mean, it had Benny Goodman, Gene Krupa, Connie Boswell.

BAWDEN: Your biggest hit ever was *Hitler's Children* [1943].

GRANVVILLE: I initially balked at doing it. It features rather unsavory episodes. In one scene, I'm tied to a post and whipped. Then my Nazi boyfriend suggests we have an illegitimate baby of pure German stock for the Fatherland that we can give away. Nobody knew it was going to be RKO's biggest profit maker of the year. How that stuff got through the censors was amazing, but I was later told because it was the Nazis we were allowed to go all out. The word got out it was very daring and, of course, audiences flocked to see it.

BAWDEN: Why did you go back to MGM in 1944 for *Andy Hardy's Blonde Trouble?*

GRANVILLE: Because the money was good. But we were flogging a dead horse here. Mickey Rooney was simply too old for this kind of thing. He'd had a hectic personal life and when he goes in to have a talk with his father—Lewis Stone—audiences just laughed. It was wartime but this was a frosh romance. I was a college girl he was taken with. There were lovely twins to look at, too—Lee and Lyn Wilde. The shooting started with the Mick in the army and it didn't look right, so the picture was delayed until he got leave to join the cast. I thought it very racial—Keye Luke plays a Chinese doctor and every one of his patients is hesitant about going to him. But those were the times. It wasn't a hit.

So you can say I was surprised MGM tried again two years later with *Love Laughs at Andy Hardy.* It was actually released in January 1947, the same year MGM also killed off *The Thin Man, Dr. Gillespie,* and *Maisie* series. Postwar audiences were far more critical and demanding. Only we were back in frosh year: no time had intervened. The cast was downhearted and it showed; we knew it was end of the line. The Mick was too old and his carousing was showing on his face. They tried again in 1958, by which time nobody cared about Andy Hardy at all.

BAWDEN: You made one of my favorite film noirs around that time, *Suspense* [1946].

GRANVILLE: We made it for King Brothers at Monogram. They'd just made *Dillinger* [1945], which reaped a fortune. The director was Frank Tuttle, who'd done *This Gun for Hire* [1942] and he made the most of our minuscule budget. The sets were awful and they rounded up a whole lot of veterans who needed the work: Eugene Pallette, George E. Stone. The ice-skater here was Belita. Couldn't act but boy, she was some skater. I was Barry Sullivan's rejected fiancée, completely devoid of glamour, and I loved that part.

BAWDEN: You were the original choice to play in *The Razor's Edge* [1946], or so I've heard.

GRANVILLE: You heard correctly. I heard about the project and phoned up [director] Eddie Goulding, who was now attached to Fox. I did a test for him that he reported was "sparkling." But Anne Baxter, who was the same age, heard about the production and told Darryl Zanuck that since she was already on contract it would make sense using her for purely economic reasons. He thought about it, agreed, and Eddie phoned me in tears saying he was only the director, what could he do? And Anne was so wonderful she copped a Supporting [Actress] Oscar and that really broke my heart. It happens all the time in Hollywood—rejection. But I really needed an A picture right about then and I didn't get one.

BAWDEN: Your last big part was in *The Guilty* [1947]. As twins!

GRANVILLE: I was up against Bette Davis and Olivia de Havilland—we all played twins around that time. One twin was nicey-nicey, the other cold-blooded to the core. Again it was for Monogram. We'd shoot ten hours a day. That's where I met Jack Wrather, who produced it, and we married that same year. It was based on a Cornell Woolrich tale and I wish we'd had more money for the sets, etc. John Litel was in it and on the first day on set he ran in shouting, "I want my daughter, Nancy!"

BAWDEN: What happened to your movie career?

GRANVILLE: I was no longer interested in acting. I'd married Jack and he was starting his own businesses and that was an exciting place to me. *Guilty of Treason* [1950] was my last movie lead for some time. As the children came along, I had less time for acting, but in the early days of live TV I'd do a few shows every year as guest star: *Armstrong Circle Theatre*, *Somerset Maugham Guild Playhouse*, *Schaefer Century Theatre*. I had Anne Baxter's part in the live TV version of *Guest in the House* on *Broadway Television Theatre* [1953]. As filmed TV came into play, I did *Schlitz Playhouse*, *Climax!*, *Ethel Barrymore Theatre*, then more live work on *U.S. Steel Hour* and *Lux Video Theatre* and a *Playhouse 90* I was proud of titled *The Velvet Alley* with Jack Klugman, Art Carney, Les Nielsen, Alexander Scourby and, in bits, Dyan Cannon and Burt Reynolds. How's that for all-star live TV?

BAWDEN: You made it back to movies in 1956.

GRANVILLE: In *The Lone Ranger* movie—movie versions of TV hits were all the rage right then—there was *Our Miss Brooks*, *Dragnet*, *Here Come the Nelsons* with Ozzie and Harriet, but none was a big success. Ours played well at the matinees for kiddies, but not at night. Critics commented on the beautiful color.

BAWDEN: Meanwhile, Jack Wrather was busy.

Robert Bray and Lassie with executive producer Bonita Granville Wrather on the set of TV's *Lassie* (1954–1974). James Bawden collection.

GRANVILLE: You can say that again! The Wrather Corp. bought the rights to *Lassie* in 1951. MGM let the contract lapse, convinced the franchise was finished. Jack disagreed and transferred the action to a family farm, casting Jan Clayton, who was in the original production of *Carousel,* as the widowed mother, Tommy Rettig as her son, Jeff, and George Cleveland as her aged father. I became first the associate producer of the CBS series *Lassie,* which debuted Sunday nights in September 1954. And later I became executive producer and we ran right through 1971.

In 1957 we had to change casts—Tommy had sprouted so and George passed away. The originals were syndicated in reruns as *Jeff's Collie*. So we restarted with Jon Provost, who was so tiny he lasted seven seasons through 1964. Originally, the new parents were Cloris Leachman and Jon Shepodd, but they only lasted a season. Brilliant actress as she is, Cloris could not bond with the dog. In came June Lockhart and Hugh Reilly and a new grandfather figure in George Chandler. CBS cancelled us in 1971 and we went through three seasons of syndication with new episodes. Campbell's soup was our sponsor and we went to them for production details and not CBS most of the time.

Jack also built all the original hotel rooms at Disneyland in conjunction with Walt Disney. The restaurant, Granville's Steak House, and the wing the Bonita Tower were named after me. He bought the rights to *The Lone Ranger* in 1954 and took over production of the series 1954–57. We also did the series *Sergeant Preston of the Yukon* [1955–1958] for CBS and Jack had hotels at Balboa and Palm Springs. He owned Muzak from 1957 to 1980 and later on he purchased Howard Hughes's *Spruce Goose* as well as the *Queen Mary*, which we now run as a tourist attraction docked at Long Beach.

BAWDEN: Can I ask what you thought of the movie version of *The Legend of the Lone Ranger* [1981]?

GRANVILLE: Oh, please! We had a handsome leading man [Klinton Spilsbury], but he couldn't really act, could he? He was dubbed by James Keach. They took all the mystery out of the character, made him commonplace. It died, really died at the box office.

BAWDEN: And you've continued as chair of the board.

GRANVILLE: Jack passed in 1984. He was a huge smoker. I wasn't feeling well so I went in for a check-up and found I had lung cancer, too, although I've always been a nonsmoker. But secondary smoke is just as dangerous, I've found out. I'm keeping going and want to preserve his heritage. And I love leaving all the decision making to my son.

Afterword

I interviewed Granville in 1986 and less than two years later, on October 11, 1988, she succumbed to cancer. The next year Disney bought Wrather Corporation and kept the hotel, but sold off all other assets that came with the purchase. It was indeed the end of an era.

Johnny Sheffield

Interview by Ron Miller

There were child stars like Shirley Temple, who made mega-millions for her movie studio and was a number one star at the box office. And there were child stars like Mickey Rooney, who grew up famous and never slipped into obscurity; Tatum O'Neal, who won an Academy Award, then fell out of favor as a grown-up actor; and Gary Coleman, who never really grew up, lived a rather tragic life, and died way too young. And then there was Johnny Sheffield, who was picked as a child to play the adopted son of Tarzan in the movies and had one of the most fabled childhoods of any juvenile star.

Born to actor Reginald Sheffield, an Englishman who'd been a child actor himself, Johnny grew up in a very classy household. His mother was a New Yorker with an Ivy League college education and a liberal outlook. His parents encouraged Johnny's interest in following his father's occupation and, at age seven, he was cast in the 1938 West Coast company of the hit Broadway show *On Borrowed Time* and was so good that he was sent to New York to replace the boy playing his role on Broadway.

With that very rich credit to his name, it's easy to understand why Johnny was a solid contender for the role of Boy in *Tarzan Finds a Son!* (1939) after his dad saw a note in a Hollywood trade paper saying they were looking for a boy to play alongside Johnny Weissmuller in the hit MGM movie series and took Johnny in for an audition.

Between 1939 and 1947, Johnny appeared in eight *Tarzan* movies at MGM and later RKO, then left to star in his own series at Monogram, *Bomba, the Jungle Boy.* That series ran to a dozen films. After filming an unsold pilot for a jungle TV series called *Bantu, the Zebra Boy,* in which he roamed the jungle riding bareback on a zebra, Sheffield gave up acting and pursued a career in business, earning his business administration degree at UCLA.

Johnny Sheffield as Bomba the Jungle Boy. Courtesy of Monogram Pictures.

Sheffield married only once—in 1959—and he had three children with wife Patricia. He settled down in Chula Vista, California, where he ran his own home construction business.

Setting the Scene

I got to know Johnny Sheffield after doing a telephone interview with him in 1994 as part of the promotion for a *Tarzan* movie festival on the American Movie Classics (AMC) cable network. We stayed in touch and exchanged frequent phone calls over the next few years.

In 1999, when I formed a website with three other retired journalists with solid entertainment writing backgrounds, I approached Johnny with the idea of writing his memoirs as a series for the website. He was happy to do so and, with my help, authored *Memoirs of a Jungle Boy*, which ran on www.thecolumnists.com in 2000.

After that, Sheffield and I really became good friends. A few years later he and wife Patti came to stay with my wife and me at our home on the Canadian border in Blaine, Washington. Johnny appeared with me on a public program in nearby Bellingham, honoring his work in the movies.

During our days together, Johnny and I talked a lot about his movie career. I've pulled together material from our original interview and our subsequent private chats for this chapter.

The Interview

MILLER: Johnny, it's almost a cliché to think "lost childhood years" when you think of a Hollywood child star, since so many of them turned out to be screwed up as adults. Your situation?

SHEFFIELD: I know you often hear about the tormented lives of Hollywood child stars. You won't hear that from me. I was blessed with an extraordinary childhood. My caring, loving, teaching parents were probably the most popular mother/father combo in my town, especially if you ever took a vote among all the children in the neighborhood.

MILLER: You had never made a movie when you stepped into the role of the little boy who's found by Tarzan in the wreckage of a plane crash in the jungle. What was it like to immediately start working with a famous movie star like Johnny Weissmuller, who was also an Olympic swimming champ?

SHEFFIELD: Can you think of anyone better to get you in shape to star in a jungle boy series? Is there anyone better prepared to teach you how to outswim a crocodile than a genuine Olympic swimming champion? I was "Little John" to him. We were close. Big John took a personal interest in me, becoming my second father and my coach.

Johnny Weissmuller was an authentic superstar. He gave off a very special light for all of us to see. It has taken fifty-plus years to fully understand how spending my formative years, seven to sixteen, under the wing of a world champion has affected my life.

MILLER: You had to plunge right into the water in your role as Boy. Did he give you any special swimming tips?

SHEFFIELD: When I couldn't swim, my jungle dad didn't say, "Boy no good; can't swim! Let him drown!" No, Tarzan actually taught me to swim. In our real life, he was like he was in the movies. Tarzan taught me I wasn't alone; I could always give out the Tarzan yell and count on him for help when things got sticky. [Sheffield could give out with a pretty authentic Tarzan yell. In fact, he demonstrated it one morning on our deck, which overlooks a golf course. If there had been any wild elephants out there, I'm sure they would have come running. Meanwhile, the early-morning golfers stood and gaped.]

MILLER: I grew up on the *Tarzan* movies and seem to remember they preached a certain fundamental set of values. Were you conscious of that yourself?

SHEFFIELD: Remember *Tarzan's New York Adventure* [1942]? When Boy was kidnapped and taken from Africa, Tarzan took action. He didn't mope around. He went down to our swimming hole, picked up a few gold nuggets to cover expenses, got on the Pan Am Clipper, and went to New York to "find Boy!" When it came to protecting his family, Tarzan was *tops*. Once it became apparent the US judicial system would fail to produce Boy, Tarzan and Jane had a family conference right in the courtroom on the thirtieth floor of the Justice Building overlooking Manhattan. I'll never forget that scene: "Jane say Tarzan find Boy?" Tarzan asks. "Yes, Tarzan," she says, eyes brimming with love, as Cheetah looks on. *Wow!* Did Tarzan go into action! Right out through the courtroom window! He swung his way through Manhattan, then dove off the Brooklyn Bridge and swam for it to rescue Boy! Will you ever forget that?

Tarzan's New York Adventure taught me the resourcefulness and humanity of Tarzan and the principle that family responsibility is the nucleus for human growth and happiness. It also taught me that the family can be vulnerable to outside influences of evil. I bet it taught you the same. This threat to the safety of Boy and the happiness of his family compelled Tarzan to get going. He reveals his values by action and is willing to risk it all for his family. The movie clearly demonstrates family values. Truth, honesty—and what we jungle folk call the "Umgawa Way"—always win out over lawlessness and greed!

From left: Cheetah, Johnny Sheffield, Johnny Weissmuller, and Maureen O'Sullivan in a posed "jungle family" photo during the *Tarzan* series of films. Courtesy of Johnny Sheffield.

MILLER: Johnny Weissmuller was known around Hollywood as quite the ladies' man. Did he teach you anything about that, too?

SHEFFIELD: When my father was teaching me about the "birds and the bees," Tarzan was teaching me about the "crocodiles and the flamingos." So by the time I reached adolescence I was pretty well informed on the subject.

I remember one day, while rehearsing a scene, Big John caught me staring at Jane's curves. I came out of it when he nudged me on the shoulder. I looked up at Big John and he was smiling. "Pretty nice, Boy, huh?" he said quietly. I had to agree, but boy, was I embarrassed. Tarzan then said for all to hear: "Boy grown up now!" I guess it was pretty obvious to the whole crew the discovery I had made. After that my education expanded quite a bit under Big John's influence.

MILLER: Did Weissmuller ever talk about his exploits with women?

SHEFFIELD: On certain days you might hear: "Brenda swims

tonight!" echoing around the soundstage. At the time Big John was train-ing a young woman swimmer named Brenda—not Brenda Joyce, who later played Jane—for a series of races. Brenda was in strict training. The idea was to reserve all her strength for the competition and that meant *no sex* just before a race. This approach was not working as Brenda was not winning. Big John told me he was going to try the opposite approach. So when he told me, "Brenda swims tonight," I knew what that meant. And she *won!* Soon the film crew caught on and they were delighted when Big John came on the set and announced: "Brenda swims tonight."

MILLER: What else did he teach you?

SHEFFIELD: Big John taught me to have *fun!* He loved to play, liked good-looking women, flashy clothes, and toys. He owned a Lincoln with the "Continental Pack" on the back. He loved that Lincoln. He drove it on the studio lot and to and from location. In the trunk he kept his golf clubs and practice balls as well as some swimming gear: trunks, face plate, and swim fins.

Behind the scenes, Big John took time to play with me. On location, when I wasn't in school, he would call me and we would go over to that Continental trunk for some golf gear and would "hit a few balls" together. Tarzan loved golf.

Big John loved to win and he gave me his winning attitude. He said to think of it this way: "When you step up to the starting mark, look down the line and you'll see there are two kinds of swimmers or golfers, card players, etc., standing there: the ones who are going to lose and *you!*" Hey, it worked for Big John.

MILLER: You grew to manhood between 1939 and 1947 when you made your last appearance as Boy in *Tarzan and the Huntress*. Did you and Weissmuller keep in touch afterward?

SHEFFIELD: Yes, we always did. We often played golf together.

MILLER: What was the last time you saw him?

SHEFFIELD: The last time I saw Big John alive I was hitting six irons on the practice fairway at the Riviera, my home golf club in Los Angeles. The word came down that my jungle father, Tarzan, was getting ready to tee off on #1 above me. When I saw Big John's foursome crossing the bar-ranca coming down the fairway toward me to make their second shots on #2, I cut loose with Boy's yell and Big John answered with his famous Tar-zan yell. All action on the golf course stopped. He left his group and came over to me and we talked. Big John watched me hit a couple, encouraged me, then hit a couple himself. It was like old times by the trunk of his Continental. I looked at him and he looked at me. We both looked down to the practice green where our shots were resting. Then we looked at each other again and had a great laugh. We both hit 'em pretty darn good. He ruffled my hair. On the way back to rejoin his foursome, he turned and smiled. It never mattered what Big John was doing, he always had time for me. That was the last time I saw my jungle father alive.

MILLER: Altogether, you made eight *Tarzan* films with Weissmuller, first at MGM and then at RKO. When you went off to college, you left the series, but then an offer came your way.

SHEFFIELD: I was approached by a young producer named Walter Mirisch who wanted to produce a series of low-budget jungle movies at Monogram Pictures based on the *Bomba* novels for boys. He wasn't much known at the time. In fact, he was still in his twenties. But he soon became one of the most successful producers in Hollywood, especially after he and his older brothers, Harold and Marvin, formed the Mirisch Company and started turning out films like *The Magnificent Seven, West Side Story, The Great Escape,* and *In the Heat of the Night.* We got along famously from the start.

MILLER: How old were you then?

SHEFFIELD: I was eighteen. My schedule for the *Bomba* films was arranged to allow me to go on with my education at UCLA. At school, we talked about man's impact on the environment, but in my make-believe world "beyond the Rift," Bomba was just trying to avoid man's impact—period.

MILLER: Your first leading lady in *Bomba, the Jungle Boy* [1949] was another grown-up child star, Peggy Ann Garner, who won a 1944 Academy Award as Best Child Actress and had the leading role in the 1945 film *A Tree Grows in Brooklyn.* How did the two of you get along?

SHEFFIELD: She was a real pro! We had a grand time together. I will never forget the scene where I show her my "digs" and pointed out how nice it would be for her to stay with me in Bomba's cave. Her line was "Very cozy." I think she made me construct a shelter for her outside. Anyway, you couldn't ask for a better reading of that line—and I soon got her dressed properly, without all that underwear.

MILLER: For the *Bomba* series, you also worked a lot with animals. Were you used to it by then?

SHEFFIELD: George Emerson, my animal trainer at Metro, taught me how to work with the animals. I pretty much knew by then what they would tolerate and what they would not. You probably noticed I first appeared with a monkey on my shoulder. That was Otto. We were a low-budget group and couldn't afford a chimp. Otto fitted in just fine. He was well trained and no advance coaching was required for me to work well with him.

MILLER: Was it a different ball game for you, working with a poverty-row studio like Monogram after MGM and RKO?

SHEFFIELD: Right away I was impressed with the team Walter had put together to make the *Bomba* films, starting with the director, Ford Beebe. He was one of the best action directors in Hollywood—a veteran of two hundred or so westerns, serials, and low-budget action pictures dating back to 1916. Ford Beebe had a full head of white hair and penetrating blue eyes that were warm and actually twinkled. When he was on the set, he wore zip-up soft leather boots and a wide-brimmed white felt western-type hat. He was my director/writer for every Bomba performance I made. I count myself very fortunate to have worked under his direction and tutelage.

MILLER: But wasn't it tough making pictures on a tight budget with all those animals running around?

SHEFFIELD: When you're making action films, working with animals, and you're on a tight budget, you must have an appreciation for the overall effect of the scene and not get carried away with every detail. Forget about it; you are never going to get the animals, the actors, and the action to conform to some dreamed-up notion of what exactly should happen. In fact, more often than not on the *Bomba* pictures, all hell would break loose as soon as the director called for action! The animals would go one way, the actors another. The fight would end up down by the river instead of under the tree. Meanwhile, the camera operator is going nuts trying to follow it all and "stay with the money."

MILLER: Though you were still a teenager, were you a pretty accomplished performer by then?

SHEFFIELD: The crew called me "One-Take Johnny." My father taught me the business well. I knew the scene, hit my mark, found my light, and knew my lines. Ford told me many times that he appreciated that from me. We all appreciated Ford. He didn't have to make a complete master shot for each scene. He would let the long shots roll until he had enough footage for the film cutter to work with. Ford had the film all cut in his head and didn't need the expense of shooting a lot of extra footage that would never be used in the movie.

This was in sharp contrast to what Mr. Dick Thorpe was permitted to do with MGM money on the *Tarzan* pictures. At Monogram we had to be fast. The director had to know what the next setup was going to be and communicate that to the crew clearly and decisively.

MILLER: If your whole movie career involves running around in little more than a loincloth, as yours did, isn't there a constant demand to stay fit?

SHEFFIELD: Let's face it, the camera puts a few pounds on you. That's bad enough when you have a round, "out-of-focus" face like mine, but Bomba ran around in a leopard skin G-string and that compounded my problem.

All my female fans have told me that if Bomba ever showed up with a flabby "bod," they would have split—abandoned me immediately—and all those theaters would have been empty. Fortunately, I had a swimmer's build, lots of athletic friends, and lived in Hollywood, the Sex Capital of the World. We could ski in the morning, surf in the afternoon, and dance at night. I never went to the gym. I didn't have to, thank God. The secrets of my Bomba fitness program were swimming, snow skiing, surfing, and dancing, so I had no excuses for not keeping in good shape.

MILLER: In 1955 *Bomba* finally came to an end. What did you think was going to happen next?

SHEFFIELD: My dad put together the pilot for *Bantu*, a weekly TV series. We put a lot into it, but it didn't sell. After *Bantu* failed, I decided to get out of the business for good.

MILLER: What was life like for you when you weren't a jungle boy anymore?

SHEFFIELD: On many evenings, I was back at the beach surfing and playing Hawaiian and Tahitian music for the girls around our beach fire. That's how I became a Southern California surf and ski bum. There were some other actors on the beach back then. Do you remember Irish McCalla, better known as TV's Sheena, Queen of the Jungle? She was there. So was Richard Jaeckel. We had plenty of luaus and loved Hawaiian and Tahitian music.

Afterword

Johnny Sheffield was doing some repair work up a ladder at his home in Chula Vista on October 15, 2010, when he slipped and fell. Though his injury was not fatal, he suffered a heart attack in the hospital and died.

Johnny Sheffield and I used to banter over the meaning of the word *umgawa*, which is uttered so frequently in his *Tarzan* movies. Though I'm sure he didn't get this from any linguistic expert, Johnny said "umgawa" was a positive word. If you look at a shapely woman, wiggle your eyebrows, and say, "Umgawa!" he assured me, she will know you're paying her a compliment. So Johnny and I used the word for our formal greetings to each other and our farewells.

And so I'm going to use it right now as my final message to my "jungle boy" pal, a bright and energetic child actor whose youthful performances are still as good as they were sixty years ago: "Umgawa, Johnny! I know you and Big Johnny are looking down at us from way up on the escarpment where only the bravest dare to go. Enjoy the view, my friend—and watch out for that damned chimpanzee who somehow found his way up there, too!"

Anne Shirley

Interview by James Bawden

Her name at birth was Dawn Paris, but she became a popular child actress under the name Dawn O'Day until 1934, when she played one of the most famous characters in children's literature—Anne Shirley from *Anne of Green Gables*—and liked that name well enough to take it as her own.

Anne Shirley had already notched some wonderful credits as Dawn O'Day. She was the child kidnapped by outlaws in Tom Mix's *Riders of the Purple Sage* (1925) and the young Anastasia in *Rasputin and the Empress* (1932). Under her new screen name, Shirley landed a number of solid roles as a teenager in films like *Steamboat round the Bend* (1935), *Stella Dallas* (1937), in which she played Barbara Stanwyck's daughter, earning an Oscar nomination, and *The Devil and Daniel Webster* (1941).

Those who remember her most vividly as the sweet and innocent Anne in *Anne of Green Gables* and its sequel *Anne of Windy Poplars* (1940) surely won't forget her metamorphosis into the sexy, naughty younger sister of Claire Trevor in 1944's *Murder, My Sweet*, the classic film noir.

Shirley retired after that scorching role and what already was a pretty full lifetime in films. She was married three times—first to actor John Payne, then to film producer Adrian Scott, and finally to screenwriter Charles Lederer, who remained her husband until his death in 1976.

Despite that sexy role in 1944, wholesomeness was always Anne Shirley's primary stock in trade.

Setting the Scene

In the summer of 1974, during one of my first trips to Los Angeles, I discovered there was a listed phone number for Anne Shirley Lederer in the Malibu directory, so I dialed the number. When a woman with a very charming manner answered, I plunged ahead and told her I'd watched the

Anne Shirley in her Oscar-nominated role as Laurel in King Vidor's 1937 *Stella Dallas*. Courtesy of United Artists.

1934 movie *Anne of Green Gables* at least half a dozen times on TV and really wanted to interview the original, authentic, one and only Anne Shirley.

"Look," she said. "Your voice sounds pleasant and I've never been interviewed in thirty years, so . . ."

And two hours later there she was, striding through the lobby of the Century Plaza Hotel: no pigtails and gingham gown, but rather salt and pepper hair and a fancy Chanel suit. She said her driver would be picking her up promptly in two hours. "So, let's get started, Bub."

The Interview

BAWDEN: Could you talk a bit about how you started out in movies?

SHIRLEY: I started out at twenty-two months, working for fashion spreads in New York magazines, and was soon in flickers. Lucky for me these were silent days because I could not speak. Many were "crawl-ons"— I can't call them walk-ons. That was all in Manhattan, but when things got tight for money, my mother moved us to Hollywood. I'd like to regale you with stories. But I only have dim memories of the director chattering away, which was possible before sound.

I do recall *The Callahans and the Murphys* [1927] when I was only nine, because Marie Dressler's breath was something else. Yes, that great lady could belt back a few and then some. There was 1928's *Sins of the Fathers*, where I was Ruth Chatterton's daughter, and then Jean Arthur [played the part] as a grown up. I don't think we ever met. I remember Ruth's lah-dee-dah British accent, that's it. I did three movies with Barbara Stanwyck: first *So Big* [1932] and *The Purchase Price* [1932]. She was extra nice to us kids and years later we made a big hit at Goldwyn [Studio]— 1937's *Stella Dallas*. She remembered me, but as Dawn. It helped that we had a connection.

BAWDEN: Why do you consider the film *Finishing School* [1934] to be the turning point in your career?

SHIRLEY: Oh, yes. A director named George Nicholls hired me as one of three ingenues for *Finishing School*. But the RKO head office gave the part to Mitzi Green, who was a big "kidlet" star of the time. But [Mitzi's] father read the script and said the part wasn't big enough, so she quit days before shooting started and I was suddenly in. Then RKO assigned Nicholls to direct *Anne of Green Gables*. It was going to be one of RKO's big pictures of the year, with location work to be done on Prince Edward Island. Of course, I'd read the book by [Canadian] author L. M. Montgomery— every girl my age had. It already was a classic.

Then RKO experienced yet another salary freeze and decreed it all had to be done on the back lot. [Some second-unit photography had already been shot on Prince Edward Island, the locale of the story.] George said he needed somebody he could trust to deliver [a performance] and remembered me.

Right at that time I really was Anne—as garrulous and gawky as she was. It made for a perfect fit. They even changed my name to the character's. And that was fine with me. It wasn't unheard of, you see: Tom Brown's name had been changed for the film *Tom Brown of Culver* [1932]. And my mother legally changed her name, too, to Mimi Shirley.

BAWDEN: What do you remember about the filming?

SHIRLEY: That fine old Broadway star O. P. Heggie was the bachelor farmer Matthew and Helen Westley was Marilla, his sister, who looked after him. I was the orphan who came to live with them. Mr. Heggie spoke so slowly, but not that way in person. He later told me it was a Broadway trick to make people pay attention. He and Helen made a pet out of me, always complimentary after a good take. I wasn't really acting, just being me and with these marvelous back lot sets to play on.

It was a huge hit, made modestly, not cheaply—an A picture that really brought in the family trade. RKO was a women's studio: that year the biggest stars were Irene Dunne, Katharine Hepburn, Ann Harding, and Constance Bennett, who left at year's end. There were the Rogers-Astaire pictures shooting, but I never had the gumption to sneak in and watch.

The picture made me Anne Shirley. Even today letters addressed to Anne Shirley, Hollywood, somehow get to me. How do I explain to those little girls watching me on TV that I'm somewhat older these days?

BAWDEN: Then you immediately went over to Fox for Will Rogers's last picture. [He died in Alaska in an airplane crash before the movie, *Steamboat round the Bend,* was released.]

SHIRLEY: He had all his dialogue up on boards. But he never looked at the boards. He'd just say what he wanted to. I was shy, so I couldn't explain the huge fights between him and [director] John Ford. The Ford stock company was there in force: brother Francis Ford, Irvin S. Cobb, Stepin Fetchit. They'd kid around between takes while I was off for some obligatory schooling. Mr. Ford never asked me back, so I'm guessing he thought me inadequate. Both men kidded me about the slacks I wore, which Mr. Rogers whispered, in all sincerity, might make some people think I was a loose woman.

BAWDEN: With the huge success of *Anne of Green Gables,* why was there no immediate sequel?

Pesky Tom Brown pulls Anne Shirley's pigtail in *Anne of Green Gables* (1934). James Bawden collection.

SHIRLEY: For the same reason there was no sequel to *Gone with the Wind* [1939] or most of the other hits of the time. Studios didn't think in those terms. But I remember one that was attempted at RKO right then—*Son of Kong*—was a real flop. We finally got around to making a sequel in 1940 when few people cared to remember the original: *Anne of Windy Poplars*. And I can report nobody ever asks me about that. The Anne character had grown up to become a schoolteacher and she encounters gossip in her new position. Michael Kanin [Garson Kanin's brother] wrote the script.

BAWDEN: Instead, I guess, they started casting you as a precocious teen in "programmers."

SHIRLEY: No! In the next, *Chasing Yesterday* [1935], Mr. Heggie and Miss Westley were back and the story was by Anatole France. I was the waif needing a custodian. The same story as Anne. But definitely not a programmer. Then I did *Chatterbox* [1936], where I'm trying to make it as an actress, just like my mother. And there was a 1936 remake of *M'Liss*, which had been a big hit for Mary Pickford. Mr. Nicholls directed both *Chatterbox* and *M'Liss*. RKO saw us as a team.

BAWDEN: What was it like to work at RKO?

SHIRLEY: Well, it was an amalgamation of several studios, so it had several lots all over town and not one big one. I'd do one scene at what used to be Pathe, then one at Radio, then back again. There wasn't as much money to spend as [at] MGM, but I thought our stories were better because you could be yourself a little more. I wouldn't have lasted long at MGM. My pictures tended to make money and as I inched towards eighteen the studio made me a sort of teenage star girls could relate to. And let's face it, I stayed on for more than ten years through many RKO presidents. They'd troop us in to meet the latest president and we'd be back a few years later. During the Depression RKO was always losing money.

BAWDEN: You got your only Oscar nomination for *Stella Dallas*. What do you remember about that one?

SHIRLEY: Just how powerful Barbara Stanwyck was. Through sheer force of personality, she could make a scene work. I was originally going to do it with Ruth Chatterton as the mother. But she'd hated [director] William Wyler so on *Dodsworth* she refused the role. And after Stanwyck was in, Sam Goldwyn upped and [replaced] Wyler with King Vidor. Ruthie heard about it and went ballistic, I'm told.

King was a lovely man. Very meticulous. He'd explain every scene, say what he was looking for. If there was a lot of tension, Missy [Stanwyck's nickname] would reply with a dirty phrase that would have everyone laughing. She was only thirty, playing at least a decade older. Later on there was a falling-out with Vidor when he nixed her for *The Fountainhead* because by that time [Stanwyck] really was in her forties. I had that happen to me and it's always humiliating.

BAWDEN: How often did people mistake you for Olivia de Havilland?

SHIRLEY: Well, I replaced her on one day's notice for *Saturday's Children* [1940] because she said she would not do remakes. The clothes fit perfectly! And we were both up for Melanie in *Gone with the Wind*. David Selznick had me test for it, but Leslie Howard was already cast and our twenty-five-year age difference just could not be explained away. When he tested with Livvie, he had a blond wig and cosmetic touches that made him look younger. But I honestly do not think I could have done that part—maybe ten years later! Livvie and I then worked together in *Government Girl* [1943] and I could see how opinionated she was. Plus she had great reserves of egotism, which every movie actress needs. I was as shy as a church mouse, I'm afraid.

BAWDEN: A lot of people say *A Man to Remember* [1939] contains your finest role.

SHIRLEY: One of the best. It was a remake of *Sweepings* [1933], which starred Lionel Barrymore. And it was better. Garson Kanin was a new director the studio was pushing along and he made it without much studio interference. And it wound up on the *New York Times* Best Ten list and I got wonderful reviews. Edward Ellis starred as a country doctor who takes in a baby—I was the grown-up girl. Edward was thin, dour, not at all sympathetic. He was the title character in the movie *The Thin Man* [1934]. Audiences warmed to him as the movie unfolded. He seemed just so natural. We worked into the night every night and the script was superior. It was by Dalton Trumbo.

BAWDEN: Another big critical hit was *All That Money Can Buy* [1941] from the Stephen Vincent Benét story *The Devil and Daniel Webster.*

SHIRLEY: Edward Arnold and Walter Huston went right at it. And there was Jane Darwell, Gene Lockhart. I was the wife of Jimmy [James] Craig, who looked like a young Clark Gable. And that ruined his chances for stardom on his own. I don't think it made much money. It was a prestigious thing.

So was *Vigil in the Night* [1940], where I played Carole Lombard's sister. It was very heavy stuff. I was a negligent nurse and a patient dies under my care. Carole told me she wanted to only play drama. She was sick of being typecast in screwball comedies. Me, I'd have given anything to do just one good comedy.

BAWDEN: Well, what about *Lady Bodyguard* [1943]? Wasn't that funny?

SHIRLEY: It was supposed to be light but it was awful. Then I did *Bombardier* [1943] and both my leading men, Randolph Scott and Pat O'Brien, had been born in the nineteenth century. I looked like I was having a fling with guys old enough to be my father. But leading men were scarce right then.

BAWDEN: It's ironical that your last film—*Murder, My Sweet*—was just about your biggest commercial hit.

SHIRLEY: I was twenty-six and I wanted out. Too shy, I guess. I'd already worked twenty-four years. I had no real life. I only lasted that long to make my mother proud of me. I did this one to wind up my contract and I loved doing it. The director, Eddie Dmytryk, told me he'd hired Dick Powell as the hardboiled detective Philip Marlowe and I gasped. Like most

From left: Claire Trevor, Miles Mander, Anne Shirley, and Dick Powell in *Murder, My Sweet* (1944). This was Shirley's final screen role. James Bawden collection.

people, I thought of Dick as a crooner. But Eddie said he had a Boy Scout's face but with deep wrinkles indicating newfound cynicism. And it gave Dick a whole new career just as I was winding up. At one point Claire Trevor and I went over to Eddie and tried to get him to let us change parts. I think I just might have managed but Claire looked too mature to play the distraught daughter, although she told me she was tired of playing hard-boiled types. Every actor hates playing what they do best.

BAWDEN: Then you just slipped away?

SHIRLEY: To a successful marriage [to Charles Lederer], and I had two kids to bring up. My daughter, Julie Payne, acts, and Daniel is a poet. I thought I might stay in the business as a dialogue director but that category has been abandoned in a foolish attempt to cut costs.

But letters? I'm getting a lot these days and all addressed to a teenager who disappeared a very long time ago. Old movie stars definitely do not fade away. We've just moved over to TV's *Late Show.*

Afterword

Husband Charles Lederer died suddenly in 1976 and Anne Shirley decided not to give any more interviews. She died of lung cancer at age seventy-five on July 4, 1993, still very much the well-heeled Beverly Hills matron. She lived long enough, though, to see *Anne of Green Gables* revived as a spectacularly popular TV production starring Canadian Megan Follows as Anne Shirley, which led to a major boom in TV versions of Lucy Maud Montgomery stories.

V

Famous Monsters
of Filmland

John Carradine

Interview by Ron Miller and Darla Miller

John Carradine spent the last half of his long, long acting career as a "name above the title" attraction in the realm of horror movies, each one seemingly more cheaply made than the last. If scholars of the cinema tend to write him off as unimportant because he starred in the likes of *Billy the Kid vs. Dracula* (1966) and *Hillbillys in a Haunted House* (1967), they should be reminded that he also was in John Ford's *Stagecoach* (1939) and *The Grapes of Wrath* (1940), Rouben Mamoulian's *Blood and Sand* (1941), and Cecil B. DeMille's *The Ten Commandments* (1956).

Those lucky enough to have seen him perform live onstage in a Shakespeare play would have little doubt that Carradine could have gained acting immortality as a fine dramatic actor of the stage. Theater was, in fact, his real passion and he put a great deal of money into his own theater endeavors over the years.

Possibly the most prolific of all modern actors, Carradine estimated that he had been in more than three hundred movies—and his versatility was obvious. He was a solid performer in scores of westerns, dozens of period costume pictures, and scads of crime dramas. In 1936 alone, he appeared in thirteen films. He costarred with Shirley Temple in *Captain January* and *Dimples,* played the lute and sang in John Ford's *Mary of Scotland* with Katharine Hepburn, and appeared in a musical (*Anything Goes* with Bing Crosby and Ethel Merman), a Foreign Legion adventure saga (*Under Two Flags*), a big-budget Technicolor romance (*The Garden of Allah*) with Charles Boyer and Marlene Dietrich, and a frontier adventure (*Daniel Boone*).

Most important, 1936 was the year he played his first really memorable villainous role—the nasty sergeant who torments Warner Baxter in John Ford's *The Prisoner of Shark Island*. After moviegoers saw him in that

John Carradine as an Italian courtier who serenades Mary Stuart in John Ford's *Mary of Scotland* (1936). James Bawden collection.

role, he was continually in great demand as one of the screen's most dastardly heavies.

Carradine was renowned for his reliability as an actor, in spite of his reputation as a heavy drinking man. He was married four times and was involved in acrimonious divorce and custody wrangles with his first two wives. He fathered three sons—David, Keith, and Robert—and adopted a fourth son, Bruce, who was his first wife's son from an earlier marriage. All became actors.

As a matter of fact, Carradine fathered one of the most successful acting dynasties in Hollywood history. Son David became a star in movies and television whose greatest fame came from his popular TV series *Kung Fu* (1972–1975). Keith is a respected movie, TV, and stage leading man who played Will Rogers in an acclaimed Broadway musical biography of the famed humorist and won an Academy Award for "I'm Easy," the song he composed and performed in Robert Altman's 1975 film *Nashville*. Robert has appeared in many popular movies and TV shows and is probably best known for his starring role in the 1984 *Revenge of the Nerds* film and its sequels. David's daughter Calista, Robert's daughter Ever, and Keith's son Cade and daughter Martha Plimpton are all actors.

Setting the Scene

Ron Miller and his wife, Darla Miller, each interviewed John Carradine on separate occasions. We have merged the interviews, but each has described the circumstances of their individual interviews.

RON MILLER: My interview with John Carradine came in 1971 while he was in rehearsal for a performance as Shylock in Shakespeare's *The Merchant of Venice* at the Comedia Repertory Theater in Palo Alto, California. We met while he was breakfasting in his room at a local hotel before leaving for the rehearsal hall. He was then sixty-five. Carradine was candid, articulate, and extremely personable. Fans of his horror movies would have been severely let down because there was nothing even the slightest bit sinister about him. Later that week, I attended the opening night performance and was delighted by his masterful performance in the classic role.

DARLA MILLER: My interview with John Carradine was in December 1978 as he was preparing to play the role of Ebenezer Scrooge in a production of *A Christmas Carol* onstage for the San Jose Theater Guild in San Jose, California. He met me for coffee in the cafeteria of the newspaper where I worked as a feature writer, the *San Jose Mercury News*. Carradine, who was then seventy-two, came wearing a long black overcoat and a stylish black hat. I felt he looked more debonair than devilish, his piercing blue eyes more kindly than sinister.

The Interview

R. MILLER: By now it seems clear that you're the cornerstone of a very impressive acting dynasty-in-progress. How important is family to you?

CARRADINE: Well, I'm half Johnny Reb, and southerners are very family conscious, you know. All my father's relatives are very conscious of the family background. They've studied genealogy of the family and they've traced us back to William the Conqueror.

R. MILLER: Tell me about your own immediate family background.

CARRADINE: My father was a Southern gentleman. He was born in Natchez, Mississippi. His father was a Methodist preacher, a very distinguished and famous one. And my father studied law. Somewhere along the line, he was a mural painter. Then he went to New York and became a journalist. He worked in that profession to the point where he was London correspondent for the Associated Press. He died when I was very small. I have a half-brother and a half-sister. My half-brother is a Ph.D. from Harvard who teaches school in Cape Cod and builds boats. My mother was a surgeon. Her last post was on the staff of the Cancer Clinic in Philadelphia. I was sent to boarding school until my mother married again, when I was ten. Then I lived with my mother and stepfather in Philadelphia.

R. MILLER: How early did you decide you were destined to be an actor?

CARRADINE: I was taken to a performance of *The Merchant of Venice* when I was fourteen and was very impressed. Shylock was played by Robert Mantell, who was then the premier Shakespearian actor in America. He had the greatest voice I ever heard in my life. I walked out of the theater on a cloud and said, "That's what I want to be!"

D. MILLER: Is it true you actually memorized the play as a teenager?

CARRADINE: I made a 25¢ bet with a school fellow that I could learn the whole damn play in a week—and I did. I was fourteen at the time. But I was thirty-eight before I ever played Shylock.

R. MILLER: Speaking of voices, you certainly have one of the great ones yourself. Was your speaking voice natural or did you have to cultivate it to make it what it is today?

CARRADINE: Oh, yes, I had to. I had a good natural voice—a good, light, clear baritone voice. And I was a singer at first, you know. I wasn't getting very far because I wasn't very good. I had no formal training and there were so many singers around the Los Angeles area when I started out. They could sing circles around me. So I quit singing and concentrated on acting. I wanted to play Shakespeare and I did some work with an old semiretired Shakespearean actor. Anyway, this old fellow took a fancy to me and one day said, "John, you're the only young actor I know who can do all the good parts. But you lack voice for them. You need a stronger and a heavier voice. And you need the last note *d-o-w-n!*" So he gave me an exercise that tore my throat right out of my neck! I thought I'd never be able to speak again! But in about a month, I noticed a difference. He said, "Don't baby your voice. Treat it roughly. You'll never have one till you've lost it half a dozen times." And so I used to go out to the Hollywood Bowl late at night or early in the morning and shout Shakespeare to twenty thousand empty seats. I did this every night for five years. By that time, I was a basso.

R. MILLER: Okay, I'm already shocked to learn that you once were a singer. Do you ever sing in public today?

CARRADINE: Of course! I've done *Paint Your Wagon* [onstage] several times and I have more songs than the lead actor. If I'd known I was going to be a bass before I was thirty, I would have stuck to singing, for there are very few of them around.

R. MILLER: I know you started in movies as early as 1930, but how long did it take before you were really successful?

CARRADINE: It was when I played the prison commandant, the tormentor of Dr. Mudd [Warner Baxter] in *The Prisoner of Shark Island*. I think it was my seventy-fifth role in a movie.

D. MILLER: How did you get along with the director, John Ford?

CARRADINE: When I first met John Ford, we didn't get along at all. He wanted me to play my role like a blithering idiot and I said no. We finally compromised. I did some of it the way he wanted, but I couldn't resist doing it my way. I figure he didn't like me for sour apples. But when we actually started shooting, we got along fine.

D. MILLER: You went on to become a regular member of Ford's so-called stock company with films like *Stagecoach*, *The Grapes of Wrath*, *Tobacco Road* [1941], and *The Man Who Shot Liberty Valance* [1962]. How did he work?

CARRADINE: Ford was a very peculiar man. You had to second-guess him all the time. He could be very cute. He could deliberately get actors mad at him to supply them with proper motivation for scenes where they were angry.

D. MILLER: What do you consider your best performance?

CARRADINE: My best performance was in *The Grapes of Wrath*. [He played the itinerant preacher.] But my favorite film was *Captains Courageous* [1937]. It probably was a personal favorite because it was a sea picture and I'm a boating man.

R. MILLER: I've seen some of your earliest appearances in horror movies of the 1930s—a small part in *The Invisible Man* [1933], the organ player for Boris Karloff's Satanic cult in *The Black Cat* [1934], and one of the hunters who finds the Frankenstein monster in the blind man's hut in *The Bride of Frankenstein* [1935]. But I've heard that you are very uncomfortable with being lumped in with the so-called horror actors like Karloff, Lugosi, and Chaney. Is that true?

CARRADINE: Oh, yes, yes! It's so ridiculous. I never played a monster in my life. I did very few of those pictures, most of them all at one period. I did them to finance my repertory company. I just sent the money right up to Equity, the stagehands' union, and the railroads and the costumers. I did it for that reason.

D. MILLER: Did you ever do a picture that you were ashamed of?

CARRADINE: There are pictures I wish I hadn't done. One of them was *Billy the Kid vs. Dracula*. I was broke and needed the money. Finally I started turning down the bad ones. My conscience took over and I'd say, "I won't read lines and vomit at the same time."

R. MILLER: Well, even though you're a well-known character actor today, it looks as if you've done quite a few films that one might say were beneath your dignity.

CARRADINE: More or less because of my responsibilities. I still have an awful [financial] load to carry. I've been carrying a heavy load for thirty years. I've got a ways to go before I can call my life my own.

R. MILLER: In the early 1930s, when you were first making a name for yourself in movies, Boris Karloff was the big name in the horror genre. I know you worked on the stage with him even before you made films together. What did you think of him and how did you two get along?

CARRADINE: Boris was a very fine actor. I have seen him do marvelous things. We did a show together onstage back then—in fact it was the only time we've ever been on the stage together. [The play was *Window Panes*, in 1929.] He played a brutalized Russian peasant. He looked like Rasputin with a typical peasant shirt and boots. It was a superb characterization. Then he did a play right after that in which he played a wily, culti-

276

John Carradine reprises his frequent vampire role in *Billy the Kid vs. Dracula* (1966). His victim is Melinda Plowman. Ron Miller collection.

vated man of the world—a Russian nobleman, a general who had some of the qualities of the prefect in *Crime and Punishment*. I said to myself: "Gee whiz! This guy's an actor—a hell of an actor!" But he never got a chance to really show what he could do on the screen. Well, he did one picture in which you could see he was a hell of an actor. It was a thing called *The Body Snatcher* [the 1945 Val Lewton production, directed by Robert Wise.] For my money, he walked away with it.

R. MILLER: Do you think playing Frankenstein's monster put his career in a box that he seldom got a chance to leave?

CARRADINE: Yes. Boris, you see, was stuck with this. I had turned it down—the Frankenstein part. We had been doing that play together in 1928. I was making $50 a week and he was getting $75. He was the heavy and I was the comedian. We played for ten weeks in Los Angeles and then Boris went back to driving a truck and I went back to pacing the boulevard, looking for another job. Then I got a call [from] Universal and I found out the role was playing a monster and I didn't have any dialogue, so I turned it down. About three months later, they got Boris. He accepted and, of course, it made him a star. But it typed him and I'm sure he has never ceased to regret this.

R. MILLER: Even though you demean the horror films, why do you think so many wonderful stage actors like Karloff, Bela Lugosi, Claude Rains, and yourself all became the real "stars" of horror?

CARRADINE: Forgetting for the moment that I have played some of this sort of thing, I would say it's the most difficult thing to do and do well. A bad actor would overdo them. Of course, I can make mistakes. I had a chance to do the monster in *The Munsters* [the 1964–1966 TV show]. Unfortunately for my pocketbook, I was doing a picture and couldn't get away. So I lost the part to Fred Gwynne. Now Fred did something with it that I wouldn't have done. I would have played the makeup [let the bizarre Frankenstein makeup set the tone for the character]. But Fred didn't. He played a real sweet guy, which makes the whole thing. And he was absolutely right about it. [Carradine did land a role in *The Munsters*, playing the occasional character of Mr. Gateman, the mortician.]

R. MILLER: Now I'm sure your horror movie fans would argue that you did something "absolutely right" yourself with your portrayal of Count Dracula, especially in your two Universal horror movies of 1944–1945, *House of Frankenstein* and *House of Dracula*.

CARRADINE: Yes. I went back to the Dracula of the book by Bram Stoker and did him with top hat, moustache, and dignity.

R. MILLER: Many of us rank your performance in *Bluebeard* [1944] as your best and most original in that sort of film.

CARRADINE: It was directed by Edgar Ulmer, who did *The Black Cat* in 1934. He created a very moody atmosphere and I had a chance to play a fully developed character and even play some rather romantic scenes. It was also the first film in which I got single star billing. It was the biggest part I ever had in a picture and certainly not the easiest to play. It wasn't a bad picture until the end, when they got those two former Mack Sennett cops in—that was completely out of left field. It very nearly ruined the whole picture.

R. MILLER: And it was one of the few pictures in which you actually got the girl—several of them.

CARRADINE: Yeah, yeah. Except that I killed them all. There was an implication that I was a successful lover, though. I very seldom have had that experience in pictures. [One of Carradine's women in *Bluebeard*, Sonia Sorel, became his second wife in 1944. Their marriage ended in divorce in 1956.]

R. MILLER: After years of playing heavies on the screen, do you think the audience always suspects you even when you're not playing a villain?

CARRADINE: Oh, yes. Just because I'm in it. For instance, they had me in a part in a Sherlock Holmes picture [1939's *Hound of the Baskervilles*] with Basil Rathbone. I was the butler. They made me wear a beard to make me look sinister. Of course, no English butler ever wore a beard. But the idea was for the audience to say, "He did it! He did it!" as soon as they saw me. But I didn't. I was only the red herring. Movies sometimes use me for just that purpose.

Afterword

Carradine continued to appear in increasingly lower-class horror movies well into the 1980s. He played the surgeon who turned Rex Reed into Raquel Welch in *Myra Breckinridge* (1970) and he was deep into self-parody as the mad scientist who unleashes a giant, crawling female breast in Woody Allen's *Everything You Always Wanted to Know about Sex (but Were Afraid to Ask)* (1972). His last major film was *Peggy Sue Got Married* (1986) and his final screen appearance was in a 1990 horror movie called *Buried Alive*. He is sometimes credited for *Bikini Drive-in* (1995), but only his photo appears in that film—as a character's grandfather.

Though Carradine received few awards during his acting career, he did win a daytime Emmy Award for his performance in a 1985 Young People's Special called *Umbrella Jack*. He has a star on Hollywood's Walk of Fame and was inducted into the Western Performers Hall of Fame at Oklahoma City's Western Heritage Museum.

On November 27, 1988, after climbing to the top of Milan's Gothic cathedral, the Duomo, Carradine was stricken and rushed to a hospital, where he died of multiple organ failures. Like frequent costar Boris Karloff, he had suffered from crippling arthritis through much of his later years. He was eighty-two at the time of his death and was still married to his fourth wife, Emily.

Lon Chaney Jr.

Interview by Ron Miller

Being born the son of one of America's most famous movie stars was a challenge to Creighton Tull Chaney, whose father, Lon Chaney, was the most acclaimed character actor of the silent movie era, a man whose name was synonymous with terror after his performances in such classic films as *The Hunchback of Notre Dame* (1923) and *The Phantom of the Opera* (1925).

The tall, rugged-looking Creighton did not seek an acting career, even though he'd been carried onstage by his famous father even in his infancy. Instead, Creighton tried a number of other careers and was quite successful in the appliance industry, where he did some pioneering work in development of thermostatic devices for the home.

But after his father's death in 1930, young Chaney considered taking advantage of the many offers he received to become an actor. It was, after all, a time of economic depression in America and it was tempting to take the money for what appeared to be simple work. Chaney at first resisted the pleas of film producers to take his father's name but finally relented, although he still refused to step into the kinds of horror movie roles that had made his father famous.

Chaney learned his new trade in westerns, serials, and adventure pictures, where his rangy physique made him loom large. By 1939, when he was cast in the pivotal role of Lennie Small in the movie version of John Steinbeck's novel and stage play *Of Mice and Men,* he was finally regarded as a serious actor who could stand on his own merits.

Then in 1941 Lon Chaney Jr. agreed to take a leading role in a horror movie at Universal, where his dad had made the classic *The Phantom of the Opera,* becoming the studio's new horror star with *Man-Made Monster,* followed by the role that became his signature in the horror field, that of the eponymous lead in *The Wolf Man* (1941). Thereafter, Universal put him into the leading roles in all of its horror franchises—he played Fran-

Lon Chaney Jr. in his most famous horror role in *The Wolf Man* (1941). Courtesy of Universal Pictures.

kenstein's monster (*The Ghost of Frankenstein*, 1942), a mummy (*The Mummy's Tomb*, 1942), and Count Dracula (*The Son of Dracula*, 1943).

Chaney rapidly became known as one of Hollywood's wilder characters, a serious drinker whose benders were legendary. By the end of the 1940s, the initial horror movie boom was over, even at Universal, and

Lon Chaney Jr. with Betty Field in *Of Mice and Men* (1939). Courtesy of United Artists.

Chaney slipped from leading roles to character parts. Still a very capable actor, he turned in some of his best work in those supporting roles, including as the reluctant old lawman in *High Noon* (1952) who doesn't help hero Gary Cooper fight off the men who've come to town to kill him on his wedding day, the old alcoholic in *Not as a Stranger* (1955), and the ex-con who talks a mob out of lynching escaped convicts Tony Curtis and Sidney Poitier in *The Defiant Ones* (1958), the latter two films directed by Stanley Kramer.

But in the last twenty years of his life, Chaney wasn't offered many roles of that quality. Instead, he fell into a long series of cheap horror films that tried to cash in on his famous name. Despite that decline, though, Chaney remained extremely popular with young fans who kept rediscovering him through his rich legacy of great films from the salad days of his long career.

Setting the Scene

Getting an interview with Lon Chaney Jr. was one of the bolder adventures of my career as a journalist because it came about in 1958 while I was still a junior in college, studying filmmaking at UCLA and sending freelance stories to my California hometown newspaper, the *Santa Cruz Sentinel,* for $20 a pop. I looked Chaney up in the Academy Players Directory and called his agency, asking for an interview, stressing the fact that I was a college student who had seen many of his films, even in that era when there was no home video or cable network like Turner Classic Movies where young people could track down movies no longer in theaters.

To my delight, Chaney agreed to the interview and gave me directions to his home in the Hollywood Hills. I had no car, so I had to call a taxi and hope I had enough money to pay my fare. As it turned out, the cab driver was a swell guy. Seeing my notebook, he asked what I was up to. When I told him, he got excited because he had once worked as a valet to Lon Chaney Sr. and remembered him with great awe and respect.

Chaney Jr. lived at the very top of Lankershim Boulevard, looking down on Universal City in the North Hollywood area of the San Fernando Valley. From his yard, you could see the famous *Phantom* stage where his dad had reigned in 1925. Chaney was waiting for us at the top of the driveway and was amused that I had come "New York style" in a taxi. When I told him the cabbie had been his dad's valet, Chaney invited the fellow in for a brief chat and shook his hand warmly.

What followed was a long and interesting chat with the extremely gracious and friendly Chaney. He was then working in a western at Universal-International called *Money, Women and Guns* (1958), but he had the afternoon off. He was really enjoying the job, he told me, because he had met several old-timers like himself on the set, guys who liked a good time and remembered the good old days.

The Interview

MILLER: There's a scene near the end of *Man of a Thousand Faces* [1957] in which your dad [played by James Cagney] is dying and hands over his makeup kit to you [played by Roger Smith], seeming to bless your following in his footsteps.

CHANEY: Never happened. They made that up.

MILLER: So your dad didn't expect you to become the next "man of a thousand faces"?

CHANEY: I don't think he saw a future in acting for me. But he did teach me a lot over the years about how to make myself up as unusual

Lon Chaney Jr. visits the set of the 1943 remake of his father's *Phantom of the Opera* at Universal Studios and meets its female star, Susanna Foster. Courtesy of Universal Pictures.

characters. Let me show you a few examples.[Chaney showed me some still photographs of himself in makeup he had personally designed, including a picture of him as the caveman he played in 1940's *One Million B.C.* and one as a mummy.]

MILLER: But you didn't get to do this for your actual scenes in the movies?

CHANEY: No, because of union rules.

MILLER: How much of an ordeal was it to go through the makeup process to become the wolf man?

CHANEY: I had to go in early in the morning and sit through four hours in the makeup chair for the scenes where I turned into a werewolf in stages—and those scenes only lasted a minute on the screen!

MILLER: Was that worse than being made up as Frankenstein's monster for *The Ghost of Frankenstein*?

CHANEY: Yes, but that Frankenstein outfit weighed eighty pounds, so it was worse to have to keep it on so long and work wearing it.

Turhan Bey (*left*) with Kharis (Lon Chaney Jr.), the living mummy, and the unconscious Elyse Knox in *The Mummy's Tomb* (1942). Courtesy of Universal Pictures.

MILLER: You played quite a few death scenes in your movies, but somehow you never really died for good.

CHANEY: It got pretty ridiculous after awhile. They would figure out some tricky way to kill me in one film and then have to think of something even more elaborate to bring me back to life in the next one.

MILLER: As funny as it was, many of your fans think of *Abbott and Costello Meet Frankenstein* [1948] as the end of the classic Universal horror era, not only for you and your costar Bela Lugosi, but for fans of Frankenstein, the wolf man, and Dracula.

CHANEY: I'd been typed before, but never as bad as that. I knew the only thing to do was to refuse all horror roles and go broke. I didn't like the idea of starving, though.

MILLER: The last new horror picture I saw you in was *The Black Sleep* [1956] with Basil Rathbone, John Carradine, and Bela Lugosi. You were practically a bit player.

CHANEY: I moaned when I saw the script for that one. I couldn't see much future in pictures like that, so I made up my mind to get untyped, whether I starved or not.

Afterword

My interview with Lon Chaney Jr. was done before portable tape recorders were readily available, so I took notes by hand. That was nearly sixty years ago and some of my notes are no longer readable, but I do remember Chaney telling me that he was extremely nervous when he replaced Broderick Crawford in the role of Lennie in the stage version of John Steinbeck's *Of Mice and Men,* so nervous that he often threw up in the wings before going on. Yet it was his stage performance that convinced film director Lewis Milestone to pick him for the role in the movie, a performance still ranked as his all-time best.

Chaney also told me many stories about how tough times were for him during the Depression years and how many menial jobs he had to take to make ends meet.

Chaney was married twice, first to Dorothy Hinckley from 1928 to 1937. She was the mother of his two sons, Lon III and Ron, both now deceased. When I visited him, I met his very nice and lovely second wife, Patsy Beck. At the end of our afternoon together, Chaney and Patsy gave me a ride to the city bus route on Santa Monica Boulevard so I could catch the bus to my apartment in West Los Angeles.

I will always remember him as a very warm and decent man. He was stone-cold sober during our interview. His drinking, though, probably helped do him in. He died on July 12, 1973, at San Clemente, California, after his liver failed and he suffered a heart attack. His body was donated to medical science. He was sixty-seven.

Chaney did manage to get a lot of nonmonster character parts in the years after our talk, but he never played a starring role again unless it was in a horror film. His last film was the ultra-cheap *Dracula vs. Frankenstein* (1971). He did work in Woody Allen's 1972 comedy *Everything You Always Wanted to Know about Sex (but Were Afraid to Ask),* but his scene was not in the final cut.

Boris Karloff

Interview by Ron Miller

If Roy Rogers was the "king of the cowboys," then Boris Karloff surely was "king of the monsters."

Born in 1887 in Dulwich, England, as William Henry Pratt, Karloff came from a family of British diplomats but passed up a career in the foreign service to become an actor, emigrating to Canada and touring with various theater companies in small towns all over North America. Though Karloff, who took the new name fairly early in his acting career, appeared on-screen in small roles from 1916 on, at first he failed to establish himself as an emerging talent on either stage or screen, and for years he often had to take menial nonacting jobs in order to survive.

Tall, with dark, sharp features, he tended to get villainous roles in silent movies, often playing ethnic types. His most notable roles were as heavies in silent serials like *Tarzan and the Golden Lion* (1927) and *King of the Kongo* (1929). His first real horror-type role was as an evil hypnotist in *The Bells* (1926) with Lionel Barrymore. He was still little known by movie fans in 1931 when he appeared in Universal's *Frankenstein* as the monster, but his performance created a phenomenal response and he was soon in demand both in Hollywood and in his native England for similar roles.

Karloff enjoyed a long, mostly lucrative career by sticking with his image as a "horror" man, but was widely known in the Hollywood community as a pillar of the British "colony" of Hollywood actors. A cultured man with a taste for gardening, he was married five times. He was a noted collector of children's literature and a doting father whose only daughter, Sara, has helped keep his legacy alive for new generations of fans.

Boris Karloff in his later days as the host of TV's *Thriller* series (1960–1962). Ron Miller collection.

Setting the Scene

Like most boys of my generation, I grew up thinking Boris Karloff was a giant of cinema because he so effectively starred in so many of my favorite scary movies.

In my earliest days in the newspaper business, while working for my hometown newspaper, the *Santa Cruz Sentinel*, I learned that Karloff would be appearing onstage in one of his favorite touring plays, Paul Osborne's *On Borrowed Time*, at the Wharf Theater in Monterey, just across the bay from Santa Cruz. It was 1961.

I called the theater and was delighted to learn that Karloff would sit for an interview during a break from the rehearsal schedule. In those days, small portable tape recorders were not readily available, so I rented a huge console reel-to-reel tape machine and lugged it to Monterey, where a very genial and welcoming Boris Karloff met me for a chat over coffee in the theater's lounge. Much to my regret, I later discovered I'd done something wrong and the tape didn't record our conversation. Fortunately, I also took notes, so what follows is my translation of what I scribbled down more than fifty years ago.

The Interview

MILLER: How did you learn you had been picked to play Frankenstein's monster?

KARLOFF: I was having lunch at the Universal commissary when they gave me the news. I was delighted because times were hard then and it was going to be one of their important films of the year.

MILLER: I was impressed the first time I saw your performance—not by how scary it was but by how you stumbled into view for the first time, looking bewildered and maybe even a little frightened, your hands groping toward the light from above.

KARLOFF: He wasn't a monster then. He was like a newborn baby, taking his first look at the world.

MILLER: Then you weren't playing him like a character in a horror movie at all?

KARLOFF: I was never really a "horror" actor because horror implies revulsion and my films were never gory or ugly. They were exciting, thrillers. I felt *Frankenstein* was more like a legend or a fairy tale.

MILLER: Sad to say, my parents wouldn't let me go see the *Frankenstein* movies until I was practically grown up. But I never heard of a kid who didn't like them.

KARLOFF: My most loyal fans have always been children. They were keen observers and always let the frightening parts thrill them while absorbing the good elements of the story. Their letters to me were always

Boris Karloff as the monster in *Frankenstein* (1931). Courtesy of Universal Pictures and the *Shock* TV package.

full of compassion for the monster. They seemed to regard him as a tragic figure.

MILLER: I've talked with other actors who told me they felt sorry for you because you've been typecast through your entire career since *Frankenstein*.

KARLOFF: I realized I was typed as a monster after the first film, but I've never minded. In fact, I've always been rather grateful to the monster for it. Any actor who becomes typed is very fortunate.

MILLER: By that you mean you've seldom been out of work since—and you usually get to play the leading role?

KARLOFF: That's right. I've been in more than fifty films since then and many television programs.

MILLER: What do you think there is about you that made you so successful in that kind of role? As I sit here talking with you, you strike me as a very charming, well-spoken English gentleman.

KARLOFF: Why, thank you. Anyway, I've never been able to figure it out. I doubt if anyone ever will.

Afterword

A college classmate of mine, a local Monterey girl, was acting in *On Borrowed Time* with Boris Karloff in the Monterey production. She told me he was the gentlest, most loveable man and was very helpful to all the other actors in the production, all of them local people.

Karloff was already beginning to suffer from severe rheumatism at the time of our interview and was slightly bowed when standing. He was not yet confined to a wheelchair, which he was in many of his roles in much later years.

At the time of our brief chat, Karloff was still hosting *Thriller,* the 1960–1962 weekly horror anthology TV series, but had not yet made the series of films with producer Roger Corman at American-International Pictures, including *The Terror* (1963) with the young Jack Nicholson. Karloff's last really important film was *Targets* (1968) for director Peter Bogdanovich, in which he played a character very much like himself, an aging star known for his horror movies. Karloff filmed four Mexican Grade Z horror movies in 1968 that were released in the early 1970s, after his death. A newer generation of youngsters knew him as the voice of the Grinch in the famous 1966 Dr. Seuss animated special, *How the Grinch Stole Christmas.*

Karloff succumbed to pneumonia at King Edward VII Hospital, Midhurst, Sussex, England, on February 2, 1969. He was eighty-one.

Anthony Perkins

Interview by Ron Miller

It must be unsettling for a young moviegoer of today to look back at the beginnings of Anthony Perkins's movie career and discover he was a boyish romantic lead to Jean Simmons in his first picture and another boyish romantic lead to Jane Fonda in her first. Even harder to figure: Perkins earned an Oscar nomination in the Supporting Actor category playing the pacifist son of Gary Cooper in *Friendly Persuasion* (1956). Perkins playing a man who didn't want to kill anyone? Who'd believe that? I mean, isn't this the screen's most memorable deranged killer, Norman Bates in Alfred Hitchcock's *Psycho* (1960)?

But that's how far off some casting ideas can be. Perkins was the theater-trained son of actor Osgood Perkins when he made his first movie in 1953, and he must have looked handsome and presentable enough for filmmakers to think he might turn into a leading man. So he played a few. In fact, Perkins even went through the "teen idol" phase that so many good-looking young actors did in the 1950s, cutting records as a pop singer, although he didn't have any hits like fellow teen idol Tab Hunter had as a singer.

But even before *Psycho,* some directors had tumbled to the fact that Perkins was able to show mental instability more convincingly than he showed leading man "normality." In one of his most acclaimed early performances, he played baseball star Jimmy Piersall, who suffered mental breakdowns, in *Fear Strikes Out* (1957). What's more, Perkins was a closeted homosexual, which may account for his lack of "heat" with some of his glamorous female costars.

In *Psycho,* Hitchcock turned Perkins loose on a character that he inhabited with such vigor that the performance remains one of the most indelible in movie history. Perkins knew he had found a vein of gold when

Anthony Perkins as Norman Bates holding the keys to the Bates Motel in *Psycho III* (1986). Courtesy of Universal Studios.

he played Norman Bates, which is why he came back to the role three times for sequels and even directed one, *Psycho III* (1986).

Although he had a few chances to break away from the screwball characters that followed Norman Bates, Perkins was always at his best playing men who seemed on the verge of coming apart at the seams. A classic example: the arsonist in *Pretty Poison* (1968).

One of his other solid credits was the screenplay for a fine movie, *The*

Anthony Perkins, still a clean-cut teen idol in *Tall Story* (1960), just before he played Norman Bates in *Psycho* (1960) and changed his image forever. That's Jane Fonda looking on. Courtesy of Warner Bros. Television.

Last of Sheila (1973), which he coauthored with Broadway genius Steven Sondheim.

Perkins varied his screen work with stage roles, including a stint in the musical *Greenwillow* (1960) and dramatic roles in *Equus* (1974) and the stage version of Thomas Wolfe's *Look Homeward, Angel* (1958).

Setting the Scene

I was living and working in the Los Angeles area, covering television and the movies for a newspaper syndicate, when I was offered an interview with Perkins, who was starring in and directing *Psycho III*. The interview took place in his office at Universal Studios. Perkins was a very affable and candid fellow, totally unpretentious and eager to share his thoughts about returning to the character of Norman Bates as both star and director.

The Interview

MILLER: I'm pretty sure you don't very often dress in your mother's clothes and attack girls in motel showers, but is there at least a trace of Norman Bates in you?

PERKINS: Norman and I really have a great deal *not* in common. Although I have to admit there are times when I feel that Norman directed the movie [*Psycho III*] while I enacted the role of Norman. And somehow we shared the responsibility.

MILLER: Are you poking a little fun at Norman and the whole *Psycho* phenomenon in this movie? For example, when Diana Scarwid checks out of the same motel room where Janet Leigh was butchered, she apologizes for leaving the shower in such a mess. And you say, "I've seen it worse!"

PERKINS: I swear to you I didn't have my tongue in my cheek. You can let cars run over me. I'll go to my grave over that one. It's all done in deadly earnest.

MILLER: But why be so serious? Hitchcock once told me you had to have a laugh every now and then in one of his pictures just to relieve the tension.

PERKINS: You can't be jocular with this material. It's a tragedy. It's about misplaced passions and obsessions. You can't have your tongue in your cheek with this one.

MILLER: C'mon, there's even a scene where Jeff Fahey checks into the Bates Motel and says he won't be staying around long—and Norman says, "Nobody ever does."

PERKINS: You see, my concept is to play it straight, even if it ends up making the audience laugh.

MILLER: Okay, I think I get you. You're saying you have to act it as if it's not funny, even if it really is.

PERKINS: There you go.

MILLER: Now that more than twenty years have gone by since the original *Psycho,* most of us now consider it to be a masterpiece of directing. You were there to witness it firsthand. Were you watching how he did it, thinking maybe someday you'd be behind the camera?

PERKINS: Maybe this doesn't speak very well about me, but I really wasn't paying much attention to what he was doing while we were making the original film. I was too egotistical at the time. Like most of the other people on the set, I made a dash for the coffee wagon the minute Hitch finished a scene. In fact, I usually led the pack. I didn't stick around to chat about the technical aspects of filmmaking.

MILLER: Okay, now you're playing Norman for the third time. Some critics have declared him to be the scariest villain in screen history. How do you see him?

PERKINS: He's essentially likeable. He's optimistic and he doesn't succumb to his own vices, his own weaknesses. He's constantly trying to find alternative ways of living and being with other people. [In the storyline of *Psycho III,* Norman has been released from the asylum where he was sent at the end of the Hitchcock film. He's trying very hard to resist the temptations that might make him pick up his butcher knife once more.] The tone is everything. The audience would bitterly resent kidding around with this material.

MILLER: Hitchcock was notoriously against doing sequels and never did one, even for his most popular films. Do you think he would approve of these *Psycho* sequels?

PERKINS: I would like to think he'd give the film his blessing, but I didn't approach this as an homage to Hitchcock. There are visual quotations from Hitchcock's work in the movie, but they would be invisible to a Bantu native who hasn't seen *Psycho.*

MILLER: How did you get the directing reins for the movie? Did you refuse to play Norman if they didn't let you direct it?

PERKINS: I know that's the rumor, but it isn't true. I loved the script and wanted to be in it from the start. However, when we were negotiating, I let it drop that I'd direct the movie for nothing if they would give me the chance.

MILLER: How have they treated you as a first-time director? Did they constantly look over your shoulder?

PERKINS: God bless Universal. For a big company that has an efficient, businesslike way of making movies, they are wonderful. From the very first moment, they asked my opinion about everything and included me in everything. In return, I included them in everything.

MILLER: How about returning to the original *Psycho* for just one question? How was Hitchcock to work with?

PERKINS: He was one of the most collaborative and collaboration-prone directors I've ever worked with. Maybe he'd just had it up to here with hearing what a dictator, what an autocrat he was. He delighted in changing his plan if you gave him a good reason. Maybe he just wanted someone to outlive him and someday sit in an office like I'm doing now and say he wasn't that way at all.

Afterword

Psycho III was generally well received and led to a fourth installment, *Psycho IV: The Beginning* (1990), which was made for television. Perkins again played Norman Bates, but did not direct. A remake of *Psycho* done in 1998 by Gus Van Sant was savaged by critics. The Norman Bates character resurfaced in two attempts at a TV series in the 1990s under the title *Bates Motel*. A third try in 2013, this time with Freddie Highmore as Norman Bates, was a success and *Bates Motel* became a popular series, telling the story of Norman and his mother (Vera Farmiga) before the events of *Psycho*.

Perkins, who was gay, had been married once and had fathered two sons. His ex-wife, Berry Berenson, was one of the passengers killed when terrorists crashed two airliners into the World Trade Center towers on September 11, 2001. Perkins died of AIDS on September 12, 1992. He was sixty.

Vincent Price

Interview by James Bawden

Vincent Price was a tall, distinguished-looking actor from St. Louis, Missouri, who was educated at Yale and earned a master's degree in theater arts from the University of London. He began his acting career onstage in London, then returned to the United States, where he quickly made his mark on the Broadway stage. When Hollywood beckoned in the late 1930s, he first was appraised as a potential leading man, but his ability to successfully play character parts became obvious and most of his film career in the 1940s was devoted to a wide variety of such roles.

Because his first film contract was with Universal Pictures, where horror movies were steady profit makers, he appeared in two classics of the genre, the 1939 *Tower of London,* in which Boris Karloff drowned him in a vat of wine, and *The Invisible Man Returns* (1940), in which he played the title role in Universal's first sequel to the 1933 hit *The Invisible Man.*

But it wasn't until Warner Bros. remade its 1933 horror film *The Mystery of the Wax Museum* as 1953's *House of Wax* that Price became closely identified with horror movies. From that point on, he was elevated to mostly "name above the title" starring roles in horror films. His key roles in *The Fly* (1958) and *Return of the Fly* (1959) inspired producer-director Roger Corman to star Price in a long and hugely profitable series of horror movies based on stories from Edgar Allan Poe. Among his other hit genre films were *The Abominable Dr. Phibes* (1971) and its sequel *Dr. Phibes Rises Again!* (1972).

Cashing in on his new role as a premier horror star, Price used it to get many comic bits in TV shows. His reputation and characteristic sinister bearing also earned him the role as on-air host for PBS's much-loved *Mystery!* series, a position he held for eight seasons before giving the job up to Diana Rigg, who had played his daughter in another immense hit film, *Theatre of Blood* (1973).

Vincent Price in his years as the on-air host of PBS's *Mystery!* Courtesy of WGBH-TV, Boston, and the *Mystery!* television series.

Those of us who met him knew Price as a very cultured and likeable man with expertise in art and gourmet cooking, fields in which he wrote several well-received books.

Setting the Scene

One of my first jobs as TV critic at the *Hamilton Spectator* in 1971 was to visit the CHCH-TV studios, where a new horror-comedy series called *The*

Hilarious House of Frightenstein was being taped. At a frantic pace. Comic Billy Van did most of the roles, aided immeasurably by Vincent Price, who was the narrator of all 131 episodes and acted in some of them. On the day I interviewed Price, he was worn out by the schedule, but still polite and humorous.

Imagine his surprise when years later I persuaded Frank Goodman, the publicity agent for PBS's *Mystery!* series, to seat me next to Price three consecutive times during the annual celebrity party for the series: in 1986, 1987, and 1988. The location was always the ballroom of the Beverly Hills Hotel. On the last occasion Price was accompanied by his wife, Coral Browne, whom I had interviewed in 1983 when she starred as herself in the British-made TV movie *An Englishman Abroad*. I remember asking her what it was like to live with Vincent Price and she told me, "The house is like a fine arts museum. Art books everywhere. And then the kitchen is filled with blenders, choppers, recipe books. Many actors live to act. Vinnie acts so he has the funds to buy more art."

Later, I did a telephone interview with Price when he was promoting his great star turn in the 1987 movie *The Whales of August*. I've combined the highlights from all of our chats.

The Interview

BAWDEN: How did you get the call to Hollywood?

PRICE: I was signed to costar with Helen Hayes in the Broadway play *Victoria Regina,* which opened right after Christmas 1935 and ran for over five hundred performances. Eight times a week we got standing ovations, and naturally the Hollywood talent scouts looked in and I got offers. After delicate negotiations, I signed with Universal and made my film debut in *Service de Luxe* [1938] starring Constance Bennett. Connie was quite a character, saying to me the first time we met, "Bad choice. Wrong studio. I'm thirty-five, you're twenty-six. It will look odd in close-ups."

My second film was on loan to Warners as Sir Walter Raleigh in *The Private Lives of Elizabeth and Essex* [1939]. The two stars, Bette Davis and Errol Flynn, loathed each other and you'll notice I'm never seen standing directly beside Errol. I'm a towering giant and he was standard sized and objected to that kind of staging. It was a Technicolor spectacle, directed with style by Mike Curtiz, who loved to berate his stars. Bette was having none of this and screamed back at him while Errol just stormed off. But the use of color was brilliant and it never hurts to have a small part in a big hit. Then Universal cast me in *Tower of London* with Basil Rathbone as Richard III and me as Duke of Clarence. Basil took exception to his hunchback and had it scaled back.

You see, Universal was a studio in steep decline. All the movies they made were bad, but none more so than my next—*Green Hell* [1940]—which I made with Doug Fairbanks Jr. and Joan Bennett. One of the critics called it the funniest of the season, but it was a jungle drama. In one scene Joan is in a coma, lying on the jungle floor, perfectly coiffed and made up with nary a smudge on her ball gown—and she's been there in a coma for days! That's when the preview audience really lost it and the laughter was tumultuous. My last Universal was *The House of the Seven Gables* [1940] with George Sanders and Margaret Lindsay, a very reasonable adaptation of the [Nathaniel] Hawthorne novel, but the studio barely released it. Then I got a break when my contract lapsed. And I was quickly signed by 20th Century-Fox.

BAWDEN: What was your first Fox flick?

PRICE: I was making two at the same time. I was Charles II in *Hudson Bay* [1940], which laid a big egg because Paul Muni overacted terribly and American audiences couldn't have cared less whether France or England won the war for that bay. I seem to remember shooting scenes of that and then switching to *Brigham Young* [1940], which really diddled with the facts. He had *one* wife here. Then it was back to *Hudson Bay*. I was Mormon founder Joseph Smith in *Brigham Young*. My contract originally gave me six months a year on Broadway, so I went back for six months in *Angel Street* opposite the brilliant Canadian actress Judith Evelyn. Decades later I did a live TV special with the very same cast!

BAWDEN: Just how long did it take to make *The Song of Bernadette* [1943]?

PRICE: Nine whole months. I had the tiny role of the prosecutor and I had to wait all that time just to do a few scenes. I was so mad I should have pronounced Jennifer Jones guilty! Of anything! Years later I'm walking on the back lot and those hideous stone houses they'd built were still standing. You know, I naïvely thought this was the way they made all pictures.

Then I was cast as William McAdoo, who was treasurer under Woodrow Wilson in Henry King's picture *Wilson* [1944]. It ran 154 minutes and Henry King, who'd also done *Bernadette*, only shot for four months this time. Nobody went to see it. It whitewashed history. Did you know Wilson was an arch racist who segregated the federal post office? Poor Alexander Knox played him as a goody and nobody believed this guff. The theme was the great unwashed American public should be ashamed of themselves for deserting the League of Nations. It lost a fortune because [studio production chief Darryl] Zanuck had fallen in love with his pet project.

BAWDEN: Tell me why you think *Laura* [1944] emerged as one of the best movies of the forties.

PRICE: I think it may well be my best-ever film. I was Shelby, who was the southern paid companion. Of course I read the script when I got it and thought the dialogue brittle and clever. I remember an early read of one of the scenes for our lovely director Rouben Mamoulian. He told me Laird Cregar would probably be Waldo but was then overruled by producer Otto Preminger, who had seen Clifton Webb, who was touring in a Noel Coward play in L.A. Laird was personally devastated and that rejection began a downward personal spiral. But Otto was right. People would have guessed right away that Laird was the killer. Clifton was a new face. He'd made silent films in the twenties but concentrated on the stage since then. I think the casting near perfect. Dame Judith Anderson was superior as Ann Treadway and I was Shelby, her paid boyfriend. Once I came on set and Judith was running lines with Cliftie because he was very nervous about this new medium. And then after about ten days Otto Preminger came on set and said he was taking over as director. And he reshot most of Rouben's material. He made everything nastier. He was a very fast shooter. He expected you to always be on your toes. The whole thing emerges as a love letter to Gene Tierney [who played Laura, the title character]. I remember Zanuck telling me she was the loveliest star he'd ever met and she was shy and insecure, just as Laura. Everybody fell in love with her. Even Judith was nice when Gene was around. And it really is a very simple picture, mostly shot in the apartments of Waldo, Laura, and Ann. No violence, really—after the murder—until the end. But a heavy whiff of menace.

BAWDEN: Then you turned around and costarred in another Gene Tierney hit, *Leave Her to Heaven* [1945].

PRICE: I know there was quite a debate between director John Stahl and Zanuck about the use of color. Zanuck thought it should be reserved for musicals. John said it would be the perfect counterpoint to the disturbed state of the heroine, Ellen. People ask me if this in any way presaged Gene's own mental deterioration. Absolutely not. That was a decade later.

Scariest scene is the drowning, which Gene rehearsed for weeks in advance without John's knowledge and she was perfect on the first take. The things we got away with! The Production Code people were up in arms, but Zanuck said this was a serious study of mental illness. Stahl very cleverly used Jeanne Crain as counterpoint. She is the normal sister and the one Cornel Wilde goes off to at the end. But the idea of winding up with the sister of the girl you were accused of killing—well, the audience just didn't get that.

When I starting reading the script I figured I had a tiny part as Gene's jilted fiancé, but then I come back as the avenging prosecutor who has a real reason to get this creep convicted. A friend saw it recently and wondered why Harland [Cornel Wilde's character] gets two years in prison. For what? And the answer is he withheld evidence.

BAWDEN: Did the great Ernst Lubitsch hire you for *A Royal Scandal* [1945]?

PRICE: No, it was the great Zanuck who insisted I be hired because I was already on payroll and needed an assignment. Lubitsch tested me and said okay. Ernst was such a sweet, sunny guy. He told me he wanted Greta Garbo for Catherine the Great, but Zanuck said she was no longer box office. Besides, Fox owed Tallulah Bankhead a picture after her triumph in *Lifeboat* [1944]. Then Ernst had a heart attack as production was only beginning. Otto Preminger was assigned and it wasn't his cup of hemlock. He absolutely refused to give Tallulah guidance and she spent all her downtime in her dressing room guzzling gin. If the first fifteen minutes seem so wonderful, that's because Lubitsch mostly directed them and then was hospitalized. Otto would direct a take and then wonder out loud, "Was that funny?" The answer was no.

BAWDEN: Were you not slated to costar in *Forever Amber* [1947]?

PRICE: I'd be back as Charles II. Zanuck paid $200,000 for the best seller. Huge for the time. And then he cast pretty little Peggy Cummins in the lead. Still a teenager, she looked all of twelve. And filming progressed for some weeks until Zanuck got nervous and the censor was called to inspect the footage and pronounced it akin to child pornography. Filming ceased and a new cast headed by Linda Darnell was assembled. Linda was Darryl's girlfriend at the time. I was replaced by George Sanders as Charles II. Poor Peggy only lasted a few more years in Hollywood and then returned to England. The picture still made Fox a huge profit, even allowing the $500,000 loss on the first aborted version.

Vincent Price in his romantic leading man days with Gene Tierney in *Dragon-wyck* (1946). Courtesy of 20th Century Fox Television.

BAWDEN: Around this time you made your favorite Fox film.

PRICE: *Shock.* Made in 1946. Directed by Alfred Werker, who nobody ever heard of before or since. Don't let anybody tell you [otherwise], but Fox made B pictures just like all the other studios. I was a crazy psychiatrist and Lynn Bari saw me murder my wife and I'm out to get her. Lynn spent her whole career as queen of the Bs. And the reason the film works is Zanuck never bothered us. He never ever watched those Fox B features. And then the movie reviewers took up the cause and it played as a top feature in many markets.

BAWDEN: Also in 1946 you were busy making *Dragonwyck*.

PRICE: It was set up by Lubitsch but he was too frail to direct, so Joe Mankiewicz directed it as a Lubitsch production. A very interesting story of the Dutch in the Upper Hudson River [area]. As shooting progressed, those two bitterly disagreed and Lubitsch just left in a huff. Then a part was written for Laird [Cregar], but he had dieted so severely he died of a heart attack. It was such a waste. It was a hit, but a moderate one. And then I made *Moss Rose,* my last Fox picture. Zanuck called me in and said in the future all actors would be freelance. The studio contract system was fading as attendance declined. I'm a Scotland Yard type trailing Peggy Cummins, who is involved in Victorian mystery and murder. Ethel Barrymore was in it. I was terrified of her until one day between takes she waddles up and whispers, "Got a smoke?"

BAWDEN: Then what happened?

PRICE: At first I felt like an orphan! I did *The Web* [1947] at U-I [Universal-International] with Ella Raines and got about half of what I was making at Fox. But I worked steadily at all studios. I'd accept any part to keep going. I was Boss Tweed in the Deanna Durbin musical *Up in Central Park* [1948] at Universal. I took the part because Fred Astaire was going to direct, but he quit on opening day of filming. Perhaps he finally read the script. I even did *Abbott And Costello Meet Frankenstein* [1948]. I came into the studio and voiced a few lines as the Invisible Man.

BAWDEN: You said in one interview how much you liked working with the reigning sex symbols?

PRICE: Lana Turner and I played complicated practical jokes on each other during the making of *The Three Musketeers* [1948]. Finally, Gene Kelly yelled at us to stop it. But we didn't. Filming in France was impossible because of postwar chaos, so do you know where we filmed most of it? Pasadena! Those huge mansions with their faux French decor were perfect. Then I did *The Bribe* [1949] with the delightful Ava Gardner and we'd make up naughty limericks every day and sing them out until Bob Taylor popped his head out of his dressing room and complained.

I made two melos [melodramas] in a row with Janie Russell at RKO. On *His Kind of Woman* [1951], we were in production six months as producer Howard Hughes kept changing the storyline and ordering new sets built. I was paid weekly and wound up making a six-figure sum. Then I stayed at RKO for *The Las Vegas Story* [1952] with Jane and Vic Mature, a much misunderstood actor, a very sweet guy who was later left a fortune by his mother, so he just up and retired early. He desperately wanted acceptance as an actor, but they kept shoving him into those biblical things. He always insisted his stunt double be hired at the same time to do all the heavy lifting in fight scenes, even when wrestling that stuffed lion in *Samson and Delilah* [1949]!

BAWDEN: Didn't you once say your favorite film actor was Ronald Colman?

PRICE: Growing up, I worshipped him for his style and that voice! Imagine my excitement when I costarred with Ronnie in *Champagne for*

Caesar [1950], a very fine comedy. Then together we made the much maligned *The Story of Mankind* [1957]. I mean, it was supposed to be funny—Hedy Lamarr as Joan of Arc, Harpo Marx as Sir Isaac Newton, Reggie Gardiner as Bill Shakespeare. But the directing was very heavy-handed and the public just didn't understand it.

BAWDEN: You say your favorite-ever movie was *The Baron of Arizona* [1950].

PRICE: It was made at Lippert, one of the cheapest studios around. Ellen Drew, a refugee from Paramount, was the costar. It was the true story of James Addison Reavis, who defrauded the American government of $25 million, and Sam Fuller shot it in record time—twenty-one days. It looks great because Jimmy Wong Howe shot it with great care. Nobody ever asks me about it and I've never seen it listed on TV.

BAWDEN: How were you cast in *The Ten Commandments* [1956]?

PRICE: I answered the phone and it was C. B. DeMille thundering, "You shall be the Egyptian architect, Baka. Do you understand me?" Everyone but [Charlton] Heston got the same salary—$25,000. And we were many months at it. Then C. B. suffered a debilitating heart attack, but still kept at it. I went into wardrobe and had the craziest duds. There was no arguing. His offices were strewn with research material. I'd do a rehearsal and C. B. would thunder, "More! More passion! More understanding!" What he was asking for was the Victorian way of acting, so I'd throw my hands around. I loved meeting and working with Eddie Robinson. I can still hear him thundering, "Moooooooses! Oh, Moooooooses!" Eddie was a great collector of art. And I suggested we be paired [as contestants] on CBS's *The $64,000 Question*. He'd never done live TV before and shook visibly just before we went on. So I threw some softball material his way and he quieted down. It was a fun experience for me, less so for him.

BAWDEN: You'd played opposite Boris Karloff in Universal's *Tower of London* in 1939 and played the title role in *The Invisible Man Returns,* but *House of Wax* was the real beginning of your career as an icon of horror movies. Can you tell me about that experience?

PRICE: Well, I've been in many horrors! *House of Wax* was hard to shoot because of the 3-D cameras. I'm always looking down because I had to hit precise locations for the effects to work. André De Toth directed, but he only had one eye. Consequently, he never could see the effects he was creating. It was a huge hit, but mostly released flat [without 3-D] so people today wonder what all the shouting was about.

Vincent Price in *House of Wax* (1953), playing his signature horror role as the wax museum operator whose models are all dead people covered in wax. With him (*from left*) are Charles Buchinsky (Bronson) and Paul Cavanagh. Courtesy of Warner Bros.

BAWDEN: After starring in another 3-D horror movie, *The Mad Magician* [1954], for Columbia, you stayed away from the genre until you had another great hit in that category—Fox's *The Fly*. What about that?

PRICE: *The Fly* was supposedly set in Montreal. In one scene I have to talk to my brother, who has been turned into a fly. I started the scene and costar Herbert Marshall was rolling around the bench laughing. Every time I'd start, great tears would cascade from him. Then I got the giggles too and that little scene took a day to film. There was a sequel with Brett Halsey. Inevitably titled *Return of the Fly*. [A third film in the original series, *Curse of the Fly*, was made in 1965, but Price did not participate.] And yes, I have seen the David Cronenberg remake [1986]. Too bloody. Too much gunk. One must leave something to the imagination, I think.

Then came *House on Haunted Hill* in 1959. Bill Castle made it quickly in black and white and used the gimmick of "Emergo" to pack movie houses. It was a skeleton which was whisked out above the screaming teen-

Vincent Price is menaced by a creature, half-man, half-housefly, in *The Fly* (1958). Courtesy of 20th Century-Fox.

agers. But the next, *The Bat* [1959], was a bust because the house we shot in wasn't big enough to seem spooky.

BAWDEN: Were you surprised by the success of the films you made for Roger Corman?

PRICE: Oh, completely. Teenagers flooded the cinemas, making AIP [American-International Pictures] huge profits. The first was *The House of Usher* [1960] and everything was done in ten days, from casting to costumes to filming. Roger shot quickly and economically and I grant it was ragged. But it struck a chord. I thought *The Pit and the Pendulum* [1961] a huge improvement. With *Tower of London* [1962], I was in a remake of a film I'd first made in 1939!

I think *Tales of Terror* [1963] quite good. I loved working with Basil Rathbone and Peter Lorre. You know, when a journalist on set asked Basil why he was doing such trash, he glared and said, "I blame it all on that Marlon Brando." Meaning the Method had destroyed our way of acting. Then we got Boris Karloff and Lorre for a merry threesome in *The Raven* [1963] and the last masterwork had Boris, Basil, Peter, and I in *Comedy of Terrors* [1963] and it was the biggest hit of all.

Can I make a comment here? I never watch horror movies myself, if I can help it. Too scary for me.

BAWDEN: Why was *The Tomb of Ligeia* [1964] your last with Corman?

PRICE: He'd been battered and bruised by the terrible lashing from the critics. I think he just lost his nerve. But he gave me a new career I'd never dreamed of. And then I did some very fine British offshoots: *The Conqueror Worm* [1968] is a brilliant little study of the English civil war, *The Oblong Box* [1969] an all-star effort.

BAWDEN: But your favorite is *Theatre of Blood* [1973]?

PRICE: Because I'm a bad theatrical actor, bumping off all the critics who ever panned me. The cast was huge: Harry Andrews, Jack Hawkins, Robert Coote, Michael Hordern, Dennis Price, Arthur Lowe, Joan Hickson—all big stars in England.

[Price's wife, actress Coral Browne, was present for that question and she added, "We met on this picture and then he kills me." Price responded: "Well, you gave me a bad review. Had to."]

BAWDEN: Katharine Hepburn asked you to join her in a season of Shakespeare at Stratford, Connecticut. Why didn't you do it?

PRICE: I told her I couldn't afford to work eight weeks for $500. I couldn't buy any more art at that price.

BAWDEN: One of your great performances in more recent years was in *The Whales of August*. Tell me about that.

PRICE: I took over from Francis Lederer, who quit after a day. The weather was freezing. We seemed to film in the smallest cottage available. With all the lights, the crew, the lack of ventilation—no wonder we couldn't breathe. Lillian Gish was a revelation. Ann Sothern was marvelous to me. I'm not going to comment on Bette Davis, except to say she was effective. To be in demand at my age is, well, it's like buying a fine piece of art.

Afterword

Vincent Price did three more feature films after *The Whales of August*. *Backtrack* (1989) was directed by Dennis Hopper and had limited release. *Arabian Knight* (1995) was an animated film that Price did voice work for before he died, but never saw. His last truly memorable role was as the kindly "mad scientist" toymaker who creates an artificial boy, played by Johnny Depp, in Tim Burton's amusing horror movie spoof *Edward Scissorhands* (1990). Burton's film was almost an official coda to Price's long career as a horror movie icon. Quite visibly frail in that film, he nevertheless gave a memorable performance.

Price died of throat cancer on October 25, 1993. He was eighty-two.

VI

Unforgettable Heavies

Ernest Borgnine

Interview by Ron Miller

Ever since antiheroes began to be celebrated in American pop culture, the traditional role of the "heavy" in motion pictures has been evolving. Actors who usually played unsavory and villainous characters started to rise out of the supporting ranks and take their places as leading characters.

No actor embodies that change more perfectly than Ernest Borgnine, a big, rough-looking man with almost porcine features who spent most of his early years in movies doing really bad stuff to others. In *From Here to Eternity* (1953), for instance, Borgnine played "Fatso" Judson, who threatens to gut hero Montgomery Clift with a knife in a classic barroom encounter and finally succeeds in mortally wounding Frank Sinatra. Equally unpleasant was the bully he played in *Bad Day at Black Rock* (1955): he torments an older man (Spencer Tracy) who has only one arm until the man, an expert in martial arts, beats the crap out of him one-handed. Borgnine was the quintessential bad guy in numerous westerns, including *The Stranger Wore a Gun* (1953), *Vera Cruz* (1954), and *Johnny Guitar* (1954), and was among the nasty warriors in *The Wild Bunch* (1969) and the World War II saga *The Dirty Dozen* (1967).

But the direction of Borgnine's career was forever changed when Rod Steiger bowed out of the 1955 film version of Paddy Chayefsky's television play *Marty* (1955) and Borgnine got the role of the shy and lonely Bronx butcher who desperately wants to find a woman who will love him. Borgnine's gentle, sensitive performance won him the Best Actor Academy Award and proved he was much, much more than just a big ugly fat guy.

The Oscar led Borgnine to many other multidimensional roles and ultimately to stardom in his own hit TV comedy series, *McHale's Navy*

Ernest Borgnine in sinister mood for the film *Who Killed the Mysterious Mr Foster?* (1970). Courtesy of TV station KGSC-TV of San Jose, California.

(1962–1966). He later starred in a couple of feature films inspired by the TV series.

In his later years, Borgnine worked regularly in TV, including the CBS series *Airwolf* and many TV movies, which usually featured him in wholesome, benign roles. He was still starring in TV movies well into his nineties.

Ernest Borgnine (*right*) torments a one-armed man (Spencer Tracy) in *Bad Day at Black Rock* (1955). Courtesy of MGM.

Setting the Scene

I met Borgnine only once, in a hurried 1973 interview in San Francisco while he was doing promotional work for his latest film, Robert Aldrich's *Emperor of the North Pole,* later retitled just *Emperor of the North*. It was an action film set in Depression-era America, with Borgnine returning to his early form as a brutal heavy—this time a railroad conductor who vows to kill any hobo trying to ride free on his train. This put him up against another classic movie heavy who also went on to heroic roles and his own Best Actor Oscar—Lee Marvin, who played the king of the hoboes.

Borgnine turned out to be disarmingly good-natured, much more like his TV character McHale than any of his screen villains.

The Interview

MILLER: For years, the very sight of you on a movie screen meant somebody was going to be in for a real bad time. How did that feel?

Ernest Borgnine in his Oscar-winning role as the timid butcher who romances Betsy Blair in *Marty* (1955). Courtesy of United Artists.

BORGNINE: People used to come up to me and say, "Oooh, how I hated you in that last picture." I felt honored because that's exactly what they were supposed to think.

MILLER: But didn't it feel much more comfortable when people came up to you after getting to know you have a warm and loveable side? Is that what happened after they saw you as Marty?

BORGNINE: It broke a mold that was long in the making. Many character actors thanked me for breaking out of type and showing that actors like me could portray a number of things—not just villains.

MILLER: So then do you think you can forgive people for relishing your return to genuine nastiness in *Emperor of the North*?

BORGNINE: They've fixed the mold, I'm sorry to say. I think I may have run the whole gamut and now I'm back to playing the real heavy again.

MILLER: Tell me about this sadistic railroad conductor.

BORGNINE: The man I play is dead set against hoboes and by golly, they're just not going to ride on his train. He becomes a psychotic, mania-

Railroad officer Ernest Borgnine (*right*) challenges a legendary hobo (Lee Marvin) in *Emperor of the North* (1973). Courtesy of 20th Century Fox Television.

cal kind of crazy man. I had to get in there and play him as the meanest, no-goodest man who ever walked in two shoes.

MILLER: Do you ever wonder why you seem able to make these mean-spirited bullies so realistic?

BORGNINE: It's kind of frightening at times. At night, I'll go home and say to my wife, "Honey, am I really that bad?"

MILLER: Do you think it's just because you're kind of a big, menacing sort of guy until you smile and start talking to people?

BORGNINE: It hurts me when people describe me as a big burly brute with tremendous huge hands. I may be big. I may be burly, but I'm not a brute. I'm probably more sensitive than the ordinary person.

MILLER: So you really don't like to eat babies or stomp on the cat's tail when you're not working?

BORGNINE: I know how to sew. I know how to cook. I love beautiful things like ceramic pottery, antiques, good music, and sunsets. Does that sound like a brute, that I should be called a meanie?

MILLER: Okay, but after they see you beating up on Lee Marvin and Keith Carradine in *Emperor of the North,* what do you think people will say?

BORGNINE: Sure, some people will call me a dirty so-and-so. But I've never gotten into an argument over remarks like that. I've never had a fight with anyone. They usually say things like that to me with a laugh. But it's probably because they don't know what I might do to them next.

Afterword

Ernest Borgnine was married five times and fathered four children. He was divorced from his first four wives, who included actress Katy Jurado and Broadway superstar Ethel Merman, whose marriage to Borgnine lasted only thirty-two days. He was still married to cosmetics executive Tova Traesnaes when he died of kidney failure in Los Angeles on July 8, 2012. He was ninety-five.

Victor Buono

Interview by Ron Miller

One of the most popular screen heavies of the 1960s and 1970s was Victor Buono, who may have been the heaviest of the heavies of his era, weighing in at 280–300 pounds. Buono came to Hollywood with a rich background in Shakespearean roles on the stage at the Globe Theater in his native San Diego. He was nominated for the Best Supporting Actor Academy Award for 1962's *What Ever Happened to Baby Jane?* for his performance as the weird musical accompanist to Bette Davis's character.

Born on February 3, 1938, Buono planned from his youth to become a doctor, but he'd been encouraged to act by his maternal grandmother, Myrtle Glied, who had been a vaudeville performer on the Orpheum circuit. He was seized by the acting bug once he was cast as Papa Barrett in a high school production of *The Barretts of Wimpole Street* and went on to play the leading role in *Hamlet* while still in high school.

Buono joined the Globe Theater Players at age eighteen and immediately was cast in stellar roles in the company in such classic plays as *Volpone* and *The Man Who Came to Dinner*. A Warner Bros. talent scout spotted him there in *Falstaff* in 1959 and arranged a screen test, which led to his first TV role, as Bongo Benny in an episode of the hit series *77 Sunset Strip*.

From then on, Buono became one of the busiest villains in both movies and television. Though he mostly landed supporting roles in movies, he did star in several, including *The Strangler* (1964) and *The Mad Butcher* (1971).

Noted for his ability to mix comedy with villainy, Buono played some of TV's most notorious bad guys with his tongue in his cheek. Among them were the grand Dr. Schubert of *The Man from Atlantis*, a Captain Nemo–style villain who roamed the seas in his super submarine, the cartoonish King Tut on the *Batman* series, and colorful Count Manzeppi on *The Wild, Wild West*. His sense of humor and razor wit also made Buono a popular late-night talk show guest.

Victor Buono as the diabolical villain Mr. Schubert in *The Man from Atlantis* (1977–1978) television series. Courtesy of NBC.

Setting the Scene

I met Victor Buono when he was appearing in a 1965 stage production of Molière's *Tartuffe* at the Comedia Repertory Theater in Palo Alto, California. He was absolutely fabulous in this stage role, commanding the stage whenever he set foot upon it. He was such a powerful stage performer that I don't believe his movie and TV fans ever experienced the real Buono if they hadn't seen him live on a theater stage.

He was the most charming and self-effacing of men. If he was haunted by the limitations of his great bulk, it certainly didn't show. He struck me as a very happy soul who was quite content in his own skin and really enjoying the great variety of comic and villainous roles that kept coming his way.

The Interview

MILLER: Like Sydney Greenstreet before you, you seem destined to be typecast as a villainous character on-screen. Your reaction?

BUONO: If you weigh more than 280 pounds, you better get out the black hat and forget about getting the girl at the end of the picture. I've been shot, stabbed, run over, and been pushed off of, out of, under, and over more things than you can imagine. I never get the girl. In fact, I'm not even allowed to have a friend.

MILLER: Given that, what do you consider the ideal role for you?

BUONO: Oh, no doubt, Shakespeare's Sir John Falstaff. But ever since I played the sinister mama's boy in *Baby Jane*, nobody wants to hire me to play Falstaff.

MILLER: Did you ever think about losing weight and slimming yourself into another category?

BUONO: I can't tell you how many times I've tried to lose weight in order to change the direction of my career. But I always give up and shoot back up to 350 pounds or so.

MILLER: I've seen you on the TV talk shows and you always seem to have a pretty amused attitude about your weight.

BUONO: What else can I do but joke about it all the time? I mean, people ask me when I eat breakfast and I usually tell them I sit down to breakfast about 8 a.m. and that usually lasts until 2 or 3 p.m.

MILLER: Does being a big guy present any problems for you doing your parts in movies or TV?

BUONO: Well, let me tell you about one incident. I was playing a bad guy on *The Untouchables* and they had to show me in a close-up, driving a car. Well, I don't drive, so they had to tie a rope to the car and have a gang of grips tow me across the set. You can imagine how much they loved doing that.

MILLER: What about your visits to wardrobe? Do they have trouble fitting you with clothes?

BUONO: Trouble? My tailors don't measure me; they survey me.

MILLER: So you don't expect to ever slim yourself down?

BUONO: Well, there's about as much chance of me losing weight as there is of the pope being named chairman of the Communist Party.

MILLER: Your villains certainly don't fit the normal dimensions of movie bad guys.

BUONO: No, I've developed my own style. I don't just torture the hero. I torture him while reciting poetry or enjoying an epicurean feast.

Afterword

Buono never married and often gave whimsical answers when asked about it. Some sources say he was gay, but others say he liked women. Let's just say that he didn't seem bothered by the fact that he never "got the girl" on-screen and draw our own conclusions about why. Buono died from a heart attack on New Year's Day in 1982 at his home in Apple Valley, California. He was just forty-three.

Jack Elam

Interview by Ron Miller

Jack Elam had one of the most offbeat and peculiar careers of any Hollywood actor of his era. He was a highly successful accountant for the Samuel Goldwyn Company and several other independent movie companies until a vision problem threatened his ability to go on with his career. So he decided to move in front of the camera, cashing in on his unwholesome and rather craggy looks to become a classic screen villain. Then, after building a solid reputation as a screen heavy, the middle-aged Elam began to take on comedic old codger roles and transformed himself into a beloved character actor more likely to provoke benign laughs than nervous tension.

Quite popular with his fellow actors, Elam earned an off-screen reputation as a drinker of heroic proportions and a shrewd poker player. In the last phase of his career, he was seen mostly on television, often in situation comedies, including ABC's *The Texas Wheelers* (1974–1975), in which he was the head of a wacky family; CBS's *Struck by Lightning* (1979), in which he played a comedic Frankenstein's monster; and NBC's *Easy Street* (1986–1987), where he appeared as voluptuous showgirl Loni Anderson's ditzy uncle.

However, diehard fans will best remember him for his countless roles in westerns, including *Rawhide* (1951), *High Noon* (1952), *Gunfight at the O.K. Corral* (1957), *Once upon a Time in the West* (1968), and *Support Your Local Sheriff* (1969).

Setting the Scene

Okay, I'll be the first to admit I've adopted some unusual pop culture heroes in my lifetime. And here, obviously, is my most outrageous example: while other boys my age were arguing whether John Wayne or Randolph Scott was the best screen cowboy, I was rooting for Jack Elam.

Jack Elam as Frank, the former Frankenstein monster, in the 1979 CBS sitcom *Struck by Lightning*. Courtesy of CBS.

"Who?" my friends would say.

"Jack Elam," I would tell them. "You know, the guy who shoots babies and laughs about it? The one who's so ugly he looks like his mom threw out the baby and kept the afterbirth? The guy who looks like he's been run over by a cattle stampede *before* he's run over by a cattle stampede?"

Well, they usually didn't remember poor Jack at all—at least not until I described him as the bad guy who had one eye that kind of rolled around in the wrong direction—then they'd say, "Oh, *that* guy!"

On-screen, Jack died with style. In his salad days, he died better than anybody else in the movies. He was gut-shot and went out kicking. He was run over by trains. He was ground up in printing presses. He was dragged to death by a horse in *The Moonlighter* (1953)—in 3-D, no less! My favorite Elam death was when he died gargling quicksand in *Lure of the Wilderness* (1952).

Ordinary bloodless gunshot wounds were too banal for anybody as mean as Jack was on-screen. He needed special pain to get what he deserved. When I saw his name in the credits for *High Noon,* I expected Gary Cooper to blow a hole in him big enough to ride a palomino through. And what a letdown it was when he turned up playing nothing but the town drunk whom Cooper lets out of jail just before he goes off to face Frank Miller and his boys. Anytime they cheated me of a great Elam death scene, I felt let down. I was really upset when he sang a song and played the guitar in *My Man and I* (1952)—without spilling a drop of anyone's blood. Yuck!

It was a hoot to try to guess how Jack would "get it" in each movie that rolled into town, most of them westerns or crime pictures—the sort of pictures that desperately needed lots of bad guys for the hero to wipe his boots on sooner or later.

Jack didn't look tough enough to give any of the movie heroes a real hard time mano a mano, so they rarely used him in fist fights. Thin to the point of emaciation, he looked as if he might need help climbing onto his horse. He was a new kind of heavy who always picked on defenseless women, kids, and cripples. What else could he do in the "bad guy" world if even baby-faced Audie Murphy could beat him up with one hand tied behind his back? Yes, I know Audie was the most decorated soldier of World War II, a genuine war hero, but he sure didn't look like one!

Still, in the right light, Jack Elam was darn sinister. When he turned that gimlet eye toward you, your blood ran cold. When he waited in ambush for Charles Bronson in *Once upon a Time in the West,* it wasn't to challenge him to a gunfight at high noon. He wanted to blow Bronson's head off, then spit in the neck hole. But, as usual, Bronson got him first. As I recall, a fly was buzzing around Elam while he waited behind cover. My guess is he stunk to high heaven and Bronson either smelled him a mile away or heard the telltale buzz.

Even if Jack wasn't very successful at killing heroes, his evil "look" created a special place for him in the movies. The 1950s ushered in a new era in cinema. The public started to yearn for more realism. It was no longer suitable to identify the bad guys simply by issuing them black hats. The new order of bad guys—led by the likes of Jack Elam, Lee Marvin, Lee Van Cleef, and Ernest Borgnine—proved their badness by shooting lawmen in the back after molesting their women, suffocating their kids, and whizzing in their lunch boxes. Jack was there to be mean as hell—then to get his ass shot off by the hero.

Ultimately, Elam grew old and acquired a butt, along with chin whiskers and, believe it or not, a genial manner. In his middle years, he started playing comic cootie-brains in pictures like *Support Your Local Sheriff*, doing the sort of roles that Arthur Hunnicutt or Chill Wills used to play. A little later, he even started playing kindly old men, usually reformed drunks or drunks trying to reform. He ended up swapping lines with the sort of kid actors he used to shoot, drown, or eat for breakfast.

Setting the Scene

The first time I actually met Jack Elam, after I'd grown up and become a TV columnist, was on the set of TV's *Eight Is Enough* (1977–1981), where he was playing scenes with kids he probably could barely tolerate, no doubt because they made more money than he and wouldn't risk any of it in a poker game. I found it bizarre to be around Jack Elam in the last stages of his career. I think he was impressed that somebody had grown up watching his movies—or even knew who he was. He was always gracious and funny.

We talked at length while he was doing the short-lived CBS sitcom *Struck by Lightning* in 1979. In that show, he played Frank, the caretaker at a rural Massachusetts inn who was really the 230-year-old Frankenstein monster. Elam thought it was a mighty joke that he'd wound up in a sitcom, playing a part that had nothing whatsoever to do with cowboys and outlaws.

And we talked a few times when he did another sitcom, NBC's *Easy Street*, in 1986, playing a seedy old character called Uncle Bully opposite sexy Loni Anderson.

My wife met him once while she was on location in the desert near Kanab, Utah, doing interviews with James Brolin and Ronny Cox, who were filming *The Car* (1977). Elam was on a nearby location doing an episode of TV's *How the West Was Won*. One of the guys from *The Car* introduced her to him as "the notorious Jack Elam." As she recalls, he managed to lift an eyelid and wink at her without breaking his concentration on the poker game he was playing with his pals. At that stage of his career, lifting an eyelid was probably a major undertaking.

But I most often saw Jack at my favorite hangout in the San Fernando Valley, the venerable Sportsmen's Lodge, where Jack had a luxury suite on the top floor—just down the street from the studio where he was doing *Easy Street.*

Jack was a drinking man, and mornings were not his best time. I remember the well-seasoned waitresses in the hotel coffee shop sort of coddling him through his breakfast ritual. The staff considered him a loveable character and they all treated him more like a hungover relative than a hungover movie star. "He's just plain folks," the waitresses used to tell me.

The last time I saw him in there he was trying to remember where he had parked his car the night before. He'd been partying somewhere in the valley and when he staggered back to his car, he'd forgotten where it was. "I looked all over for it, but couldn't find it nowhere," he grumbled. "So I took a cab over here."

"That's all right, darlin'," one venerable waitress assured him. "We'll help you find it after breakfast. Now you'd better eat something, Jack."

On that last day I saw him in person, he gave me a little high-five sign as he took off to try to track down his missing car. I think it was his way of saying, "Hang in there, buddy. I'll see you again sometime."

And I do see Jack quite a lot these days, rerunning so many of his classic movies and TV episodes on home video. He was one of a kind and there'll never be another quite like him. The interview that follows was distilled from all my separate talks with Jack Elam.

The Interview

MILLER: I grew up watching you as one of the meanest men in the movies, but now you've sort of turned into Walter Brennan as he was in *The Real McCoys* [1957–1963]!

ELAM: That's funny. I worked with Walter Brennan in *Support Your Local Sheriff* and one day he took me aside and said, "I'm getting old. One of these days I'm gonna kick off and you're going to start working steady."

MILLER: How did it all begin? How does a guy go from doing the taxes for the companies making westerns to being the bad guy in front of the camera in those westerns?

ELAM: I was doing pretty well doing the books for various producers, but it was putting a heavy strain on my one good eye. The doctor told me to either find another line of work or go blind. I knew an assistant director on the Hopalong Cassidy pictures named George "Dink" Templeton. He planned to make young John Barrymore Jr. the star in a series of low-budget westerns and asked me to help him round up the financing. So I made a deal with him. I would get him the financing if, in return, he would let me play a heavy in those pictures.

MILLER: Why did you think you could play a movie villain without any acting experience?

ELAM: I'd been on the sets of movies like that for so long that the idea of going in front of the camera didn't intimidate me. Anyway, I think acting is nothing more than not being nervous while you're working. I figured I could look mean and ugly on camera because I looked mean and ugly off camera.

MILLER: So he put you in *The Sundowners* and *High Lonesome* in 1950, but Barrymore Jr. didn't become a real star from those pictures while you eventually did.

ELAM: Being a heavy is the easiest thing in the world. You can make all the mistakes you want and nobody notices. If you don't carry off the heavy, you can still get by on your looks.

MILLER: In my memory, your first really mean and nasty role was in *Rawhide* [1951] with Tyrone Power. You were really, really nasty to Susan Hayward.

ELAM: I shot a one-year-old baby in that one. That has to be the bottom of the line for me.

MILLER: It also looked as if you were bent on raping Susan Hayward.

ELAM: I don't like the word *rape*. I prefer "stealing girls' goodies." Anyway, I never actually done it on film, but I [dragged] quite a few of them off into the bushes.

MILLER: My friends and I used to make bets on how you were going to die in your next picture. My favorite was *Lure of the Wilderness,* where you drowned in quicksand, although you didn't look like you were having a real good time being dragged over rocks by a horse in 3-D in *The Moonlighter.*

ELAM: You name it and I've done it. I've been pitch-forked, beaten to death, kicked to death, shot, hung. Those deaths are really not that easy. I really got hurt on some of them.

MILLER: Some fans think your best-ever scene in a movie was the one in the opening of Sergio Leone's *Once upon a Time in the West* where you're waiting at the train station to kill Charles Bronson and amuse yourself by trying to catch a fly in the barrel of your gun.

ELAM: The fly took a day and a half. Leone wanted me to catch a fly that way and I told him you can't catch a fly that way. The barrel of the gun was no larger than your little finger. But he said, "Catch a fly!" So I sat there a day and a half trying. The prop man finally got one on a string, but Leone said, "No, I've got to have reality!" They had everything in the world strung all over my face to draw flies—honey, apricot jam, pineapple juice. And we finally got one.

MILLER: James Arness must have really liked you because I think your twenty-four guest appearances on *Gunsmoke* was the all-time record. And you were pretty much a regular in John Wayne's later westerns.

ELAM: We played poker all day long on his sets. It was John's idea that if you relaxed between takes, you did better work. It relieves tension and it's more pleasant. We had many very good times together.

MILLER: After *Rawhide,* 20th Century-Fox put you under contract and thought you might be developed into an antihero the way it developed Richard Widmark after his nasty villain role in *Kiss of Death* [1947]. What happened?

ELAM: After two years of trying, they never could find anything I was pretty enough for.

MILLER: Did it bother you to see so many of your fellow screen heavies like Ernest Borgnine, Lee Marvin, and Lee Van Cleef turn into heroes on the screen?

ELAM: If those guys are heroes, then man, I'm in a lot of trouble!

MILLER: Do you think times have changed and moviegoers now don't want to see the pretty boys as heroes?

ELAM: The tougher you are, the better they like it. The guys can bring their girlfriends to the movies and say, "If you think I'm ugly, take a look at him!"

MILLER: In your so-called salad days, you looked like you weren't even eating salads. You were so skinny you didn't have enough butt to fill a saddle, but now you look pretty normal.

ELAM: I didn't weigh over 145 pounds until I was fifty. I've been skinny all my life and this is a pleasant change of pace. I was tired of being the guy on the beach they all kick sand on. I'm not going on a diet. I'm enjoying it.

MILLER: How did you make the transformation from villainy to comedy?

ELAM: It's just the natural osmosis of getting old. I don't know that I have that much choice. And I'm not so sure I haven't done some of those psychotic heavies in a way that turned out to be comedy when I got through with them. If you're doing comedy, though, you had better sit pretty tight on your timing. If you're not funny, you're not funny—and that's all there is to it.

MILLER: So you're happy with your new image as a curmudgeonly old sourdough?

ELAM: My main interest is that it gets me off a horse. I'm getting too old for this horse stuff.

Afterword

In 1994, Elam was inducted into the Hall of Great Western Performers at the National Cowboy and Western Heritage Museum in Oklahoma City, Oklahoma.

He was married twice, first to Jean, who died in 1961, and then to Margaret Jennison, who survived him. He had two daughters and a son. He finally retired to a rural property in Ashland, Oregon, where he died of congestive heart failure on October 20, 2003. He was eighty-six.

Lee Marvin

Interview by Ron Miller

Lee Marvin was the quintessential Hollywood bad guy who was turned into a screen hero during the era in which antiheroes began to blossom in the wake of Humphrey Bogart's Rick from *Casablanca* (1942).

Tall, rugged-looking, and prematurely gray, Marvin first established himself as one of the nastiest of all movie villains, most notoriously in Fritz Lang's gloomy noir *The Big Heat* (1953), in which he scalded the face of Gloria Grahame with blazing hot coffee; in Laslo Benedek's *The Wild One* (1953), where he was the meanest of Marlon Brando's biker gang rivals; in John Sturges's *Bad Day at Black Rock* (1955), in which he tried to ram one-armed Spencer Tracy's car off the road; and in John Ford's *The Man Who Shot Liberty Valance* (1962) as the murderous outlaw Liberty whom both men and women hid from whenever he came to town. His one prolonged break from screen nastiness came with his leading role of a tough cop in NBC's weekly television series *The M Squad* (1957–1960).

Marvin had learned a lot about acting since he worked his way up from being an extra in the early 1950s, and by 1965 he was able to parody himself in the comic western *Cat Ballou,* playing dual roles: a drunken gunslinger in serious need of rehab and a vicious outlaw with a tin nose who's like the second coming of Liberty Valance. For his marvelous performance, Marvin won the Best Actor Academy Award.

After that, Marvin quickly moved up to leading roles in action movies, usually in firm antihero categories. Among his biggest hits in this post-villain period was Robert Aldrich's *The Dirty Dozen* (1967), in which he played Major Reisman, leader of the team made up of the army's worst bad guys of World War II, sent to perform an impossible mission against the Nazis. Marvin was quite at home in such military roles because he was a World War II Marine Corps veteran himself and in the early days of his career often played soldiers or sailors in bit roles. One of his last big roles

331

Lee Marvin, circa 1964. Ron Miller collection.

was that of the sergeant in Samuel Fuller's *The Big Red One* (1980), which was based largely on Fuller's own war experiences.

On the personal side, Marvin was a much larger than life personality and a drinker of heroic dimensions. Tales of the epic drinking bouts he

Lee Marvin as a drunken gunslinger atop a drunken horse in *Cat Ballou* (1965), the comic western in which he played dual roles and for which he won the Best Actor Oscar. Courtesy of Columbia Pictures.

staged with Richard Burton while making *The Klansman* (1974) are legendary.

Marvin was married twice, first to Betty Ebeling from 1951 1967. After their divorce, he married a former sweetheart, Pamela Feeley, in

1970. Their marriage survived the notorious 1971 "palimony" lawsuit in which Marvin's former live-in girlfriend Michelle Triola sued him for a share of his income. In 1981, an appeals court ruled that Marvin owed her nothing.

Setting the Scene

My interview with Lee Marvin was unprecedented, probably the most complex interview I ever did with any celebrity, bar none. I was offered the opportunity to talk with him late in 1985 when he was preparing to do *The Delta Force* (1986) in Israel. He had most recently been seen in the NBC TV movie *The Dirty Dozen: The Next Mission* (1985). The offer came because I was flying to Tucson, Arizona, anyway to do interviews on the set of the TV remake of the western *Stagecoach* and Marvin, who lived on a desert site near Tucson, was willing to sit for an interview.

I must admit I had trepidations about talking with Marvin. I'd heard several horror stories about his animosity to reporters and his ornery nature when loaded with booze. He had been smeared all over the tabloids for years because of the palimony lawsuit and was known to be even warier of reporters for that reason. But I had always admired Marvin's work on-screen, so I accepted the offer, called him, and settled on a time. Then the bad stuff started to happen.

I was unable to get a rental car from any of the well-known agencies. At the last possible minute, I managed to get one from Rent-a-Wreck, which specializes in renting rehabilitated vintage cars. But one block from the agency, the dilapidated rental broke down. I needed at least an hour to get out to Marvin's house and I now had less than that—and no car. Finally, Rent-a-Wreck agreed to lend me their repair van full of auto parts. So, exactly one hour late for my appointment with Marvin, I wheeled up his driveway in a Rent-a-Wreck repair van. When he understood who I was, he very nearly died laughing.

My misfortune turned out to be fortuitous. Shrewdly guessing I was not having my best day Marvin couldn't have been nicer. His wife, Pam, made us a delicious lunch. We all sat down and laughed about my day—and about the day before, when a water pipe had burst in my hotel room and flooded the place while I was stranded until after midnight on the set of *Stagecoach,* waiting for a ride back to the hotel with the film's star, Willie Nelson.

Before we began our formal interview, Marvin took me to one of his outbuildings to show me his large assortment of sportfishing trophies and the mounted specimens of marlin he had hooked off the coast of Baja Mexico. Then we sat down and watched a movie, *Operation Thunderbolt* (1977), which had been directed by Menahem Golan, the director of Marvin's new film, *The Delta Force* (1986). He wanted me to see what a fine action director Golan was.

During this long and fruitful day together, Lee Marvin was stone-cold sober and as friendly and likeable as any actor I've ever met in my years as an entertainment writer.

The Interview

MILLER: You enlisted in the Marine Corps in 1942, not long after your eighteenth birthday. You obviously saw plenty of action and were severely wounded in the battle for the island of Saipan in the South Pacific. What happened?

MARVIN: It wasn't pretty. I was shot in the butt by a machine gun and one of the bullets severed my sciatic nerve. I was given a medical discharge.

MILLER: Your bio explains that you began acting when you were working on a plumbing job at a community theater in upstate New York and were asked to step in for an actor who got sick while the company was rehearsing a play. You liked it and did more and ended up getting a small role in a Broadway show. How did that lead you to Hollywood?

MARVIN: They were making a lot of war films in Hollywood in those days and they needed extras, so a lot of us veterans trooped out there for the day work. You weren't being paid much so you could afford to tell the director if he was doing something wrong. Some of them liked that. As an extra, I got to meet many directors. For instance, I was in Fred Zinnemann's *Teresa* [1951], earning $16 a day.

MILLER: Your first credited role was in Henry Hathaway's *You're in the Navy Now* [1951], playing a radioman on a ship. I notice there was a fellow named Charles Buchinsky in the cast. That would be Charles Bronson, right? Did either of you have any idea you'd someday wind up being movie heroes?

MARVIN: When Charlie and I made our first picture for Hathaway, we looked at each other and knew: here are two guys who have to be heavies. I mean, we couldn't wear an Arrow shirt in a magazine ad, right? They were still doing Tyrone Power and John Payne films then.

MILLER: Why do you think that kind of pretty boy leading man faded away and the tough guys like you and Bronson came to the top?

MARVIN: Too many guys came home from the war and told their friends and families what it was really like, that all heroes weren't good looking. Anyway, I didn't have any idea about being a leading man. I was just going along with getting a job and keeping it.

MILLER: Are you happy now that you didn't look like one of those magazine cover boys?

MARVIN: I'm mature now. When I was twenty-seven or twenty-eight, a good-looking guy was Prince Charming. I didn't get any of those parts. The bad guys were the more interesting parts anyway.

MILLER: So the rise of the Lee Marvins and Charlie Bronsons is due to the coming of greater realism in the aftermath of the horrors of a world war?

MARVIN: That's right. It's not just a change in how we see heroism. In love stories, both the boy and girl would have to live happily ever after in the old days. We did all that in the 1920s and 1930s. The real facts of life are much more evident to kids today.

MILLER: You got your first leading role in a war picture, Edward Dmytrk's *Eight Iron Men* in 1952. How was he to work for?

MARVIN: We argued a lot, but it was always artistic and not egotistical stuff.

MILLER: But the film that really put you on the map was Fritz Lang's *The Big Heat*. I've heard horror stories about Lang. Your opinion?

MARVIN: I was making *The Wild One* at Columbia and they sent me over to meet him. He says, "Go down and get a haircut and a shave, then come back." When I come back, I see a desk in the corner of the sound-stage with a silver bucket on it, filled with ice and a bottle of champagne. I ask him if there's anything I can do for him [as an audition] and he says, "You're actor. I don't worry about you." Then he points across the sound-stage at Glenn Ford [the film's star]. "It's that son of a bitch I worry about!" And I said to myself, "Jesus, he likes me better than the leading man!" So I was all for him. Then about six weeks later, a new actor comes on the set— he's standing by the champagne bucket and I see Lang pointing over at me and telling him something.

MILLER: You roughed up Gloria Grahame pretty badly in that movie. Was that his idea?

MARVIN: In one scene, I grab her and swing her around and Lang says to her, "You didn't scream! You must scream!" We must have done twenty takes trying to get this scene. Lang says, "Hurt her! She must scream!" He says, "Break her fucking arm!" By then I was too weak to do it. That's the way he was.

MILLER: In contrast, who was the direct opposite of Fritz Lang?

MARVIN: Josh Logan [who directed Marvin in 1969's *Paint Your Wagon*] was probably the extreme of talking to the artist. He's a gentleman, a beautiful guy. He would admit to you when he didn't know what to do. I'd say, "Well, we have to do something, Josh!" He would expose his vulnerability to his actors. So if the actor was insecure, he'd take that as weakness. If you were secure, you'd take that as honesty, him just trying to get to the best way of possibly doing this. He knew what a scene was—and when it wasn't—working from his theatrical training.

MILLER: How about John Ford, for whom you made both *The Man Who Shot Liberty Valance* and *Donovan's Reef* [1963]?

MARVIN: Ford had a definite idea of what he wanted and if the actor didn't bring it to him, he'd give it to the actor. He had a hard-line policy on the set and he kept it going.

MILLER: Was the impact of *Cat Ballou* as big a surprise to you as it was to some people?

MARVIN: Yeah. The book was not a comedy. They'd had a hundred scripts written from it and they'd had it for twenty-odd years, so they wanted to get rid of it. When I read the script I loved it. But I saw it as a tragedy. It was only a $1.1 million budget with a twenty-eight-day schedule. We went two days over and everybody was going to get fired. Then it was this big hit. It was just one of the quirks of the business.

MILLER: It was only the second film from director Elliot Silverstein, but even with the big box office and the Oscar for you, he only did a few more films.

MARVIN: I don't know what happened to Elliot. Jesus, he was so brilliant! An amazing guy!

MILLER: You've tried to do some risky things, but they seem to want you back in the same kind of action roles.

MARVIN: All actors try to think they're not repeating themselves. You try not to. I say, "No. I've already done that." But you look back and an awful lot of it does look similar, doesn't it? To be talked about, something has to be commercially successful. I mean, how many people have seen me in *The Iceman Cometh* [1973]?

MILLER: Is one of the things you said no to another sequel to *The Dirty Dozen?*

MARVIN: They're doing more, but I won't be involved. The first *Dirty Dozen* took us five to six months. *Dirty Dozen: The Next Mission* was a five-week job. The original plan was the sequel would be shown on American television, then be released overseas as a feature film, which would change the monetary income. But I did the first sequel out of gratitude to Robert Aldrich [who directed the original], but he has just died. They've improved the money [offered], but it's just that we've done it already. I mean, it's getting a little ridiculous at my age. I'm still a major in the army? Anyway, I'm not going for the mountain of gold.

MILLER: I know it's an unpleasant topic, but do you think the whole palimony thing hurt you at all at the box office?

MARVIN: Hell, no. It made me a leading man.

MILLER: How did you get involved with *Delta Force* and a location shoot in Israel?

MARVIN: Menahem Golan just called me up and told me the story in fifteen minutes. He's a great storyteller. He's going first class all the way. I'm very impressed with the guy.

MILLER: So it's Chuck Norris and you against the terrorists? Sounds like a bloodbath.

MARVIN: The body count doesn't start to really mount until the last third. With my brains and his brawn, we got 'em!

MILLER: Why did you decide to leave Hollywood and move out here in the desert?

MARVIN: I'd worked out here several times and always thought it would be a great place to have a day off. We rented here for a year, liked it, and then bought the place. We've been living here about twelve years now. I don't shop and I'm not a nightclubber, so why would I want to live in Los Angeles? It's a little hard to see all the movies living out here because they don't have any art houses, but we rent a lot of tapes.

MILLER: You have your Oscar and you still get big roles offered to you, but are there any things you still want to do that you haven't done yet?

MARVIN: I've never had a master plan for my career. Don't have it now and didn't have it back when. I'm kind of laid back. If anything's good and the people working on it think I'd be good in it, they'll call me. I'm sure there's stuff I'd like to do, but if I made mention of it, five hundred hacks would be out there knocking it out tonight.

Lee Marvin in combat gear for Samuel Fuller's 1980 *The Big Red One*. Courtesy of Lorimar Productions.

Afterword

Lee Marvin graciously bid me good-bye and thanked me for spending the day with him. He asked me to say hello to actress Elizabeth Ashley if I saw her on the set of *Stagecoach* because "she's a great gal and we had a super time together making *Great Scout and Cathouse Thursday*" (1975).

Marvin had a son and three daughters with his first wife. His youngest daughter, Claudia, died in 2012 and son Christopher died in 2013.

In 1987, Marvin suffered severe stomach pains and was admitted to a Tucson hospital where he underwent abdominal surgery. He was kept in the hospital for a couple of weeks because he had flulike symptoms and was in a rundown condition. While there, he suffered a heart attack and died on August 29. He was sixty-three. He's buried at Arlington National Cemetery in Virginia. In 1997, Pamela Marvin published a book about their life together, *Lee: A Romance*.

VII

Great Character Actors

Richard Farnsworth

Interview by Ron Miller

Richard Farnsworth always seemed a trifle amused by the fact that some people considered him a movie star. He gave the impression that his whole acting career was some kind of scam he ran on Hollywood in between horse-wrangling jobs. But fortunately, he left behind a filmed record of what he did in front of the cameras. And make no mistake, Farnsworth had picked up a lot of knowledge about acting over the years—enough, in fact, to earn lots of rave reviews and two Oscar nominations.

For pretty much the first forty years of his movie career, Farnsworth was a stuntman who specialized in stunts involving horses. Then in 1978, after several years playing bit parts, he finally landed a sizeable role in a major motion picture—*Comes a Horseman* with Jane Fonda—and Hollywood, along with the moviegoing public, sat up and took notice of him for the first time. For that performance, Farnsworth earned a Best Supporting Actor Oscar nomination. Though he lost to Christopher Walken in *The Deer Hunter,* the clamor around him led to a strong new career as an actor who didn't have to fall off his horse to earn a living anymore.

Farnsworth wasn't the first stuntman to become a movie star. In fact, one of his old buddies, Ben Johnson, became an actor in 1949's *Mighty Joe Young* and later won Best Supporting Actor for *The Last Picture Show* (1971). Johnson's achievement inspired Farnsworth to give it a try himself.

Like Johnson, Farnsworth even progressed to leading roles in a few of his subsequent films, including *The Grey Fox* (1982) and his final film, *The Straight Story* (1999), for which he earned another Oscar nomination, this time for Best Actor.

Yet Farnsworth never lost his love of horses nor his appreciation of the hardy men and women who rode them in movies. He had been a leader in

Richard Farnsworth in *The Grey Fox* (1982). Courtesy of TV station KTVU in Oakland, California.

the world of stunt work and spent a great deal of time laboring to make it a safer and more rewarding profession for himself and his colleagues.

Setting the Scene

Richard Farnsworth was one of my personal favorites—as an actor and as a man. I enjoyed him so much on-screen that I would go out of my way to see anything he chose to do. He never disappointed me. He was at his best playing quiet men of great courage and sterling character, although I think perhaps his all-time best performance was as the charming old train robber Bill Miner in *The Grey Fox*, a performance that earned him the Canadian equivalent of the Oscar.

I had never heard of Farnsworth until I saw him in *Comes a Horseman*, a western in which he played his first major supporting role—an aging ranch hand, circa 1940, facing the end of his era as private range land was being taken over by huge ranch interests. But once I sat down with Farnsworth to find out what he'd been doing in the first sixty years of his life, I learned I'd been watching him for years—I just didn't know it. For instance, he was the stunt rider for Montgomery Clift in *Red River* (1948), doubled Guy Madison in his *Adventures of Wild Bill Hickok* (1951–1958) TV series, and did the same for Steve McQueen in the *Wanted: Dead or Alive* series (1958–1961). He even persuaded moviegoers he was Jerry Lewis in *Pardners* (1956).

We met for lunch at the large riding club and stables in Burbank, California, where Farnsworth hung out to shoot the breeze with so many of his friends who shared a love for horses. He was a genial, down-to-earth guy without a trace of "movie star" aura, and it was a kick to sit there with him while dozens of people stopped to say hello and wish him well.

The Interview

MILLER: I know you were still in your teens when you appeared in your first movie. How did that come about?

FARNSWORTH: I had been working with polo horses in Ventura [California] and many of them were owned by movie people. I heard they were looking for riders to work as extras in the new Gary Cooper picture, *The Adventures of Marco Polo* [1938], so I looked into it. They hired a bunch of us kids because they needed about five hundred riders. I was then working in the polo club horse barn for $7 a week and board, so the movie work looked pretty good to me.

MILLER: Did you think this would lead to a movie acting career?

FARNSWORTH: I never had any aspirations of that kind, but after working in the picture I decided stunt work was something I could do. There was nothing dull about it. I was a bronc rider in those days. I was a good athlete and could do just about anything they wanted.

MILLER: Wasn't it a lot more dangerous occupation back then?

FARNSWORTH: Well, those old-time directors were much more likely to ask you to risk your life. Because of the money, if one guy wouldn't do it, somebody else would. A lot of guys got hurt. It was a business where if you didn't want to do it, somebody else would put your clothes on and do it for you.

MILLER: How involved were you in bringing about changes to make it safer?

FARNSWORTH: I was a part of the Stuntmen's Association when it started. I think I was the vice president. It did more than anything else to improve the image of the stuntman. Before that, people had this idea we were all guys with a death wish—or else we were drunks who would do anything for a dollar.

MILLER: Did you have your own trained horses to do those stunts and the awful spills stuntmen did in those old films?

FARNSWORTH: At first you just got on the horses that were there. Later I developed my own "falling horses" for that kind of thing. There were some directors who would sit down and plan out things, but others just wanted to go out and shoot some action and didn't care how they got it.

MILLER: I've been told that Ben Johnson's journey from stunt rider to Oscar-winning actor was an inspiration to you.

FARNSWORTH: We were stuntmen together. He was from Oklahoma and came out here with Howard Hughes to make *The Outlaw* [filmed in 1941 but not released until 1943]. He got started in acting way before I did. His first starring role was in *Mighty Joe Young* while I was one of the cowboys who roped the big gorilla. They had this big mechanical gorilla arm that was about eight feet long. All you could see was the arm. We would rope the arm and a guy off camera would pull a lever and the arm would yank us off our horses.

MILLER: What did Ben tell you about his try at being a movie star?

FARNSWORTH: He was scared to death, but he did good. He called me when I got nominated [for an Oscar] and told me I was robbed!

MILLER: Tell me about some of your other early jobs in movies.

FARNSWORTH: I did a lot of stunts on *The Conqueror* [1956] with John Wayne. I played a Mongol with a Chinese moustache and goatee. We worked in St. George, Utah, where they had done nuclear testing and a lot of guys died later on and they thought that radiation had something to do with it.

And I was one of Kirk Douglas's sidekicks in *Spartacus* [1960]. I was on that picture for a year—and I never even got on a horse! I was strictly on the ground. I fought as a gladiator using a trident and a net. I was good at that. That was me fighting Woody Strode. I also worked as an archer in many films, including *The Professionals* [1966]. I taught Woody how to use a bow.

MILLER: You worked in some great westerns, including *Red River,* and most of the TV western shows. Were there any movie stars who were actually good riders?

FARNSWORTH: There were four good riders. Joel McCrea was probably the best. Bob Taylor was a good horseman who had his own horses. [Gary] Cooper could ride and [John] Wayne. Those are the ones who could get it done.

MILLER: Did you often double the leading men, doing their stunts for them?

FARNSWORTH: Oh, sure. I doubled for the singing cowboy Jimmy Wakely and doubled Wild Bill Elliott in four *Red Ryder* westerns. My doubling was mostly in bucking horse scenes. Other guys doubled them for their fights.

MILLER: Now that you're well established as an actor, what do you think of the stunt work you see being done today?

FARNSWORTH: The young fellas haven't had the chance to be around livestock as much as we did. The wagon drivers and horsemen are harder to find. There are still some good horseback stuntmen around, but not as many as there used to be because they're not making westerns anymore. Today's youngsters doing stunts come mainly from the motorcycle and car wreck part of it.

MILLER: How did you finally segue into acting?

FARNSWORTH: I'd done quite a few bits. I was scared of the camera—not physically, but just scared to death to have to try and act. I had some lines thrown at me like "Get a rope!" or "Hangin's too good for him!" I just figured to stay as a stuntman because I made a good living at it. But I figured I'd probably have to go out of the business because of my age sooner or later, so I gave it a try.

MILLER: So exactly how did *Comes a Horseman* come about?

FARNSWORTH: I'd done some things for [director Alan J.] Pakula in a picture he produced called *The Stalking Moon* [1969] with Gregory Peck. I was a cavalry officer. I charged down a hill and hollered some dialogue. I guess it was because of my age. [Pakula] said, "Hey, that old guy rides pretty good for an actor." And somebody else said, "He isn't an actor. He's a stuntman." So he offered me the role in his movie.

MILLER: Were you surprised to get that nice a part?

FARNSWORTH: It was only a fluke. I wanted to turn it down when they shoved all that dialogue at me, but my wife said to go ahead and try it. So I did and it worked out fine.

MILLER: How was it to work with Jane Fonda?

FARNSWORTH: Jane helped me a lot. She knew I'd worked with her dad [Henry Fonda]. She's a real pro. I've never had anybody coach me, but if you're working with someone who looks at you and really means it, it's easy to come back with your lines.

MILLER: How big a challenge was it when you finally wound up playing the leading role in a movie in *The Grey Fox*?

FARNSWORTH: I identified with that character pretty well. It was the easiest role I ever tried to play. Everything just fit without reaching. It was just one of those things. I guess I was just born to play that role.

MILLER: How do you go about the process of acting?

FARNSWORTH: I never pretend. I don't think I've ever done a role that was that different from me. I know I've got something that's a little different, but I don't know what it is. I know I'm not a good actor and I don't profess to be.

MILLER: Are there things you won't do?

FARNSWORTH: I couldn't play a meanie. No way in the world. I have to be careful what I take. Obscenity is one thing I won't do. I usually cut those words [profanity]. I don't believe in throwing in those words just because you can. I've turned down jobs because I wouldn't do that.

MILLER: You got to play a really nice man in TV's *Anne of Green Gables* [1985]. Are you okay with playing grandpa types?

FARNSWORTH: I *am* a grandpa type. I have grandchildren, so I like the grandpa parts. I don't really care about all this action stuff. I did that all my life.

MILLER: Looking back, would you have gone into acting a lot earlier if you'd known how successful you would be?

FARNSWORTH: I think I would do it just the way I've done it. It's nice to be recognized, but I would have survived either way.

Afterword

Director David Lynch gave Farnsworth his best role in a decade in 1999's *The Straight Story,* the whimsical true account of an elderly man's long trek to see his estranged brother, a cross-country journey that he makes riding his own power lawnmower because he can no longer legally drive a car. His performance was so natural, so emotionally touching that many picked it as the best of the year—and he earned an Oscar nomination in the leading actor category.

Farnsworth was married once, to Margaret Hill, who died in 1985. They had two children—a son, Diamond, and daughter, Missy. Despite a healthy lifestyle that kept him a very robust individual well into his old age, Farnsworth was diagnosed with terminal cancer in 2000 and took his own life by gunshot in his Lincoln, New Mexico, home on October 6, 2000. He was eighty.

It's painful to know that Farnsworth was in such low spirits that he decided to take his own life. Yet I can understand why he felt this was the right time to write his own finish. He would never get another role like the plucky, determined Mr. Straight. He probably wanted us to remember him that way and not the way his story otherwise was sure to end.

Hurd Hatfield

Interview by James Bawden

Hurd Hatfield occupies a unique place in Hollywood history: he played the starring role in a major MGM film of the 1940s, for which he received uniformly good reviews, then slipped away into obscurity with a series of lesser roles in a mixed bag of movies, good and bad. Handsome and well trained in theater in both England and on Broadway, Hatfield is known primarily for the 1945 film version of Oscar Wilde's *The Picture of Dorian Gray*—and that's about it.

Setting the Scene

Sometimes meeting a golden age movie star is a serendipitous occasion. In 1986 I scheduled an interview with an old friend, actor Keir Dullea, who was starring in a new made-for-cable TV series, *Loving Friends and Perfect Couples,* which was due to be syndicated on American TV. It starred such TV names as James Carroll Jordan from *Rich Man, Poor Man* and Bruce Fairbairn from *The Rookies* and ran on Global TV, where it was valued as badly needed Canadian-made television.

Dullea was in the commissary and seated next to him was an actor I'd always wanted to meet—Hurd Hatfield. Hatfield was guest-starring as a devilish character. Dullea introduced him to me. After I'd finished my other interviews I drove with Hatfield back to his hotel. There we shared high tea as he talked about his very strange Hollywood career.

The Interview

HATFIELD: All anybody wants to talk about is *The Picture of Dorian Gray*!

BAWDEN: Well, why not? It's a subversive masterpiece. How did it get made at a studio as conservative as MGM? And how did you get to star in it?

Hurd Hatfield with Donna Reed in *The Picture of Dorian Gray* (1945). Courtesy of MGM.

HATFIELD: Well, I'd been studying theater in England, but I was back in San Francisco touring in a Dostoevsky play I'd starred in on Broadway. I was spotted by an MGM scout who signed me to a contract after I made a "silent test"—meaning no dialogue, just a look at my facial features. Within days I was on the train for Culver City, where I was promptly plopped into a Katharine Hepburn vehicle titled *Dragon Seed* [1944]. She was a valiant Chinese rebel leading an insurgency against the Japanese. I played her brother-in-law, Lao San Tan, Turhan Bey was her husband, and Walter Huston was the father. A whole herd of Caucasians and we had to wear those things over our eyelids and talk in very strange English. Today I look at it and it's a real hoot. Kate is a Chinese peasant with a Bryn Mawr accent. I met her recently in New York City at a fund-raiser and said, "Good afternoon, sister-in-law" and she laughed like crazy.

BAWDEN: How did you get to star as Dorian Gray?

HATFIELD: Every actor was tested. Even Van Johnson! But the director, Albert Lewin, asked me back for a second test, which startled me. I was not as Oscar Wilde described Dorian. I wasn't blond. I didn't have angelic features. But Albert liked the passiveness of my expression—or so he said. He had directed a fantastic version of *The Moon and Sixpence* [1942] and MGM gave him virtual carte blanche. The powerful producer Pandro Berman was called in and he made the call. No young British actors were available; they were back in Europe, fighting for their empire.

You know, Albert only made six movies as a director; all are what we call art house films. He followed with *The Private Affairs of Bel Ami* [1947] and then *Pandora and the Flying Dutchman* [1951]. Then he made *Saadia* [1954] and finished with *The Living Idol* [1957]. We saluted him in New York in 1968 and he died that year of pneumonia at seventy-three.

BAWDEN: So why was Dorian Gray such a commercial hit?

HATFIELD: It was not completely faithful to the novel. But Lewin certainly tried. Everything sinister is only hinted at darkly. I played him as a narcissist. Nothing that happens to others ever bothers him. You know at the end Lewin fought like blazes to stop that one Technicolor shot of the degenerate picture. But Pandro overruled him, saying it was good box office. Albert also did the screenplay. Much of the dialogue is word-for-word the same. He asked for Harry Stradling as cinematographer. And the settings are completely Victorian and not a Hollywood variety. He inspected each stick of furniture. One little bowl he brought from his home.

Angela Lansbury won her second supporting Oscar nomination in a row. George Saunders is magnificent as nasty Lord Henry Wotton. Donna Reed is so beautiful in a demure way as Gladys. Cedric Hardwicke was hired at a high price as the narrator. The biggest story change was Sybil. In the novel, she is a Shakespearean actress, here a music hall singer. But Angie and I became friends forever. I introduced her to her second husband. She keeps using me on [her TV series] *Murder, She Wrote*.

I don't think MGM president Louis B. Mayer understood the subtext. When he was told he became furious. But the box office was solid. It really stands up. But I never really had a future at MGM because of Mayer's wrath.

BAWDEN: Then you were loaned out for Jean Renoir's *Diary of a Chambermaid* [1946]?

HATFIELD: Another artsy picture. And when released it had very few play dates. When [Luis] Bunuel made his version a decade later, Renoir protested and Bunuel said he'd never even heard of it. Paulette Goddard was in her phase of trying to be a great actress. It costarred her current husband, Burgess Meredith. I was a consumptive in love with this fey creature. The censors insisted on heavy edits and it sort of escaped into a limited release.

BAWDEN: Then it was back to MGM for *The Beginning or the End* [1947].

HATFIELD: MGM's attempt to explain the atomic bomb. An all-star thingy. I was seventh billed after the likes of Brian Donlevy and Audrey Totter. Norman Taurog, who generally directed kid actors, was in charge. Bobby Walker was the hero. It was brought to the attention of the studio by Donna Reed, whose high school teacher was involved in the Manhattan Project. It was very idealistic. But nobody has seen it recently.

BAWDEN: Then it was off to Warners for *The Unsuspected* [1947]?

HATFIELD: By this time MGM had given up on me and they loaned me and Audrey Totter to Warners. Originally it was going to star Lauren Bacall, but she got nervous being without husband Humphrey Bogart and left. Warners brought in Joan Caulfield from Paramount. They had just loaned their star Geraldine Fitzgerald to Paramount and could choose any Paramount leading lady in return. Claude Rains got second billing. A diminutive man, but a hoot to work with. Had a mesmerizing accent and flamboyant acting style. Connie Bennett was always rolling her eyes at his scene-stealing. Director Mike Curtiz used shadows all over the place. Most was shot on vast studio sets. The nominal leading man was Michael North, who later became a top agent. We were waiting around for the next scene and Audrey whispers, "From MGM drivel to Warners trash." I'm afraid I got the giggles.

BAWDEN: Then came *Joan of Arc* [1948].

HATFIELD: More expensive than *Gone with the Wind*, which also was directed by Victor Fleming. Huge medieval sets all over the place. Vast armies of villagers villaging. Great suits of armor made for the battle scenes. Fleming and our star Ingrid Bergman were an item during it. But he was also a sick man who sometimes was so weak he couldn't get out of his director's chair. It's not a bad movie. I didn't find it compelling. Ingrid wasn't right. I was Father Pasquerel, chaplain to Joan. It never recovered its costs. It really never would.

BAWDEN: Then you left movies.

HATFIELD: I did two B flicks: *The Checkered Coat* [1950] and *Chinatown at Midnight* [1950]. Asked for my release and went back to Broadway, where I always belonged.

BAWDEN: You got very busy on live television.

HATFIELD: At last I'd found my home. Never had a moment's attack of nerves. I'd open and close in a play and all within the confines of a TV studio. And without an audience to feed off. It was in August 1950 that I did *The Importance of Being Earnest* on *Masterpiece Playhouse* on NBC and then *The Rivals* with Mary Boland and Diana Douglas [Kirk's wife] a few weeks later.

BAWDEN: You were very busy.

HATFIELD: In 1953 I did *The Hasty Heart* on *Broadway Television Theater* opposite John Dall, another refugee from Hollywood. Bob Montgomery used me on his show in a two-part adaptation of *Hunchback of Notre Dame*—Bob Ellenstein was Quasimodo.

When filmed series came in I was on *Alfred Hitchcock, Lux Playhouse*. You name it. I was on virtually every series. And I also thrived on Broadway. I was in the original production of *Anastasia* with Viveca Lindfors. I remember the night Ingrid Bergman dropped by after the performance to ask Viveca for tips. Ingrid had just gotten the movie lead! Viveca was beet red with fury!

BAWDEN: But you continued making movies.

HATFIELD: It was Arthur Penn who coaxed me back to play a wonderful character named Moultrie in his bizarre western *The Left Handed Gun* [1958] with Paul Newman as Billy the Kid. And he asked me back to play one Ed Castle in the fascinating Warren Beatty starrer *Mickey One* [1965]. I had a whale of a time as Pontius Pilate, who I played as most fastidious in *King of Kings* [1961], directed by that wonderful madman Nick Ray. We had a ball feasting in Madrid during many months of production as they kept rewriting the Bible.

I somehow felt I belonged to other ages. I was Arias in *El Cid* [1962], a very intelligent spectacle, and much later I spent more time in the Old Testament as Ahimelech in *King David* [1985]. I still remember Richard Gere dancing down that dusty road, dressed in what seemed to be a big diaper. I acted as much as I wanted to, still do. It pays the big bills.

BAWDEN: And your life today?

HATFIELD: I have a gorgeous country home in Ireland. Angie [Lansbury] used to live next door but she has moved permanently back to Hollywood and I've done three *Murder, She Wrote* [episodes] so far. I can only appear once a year because it's always as a different character. She's one star who never forgets old friends. I never was asked to guest on *The Donna*

Reed Show. What character would I play? And that's why I'm in Toronto this week, although I have one strict rule: no nude scenes at my time of life, please!

Afterword

Hurd Hatfield died of a heart attack at his Monkstown estate, County Cork, Ireland, on December 26, 1998. He was eighty-one.

John Houseman

Interview by James Bawden and Ron Miller

John Houseman surely had one of the most offbeat and amazing careers in show business ever. He was doing quite well in the grain business until he lost his shirt in the 1929 stock market crash and had to cast about for a new way to make a living. He had dabbled in writing for the stage in his school days in England, so he knocked out a few plays to see what would happen. This led to a most fortuitous partnership with a young theater man named Orson Welles, and together they formed the now-legendary Mercury Theatre ensemble.

Along with Welles, Houseman produced the famous *War of the Worlds* radio broadcast that panicked America in 1938, and he was a key member of the production team for Welles's first movie, *Citizen Kane* (1941), now widely respected as the greatest of all American movies.

Houseman's accomplishments didn't stop there: he turned to acting, winning an Academy Award for the role of Professor Kingsfield in *The Paper Chase* (1973).

Houseman was married twice, first to actress Zita Johann (1929–1933), who was Boris Karloff's leading lady in *The Mummy* (1932), and then to Joan Courtney from 1952 until his death. He had two sons with Joan—John M., who's an anthropologist in Paris, and Charles S., a New Hampshire artist.

Setting the Scene

Both of us conducted separate interviews with John Houseman over the years. We have combined them for this presentation, but here we offer our individual memories of the circumstances of those interviews.

BAWDEN: When I made an appointment in 1981 to interview John Houseman in his lunch break during the Toronto filming of *Bells,* starring

John Houseman as Professor Kingsfield with James Stephens as Mr. Hart in the TV version of *The Paper Chase,* circa 1978. Courtesy of 20th Century Fox Television and CBS.

Richard Chamberlain and directed by Michael Anderson, the topic was, naturally, supposed to be the new movie. But our conversation went on past lunch break as it became apparent that Houseman wasn't entirely thrilled with his latest project and would rather talk about practically anything else. (The movie was released in 1982 as *Murder by Phone* and was a big flop.)

That was fine with me. Houseman was one of the most accomplished producers in show business history—and an Academy Award winner as an actor—so that gave me lots of things to ask him about.

MILLER: I first chatted with John Houseman after he gave a press conference with TV columnists in 1978 when *The Paper Chase* was coming to television as a weekly CBS series. Later, when *The Paper Chase* was revived by the Showtime pay cable network, I talked with him again on several occasions, the last time in 1986 when it appeared the television run of the series had come to an end.

As I wrote about our first encounter, I always felt as if I'd better polish my shoes on the back of my pants leg and make sure my fingernails were clean before meeting John Houseman because he seemed like such a complete gentleman. It was indeed a pleasure to discover that he was a much more down-to-earth kind of guy, although I never got to the point where I felt I could slap him on the back and call him "Johnny" when we got together.

The Interview

BAWDEN: I'm never sure what producers do.

HOUSEMAN: When you find out, tell me and then we'll both know.

BAWDEN: I just have to ask you about the so-called night that panicked America and Orson Welles's 1938 *War of the Worlds* radio drama since I'm talking to one of the key participants.

HOUSEMAN: May I plead not guilty? The facts are simply this: the Mercury Theatre on CBS was averaging an audience of 3.9 percent every Sunday night. Over at NBC the audience for Edgar Bergen and Charlie McCarthy was 35 percent. End of discussion. How could we panic America? We were about to be cancelled. And the only script half ready that week was one by a newcomer, Howard Koch, based on H. G. Wells's *The War of the Worlds*. I clearly remember the date: Sunday, October 30, 1938. It was Orson's idea to make it into what I call the first docudrama with a radio announcer. The program started with a full disclaimer. But that week a particularly inept male singer was featured on Bergen/McCarthy and the audience kept straying away. What they heard at CBS alarmed them. They thought it was the real stuff! It certainly did the trick. By 8:32 all of America was panicking and here we were in a CBS radio room doing a live broadcast, completely unaware. At the end, police rushed us and interrogated us for hours, but we were never actually arrested. We thought CBS would suspend us and they did consider it for a bit.

Instead we finally got a sponsor—Campbell soups! And our ratings soared because people were expecting that sort of thing every week. Instead we were giving them things like *Jane Eyre*. But it got Orson noticed. And he was soon off to Hollywood and RKO.

BAWDEN: You went, too.

HOUSEMAN: I had other things to finish in New York and when I got out there I found a very depressed Orson. He'd been working for weeks on an adaptation of *Heart of Darkness* [the Joseph Conrad novel], which RKO most assuredly did not want. His option was running out. In desperation we contacted Herman Mankiewicz and he had this idea about an epic on a newspaper tycoon. Of course, it was William Randolph Hearst. [The film ultimately became Welles's *Citizen Kane*.] To say that Herman drank a bit is an understatement. So I was deputized to babysit Mank and take him to a remote ranch near Victorville in the San Bernardino Mountains. Mank was in the back of a studio convertible and a nurse went along to restrain him. My job was to get him to actually write it all down. I mean, he'd been near Hearst and that gang for decades. He had been to San Simeon many times. Who in Hollywood hadn't? In part he'd already tackled the story with *The Power and the Glory* [1933], which starred Spencer Tracy. He finished it. And 90 percent of the script remained his even after Orson got through with his tinkering. Of course, Orson always wanted all the credit.

BAWDEN: During filming you slipped away?

HOUSEMAN: David Selznick headhunted me and off I went. He was thinking of doing a new version of *Jane Eyre* with his new discovery, Joan Fontaine, who had just won an Oscar. But David had head problems. He'd just produced two films—*Gone with the Wind* [1939] and *Rebecca* [1940]—and they'd won him consecutive Best Picture Oscars. He simply couldn't commit to our *Jane* and finally he sold all of us to Fox for a huge amount: me, Joan, our script, and director Robert Stevenson.

In his own way, he was another Orson. Both sucked the oxygen out of a room. With David, a story conference would start at 2 p.m., then we'd break for dinner at Ciro's, where he'd order for us all and then try to show the chef how to cook it. At 3 a.m. he'd still be at it while I was desperately needing sleep. But I wasn't on Benzedrine as he was.

BAWDEN: How did you get to Paramount?

HOUSEMAN: They needed a quality producer. I needed the job. After Orson and David, it was ever so romantic to be on my own. I was given titles which I might not have chosen. First I was assigned to *The Unseen*

[1945]. What?! You've heard of it and you like it? Amazing! It was a sort of follow-up to *The Uninvited* [1944], which had been a big hit for the studio's newcomer Gail Russell. And I might add she was extremely sweet but highly excitable. She had to have a drink just to step onto any soundstage. Completely introverted. So of course they made her an actress based on her physical beauty. I thought because of her instincts she might become a very great actress, but she slipped into alcoholism and died at thirty-eight. *The Unseen* was from an Ethel Lina White potboiler. She also wrote [the book that became Hitchcock's] *The Lady Vanishes* [1938], you know. Paramount just would not use the original title: *Her Heart in Her Throat,* which is understandable. Joel McCrea was the big suspect. It was all set in his gloomy Boston mansion. Kindly Herbert Marshall was the real killer. But you know all that because you've seen it.

BAWDEN: Another film you produced in that period, *Miss Susie Slagel's* [1946], was an odd choice for you.

HOUSEMAN: Again, I had no choice. Paramount had this property kicking around for years. It was supposed to be a light drama set at a boardinghouse in 1910 Baltimore and looking at the antics of Johns Hopkins medical students. Two young Paramount girls, Veronica Lake and Joan Caulfield, were top billed. There was just one problem: they loathed each other and that occasionally showed up on-screen. Sonny Tufts was the big male lead! No, I'm not kidding.

Another kid was Lloyd Bridges. We had the wonderful Lillian Gish as the spinster running the boardinghouse. After filming, a screening was arranged for the Paramount head, Y. Frank Freeman, and he went ballistic. In one scene Frank charged he'd seen "nigras and white boys" in the same infirmary. Side by side! That would never do for our southern exhibitors. So the set had to be reconstructed at great expense and reshot with a segregated bed allotment—half the "nigra" extras were fired, the rest segregated into another wing of the clinic. And we still managed to make money.

BAWDEN: Then came your big Paramount hit, *The Blue Dahlia* [1946].

HOUSEMAN: A reteaming of Alan Ladd and Veronica Lake. He was the biggest Paramount star of his day. She was only popular beside him, really. They were little people. He might have hit five feet, five inches on a breezy day. She barely hit five feet. What made Alan such a tremendous star was his voice, which he'd honed in dozens of live radio assignments. She had cut her peekaboo bangs during the war. Girls working on assembly lines were having their long hair get tangled in the machinery with dire results. She cut it out of patriotism, but it killed her sexiness. Am I allowed to say Raymond Chandler called her "Moronica" Lake to her face? And she just laughed it off. This was her last big hit, but Bill Bendix stole every scene he was in. He was a G.I. suffering from mental problems. Doris Dowling was great as Laddie's suffering wife. It's just about the most entertaining film noir around.

BAWDEN: Why did you leave Paramount?

HOUSEMAN: It wasn't the greatest place to work. And I had this lovely offer from Universal to make a film version of *Letter from an Unknown Woman*. I'd be working again with Howard Koch, who adapted the Stefan Zweig novel. We had Joan Fontaine in the lead. We had Max Ophuls as director. Then it all went wrong. Max simply couldn't hurry up. We went way over budget while he kept filming eighty takes of Joan simply climbing the stairs. The public loathed it because it was so anti everything 1948 audiences were taught to think about. Universal hacked it to shreds and released it without any campaign and, look closely, I think Max's name is even misspelled in the opening credits. And do you know, people come up to this day and say it's their favorite film.

BAWDEN: How did *The Bad and the Beautiful* [1952] start out?

HOUSEMAN: It was a look at the classical Hollywood system and how that system was crumbling. Kirk Douglas played an amalgam of many characters. The studio head, played by Walter Pidgeon, was actually Harry Cohn. Douglas most certainly was not David Selznick, but David thought so and sent out letters—such was his egotism. Lana Turner played an actress patterned after tragic Diana Barrymore. It was directed in a high style by Vincente Minnelli, whose pictures always looked great. The wonder was how well he made the black and white glisten. And it did get a Best Picture Oscar nomination, and of the cast Gloria Grahame won for Supporting Actress, which shocked us all. Her part was so tiny.

BAWDEN: How did *Julius Caesar* [1953] come about?

HOUSEMAN: I guess it was partly my idea. I'd done a lot of Shakespeare onstage. And Joe Mankiewicz was tickled with the unusual subject matter. It all depended on getting Marlon Brando on board. Think of it, Stanley Kowalski as Marc Anthony! And he said, [with] some trepidation, he'd try. There ensued long sessions with Johnny Gielgud, who said he'd teach him the cadence. I'm afraid it just wasn't enough time, but Marlon is such a brilliant actor he could fake it a bit. Gielgud himself was brilliant as

Cassius, but it was James Mason as Brutus who truly excelled. We had that old ham Louis Calhern as Caesar and he was wonderfully ripe. Deborah Kerr and Greer Garson did cameos as Portia and Calpurnia. It did work and we even made some money. But that was as far as MGM would go. When Olivier and Leigh subsequently wanted to film *Macbeth,* it was quickly turned down.

BAWDEN: How did *Executive Suite* [1954] come about?

HOUSEMAN: Well, MGM powers thought a movie about business would be free from any blacklisting nastiness! The novel was vast, so I got a young guy, Ernest Lehman, to write a script that concentrated on just seven characters. I got Robert Wise, who I had known a bit at RKO, because I needed a no-nonsense director. Our biggest star was Bill Holden as the rising young executive and June Allyson was his wife. The great Barbara Stanwyck took third billing and a relatively small part because she got the biggest screaming scene. And we added Freddie March, Walter Pidgeon, Paul Douglas, Shelley Winters, Louis Calhern. Nina Foch swears she threw the script at me when I asked her to be the secretary because the character only gets about twenty lines. But she's always there, the voice of conscience, and she was the only one to win an Oscar nomination. We spent $700,000 on star salaries and just $350,000 on making the film. After viewing the first cut, I decided not to add any music. It played without any musical score because none was needed.

BAWDEN: You also made *Her Twelve Men* [1954] simultaneously?

HOUSEMAN: I just knew you would toss that title at me! It turned out to be Greer Garson's farewell to MGM. I did it as a favor to her, just as she'd done her *Julius Caesar* cameo as a favor to me. Of course, it was a sugary thing, but I added Robert Ryan for some heaviness and the director was Robert Z. "Pop" Leonard. It came and went and made a few sou for the studio and then Greer left Leo the Lion after fifteen years of high-priced servitude.

BAWDEN: Some would consider *Lust for Life* [1956] your best picture.

HOUSEMAN: It was made in record time. MGM had long held the rights but always diddled with a production date. I was busy winding up a very silly Minnelli soaper called *The Cobweb* [1955], an all-star insanity story that nobody took seriously. Did you know Vince [Minnelli] turned down Jimmy Dean for the young lead? That was before *Rebel without a Cause* came out, by the way. It was one of Vincente's rare missteps.

Then I also had to produce Fritz Lang's *Moonfleet* [1955]. The story was crackers about smugglers, a gypsy girl, a mad mistress, a little boy played by Jon Whitely, who was hot, coming off *The Little Kidnappers* [1953], plus Stewart Granger, Joan Greenwood, George Sanders. And Fritz with his monocle, cracking his whip. It failed miserably but then I was free to tackle *Lust for Life*.

Moulin Rouge [1952] was such a hit MGM decided to proceed, but its ten-year option had only nine more months to run. Vincente was finishing *Kismet* [1955], but author Irving Stone refused to grant an extension. In March we decided we had to photograph all the European summer scenes by June or it would all be lost. We got Norman Corwin to write the screenplay because he could work in a hurry. By great luck Kirk Douglas was free. Even his hair was the right color. Anthony Quinn came on board as Gauguin and, in a nine-minute turn, walked away with the notices and a Supporting Oscar. We tried to do everything to stop it being made in CinemaScope but to no avail. At least Vincente could compose in that ratio and not have the images cropped out by somebody else. And I don't know how, but by God, it all came together and we had what I consider a mini-masterpiece.

MILLER: Most people don't remember it, but didn't you make your acting debut on-screen in *Seven Days in May* [1964]?

HOUSEMAN: I played a small part as a treasonous admiral. [Director] John Frankenheimer sort of did it as a joke. I worked half a day and that was it. I didn't do it again for ten years.

BAWDEN: How did you get to play Charles Kingsfield Jr. in *The Paper Chase*—both the 1973 movie and subsequent TV series?

HOUSEMAN: I had outlived most of my contemporaries. Nobody had the strength to tackle it. But it's crazy I had never contemplated acting except in that uncredited cameo in *Seven Days in May*. I'd been teaching acting to would-be actors. And I absorbed all the lessons of working with the greats and directing Shakespeare for the stage. It really was a small-budgeted thing with Timothy Bottoms and Lindsay Wagner as the stars. James Bridges wrote and directed it and gave me firm direction, which I needed. And I played very tough. Most people think I'm like that in real life, but I'm not.

CBS fell in love with the concept. And green-lighted a series that ran parts of three seasons, starting in 1978. We shot the movie with the University of Toronto standing in for Harvard. But the TV stuff was back lot,

I'm sad to say. We got a brilliant young actor, James Stephens, who was wonderful [as student James Hart].

We started in September '78 on CBS—Tuesdays at 8 opposite *Happy Days*. Desperate, I phoned the CBS president and pleaded for a time change. After all, when I produced many *Playhouse 90* episodes in 1959, we got bounced because ABC's *The Untouchables* creamed us. They relented and in February 1979 we were moved to Tuesdays at 10—opposite *Starsky and Hutch*! One just cannot win in this business. [Later *The Paper Chase* was revived on Showtime and did well. The first complete series also ran on PBS after its CBS run.]

MILLER: In the TV version of *Paper Chase*, you do some pretty fanciful dream sequences that put Kingsfield in some amusing situations. Your reaction to those?

HOUSEMAN: I never say no to people who ask me to do anything. I adore the dream sequences. We ran into the normal resistance of all establishments to fantasy, but I suspect that if tests were made they would find the audience enjoys them very much, too.

MILLER: After you won the Oscar, you started to play a lot of nasty characters in movies like *Three Days of the Condor* [1979], *St. Ives* [1976], and *Rollerball* [1975].

HOUSEMAN: I call them "my malignant old gentlemen." Obviously, malignant types are more fun to play than kindly old gentlemen.

MILLER: You also tackled the role of Winston Churchill in TV's *Truman at Potsdam* [1976].

HOUSEMAN: That was challenging. I'd never played a real person, let alone one who smoked cigars. I don't smoke, you see, and every day I had to smoke two or three of those huge special Churchill cigars. I used to throw up regularly.

MILLER: And in *St. Ives* you did something I find it hard to imagine you doing: you dyed your hair red!

HOUSEMAN: It was so appalling, so outrageous! That character was such fun. I'm sorry to say that some of the things that made it fun ended up on the cutting-room floor. I never understood what was going on in the picture, but I enjoyed it.

MILLER: How does it feel after all these years to be recognized in public like, well, a movie star?

HOUSEMAN: Every day I'm approached on the street by fans, some of them of high school age. I not only get a reaction from the old gentlemen with beards at the Harvard Club, but even young kids come up to me. They always want to tell me how they had a teacher in school who persecuted them and to whom they are very grateful for what he made them do in class.

MILLER: How would you sum up Professor Kingsfield?

HOUSEMAN: Kingsfield is a very special phenomenon. He fulfills the American desire for an image of authority, but not malignant authority. He's like so many strict teachers who were responsible for developing young people into human beings.

BAWDEN: Do you mind if I needle you a bit about doing all those TV commercials, especially the one on behalf of hamburgers?

HOUSEMAN: But I like hamburgers! [Spoken gruffly, Kingsfield-style, but with a twinkle in the eye, Houseman-style.]

Afterword

John Houseman did other TV series, including the sitcom *Silver Spoons* (1982–1987). His last great TV role, aside from Kingsfield, was the doomed Jewish Holocaust victim Aaron Jastrow in the miniseries *The Winds of War* (1983). In the sequel, *War and Remembrance* (1988–1989), Houseman was replaced by his friend John Gielgud.

Houseman died from spinal cancer at his Malibu home on October 31, 1988. He was eighty-six.

Raymond Massey

Interview by James Bawden

Raymond Massey was quite comfortable as both a leading man and a brilliant character actor in supporting roles. He had a long and distinguished career in the theater as well as in motion pictures and was a familiar screen presence in his native Canada, the United States, and England, where he learned much of his craft.

Massey was born in Toronto in 1896 to one of Canada's most prominent families. His older brother, Vincent, was the country's first Canadian-born governor-general. Raymond studied at the University of Toronto and at Oxford University. He served four years in the Canadian Army before a brief stint working at the family's agricultural implements factory. In 1924 he left for the London stage, where he thrived for the next fifteen years.

Massey's film career was extensive, and he also became a frequent performer on television in the United States, where a generation of younger fans probably know him best as Dr. Gillespie in the *Dr. Kildare* series (1961–1966) with Richard Chamberlain.

Setting the Scene

I always enjoyed my afternoons with Raymond Massey. As the scion of one of Toronto's most eminent families, he frequently returned to his hometown in the 1970s. I met him there three times over the years. Once he decided to take me to lunch at the Bombay Bicycle Club, which was situated in the former Massey mansion on Jarvis Street. But at the last moment, he changed his mind and we lunched instead via room service at his hotel. He said there were "too many ghosts of the past" for him in the family manse.

On another occasion, Massey stopped the taxi we were in to show me the facade of Massey Hall, which the family had donated to the City of

Raymond Massey in a studio portrait from *Things to Come* (1936). James Bawden collection.

Toronto. Massey pointed up to one blank stone and said it had been sand-blasted to remove the title "Massey Music Hall" because his Victorian grandfather had been told what music halls were like and was aghast.

The Interview

BAWDEN: Your first movie role was Sherlock Holmes in the 1931 British film *The Speckled Band*?

MASSEY: I got the job because Sir Gerald Du Maurier recommended me. He was the first choice but said, "I'm feeling rather tired, old chap, so you try it on, will you?" I had done an unsuccessful screen test for a 1928 British effort called *The Constant Nymph*. Very disappointing. Filled my mouth with cotton wool because I looked too thin in the face. I did the picture *The Speckled Band* because I needed the work. Worst-ever Holmes. Awful. The film was shot very quickly, but over seven weeks—as the money became available. In our version all the Victorian bric-a-brac was tossed out and Holmes resided in a modern apartment with a secretary and Dictaphone! The girlie in jeopardy was Angela Baddeley—that's right, Mrs. Bridges in *Upstairs, Downstairs* forty years later!

Almost a year later, there I was in L.A. in *The Old Dark House* [1932], with a Universal contract in my pocket. Turns out the Holmes movie was a big hit in the US.

BAWDEN: *The Old Dark House* is now considered a classic.

MASSEY: Never saw the thing. Thought it was a crazy plot—based on a J. B. Priestley play [*Benighted*], you know. What a cast of unknowns! Charles Laughton was in it. I'd directed him in 1929 in *The Silver Tassie* [onstage] and he could get temperamental. He positively loathed Boris Karloff, who was rumored to be part Indian. Charles was a white supremacist. Melvyn Douglas, Gloria Stuart, Lillian Bond—a real fine cast. The director, Jimmy [James] Whale, was just plain strange. [Whale had just done *Frankenstein*, one of Universal's biggest hits.] The film didn't appeal to many, but now, all these years later, is considered a classic. I was being screwed around by Junior Laemmle [studio head Carl Laemmle Jr.], who never used me again, just let me stew on the lot. I played golf on the studio golf course most days. Nothing to do. I just cut and ran—right back to Broadway and a new Kit [Katherine] Cornell play called *Alien Corn*.

BAWDEN: It was almost three years before your next film, *The Scarlet Pimpernel* [1935].

MASSEY: I was very busy on the stage [in 1934], both on Broadway and the West End [London]. Then producer Alex Korda saw me and offered a short-run contract. He thought I'd be good as the scowling French revolutionary Chauvelin. Leslie Howard was the star, Merle Oberon [played] his wife, and Nigel Bruce was the Prince of Wales. It was shot at Alex's Elstree Studios, an hour from the West End by subway. So Alex gave [me] a limo and a driver so I'd get an hour's sleep before I stepped onstage. I asked Gladys Cooper for permission [to work on the movie]. We were then doing *The Shining Hour* [onstage]—and she was also the manager. She told me she'd signed [to do a movie at the same time], so she then had to grant my request.

I learned so much working with Leslie Howard. He'd whisper between takes, "Tone it back a bit, old chap." To me he never seemed to do much. Then I watched the rushes and he'd effortlessly stolen the scene. Most British films at the time were truly rotten—we called them "quota quickies" because a certain quota of every cinema's fare had to be British product. So the theaters played the quickies all day . . . to no audiences, and at night people turned out to see the latest American imports.

Alex topped all that with his lavish films—well mounted, beautifully photographed, with big casts. On *Pimpernel,* Roland Brown was our director and he walked out after one day of enduring Alex's insults. So Alex directed some scenes and so did Harold Young, who got the credit. The cameraman was another American, Hal Rosson, who created such beautiful scenes the audiences would whisper, "Aaaaaaah!" Leslie added humor to what was essentially a chase tale—with my character forever two steps behind the elusive Pimpernel.

BAWDEN: Then in 1936 came what you've told me you consider your biggest, if not best, film.

MASSEY: *The Shape of Things to Come* [known in the United States as *Things to Come*]. Alex plowed all his financial resources into that one. I immediately read the H. G. Wells novel and was eager to make it until the script arrived and all the humor was left out and great gobs of socialism substituted. But Wells's contract said he had complete control of content and what he chose to do was use the film as a great educational experiment. He was always on set. We had great talks. The sets were huge. And H. G. started making script changes so the cinematic possibilities of the story would shine through. Ned Martin did the special effects; Georges Périnal was the cameraman. I ask you to look at the launching to the moon part and you'll see how closely it anticipates NASA's mission. I had two parts— the First World War airman and his grandson thirty years later. But three years later we were all at war again, despite all of H. G.'s admonitions.

BAWDEN: How did you manage to wind up back in Hollywood five years after vowing never to return?

MASSEY: It was all Leslie Howard's fault. He talked me up something fierce to David O. Selznick, who got interested enough to offer me the plum part of Prince Michael in his new version of *The Prisoner of Zenda*

[1937]. And the money was very nice, too, although I'd just had a big Broadway hit in *Ethan Frome* with Ruth Gordon.

David's cast was starry enough: Ronnie Colman, who was just as much a minimalist actor as Leslie; Madeleine Carroll as our beautiful Flavia; Mary Astor as Antoinette; Doug Fairbanks Jr. as Prince Rupert. It was a busy production, David was always ordering retakes, and after our wonderful director, John Cromwell, left, W. S. Van Dyke shot even more retakes. Sidney Howard was writing *Gone with the Wind* at the time for David and made the mistake of venturing onto the set one afternoon and David immediately ordered him to rewrite the mammoth engagement party scene. The photography by Jimmy Wong Howe was very opulent. It made you believe you were in that mythical kingdom. And there's nothing wrong about being in such a big hit.

BAWDEN: Then you went to Sam Goldwyn for *The Hurricane* [1937]. How did that happen?

MASSEY: My agent had insisted on a one-picture deal with David and then Sam Goldwyn bit and took a one-picture option. He tried to expand it into a full contract, but I figured it was more profitable to freelance, which made Sam mad as blazes. He spent the entire picture yelling at [director] Jack Ford, who had a real Irish temper and yelled back. Jack told me he'd only taken the job for the trip to Hawaii. Instead Sam built his South Pacific island on the back lot—the trees were papier-mâché and one day under the intense heat from the arc lights one of the trees crumpled and hit Mary Astor on the noggin.

I got the part because the first choice, Basil Rathbone, decided he'd played enough villains and was on the lookout for leading man roles. I wanted to stay nasty, as I certainly was here as Governor De Laage. Mary was my wife and the native kids were played by Dorothy Lamour and Jon Hall, who became big stars off of this one.

BAWDEN: You immediately hustled back to England for *Drums* [1938].

MASSEY: Another great snarling villain. It was a Sabu picture. He had become all the rage after being discovered by Robert Flaherty for *Elephant Boy*. A beautiful, strangely serene young lad and for a few years a box office sensation. Alex Korda did this one, my third in a row for United Artists producers. I put on the dark pancake [makeup] and did my thing. The fact it was all very racist never entered my mind at the time, although there were ominous stirrings in India, where the film was not popular. But it

Abraham Lincoln (Raymond Massey) shakes hands with Senator Stephen Douglas (Gene Lockhart) in *Abe Lincoln in Illinois* (1940). Courtesy of RKO Pictures.

reinforced our British stereotypes that we were training a new generation of progressive Indian leaders. Nobody could have known a decade later India would be free of the British for good. So *Drums* these days seems like dated propaganda for an empire that no longer exists.

BAWDEN: Then you had huge successes, first on the London stage in *Idiot's Delight* and then on Broadway in *Abe Lincoln in Illinois*. Then came the film version as Lincoln.

MASSEY: Only Henry Fonda and Jack Ford beat us to it. [Fonda starred in John Ford's *Young Mr. Lincoln* in 1939, a year before Massey's Lincoln film came out.] So a second Lincoln film in a year was a predictable failure at the box office. Ford took huge liberties with the material, particularly by making Lincoln so young and handsome. Ours was more prosaic and faithful to history—and I admit it's a tad dull after the Ford theatrics. When we opened [the stage version] at the Plymouth Theater in October 1938, I was still having trouble finding my Lincoln. He came to me that first night and I never had stage jitters as I usually did on opening nights. Playwright Bob Sherwood said he was positive Honest Abe would have been wowed.

BAWDEN: But you were upset by the cutting of a scene from the movie version—the one in which a prayer is said for the sick prairie boy?

MASSEY: I couldn't understand it. It was central to understanding Lincoln's character. I phoned Bob Sherwood [who wrote the play] and he couldn't explain it. Then I phoned producer Max Gordon and he yelled back to mind my own business. Most of the rest of the picture was okay. I always get a chuckle out of the presence of four Canadian actors doing the Lincoln-Douglas debates: Me, Gene Lockhart, Doug Dumbrille, John Qualen. But nobody noticed it at the time.

But I'll tell you about the premiere in Washington. First, I absolutely refused to arrive in costume as the RKO publicity department had suggested. Then I told Mrs. [First Lady Eleanor] Roosevelt how disappointed we all were that it was running in segregated cinemas. Washington had Jim Crow laws everywhere. She went to the event as planned, although there were pickets outside protesting [that] black people were barred from the event. I wonder how Lincoln would have thought of all of this.

BAWDEN: How did you get to Warners for a fifteen-year run as the studio's top character star?

MASSEY: I got a script called *Santa Fe Trail*. Loved doing westerns because everything was outdoors. And there was sheer fun in moving from Lincoln to John Brown. How strange is that anyway? I also played John Brown onstage in the Benét play *John Brown's Body* and again in the movie *Seven Angry Men* [1955]. What a great roaring part. Mike Curtiz was the director, amazing with action, and one day he really did roar, "Aim the empty horses the other way!"

I then did a play revival—*The Doctor's Dilemma* [1941] with Kit Cornell—and signed with WB for security. I'd do one movie or two, but for six consecutive months only. Then I could do a play until the next year. My wife, Dorothy, was convinced I'd made a big mistake.

BAWDEN: But first you returned to Canada for your only Canadian movie, *The 49th Parallel* [a 1941 film also known as *The Invaders*]. How did that come about?

MASSEY: My brother Vincent, Canada's high commissioner in London, sent me a wire to meet [producer-director] Michael Powell, then in L.A. He was about to begin this amazing odyssey—a film shot right across Canada. It concerned a bunch of Nazi saboteurs [headed by Eric Portman] who land in Hudson Bay. First they attack trappers [Laurence Olivier and Finlay Currie]. Then they meet a Hutterite girl in Manitoba [Elisabeth Bergner]. Then it's a pacifist in the Rockies [Leslie Howard]. Just as the last Nazi alive gets over the Peace Bridge at Niagara Falls, I appear—a draft deserter who finally does the right thing.

I only had five days to do my part, which was shot in a real railroad car. Stationed right beside the Falls. For other scenes Mike shot the exteriors and medium shots on actual locations, with the interiors to be finished in England. That's Elisabeth [Bergner] you see in long shots, but she absolutely refused to return to London because she was on the Nazis' most wanted list. So Glynis Johns stepped in and finished those scenes. She's in all the interiors, and the long-range exteriors are still Elisabeth. Glynis was twenty-seven years Elisabeth's junior! Larry and Leslie also did their scenes in England. With stand-ins for the long shots filmed in Canada. But no matter, the film was a huge hit. It was the first time Canadians had seen themselves on the screen and not in some blithering *Rose Marie* caricature.

BAWDEN: Your first picture under contract to WB was *Dangerously They Live* [1941]?

MASSEY: A terrible film. My wife kept telling me I'd made a mistake. Then came *Arsenic and Old Lace*. I know you're going to ask me why it took three years to be released. So here's the story: [director] Frank Capra was going into the U.S. Army, so he only had the summer of '41 to make it. WB took many of the cast members from the play, still running on Broadway. But the producers refused to free Boris Karloff, who was playing the nasty brother, Jonathan, because he was the big box office attraction. I tested for Capra and won this wonderful role [Karloff's part] and Warners added Cary Grant as Mortimer Brewster plus Priscilla Lane as his fiancée, Elaine Harper. Everybody was convinced it would be a huge hit and we had such fun making it. I'd already played a disturbed man in my worst-ever play performance, *The Black Ace*. So as Jonathan Brewster I simply played Randolph Calthorpe. I did not imitate Boris Karloff, as some people charged—but never to my face.

WB had a deal [requiring] the play to close before the movie could be released. The armed services watched this one in 1942 and then came 1943 and still the movie was dormant. The play kept packing them in for two years after our film version was made and when it was released in 1944, it didn't have the impact it might have had three years earlier. Cary Grant claimed he'd physically changed. Priscilla Lane had left Warners two years earlier and Jack Carson, in a small role, had since become a big star. But I still enjoy watching it on TV because it's one of my few comedies.

BAWDEN: You also made two movies with Humphrey Bogart.

MASSEY: *Action in the North Atlantic* [1943] was where we met. Adored the man. Best movie actor of all time. He'd served a twenty-year apprenticeship on the stage and in movies as the second lead. Not a tough guy at all, but came from a socialite family. The entire effort was studio bound. We never went near a real ship. Bogie made every gesture seem so damned easy that we were overacting in the same scene. Two ships were built on separate Warners soundstages. Two fully functioning ships! Every action was done against back projection. There were miniatures for some battle scenes and a shot could take forever to set up. One day Bogie was bored and bet me his stunt double was more courageous than mine. So we had the guys diving into the studio tank until both were exhausted. They got paid extra for it—out of our own pockets, I might add. We made another, a very boring thing called *Chain Lightning* [1950].

BAWDEN: You were very busy in those days. Take me through the titles from this list.

MASSEY: *Reap the Wild Wind* [1942]? I was on loan-out to Paramount and loved [the film's director] Cecil B. DeMille, who was a devotee of ham acting. I really put it on in that one. It was sheer fun to be so nasty. *The Woman in the Window* [1944]? I discovered just how great a movie actor Edward G. Robinson was, the way he could get the audience's attention by fondling objects, the way he rat-tat-tatted out the lines. Amazing. *Hotel Berlin* [1945]? It was in general release as the war ended but I liked my sadistic Nazi general and the picture really was a redoing of *Grand Hotel* [1932].

BAWDEN: One of your best-ever performances was as the American patriot in *Stairway to Heaven* [1946].

MASSEY: One of my favorite movies, actually. The realization was superb. David Niven was an RAF pilot who bails out, gets washed ashore, is attended by a doctor played by Roger Livesey, and romances Kim Hunter. [In the story, Niven's fate is in the hands of a heavenly jury, including figures from British and American history.] I played the first American colonial killed [by the British] in the Revolutionary War, a wonderful part to glower, great speeches. People still ask me about it. Michael [Powell] had one more part for me—1961's *The Queen's Guard*, which I did to act opposite my son Daniel.

BAWDEN: Then it was back to Warners.

MASSEY: I always pleaded off working with Bette Davis, with her temperament. Joan Crawford was something else again. The movie was *Possessed* [1947] and I discovered the secret of Joan's longevity: she was the best technician I'd ever met. Could match close-ups and long shots flawlessly. Knew everything about lighting, camera lenses, and dressed for the camera and not the other actors. Her face photographed superbly, captured and held the light. She was playing a schizophrenic nurse tending my terminally ill wife. Curtis Bernhardt directed and he wisely refused to go the melodrama route. The wife is never shown, only heard through half-closed doors.

First scenes were shot on downtown L.A. streets as dawn breaks and we see a mentally confused Joan leaving a streetcar, walking to early morning confession. Joan loved to talk about one day tackling the theater, but I knew she never would. For one thing, she had an innate fear of people. And she did have a sense of humor. When Curt [Bernhardt] addressed her as "Bette" during one scene, she threw the glass of champagne she was holding at him. One more thing: during the big party scene she insisted all the crew dress up, too, so she'd be in the right mood, and then when we were waltzing, she insisted she lead. After all, she was the star.

BAWDEN: Your opinion of *The Fountainhead* [1949], please!

MASSEY: Claptrap. Didn't work. Gary Cooper had signed for the lead and he wanted his girl, Pat Neal, in. This meant Barbara Stanwyck was eased out by director King Vidor and she walked out of the studio in rage. But Coop was twenty years too old and he wasn't smart enough. This part wasn't for a Mr. Deeds, but a cold, calculating adventurer and Gary was always pure on the screen. Young Pat didn't have the right kind of sex appeal. It just didn't work, and [the book's author] Ayn Rand's philosophy was frankly gibberish as far as I'm concerned.

BAWDEN: You told me you liked doing westerns at Warners. Why?

MASSEY: Because it got me out of the back lot and into the great outdoors. Well, actually, we shot at the Warners ranch. *Barricade* [1950] was a reworking of *The Sea Wolf*. *Dallas* [1950] with Coop was okay; *Sugarfoot* [1951] and *Carson City* [1952] were with Randy Scott, who was a big box office draw around that time. One of his oaters would be made easily in four weeks at the most. WB lent me out for *David and Bathsheba* [1952] and I could rant as an Old Testament prophet.

BAWDEN: How often do people ask you about James Dean?

MASSEY: In every interview! At every party! That movie [*East of Eden* (1955) in which Massey played Dean's father] has a life of its own, but Jimmy was dead by the time it went into release. Did he give a coherent performance? No! He was studying the Method, which might have left him as mixed up as Monty Clift, if he'd lived longer.

The success of that film is due to [director] Elia Kazan. He'd add some bit of unrehearsed business to a take to surprise Jimmy and—presto!—we'd have our scene. Jimmy couldn't do the same take twice because he had no training. There is a great performance buried in it: Jo Van Fleet as the mother. She's a force unto herself and in scenes with Jimmy, she just blows him away. [Van Fleet won the Best Supporting Actress Oscar for her performance.]

In that scene where he rushed into the train car to toss down the lettuce? Jimmy went up and we just stood there for the longest time. Then Burl [Ives] turned to me and said, "Guess Jimmy's got to hate that ice." I'm not discounting the truly amazing reception of the movie. But it was all due to Kazan's methodically gathering snippet after snippet of usable film. Jimmy couldn't give a sustained performance, you see.

BAWDEN: Why did you turn to television and *Dr. Kildare?*

MASSEY: I'd loved live TV. I did the Lincoln play live on CBS in 1949. We did it from CBS studios atop Grand Central Station. Remember, it was live and as the train in the last scene is pulling out of the station with me and Ruth Gordon, all the well-wishers were supposed to shout, "Goodbye, Mr. Lincoln!" Except one old doll, who shouted, "And you, too, Mr. Massey! Good-bye, Mr. Massey." Got me so mad—when the red light was out I chased her right up the street.

By 1961, we'd moved permanently to Beverly Hills and the movie pickings became thinner as the years went on. Always said I wouldn't do a series. But Dr. Gillespie was a great role. I wasn't on call all week. I'd have days off. My job would be to rush into a scene and argue ethics with Dick Chamberlain as Dr. Kildare. I got recognized on the street by people who'd never been to the theater and only vaguely remembered me from movies. One more thing: MGM made this one with real care.

I've got a Dick Chamberlain story for you. Included him in some of our posh parties. And one night Cedric Hardwicke had a couple and started berating Dick with the best career advice he ever got. He said, "Young man, you are a star, but you do not yet know how to act." So when the show folded Dick went into English repertory for several years, played all sorts of parts, and became a very credible actor as well as romantic lead.

Richard Chamberlain as Dr. Kildare and Raymond Massey as Dr. Gillespie in NBC's series *Dr. Kildare* (1961–1966). Courtesy of NBC.

BAWDEN: You tell an interesting story about why you retired from acting.

MASSEY: It was 1975. I'd virtually retired when the invitation came forth to costar in a revival of *The Night of the Iguana* opposite Dorothy McGuire and Dick Chamberlain and Eleanor Parker at the Dorothy Chandler Pavilion in L.A. On the second preview I froze, couldn't remember a damned thing. Was it because [the playwright] Tennessee Williams was sitting in the audience? I thought he'd tear me apart afterwards, but he came to my dressing room and was very sweet. I was taking medication for migraines and that night I came up blank. Had to make up a lot of verse and with the author right there! But I was seventy-nine and I thought to myself that this really is it. My working days as an actor were just about over. I finished the run, never again blanked out. But it was time to go, to drop back into the black hole of being simply an eager devotee of other people's acting.

Afterword

Raymond Massey was married three times. The first two marriages ended in divorce. His first wife, Margery, bore him a son, Geoffrey, who became an architect. His second wife, Adrianne Allen, was an actress and their two children, Anna and Daniel, have had important acting careers. His marriage to Dorothy Whitney lasted until her death in 1982. She had been his lawyer in his divorce from Adrianne Allen, and her husband, William Dwight Whitney, had represented Adrianne—and later married her. That bizarre set of circumstances was used as the plot for the famous Spencer Tracy–Katharine Hepburn movie *Adam's Rib* (1949).

Massey died of pneumonia on July 29, 1983, in Los Angeles. He was eighty-six. He'll be remembered as a famous movie star in America as well as in England and his native Canada.

Reginald Owen

Interview by Ron Miller

When they rank the all-time great character actors in Hollywood history, surely Reginald Owen's name will be right near the top. This gifted English-born and English-trained stage actor had a remarkable career that stretched from his screen debut in 1929 opposite the legendary Jeanne Eagels in *The Letter* all the way into the 1960s, when he was still in fine form as Admiral Boom in Disney's *Mary Poppins*.

Among his most celebrated roles was his performance as Sherlock Holmes in *A Study in Scarlet* (1933), which he undertook, amazingly, right after he had played Dr. Watson to Clive Brook's Holmes in the 1932 *Sherlock Holmes*. Probably his most acclaimed performance was as Ebenezer Scrooge in MGM'S 1938 *A Christmas Carol*.

As a longtime MGM contract player, Owen costarred with Greta Garbo, Clark Gable, Joan Crawford, Spencer Tracy, Katharine Hepburn, and nearly every other major star who ever worked at the studio.

Tall, dignified, and distinctly British, Owen was a beloved member of Hollywood's British colony" and continued working busily into his eighties.

Setting the Scene

I met Reginald Owen in 1971 when he was acting in a play he had written—*The Female Animal*—which was being produced in a regional theater, the Manhattan Playhouse, in East Palo Alto, near Stanford University. Then eighty-two years old, Owen was the most genial of characters, a man who seemed thoroughly pleased with the course of his long career and still eager to be directly involved with his audience.

Reginald Owen as Ebenezer Scrooge and child actor Terry Kilburn as Tiny Tim in MGM's 1938 *A Christmas Carol*. Courtesy of MGM.

The Interview

MILLER: You were trained as an actor in your native England at the Royal Academy of Dramatic Arts and made your professional stage debut at eighteen, but what brought you to America?

OWEN: I was offered the chance to play the prince in Molnar's *The Swan* on Broadway with Basil Rathbone and Eva Le Gallienne. It was well received and I was offered a screen test at Paramount, where they were anxious to find actors with voices that would work in the new talking pictures.

MILLER: That led to your being cast in a major Hollywood film—*The Letter* with Jeanne Eagels. It was one of the first talking pictures and very successful, which made you in demand for movies on both sides of the Atlantic. Did that set you up nicely in movies?

OWEN: Not everybody thought I could play comedy. That changed when Frank Capra cast me in *Platinum Blonde* [1931] with Jean Harlow and I displayed my flair for comedy. That's when I was really in demand.

MILLER: When you signed a contract with MGM, that obviously convinced you to pursue your acting career primarily in America. How did you like working for the studio?

OWEN: I was treated very well at Metro. I never had any trouble with any director or executive. They were very courteous to me. I worked steadily in picture after picture. It seemed like I was working fifty-six weeks a year—and I thrived on it.

MILLER: Though you occasionally landed leading roles, were you disappointed that they preferred to keep you in supporting roles?

OWEN: Not long after they signed me up, they decided not to make me a star so I could go on being a character actor. I never minded. I never wanted to be a star anyway. That was fine with me. I got plenty of work and they paid me very well. I always liked eccentric parts. Give me a moustache, a beard, or even an eyeglass and I'm fine. The only time I ever get uncomfortable is when I'm playing myself.

MILLER: I don't think that happened very often anyway. Your credits are a roster of your versatility. You've played kings, dukes, gentlemen of all types, and were a nasty villain in *Call of the Wild* [1935]. And, of course, the all-time grinch: Ebenezer Scrooge in *A Christmas Carol*.

OWEN: And that's my favorite role.

MILLER: You had the unique opportunity to work with the mysterious Greta Garbo in three pictures—*Queen Christina* [1933], *Anna Karenina* [1935], and *Conquest* [1937]. What was she like?

OWEN: Her shyness wasn't put on for the press. She was extremely shy, but a very likeable person. I remember the first day of shooting on *Anna Karenina*, she had them put up a screen so nobody could see her acting except those of us involved in the scene. She showed up wearing thick stockings and sneakers, but when she changed into her costume she looked like a million dollars. She was a truly beautiful woman!

MILLER: Some legendary tales are told about studio chief Louis B. Mayer, not all of them complimentary. He was your boss for more than twenty years. How did you get along with him?

OWEN: He had an immense pride in the people who worked under his management. I never knew him to interfere with his directors or his actors. He was the executive par excellence.

MILLER: How did it feel when your MGM contract finally came to an end after such a long run?

OWEN: I didn't go out in good style. I've made about 150 movies, but my last one at MGM was the worst I ever made. I won't even mention the title. [Probably the 1954 *The Great Diamond Robbery* with Red Skelton.] All I remember is I lugged a bass fiddle around through the whole thing.

MILLER: Now at eighty-two you're starting a new career as a playwright?

OWEN: No, this isn't my first play. I wrote a comedy called *Jack's Up*, which was produced in the 1930s in Providence, Rhode Island, and died there from audience anemia. It was supposed to be a comedy, but nobody was laughing. Well, I take that back. At the end of the first act, I was seducing a young girl who was supposed to hit me over the head with a breakaway bottle and knock me out. But when the performance began, we couldn't find the breakaway bottle and had to use a rubber one. I instructed her carefully not to hit me too hard, but in her excitement, she dropped the bottle. We got the only laugh of the evening when the bottle bounced all over the place and finally dropped into the footlights.

MILLER: Have you any notions of retiring from acting and just enjoying your home life?

OWEN: I'll never retire. I like to work and play golf. As for my home life, it's quite normal. I never did see any of those Hollywood orgies you always hear about.

Afterword

Reginald Owen was married three times and was still with third wife, Barbara, whom he married in 1956, when he died from a heart attack on November 5, 1972, in Boise, Idaho. He was eighty-five.

Jay Robinson

Interview by Ron Miller

Few character actors in movie history have enjoyed the sensational screen debut afforded young Jay Robinson, a little-known stage actor who turned in a riveting performance as the despotic Roman emperor Caligula in 20th Century-Fox's biggest production of 1953, the biblical blockbuster *The Robe*, which introduced the wide-screen CinemaScope process and revolutionized the way movies were presented to moviegoers. Portraying Caligula as a corrupt, power-mad ruler bordering on the edge of lunacy, Robinson virtually blew everybody else off the screen, earning a special niche in the history of screen villainy when he sent the stars of the picture—Richard Burton and Jean Simmons—to their deaths in the film's dramatic finale. His performance was extravagantly praised by critics—the *New York Times'* Bosley Crowther called it one of the ten finest ever put on the screen.

Robinson's dazzling debut earned him a chance to reprise the role in the big-budget sequel *Demetrius and the Gladiators* in 1954, which led to his being cast in another historical epic, 1955's *The Virgin Queen* with Bette Davis.

But in just a few years, Robinson was a forgotten man, done in by his own arrogance and his addiction to drugs. Off the screen for several years, Robinson finally emerged from drug rehabilitation, cured of his addiction and humbled by his ordeal—ready to resume his career in films and on television.

Yet lightning wasn't about to strike twice for Robinson, who never regained the fame he had achieved at age twenty-three in *The Robe*.

Setting the Scene

I met Robinson in 1982 in an interview arranged by KTVU-TV, an Oakland, California, local independent station, now a Fox network affiliate,

Jay Robinson as Emperor Caligula in *The Robe* (1953). Courtesy of 20th Century Fox.

that had scheduled a special screening of *The Robe* in prime time and had hired Robinson to help promote the event.

He was good-natured, far from arrogant, and considerably contrite about the damage he had done to his promising career nearly thirty years earlier.

The Interview

MILLER: What had you been doing before you were cast in *The Robe*?

ROBINSON: I was suffering from my first real defeat. I had just produced a play on Broadway that had flopped rather badly. I wanted to go off and lick my wounds. I got off a bus in downtown Los Angeles and checked into the old Biltmore Hotel. As long as I was in town, I decided to see if anything was doing, so I picked an agent's name out of the yellow pages.

MILLER: If memory serves, the agent you picked was Peter Shaw, who was the husband of actress Angela Lansbury.

ROBINSON: That's right. I gave him a list of my theater credits and he told me to stay by the phone because he might have some work for me.

MILLER: Had you read anything about *The Robe* before that day? Had you read the best-selling novel by Lloyd C. Douglas or heard that the studio was putting everything it had into a multimillion-dollar wide-screen production in an attempt to lure moviegoers away from their TV sets?

ROBINSON: All that meant nothing to me because I had no desire to be in a movie. I was a stage actor, looking for work in theater. I hadn't read the book and knew nothing about Caligula.

MILLER: So how did an unknown twenty-three-year-old wind up landing one of the plum roles of the decade?

ROBINSON: They had already cast the role with an actor named John Buckmaster, but he wasn't working out. They decided to replace him and Peter Shaw knew they were still looking for someone after talking to just about everybody else in town. Peter talked me into meeting the studio casting people. Two days later they did a screen test and [studio boss] Darryl F. Zanuck hired me on the spot.

MILLER: So what did Zanuck see that convinced him?

ROBINSON: I don't know. It was very strange. I just felt an affinity for the character. I picked up the script and instinctively hit just what they wanted. Zanuck signed me to a contract at $3,000 a week and rushed me into the sequel.

MILLER: How did you fit in at the studio? I can't imagine there was anybody else under contract that was quite like you.

ROBINSON: I was like David Bowie suddenly thrust back into the 1950s! The other young actors of the period were pretty straight types like Robert Wagner, Tab Hunter, and Jeffrey Hunter. And here was I—this bizarre, strange, flamboyant creature. I don't think 20th had any idea what to do with me.

MILLER: What sort of roles did they have in mind after Caligula?

ROBINSON: They announced I was going to play the pharaoh in *The Egyptian* [1954], Napoleon in *Desiree* [1954], and John Wilkes Booth in *Prince of Players* [1955], but none of those roles came to pass. [Edmund Purdom did *The Egyptian*, Marlon Brando did *Desiree*, and John Derek played Booth in *Prince of Players*.] They also turned down loan-out requests for me from other studios and barred me from doing any theater work.

MILLER: How did you get along with Zanuck, who must have thought highly of you, at least at first?

ROBINSON: Zanuck held me in a vicelike grip. In those days you had to do exactly what they said. You even dated who they wanted you to date, lived where they wanted you to live, and couldn't leave the county without calling the studio. They just paid me my $3,000 every Friday and told me to buy a house in Bel Air.

MILLER: Well, sooner or later, I have to ask you what went so wrong that your whole career suddenly fell apart.

ROBINSON: It was just an incredible case of too much, too soon. I was surrounded by the worst sycophants, who were saying I was great, wonderful, brilliant. I believed my own publicity. That's the way it went on until I began to play the role of Caligula in my lifestyle off-screen.

MILLER: In 1958 police raided your Bel Air home and arrested you for possession of methadone. You were convicted and sentenced to a year in jail, but remained free on bail.

ROBINSON: Before *The Robe*, I was just a kid, totally dedicated to theater. I neither smoked nor drank and did no drugs of any kind. But I'd been on drugs for three years when I was arrested. My father was so upset by what happened that he suffered a fatal heart attack at the preliminary hearing. I went into rehab and was off drugs completely by 1960. I met and married my wife, Pauline, that year. I tried to get my career started again, but all doors were closed to me.

MILLER: How did you make a living?

ROBINSON: I could only get these menial jobs. I cleaned cages at the zoo. I worked as a fry cook. I managed a rooming house on skid row. Things got worse. I thought my conviction had been overturned, but it wasn't. I found that out when I applied for a job as a psychiatric technician at a state hospital. They ran my I.D. and the next thing I knew I was arrested on a fugitive warrant. I had a jury trial, was convicted and sent to state prison, where I served fifteen months before being paroled.

MILLER: How did things change for you once you were drug free, out of prison, and ready to work again?

ROBINSON: I found the industry was more tolerant of such things. Knowing what I've been through, it's incredible to see the casual attitude about these things today. Nobody gets upset about drug use until there's a tragic death like John Belushi or Freddie Prinze. Bette Davis, who remembered me from *The Virgin Queen*, went to bat for me and got me a job in her film *Bunny O'Hare* [1972]. Then Warren Beatty offered me the job of the beauty shop operator in his *Shampoo* [1975]. I started to get work in

TV shows like *Barney Miller* and I played a drag queen in *Partners* [1982] with Ryan O'Neal and John Hurt.

MILLER: Do you think you have to find a big role as showy as Caligula to get back on everybody's A list?

ROBINSON: I don't know. There are so many young people who don't even know me now. It's a little disconcerting in a way. Even now, I haven't mellowed out to the point where I can take it all in stride. If two or three months go by and I don't work, I always get the feeling that I'm never going to work again. I feel I'm at the height of my powers as an actor and that the great roles are still ahead. I've got to hold onto that dream, that it's all going to happen again as it did once before. I know I can handle it now.

Afterword

Jay Robinson continued to work, mostly in television, through the 1990s, but never got that showcase role to put him back on top. He died of congestive heart failure at his home in Sherman Oaks, California, on September 27, 2013. He was eighty-three.

Rod Steiger

Interview by Ron Miller

Rod Steiger was one of the first stage-trained Method actors to make a serious impact in movies of the 1950s and 1960s. He first appeared in a small role in the 1951 film *Teresa,* but soon was attracting much more attention with his performances in live television dramas out of New York, most notably in the title role of the original telecast of Paddy Chayefsky's *Marty* in 1953.

Though the role went to Ernest Borgnine when *Marty* became a feature film in 1955, winning the Best Picture Academy Award and the Best Actor award for Borgnine, Steiger had already established himself in movies as a top-rank character actor with his Oscar-nominated supporting performance in Elia Kazan's 1954 *On the Waterfront,* which won that year's Best Picture award and Oscars for leading man Marlon Brando and supporting actress Eva Marie Saint.

With his stocky frame and round face, Steiger wasn't cut in the mold of a leading man. Yet he was so respected as an actor that he frequently alternated between strong supporting roles in major films, such as the 1955 musical *Oklahoma!,* and occasional leading roles in westerns like *Run of the Arrow* (1957) and crime dramas like *Al Capone* (1960). In 1965 he was nominated for an Oscar for the title role in Sidney Lumet's *The Pawnbroker.*

In 1967 Steiger finally won the Best Actor Oscar for his acclaimed performance as the redneck sheriff in Norman Jewison's *In the Heat of the Night,* which also won the Best Picture Oscar that year. For the rest of his career, he continued to play strong supporting roles in A films and often leading roles in independent films like *The Pawnbroker.*

Steiger remained bitter most of his life about losing the role in the movie version of *Marty* to Ernest Borgnine, but he always claimed his greatest mistake was turning down the part of General George Patton in

Rod Steiger in *The Amityville Horror* (1979). Ron Miller collection.

1970's *Patton,* supposedly because he didn't want to play a role that glorified war. George C. Scott took the role instead and won the Best Actor Academy Award.

Steiger's personal life was also rife with problems. He was married five times, the first four ending in divorce. He had serious health problems during the last phase of his career, and fought a weight problem most of his life.

Setting the Scene

I had two one-on-one interviews with Rod Steiger. The first was in 1984 on the set of *Jackie Collins' Hollywood Wives,* the ABC television miniseries in which Steiger played a studio powerbroker. The second was in 1991 over a late lunch at the famous Polo Lounge of the Beverly Hills Hotel set up to discuss his leading role in the NBC TV movie *In the Line of Duty: Manhunt in the Dakotas,* in which Steiger played real-life religious fanatic and federal fugitive Gordon Kahl of the notorious Posse Comitatus.

Both times Steiger was friendly and quite candid, though he routinely deflected the conversation away from discussion of what he called his "process" in developing a character.

I was amused that Steiger, who was always a little pudgy, chose from the dessert cart a wickedly large plate of something floating in a rich sauce and dug into it quite eagerly. Possibly noting my skeptical look, Steiger said, "I've been on a diet all my life." He was making it clear this was one of those days when he wasn't going to abide by it.

The Interview

MILLER: You've had some recent health issues, including a coronary bypass. How are you feeling?

STEIGER: When I start sounding self-pitying, I have to remind myself I don't have a hose up my rear and an oxygen tube in my nose. I'm not back in the hospital. Until that day, I have nothing to complain about.

MILLER: You've always been known for a rather intense pursuit of your career goals. Now that you're in your sixties, do you feel the same way about your career goals?

STEIGER: I feel more alive when I'm tackling a challenging role, but unfortunately I worked harder on my professional life than I did on my personal life—or I wouldn't have had four marriages. [Steiger was still with his fourth wife, Paula Ellis, at the time of our interview. He credited her with getting him out of a suicidal depressive state after they married in 1986.] I got so involved with the challenge of trying to create that I paid little attention to the people around me and my personal relationships.

MILLER: Some leading men tend to play themselves on-screen and fashion a screen persona that reflects their own off-screen persona. But

Rod Steiger (*left*) with Marlon Brando in the famous taxicab sequence in *On the Waterfront* (1954). Courtesy of Columbia Pictures.

you've always been a versatile character actor. Does it bother you that you've played so many tough guys and all-around unpleasant characters?

STEIGER: I've seldom been able to show my gentle or vulnerable side in a movie.

MILLER: I've seen some of your early TV work, which included a lot of likeable characters, most especially Marty Piletti in the original *Marty*. Lots of people probably still think Ernie Borgnine beat you out of the role in the movie version of *Marty*, but I understand you actually were the first choice and turned it down. Why?

STEIGER: The producers wanted to sign me up for seven years. I didn't want them to have that control over me.

MILLER: You were very hot the year the *Marty* movie came out, even though Borgnine won the Oscar and not you. You were coming off that amazing performance in Elia Kazan's *On the Waterfront*, for which many thought you deserved the Supporting Actor Oscar. [Steiger was nominated, but so were costars Lee J. Cobb and Karl Malden. The conventional wisdom is that they split the vote, allowing Edmond O'Brien to win for *The Barefoot Contessa*.] Why didn't Kazan ever use you again?

STEIGER: Because I refused to work with him again. He cooperated with the House Un-American Activities Committee's Communist witch hunt. I had a friend who committed suicide over being blacklisted. I could never look him [Kazan] in the eye again.

MILLER: Another great Steiger performance of that period was your portrayal of the movie studio boss in *The Big Knife* [1955]. Is it true the author, Clifford Odets, based your character on MGM's Louis B. Mayer?

STEIGER: He was such a peculiar character, but I didn't know he was supposed to be L. B. Mayer. He was before my time.

MILLER: But you played another studio boss, Oliver Easterne, in TV's *Hollywood Wives*. Your costar, Stefanie Powers, told me she thought the novelist, Jackie Collins, based him on a combination of Jack Warner [Warner Bros.' chief] and Harry Cohn [head of Columbia Pictures]. Your impression?

STEIGER: I certainly saw Harry Cohn in the character. I was never under contract to him, but I was around him a lot when I made *On the Waterfront* and *The Harder They Fall* [1956]. [Both movies were made at Cohn's Columbia Pictures.] He was a very, very strong person. If you talked back to him and you were right, he respected you and liked you. If you talked back to him and you weren't right, he fired you.

MILLER: I'm one of the people who think you hit an all-time high with your performance in Sidney Lumet's *The Pawnbroker*, but it was pretty much an art house film that many people found too depressing. You were nominated for the Best Actor Academy Award, but didn't get it that year. Did you feel vindicated when you finally won your Oscar for *In the Heat of the Night* two years later?

STEIGER: Naturally it felt good, but people think winning the Oscar means you get to pick and choose your roles from then on. It's not that way at all. The Oscar lasts you about a week and a half. If you don't find something good to follow it up, it doesn't mean anything.

MILLER: What did you think when you first looked at your *In the Heat of the Night* role and saw you were a redneck, racist lawman who has to overcome his prejudice and learn to respect a big-city urban detective who's black?

STEIGER: I thought of them as two gunfighters, loners who meet

Rod Steiger as W. C. Fields in *W.C. Fields and Me* (1976). Courtesy of Universal Studios.

through their actions rather than intellectual discourse and begin to respect each other, regardless of color.

MILLER: You must have been disappointed when your follow-up film, the black comedy about a serial killer, *No Way to Treat a Lady* [1968], was a box office dud and your resourceful performance pretty much ignored.

STEIGER: I was very hurt with the mixed reviews, but now it's becoming a cult film.

MILLER: When you think back on some of the challenges you've taken with roles, I guess playing W. C. Fields in *W.C. Fields and Me* [1976] must be right up at the top of your list. You not only had to master an impression of Fields, but you had to learn how to juggle like he did.

STEIGER: I was doing a farewell speech, as Fields, to the crew when we wrapped up filming and somebody told me Carlotta Monti was there. [Monti was Fields's mistress for years and the movie was based on her memoir about her time with him.] I nearly died when I heard that. But she came up to me, started to cry, and called me by his nickname: "Woody! Oh, my God, you're my Woody!"

MILLER: How do you apply the Method when you're playing a character who might be pretty unsavory?

STEIGER: It has nothing to do with Method. I just was taught to identify deeply and personally with the character I'm doing and not to judge him as either a villain or a hero.

MILLER: You've done several television movies, but you've avoided doing a series, even when they turned your most famous movie, *In the Heat of the Night*, into a weekly series. Any reservations about doing things like that?

STEIGER: I'd rather starve on $1 million a year [his average annual income then] than make $12 million and have no self-respect. I can starve beautifully and I hope I'm lucky enough to keep starving that well all the years I have left.

Afterword

Rod Steiger was divorced from Paula Ellis in 1997 and was married to fifth wife Joan Benedict when he died from pneumonia and complications from surgery for a gall bladder tumor on July 9, 2002, at age seventy-seven. He had a daughter, opera singer Anna Steiger, by second wife Claire Bloom and a son, Michael, by Paula Ellis.

Acknowledgments

None of the chapters in this book are reprints of previously published material, although most of the interviews were originally conducted for the newspapers and magazines that regularly published the authors' articles and columns. Each interview has been updated and reformatted to include previously unpublished material taken directly from the original tape recordings and notes made by the authors.

Earlier versions of James Bawden's interviews with Bette Davis, Henry Fonda, Raymond Massey, and Vincent Price appeared in the *Hamilton Spectator*. Earlier versions of Bawden's interviews with Bette Davis, Yvonne De Carlo, Bonita Granville, Hurd Hatfield, John Houseman, Walter Pidgeon, Jane Russell, Alexis Smith, James Stewart, Cornel Wilde, Esther Williams, and Robert Young appeared in the *Toronto Star*. An earlier version of Bawden's interview with Anne Shirley appeared in *Filmograph* magazine. Earlier versions of Bawden's interviews with Yvonne De Carlo and Janet Leigh appeared in *Films in Review* magazine. Earlier versions of Bawden's interviews with Joan Leslie, Raymond Massey, Patricia Neal, Walter Pidgeon, Jean Simmons, Alexis Smith, Jane Wyatt, and Robert Young appeared in *Films of the Golden Age* magazine.

Earlier versions of Ron Miller's interviews with Lon Chaney Jr., Anthony Dexter, and Boris Karloff appeared in the *Santa Cruz Sentinel*. An earlier version of Miller's interview with Buster Keaton appeared in *Lyke*, the campus magazine of San Jose State College. Earlier versions of Miller's interviews with Ernest Borgnine, Victor Buono, John Carradine, Jack Elam, Richard Farnsworth, John Houseman, Lee Marvin, Victor Mature, Maureen O'Sullivan, Reginald Owen, Robert Preston, Jay Robinson, Johnny Sheffield, Rod Steiger, and Elizabeth Taylor appeared in the *San Jose Mercury News* and in numerous newspapers reached by the Knight Ridder syndicate. Other interviews with Johnny Sheffield first appeared in the online magazine *TheColumnists.com*. An earlier version of Ron Miller's interview with John Carradine appeared in *Castle of Frankenstein* magazine. Portions of Darla Miller's interview with Carradine appeared in the *San Jose Mercury News*.

Portions of interviews by both Bawden and Miller also appeared in career tributes and obituaries of the stars published in the online magazine *TheColumnists.com* between 1999 and 2013.

The authors want to pay special acknowledgment to the distinguished film historian and author Patrick McGilligan, Screen Classics series editor at the University Press of Kentucky, who first solicited our work for publication and was responsible for bringing our first collection of interviews—*Conversations with Classic Film Stars* (2016)—to the publisher's attention.

We also want to express our deepest thanks to the respected film scholars Sheila Benson and James Robert Parish for their invaluable endorsement of our first book and to the acclaimed journalist Robert Lindsey, author of *The Falcon and the Snowman* and other major works, for his online endorsement and support of our first book.

We also want to express our appreciation to Dollie Banner of Jerry Ohlinger Movie Materials in New York City for her crucial assistance in providing the missing elements of our photo selection for this book.

And we want to especially express our deep appreciation to our chief editor at the University Press of Kentucky, Anne Dean Dotson, and her superb staff for their great help in making our first book as a team such a pleasure and a positive learning experience for both of us.

Finally, we want to once more thank the great stars who so kindly granted us the time to talk with them privately about their careers, often on numerous occasions. We will never forget our times with them and we hope the record of our chats will please their many fans, who also will never forget them.

About the Authors

James Bawden and Ron Miller met more than forty years ago at a convention of television columnists in Los Angeles, discovered they shared a love of films from Hollywood's golden age, and have been friends ever since. After their retirement from their newspaper jobs, they worked together on the former website www.thecolumnists.com and collaborated on their first book together, *Conversations with Classic Film Stars* (2016). This is the second of several planned collections of interviews they have done with actors and other filmmakers.

Bawden earned bachelor's degrees in history from the University of Toronto (1968) and in journalism from Carleton University (1970) and has a master's degree in history and politics from Laurier University (1975). He was the television columnist for the *Hamilton Spectator* in Ontario, then moved on to be the TV columnist for Canada's largest newspaper, the *Toronto Star*. He has written for many film magazines and journals, including *Films in Review*. He lives in Toronto.

Miller was born and raised in Santa Cruz, California. He earned a bachelor's degree in journalism from San Jose State College (1961). Before becoming an entertainment writer, he was a news reporter and news bureau chief at the *San Jose Mercury News*. From 1977 to 1999 he was a nationally syndicated television columnist for the paper and the Knight Ridder newspaper chain. In 1994 he won a National Headliner Award for his columns, and he is a former national president of the Television Critics Association.

Miller is the coauthor of *Masterpiece Theatre* (1995) with Terrence O'Flaherty and sole author of *Mystery! A Celebration* (1996) and *Mystery Classics on Film* (2017). As a fiction writer, he has published a dozen short stories in national magazines. He lives in Blaine, Washington, with his wife, Darla.

Index

SCREEN CLASSICS

Screen Classics is a series of critical biographies, film histories, and analytical studies focusing on neglected filmmakers and important screen artists and subjects, from the era of silent cinema to the golden age of Hollywood to the international generation of today. Books in the Screen Classics series are intended for scholars and general readers alike. The contributing authors are established figures in their respective fields. This series also serves the purpose of advancing scholarship on film personalities and themes with ties to Kentucky.

SERIES EDITOR: Patrick McGilligan

BOOKS IN THE SERIES